"I Saw the Heaven Opened"
A Commentary on Revelation

By Daniel H. King, Sr.

© **Truth Publications, Inc.** 2018. All rights reserved. No part of this book may be reproduced in any form without written permission from the publisher. Printed in the United States of America.

ISBN 10: 1-58427-456-5

ISBN 13: 978-1-58427-456-8

Cover photo and graphics: istockphoto.com; sky photo used throughout the book: istockphoto.com; Patmos photo on page 31: by Kyle Pope; Seven Churches of Asia Map on page 56: by Kyle Pope; Temple of Domitian in Ephesus photo: istockphoto.com.

Truth Publications, Inc.
CEI Bookstore
220 S. Marion St., Athens, AL 35611
855-492-6657
sales@truthpublications.com
www.truthbooks.com

Table of Contents

Preface 7
Introduction to John's Book of Revelation 13
    What Do We Know about the Writer? 21
    What Can We Say about the Place of Writing? 31
    What Do We Know about the Setting and Date of
        Composition? 35
    What Was the Original Destination of the Book? To Whom
        Was it Penned? 55
    What is this Strange and Mysterious Book? 64
        A. The Type of Literature 64
        B. Purpose of the Book 89
    How to Read This Book of Symbols 90
    Great Themes in the Book 91
        A. Relationship between Church and State 92
        B. Martyrdom and Persecution 94
        C. Warfare and Victory 96
    Approaches to the Interpretation of Revelation 98

Chapter One
The Letters to the Seven Churches of Asia (Part 1) 108
    A. The Introduction (1:1-3) 108
    B. The Formal Greeting and Opening Address (1:4-8) 112
    C. The Vision of Christ among the Churches (1:9-20) 114
    D. The Letters to the Seven Congregations of Asia Minor
       (2:1-3:22) 118
       Letter to Ephesus (2:1-7) 120
       Letter to Smyrna (2:8-11) 130
       Letter to Pergamum (2:12-17) 137

Chapter Two
The Letters to the Seven Churches of Asia (Part 2) 148
    Letter to Thyatira (2:18-29) 148
    Letter to Sardis (3:1-6) 153
    Letter to Philadelphia (3:7-13) 158
    Letter to Laodicea (3:14-22) 163

Chapter Three
Cycle One: The Seal Sequence (4:1-8:1) 172
    A. The Throne Scene: A Vision of the Court of Heaven (4:1-11) 173
    B. Opening the Seals of the Closely Sealed Book (5:1-14) 176
    C. The First Six Seals Opened (6:1-17) 179
    D. Sealing of the 144,000 and the Innumerable Multitude (7:1-17) 195
    E. The Majestic Silence (8:1) 200

Chapter Four
Cycle Two: The Trumpet Sequence (8:2-11:19) 203
    A. Seven Angels and Seven Trumpets (8:2-6) 205
    B. Woes upon Nature (8:7-13) 208
    C. Woes upon Mankind (9:1-21) 215
    D. The Interlude Visions (10:1–11:2) 222
    E. The Two Martyr/Witnesses (11:3-14) 229
    F. The Final Trumpet Blasts (11:15-18) 233
    G. The Vision of the Ark of the Covenant (11:19) 236

Chapter Five
Cycle Three: The Beast Sequence (12:1-14:20). 241
    A. Seven Figures 241
    B. The Vision of the Woman and the Dragon (12:1-17) 242
    C. The Vision of the First Beast (13:1-10) 247
    D. The Vision of the Second Beast (13:11-18) 254
    E. The Triumphant Saints on Mount Zion (14:1-20) 259

Table of Contents

Chapter Six
Cycle Four: The Bowl Sequence (15:1-16:21) 266
    A. The Victorious Saints by the Fiery Sea and the Seven Angels
        with Their Seven Bowls (15:1-8) 267
    B. The Bowls Are Poured Out (16:1-21) 271

Chapter Seven
Cycle Five: The Judgment of the Harlot (17:1-19:21) 281
    A. The Harlot Imagery 282
    B. Vision of the Mysterious Harlot (17:1-18) 283
    C. Judgment upon the Harlot (18:1-24) 295
    D. Judgment upon the Beasts (19:1-21) 301

Chapter Eight
Cycle Six: The Final Victory (20:1-15) 312
    A. The Grand Finale 312
    B. Victory for the Martyrs (20:1-6) 313
    C. Gog and Magog (20:7-10) 321
    D. The Great White Throne (20:11-15) 325

Chapter Nine
Cycle Seven: The Reward of the Faithful (21:1-22:5) 331
    A. The Glorious Future for God's Faithful People (21:1-8) 331
    B. God's New Age (21:9–22:5) 339

Chapter Ten
    The Epilogue (22:6-21) 350
    Conclusion 361
    Afterward 362

Works Consulted 366

Preface

Like a host of other students of the book of Revelation, our own enthusiasm over this wonderful series of heavenly visions given to the Apostle John was first awakened by a course of study at the feet of Professor W. B. West, Jr. Dr. West was the founding dean at the Harding Graduate School of Religion (now known as the Harding School of Theology) in Memphis, Tennessee, and the present writer studied with him in the early 1970s. Not to say that this was our first in-depth study of the book, for we had made a careful investigation of it earlier while reading Foy E. Wallace's commentary on Revelation during our time at David Lipscomb College two years previous.

That first effort ended in frustration, however. Far too many questions were left unaddressed by Wallace's conclusions, even though Wallace had emphasized with great assiduousness the folly so patently obvious in all of the futuristic readings of the book, and had made his case most persuasively. It could be fairly observed that Wallace was abundantly clear on what the book *did not* mean, but not nearly so clear on what in fact it *did* mean.

Dr. West, however, shared with his students a different and altogether unique perspective on the work that for most of us was thoroughly enlightening. It was as if the covers were pulled back from these many mysterious symbols and the light of understanding had shown through. His approach was fascinating but amazingly simple. Students were immediately seized with the notion, "Why didn't I think of that?" Once presented with this approach, that is precisely how it appeared to us all. The obvious answer to that question, however, is that there is so much fog in the air around the book of Revelation, put there by the speculations and ruminations of hosts of students and scholars over the many years of its existence, that the manifestly obvious does not appear nearly so apparent to most readers in our own time.

West argued for reading the book "through first century glasses" rather than opting for a reading that highlighted modern considerations, especially in regard to culture and history. He taught us to read the book in the way that those first early Christians would have read and understood it, and he argued that we ought to attempt to apply it primarily to their particular circumstances and spiritual needs rather than, as so many do, to our own. Applying it to our own situation was important, of course, but only as a secondary matter rather than the major one. Too often, precisely the opposite is the case. Present-day geopolitical realities and dangers are read *into* the book, along with cultural norms, rather than from it. (Such matters would have to be read into it, for none of these things are actually found therein.) This only leads to confusion. First, West pointed out, it had to be seen in the light of the persecuted disciples of Christ who lived and worshipped in Asia Minor in the age of the Roman emperors and of the idolatrous emperor cult which is alluded to in the book and so menacingly threatened them at the time. That religious affiliation and its forced adherence proved to be a terrible bane to the Christian teaching and lifestyle that they had pledged first allegiance to when they were baptized into Christ and identified themselves with the church of Christ. Until and unless the reader has come to appreciate this truth, he is not very likely ever to understand this material, written as it was to address the challenges that this immensely popular, but patently false religion represented for Christianity.

John meant for his record of the visions he saw on Patmos to be understood. He knew that it was written in the challenging language of signs and symbols, for he himself said so (Rev. 1:1-3). Yet, even though he used figures of speech and delicately stylized pictures of all sorts of things in his presentation, he nevertheless wanted those members of the seven churches of Asia Minor to "get it" and take away from their reading of the content of the Apocalypse a genuine message from Jesus Christ. A message of comfort and encouragement. A message of hope and victory. Unfortunately, over the years much of what he had to say to them has been lost in the heavy mists of empty speculation and tortured interpretation which has been applied mercilessly to this extraordinarily simple book. It was never meant to be as complicated as many expositors have made it out to be.

We remember Dr. West saying repeatedly, with a twinkle in his eye, "Revelation is the easiest book in the Bible." We are not certain that we are as

Preface

fully convinced of that proposition as he apparently was, but it was certainly understandable and comprehensible when examined on those terms. John meant to get his message across to his audience in broad generalities, and he did so for those who are willing to look at the contents of the book through the eyes of those who first read its message and applied it to their own situation.

Unfortunately W. B. West never wrote the commentary he spoke so often about writing. However, after his passing in 1994 Bob Prichard put his brief commentary notes (158 pages) into print in a book published by the Gospel Advocate Company, entitled, *Revelation through First Century Glasses* (1997). West influenced an entire generation of students of the book of Revelation through his delightfully challenging way of looking at this interesting literary document. This author was one of those students. We would be remiss if we were not to express deep and abiding appreciation for Dr. West and his early help with our study. We never speak about this book, write or teach on its meaning without silently giving thanks to God for the influence Dr. West has had on our research throughout the years.

This present work represents the realization of the aspiration of a lifetime. It has always been this author's plan to write this book. Of course, as it is often said, "Life happens in the meantime." And so, other matters have too often crowded it out and intruded into the process, and the realization of that plan has certainly been put off for too long. But, of course, we have frequently taught the book of Revelation and preached and lectured on topics related to it for nearly five decades since those first early investigations. In 2010 a workbook which we developed for the *Bible Text Book* series of class materials published by Truth Publications, Inc., became the inspiration and subsequently the formal basis for the present study of John's Apocalypse. Our immediate thought after its publication was that we needed to write a follow-up study for teachers of that material, something that would delve more deeply into the background and provide teachers additional illustrative information and evidence for many of our generalizations and conclusions. Since that time we have worked on "fleshing out" the material presented in that class book and putting it into a fuller and more versatile package for a larger readership. The reader will have to judge for himself how successful we have been in providing a useful guide to the content of the apostle John's most challenging literary work. It is our fervent prayer that it will fulfill that mission.

The author of this book is generally responsible for the translation of the text into English. Hence, the translation is our own, utilizing language the frequent peruser of the English Bible should be accustomed to reading. In the process of producing this rendering, we have attempted to remain in line with the older versions such as the KJV and the ASV, so as not to confuse the reader, while removing older and out-of-use linguistic phenomena, and at the same time clarifying certain expressions by the employment of a few modern idioms. Users of the older versions, and there are many of them still out there, will probably find themselves quite comfortable with our product. We have tried consciously not to depart too far from what they are accustomed to reading, while at the same time making it more readable and accurate in terms of modern parlance.

The reader should also understand from the outset that this book is not intended as a verse-by-verse treatment of the Revelation. There are many excellent works currently available that perform this function extremely well. They are intended for the advanced reader and the scholar, not for the introductory student. This book is a thematic treatment of Revelation. It is meant for the ordinary reader, the non-scholar. It purports to take note of the main lines of thought that John intends to set before his audience in his report about the visions that were shown to him. As such it will not attempt to explain every facet of every image that is pictured in the Apocalypse. This is not our goal. We would much prefer to have the reader finish reading this book and say that they understand the book of Revelation than to have them say that they understand every aspect of a particular vision of the book of Revelation. It is much to be preferred that the student be able to appreciate the big picture, the main line of thought, and the general intention of the author. In our view, the thematic method has much that commends it, for the verse-by-verse approach can be rather dizzying when trying to negotiate hundreds of individual items, intricate symbols, each begging for at least a modicum of explanation and some small amount of commentary to set it in its context and apprehend its significance. Hence, we have opted for the present approach to the book in order to benefit the average reader. Admittedly, there are some occasions in the book where we have entered into scholarly dialogue about some feature of special interest to this author in particular, usually having to do with archaeological materials from the ancient world which throw light on some aspect of the content of the work, or else some linguistic phenomenon that is interesting and

Preface

worth noting. Other than these two areas of our own intense interest, we have shied away from those kinds of investigations. They do not usually benefit the ordinary reader, and may well discourage them from further study. Certainly we do not want to be guilty of that.

Finally, it is important that we express our appreciation to those who have made this book a possibility. Thanks are due to the Board of Directors of Truth Publications, Inc., and in particular to my old friend and longtime associate Mike Willis for his considerable editorial skills in bringing this book to its final form. Too, as regards the other fellow members of the editorial committee of the company, Mark Mayberry and Kyle Pope, we would like to take special mention of them, since they will no doubt make considerable contributions to the final product when it is finished. In addition, they are responsible for the other equally important phases of publishing this book, along with hundreds of other books and articles for so many other extraordinary writers and their reading audience. Thanks for all of your hard work, fellows.

I also want to take a moment to thank my beloved bride of 50 years, Donna Jean Chapman King, for her love and patience throughout the years of our work together in the Kingdom of Heaven. She has been amazingly patient with me throughout these many years of being a "book worm" who is always reading or writing books, essays, and articles that pertain somehow or other to the Bible. That has been one of the great passions of my life, and she has often had to play "second fiddle" to some literary endeavor to which I am wed at a particular point in time. She has been such a blessing to my life. I thank God for her every day and hope that we have many more years to enjoy one another's company and assist each other in the work of Christ and the church in the world.

It is our hope that some small amount of good will come from this effort. Remember this, from start to finish: John's book needs to be demystified! Revelation was intended to be understood and appreciated, not avoided because of its perplexities and unintelligible content. If we can wrap our minds around that idea at the beginning, our approach will attempt to make it so and create an atmosphere of pleasurable reading and enjoyable study rather than of bewilderment and confusion for the new student. That is our plan. On our part, we certainly have no desire to add additional incoherence or ambiguity to this beautiful book of encouraging imagery, originally intended for the reassurance and edification of the persecuted church. What it was for them then, it should be for us today. We should take great pleasure in reading and studying it, just as we believe those first early disciples did as they made their way through the magnificent drama that is the Revelation.

If it is true that, "All is well that ends well," then all is assuredly well at the end of the Revelation because the book ends very well indeed for the church of which Jesus Christ is Savior and Lord. This fact must not be missed. We should read the book and be comforted by its pictures of the future. The visions contained in it were never, ever, meant to be frightening in their aspect for the faithful believer. Precisely the opposite! And unless that is seen to be so at the conclusion of our study of the Revelation, then something about our approach to the material has most unfortunately, but very effectively, defeated the intended goal of the original writer.

So, enjoy John's book of prophecy. Read it with pleasure. Breathe it in deeply and experience the encompassing exuberance of it. It was meant to encourage your faith and spur you on to faithful service for Jesus Christ in spite of whatever opposition may arise in an attempt to frustrate you or cause you to be discouraged. John has revealed the end of the story, so that all doubt and disbelief ought to be cast aside. The Lord will be victorious over them all! All enemies will fall before him. It may take some time, but they will inevitably be humbled before the Almighty God who fashioned heaven and earth. If God could bring mighty Rome to her knees before his Christ, any new ones who appear will just as easily be vanquished with time. So, be patient and stay steadfast in your faith. The heavenly city awaits!

On our part, we only hope that this small book will contribute something to the worthy purpose of allowing John to speak with clarity and decisiveness to those of our own time who are suffering under the cruel hand of tyrants, oppressors and persecutors: the Lord is on His way to the rescue! Just be patient until He arrives! And, until Jesus comes again in glory and great power, we must learn to say with confidence and with John's expectant enthusiasm, after he had viewed all of the scenes of the Apocalypse in their fullness: "Amen (Even so), come, Lord Jesus!" (Rev. 22:21).

Introduction to John's Book of Revelation

Revelation is a remarkable book. In the Bible it stands virtually alone in a special class almost by itself. And at the same time it utilizes a whole host of concepts, figures, and themes that are present elsewhere in Scripture. Thus, on the one hand it could be said that John's Revelation is undoubtedly one of the most magnificent literary endeavors in the biblical corpus of materials, and yet on the other this interesting amalgam of symbols is so different from the rest of the Bible that it is a total mystery to most people who read it today. Is that not ironic? The latter problem has proven its undoing for many readers. They simply are not willing to do the hard work necessary to get inside of the mind of the author and into the world that was contemporary with him. Thus, it has often been said that the book of Revelation has suffered more from misuse and neglect than any other book of the Bible. Because it is written in language that is highly symbolic, and presents to its readership visions that are filled with all sorts of shockingly vivid imagery, it is mystifying to the great majority of us, and most of us feel that there are many things about it we just do not understand. One author remarked in his own frustration with the contents and its long history of often downright silly misinterpretation:

> Few writings in all of literature have been so obsessively read with such generally disastrous results as the Book of Revelation. Its history of interpretation is largely a story of tragic misinterpretation, resulting from a fundamental misapprehension of the work's literary form and purpose. Insofar as its arcane symbols have fed the treasury of poets, its influence has been benign. More often, these same symbols have nurtured delusionary systems, both private and public, to the destruction of the fashioners and to the discredit of the writing (Johnson, 512).

One thing that is a potential key to our sad plight is that we are not accustomed to this sort of "heavy" and "freighted" symbolism. Certainly much less so than the ancients were. Assuredly it requires much more thought and interpretive skill than, say, the straightforward historical narratives of Acts or the uncomplicated and undemanding epistolary style of an unadorned and unpretentious letter like Paul wrote to the Christian slave-owner Philemon about his run-away slave Onesimus, or the young preacher Titus in regard to his duties as a minister of the gospel. Since we all tend to be a little lazy at times, we therefore tend to take the easiest courses in the College of Spiritual Development and avoid the advanced ones when we can. So, we study Acts, Titus, and Philemon, and neglect the Revelation of John. That is certainly the easy way out of this conundrum. But avoiding Revelation is not the best plan. Even aside from the symbolic sections, the work is rich with content. There is much in the book that needs to be known by the mature Christian. A little work and study will pay rich dividends to the one who spends the time and makes the effort to tap its treasure-trove of spiritual resources.

Also, because through the ages of its interpretation it has served as a sort of magnet and hence a playground for extremists and fanatics who have forced upon it all kinds of strange and bizarre interpretations, we have tended to shy away and sometimes steer clear of it altogether. Adding multiple confusing interpretations to the mix has led only to further befuddlement. As a result, some of us even fear to attempt to probe the depths of its many intricacies and profundities. On account of the nature of the material found in this book, in almost every era of extreme emergency, of political uncertainty, or international crisis the book of Revelation has become the bastion for the religious "lunatic fringe" of the time. It is their "go to" book whenever the world seems to be nearing the precipice. The august Professor Hendriksen, for example, in his 1949 lectures on Revelation (12) laughingly ruminated about a popular journal during World War II which published a lengthy series of eagerly read articles whose author "on the basis of prophecy" endeavored to furnish detailed information about the future progress of that horrible conflict and its final outcome. "It so happened that the actual course of events belied his predictions: Italy did not 'win the war!'"

Introduction to John's Book of Revelation

More recently, the fall of the iron curtain and of communism within the old eastern bloc countries has frustrated another entire generation of speculators on the meaning of the book. Soviet Russia collapsed and with it the premises and projections of a plethora of speculative books that made of it the ultimate anti-Christian power whose military ambitions were to bring about the Battle of Armageddon and the consummation of the age! What a dreadful waste of pen and ink! One wonders whether the Lord will allow the world to stand long enough to frustrate the more recent millennialism which views the book in terms of Islamic extremism. Who can tell?

Even well-meaning and sincere students of the Word have missed its significance, as this early quotation from Justin Martyr, who lived in Ephesus and later in Rome, writing about AD 155-160 suggests. He was one of the few early churchmen who believed that John's book actually taught millennialism:

> And, further, a man among us named John, one of the apostles of Christ, prophesied in a Revelation made to him that they who have believed our Christ will spend a thousand years in Jerusalem, and that afterwards the universal, and, in one word, eternal resurrection of all at once, will take place, and also the judgment (*Dialogue with Trypho* 81).

Justin Martyr was no doubt an erudite and pious fellow, but a too-shallow reading of Revelation can confuse even the best of men! And Justin was certainly bewildered by John's words on this thorny question. On the other hand, when we have equipped ourselves properly with the right tools of interpretation, namely an appreciation of the historic circumstances of the clash between Christ and Caesar, the church and Rome, and an understanding of the general method of the writers of the Jewish apocalyptic literature who preceded the writing of John (initiated by Daniel, Ezekiel, and Zechariah), then there is no reason that we should feel in the least threatened by the study of this great book. Justin's problem seems to have centered around this latter aspect. He was not sufficiently aware of the methodology which was employed in the writing and interpretation of that body of literature. Literalizing passages that are filled with symbols, and thus were never meant to be taken literally, has proven disastrous for more than one student of the Revelation over its long history. Unfortunately,

Justin fell prey to this error. Many have followed him in this mistaken approach to that particular text (Rev. 20:1ff.

As Leon Morris said, "It is of utmost importance for modern man that he does not lose touch with the eternal realities so stressed in Revelation" (Morris, 15-16). Perhaps there has never been an age for which its eternal teaching is more relevant than our own. For these are days when the decisions of the great powers of our world have far-reaching effects on ordinary men and women, and we feel quite helpless as we experience it. And even though we may have no great interest in political ideologies, we find that our lives are immeasurably affected by decisions reached in the world's capitals, Moscow and Washington, London and Beijing, places and circumstances in which we have no voice at all and no ability to determine the ultimate outcome. We are led to ask the question, "Are we then no more than pawns caught up in a strategic geopolitical war of ideologies?" Massively powerful nuclear weapons are lined up on each side in a hundred different directions, constantly threatening both guilty and innocent alike, with some leaders being insane tyrants seemingly ready to push the button over any apparent slight and plunge the entire planet into nuclear holocaust.

No one wants such a nuclear inferno or the "nuclear winter" that is sure to follow, with potentially all life being snuffed out on the earth, and yet some who are in control seem oblivious to the present and future ramifications of their risky decisions. Is there something demonic about these evil forces which even our most powerful statesmen seem unable to control? It is hard to tell for sure. And yet, this is the world that we are presently living in!

The book of Revelation resoundingly speaks with reassurance and hope to an age which is tortured by complicated and thorny problems like these, for it was written to a voiceless minority of religious people who were at their particular historical moment massively overwhelmed and painfully tortured by the subtleties, ironies, and ugly realities of geopolitical power. Indeed, it has been called, not unjustly, "a theology of power" (cf. Morris,16). We would adjust this title and make of it "a theology of power for the sake of the powerless." The church represented a tiny minority of the population almost entirely devoid of regulatory or administrative influence and bereft of political strength. God was the solitary source of their power. And so, to Him they were forced to look with anticipation, praying that He would

Introduction to John's Book of Revelation

hear their appeals and act on their behalf. There was no other alternative for them. God was their only hope. The Revelation speaks to that inner longing of the human soul when it is out of alternatives. It shouts to the heavens that God not only has the power to act on their behalf, but in fact will do so convincingly. God will judge the wicked and reward the righteous, but it is incumbent upon the believer to wait patiently for Him to do so, and in the meantime, not lose hope or permit his faith to fail.

This book also has much to teach us, as Christians, that is helpful and useful in our everyday service to the Lord, and we must not get lost in the symbols and images which are found in such profusion in the book to the point where we lose sight of this important fact. The seven letters to the seven churches of Asia are, by themselves, filled with important insights into the relationship of Christ with those congregations of disciples which have associated themselves with his cause. "I know thy works" is a phrase that is repeated throughout the letters, suggesting that the Lord (who at times seems to be so very far away) is intimate with all that is happening in the church in the present hour. He walks amidst the seven lampstands (which represent the churches) and knows of their flaws and is fully aware of their strong points. He is proud of their accomplishments. At the same time, He condemns their sins and encourages them towards repentance, with the assurance that forgiveness will always be forthcoming and full restoration is available. He sympathizes with their fears and weaknesses, and encourages them to be patient and to bear up under the heavy load of their immediate burdens. He understands their temptations and commiserates with their many onerous problems. Such teaching is of enormous benefit to the daily life of the child of God, and it is found in the book of Revelation, a book which many people fear to read and thus refuse to study! What a tragic loss!

At the same time, in this work the reader is carried off into another dimension, vastly different from our own. It is not the time-and-space world with which we are all so familiar, but into the sphere of what lies behind the scenes of what happens on the plain of the ordinary. One is carried, not into some never-never land of fancy, but into the Ever-ever land of God's eternal Values and Judgments (cf. Phillips, 9). Hence, he shares in what is real to God, divine reality. With its beautiful picturesque portraits of heaven itself, no book in all of the Bible has made heaven seem more authentic and more desirable than this book has. As A. M. Hunter wrote: "Revelation, beyond all other books, has made people feel that heaven is real; and in the strength of that blessed conviction go forth anew to do battle with the world and all of its evils" (Hunter, 113).

Thus, even though we cannot see heaven with our physical eyes, we can visit it in the symbols and figures of the book of Revelation, and on account of those beautiful portraits desire it with all of our hearts and work and labor for the Master that much more diligently to attain its glories when our life on earth is finished. Moreover, even though we cannot see behind the scenes of world history to understand the complex and sometimes confusing powers of both good and evil that are endeavoring in the course of these struggles to achieve spiritual dominance, in the Apocalypse these struggles are revealed to us. We see what those first disciples saw. What the Revelation revealed to them it reveals to us also. When we are able to unravel the meaning of the symbols of the book, we understand the struggle taking place between the forces of good and evil in the world. Their world and ours.

Just as those truths were revealed to the suffering bands of Christians in Asia Minor during the Roman persecution of their movement by those elements attempting to force upon them the worship of the Roman Emperor, they are made known to us also. Pagan idolatry has been replaced in our own time with radical Islamic ideology or else secular humanism with its panoply of evils dragged along in its wake. The names and ideas have all changed, but the spiritual forces are identical. God and Satan are at odds with one another. Just as they have always been. It was so in the days of the prophet Daniel when he saw the great powers of his day portrayed as enormous and threatening beasts, and it was so when John saw them pictured as a beast with ten horns and seven heads.

In the end the "Great Red Dragon" (Rev. 12:3ff.) was behind it all pulling the strings and manipulating the main characters of the drama. Who was this dark and frightening figure (then and now)? John tells us: he is "the old serpent, he that is called the Devil, and Satan, the deceiver of the whole world" (12:9). Complex geopolitical realities play out in the newspapers and in the media of our time, but always we know that the

Introduction to John's Book of Revelation

same struggle is ongoing. Evil and good are in a continuous struggle for dominance. John tells us who the combatants are. And he reveals to us the way the whole thing is to end. There is no ambivalence on this matter. The end is absolutely certain. Evil will be defeated. God and good will be triumphant. Along the way as events play themselves out it may seem to be the other way around. Frequently evil will appear to have the upper hand, but if we believe John's Revelation, we know with absolute clarity that God will be victorious, and God's people will be victorious with him. God will win and we will win.

In fact, seen in this light, studying the Revelation can become for us a joyful and faith-building experience. It can arm us with the knowledge which will carry us through our own personal dilemmas and crises and even the sometimes frightening and overwhelming events of contemporary world history. It will also provide us with a consciousness of God's ultimate control of things both in our own lives and in the destiny of this world's great nations. This was true for the content of this book for the seven churches of Asia at the end of the first century, and it should be so for us also. It built up their faith and gave them hope. It ought to do the same for ours as well. But, admittedly, on our part it will take a bit of effort to wade through the intricate symbolism to get to the messages this part of the Word of God has to communicate to us. If we work at it, though, we will be rewarded handsomely.

Finally, it must be remembered that, in spite of the heavy symbolism in which John wrote this book, he expected the ordinary men and women of the churches of Asia Minor to understand what he had written, even though they were not Bible scholars, trained historians, much less theological experts. There is no evidence that they found it necessary to organize study groups or "brain trusts" in order to discuss and come to a consensus in regard to its symbols or their meaning. Nor did they seal up the book for later centuries, when it might be better understood in terms of events which had already unfolded (compare 22:10 with Dan. 12:4, 9). The basic issue for them was not what the essential meaning of the book might be, which was altogether transparent in their situation at the time (just as it ought to be for us in our own), but whether or not they would respond to its call for the kind of wholehearted faithfulness advocated by

John as essential in those perilous times, even to the point of dying for the faith (2:10). This is what the book calls for on the part of the reader. Not brilliance or cunning, but loyalty to God at whatever personal cost. M. E. Boring has observed rightly:

> John's claim that this vision of reality is not our own achievement, the result of our own calculation, but is *revealed*, intensifies a claim latent in all the Bible, a claim to address us with a word from Beyond, a word we naturally resist. Revelation not only claims something about itself, it makes a claim on the reader, a claim we may not want to hear. This native resistance to the call to discipleship may be the ultimate barrier to understanding the message of Revelation. True understanding of Revelation requires belonging to the community in which the same Spirit that inspired John's message continues to be active. This is not an alternative to historical understanding, but it does go beyond it (Boring, 46-47).

Over the many centuries since the apostle penned this magnificent work of apocalyptic literature, the church's best thinkers have artfully developed many different ways of interpreting and understanding this book. Some of those strike close to home while others are far wide of the mark in terms of the writer's original purpose. But, laying all this aside for the moment, "where the rubber meets the road" for John was not whether a reader has the insight or skill to peel away the imagery to get to the theological overtones of his freighted symbols, but whether one has the courage to face the challenge of the book itself, the challenge of faithfulness to our Savior in a time of danger or even death. Are we willing to be faithful to Christ, despite the persecutions and controversies of our own time and unique historical circumstances? That is the real challenge of the book of Revelation. That is the actual purpose of the book.

These other considerations may be interesting and even heady at times, but in many instances they represent only distractions from the writer's original intent. John was telling the Christians of Asia Minor to remain steadfast in the face of whatever physical or psychological terror came their way. But he was also guaranteeing them that, even if they suffered terribly or perished on account of their tenacity, God would punish their oppressors eventually, and reward them eternally. What awaited their molesters would prove to be beyond terrible. What awaited God's faithful would prove to be beyond wonderful.

Introduction to John's Book of Revelation

What Do We Know about the Writer?

The early church was convinced that the apostle John, the brother of James, was the author of the book they called "Revelation." The evidence of this is early and plentiful. Papias (*circa* AD 70-163) was probably the first writer to make direct use of the document. And although the fragments of that author's *Expositions of the Oracles of the Lord*, preserved in the writing of Eusebius, do not mention such use, there is allusion to his acquaintance with and high regard for the Apocalypse in Andreas' commentary on the last book of Scripture, penned in the sixth century. Additional independent testimony for recognition of the book as a genuine work of John, comes from Irenaeus (*Against Heresies* 5.30.1), who spoke of the certification of the true text of Revelation 13:18 by men who saw the Apostle face to face. Justin Martyr, who taught at Ephesus shortly after his conversion in 130 noted that, "A certain man among us, whose name was John, one of the apostles of Christ, prophesied in a revelation made to him, that those who believed in our Christ would spend a thousand years in Jerusalem" (*Dialogue* 81). And even though he misread the force of the teaching of Revelation 20, it is certain nevertheless that since he was in the area where the Revelation was first circulated barely four decades previous to his handling of the document, Justin is a very powerful witness in regard to the authorship of the material.

Interestingly enough, in spite of the peculiar nature of the contents of the book, filled as it was with mysterious symbolism, it was immediately recognized as being inspired Scripture and understood that it ought to be treated as such. This is especially noteworthy because every part of the New Testament canon was not so fortunate as it was during those early years. There was considerable competition in some instances in regard to the recognition of the status of genuineness and canonicity of all documents claiming such identification. This was so on account of the fact that some of the letters, especially the general epistles like James, were first read and safeguarded not by the larger Gentile congregations but by out-of-the-mainstream Jewish Christians and their congregations who were scattered and persecuted after the destruction of Jerusalem in AD 70 (having the dreadful misfortune of being both Jewish and Christian in an unfriendly Greco-Roman environment after Rome had tired of Jewish churlishness and rebellion and was beginning to weary of the Christians and their strange ways as well). Also complicating matters was the fact that they fought for recognition in a situation where there were very many apocryphal and pseudepigraphical documents that were appearing among the Christians in order to promulgate or promote some strange new doctrine pertaining to some particular aspect of the Christian system. Yet, the Revelation seems to have been little affected by any of this. It was recognized as Scripture early and often, and that in spite of the utter strangeness and alien methods employed by the writer in communicating his message.

The evidence of this is powerful and plentiful. In our view there is only one thing that is able fully to explain this phenomenon, and that is its early attachment to a figure who locally was considered a hero of the faith and was personally known to many people in the region. The earliest written extra-biblical tradition attaching John to the city of Ephesus is found in the writings of Irenaeus (*Against Heresies* 2.22.51; 3.3.4; 5.30.1; 5.33.3). There he tells the story of "John, the disciple of the Lord, going to bathe at Ephesus, and perceiving Cerinthus within, rushed out of the bath-house without bathing, exclaiming, 'Let us fly, lest even the bath-house fall down, because Cerinthus, the enemy of the truth, is within.'" Cerinthus was a well-known heretic who promoted his false doctrines widely and effectively. John apparently wanted nothing whatsoever to do with him and wished not be found in the vicinity of the man. This tale has a ring of truth about it, and there seems to be no good reason for doubting its veracity.

Irenaeus lived in the second century, of course, but as a young man it is said that he had met the grand martyr of the faith, Polycarp, and had been taught by him. Tertullian noted that Polycarp was appointed to his office as a bishop at Smyrna by the apostle John himself (*Prescription Against Heretics* 32). Irenaeus not only claims repeatedly that the apostle John spent the closing years of his life at Ephesus, but in proof of this proposition refers to the testimony of the presbyters, who he claimed had seen him in Asia, and especially to the personal testimony of Polycarp. Both Irenaeus and later also Eusebius (*Church History* 3.39.2) considered him to have been the personal teacher of Papias. John, in fact, is said to have lived a very long life and even to have survived "till the days of Trajan" (AD 98-117). Irenaeus also preserved this tradition for later generations (*Against Heresies* 2.22.5; 3.3.4; and both passages are quoted in Eusebius' *Church History*

3.23.3-4). These stories, although they are not found in the text of written Scripture, nevertheless have the ring of truth about them since there is nothing outrageous or unbelievable and thus they may well take the reader back to the era of John and may also attest to various circumstances and events surrounding his days at Ephesus in the final decade(s) of his life. They also provide very strong evidence for the writing of the Revelation at the very end of the first century AD, establishing that he lived long enough and dwelt in the very vicinity mentioned in the book (Patmos was but 63 miles, or 101 kilometers offshore from Ephesus).

So, John's association with the area goes beyond his connection with the island of Patmos (Rev. 1:9) in the Mediterranean not far from Ephesus in Asia Minor. Moreover, three hundred years after his death a small chapel was constructed over the site of what was historically connected with his grave on the southern slope of Ayosolug Hill near Ephesus, and eventually in the era of the Emperor Justinian (AD 527-565) a beautiful basilica was constructed there. It still bears the name "The Basilica of Saint John." For a time it was utilized as a mosque after the Turkish invasion, but it was destroyed by an earthquake during the fourteenth century. Its ruins are still standing today, containing impressive 10th-century frescoes of Jesus, John, and others. So, the tradition of John's presence in Ephesus after the scattering of the apostles from Jerusalem dates very early and, in our estimation at least, is beyond successful denial (Clemen, 643-676). The extreme skepticism which denies even the presence of the apostle John in the city of Ephesus, is a relatively modern perspective and has nothing that commends it. The tradition of the "beloved disciple" in that city "down to the times of Trajan" is ancient, widespread, and almost uncontradicted in the earliest days of the church. The counter evidence, on the other hand, is quite simply trivial and hardly worth serious consideration. As Carl von Weizsäcker observed: "The proof given by Irenaeus from Polycarp . . . is more than tradition, it is direct documentary evidence" (von Weizsäcker, 2: 168).

In our view it is especially noteworthy that the strong tradition in the region that John lived to old age and died, apparently of natural causes associated with extreme old age, is especially striking since some viewed the Lord's words to the two brothers James and John as a prediction of their eventual martyrdom (Matt. 20:23; Mark 10:35ff.), and this would have created a possible contradiction, since only James is said to have been martyred (Acts 12:2). This may well have been the inspiration of the theory held by some writers of the early centuries that John died at Jerusalem at the hand of the Jews as well as the tradition that he was almost boiled alive in a cauldron of oil during the reign of Domitian (see Tertullian, *The Prescription Against Heretics*, 36: "the apostle John was first plunged, unhurt, into boiling oil, and thence remitted to his island-exile"; cf. Badham, 3: 729-740; and, 8: 539-554).

The earliest specific reference to the Apocalypse as Scripture *per se* is found in the Letter of the Churches of Lyons (Lugdunum) and Vienna in Gaul which was directed to the congregations of the Asia Minor region. Within that document the statement is made that the unrighteous hatred shown in the persecution which then raged against the Christians of their communities fulfilled the Scripture. The quotation of Revelation 22:11 then follows (Eusebius, *Church History* 5.1.58). Tertullian of North Africa, like Irenaeus, was also in the habit of quoting from the Revelation and noting that it was the work of the apostle John. The Canon Muratori, a Latin translation of a Greek original dating from about 170, included John's Revelation, noting that although the writer penned his letters to seven churches, in fact, in those letters he speaks to all of them (cf. Harrison, 428). This is especially interesting and very potent evidence for the legitimacy of the Revelation because this is the same region to which John penned the seven letters which are couched in the early chapters of the book. So, not only is this evidence of the recognition by people from the specific region where the work originated that it is wholly genuine, but it also provides us with powerful proof that the apostle John was its author.

Now, the author of the Apocalypse identifies himself simply as John. He provides no further enlargement upon this straightforward introduction of himself. He says that this book is the "revelation of Jesus Christ which God gave him to show to his servants . . . and he sent and signified it to his servant John" (1:1). The epistolary introduction of 1:4 reads: "John to the seven churches that are in Asia." Later, he calls himself, "John, your brother and partaker with you in the tribulation and kingdom and patience" (v. 9). He is merely John, a brother in Christ, and a fellow sufferer with those who were then experiencing tribulation for the cause of Christ. The simplic-

Introduction to John's Book of Revelation

ity and directness of this preface is noteworthy. It tells us something very important about the relationship of the writer and the readers.

This writer was so well known to the readers that he needed to say no more than this. Apparently it could be assumed that there could be no possibility of a mistaken identity. He did not need to claim apostleship as a title or office in the church. They knew who and what he was. It was not necessary for him to inform them of his close personal relationship with Jesus as his disciple and close friend. They already knew all of this, and perhaps much more besides. The author's matter-of-fact approach and his extensive knowledge of the precise conditions which existed in each of the seven churches indicate that he wrote as a person of authority to Christian communities which were in some sense under his jurisdiction. The name John appears four times in the book. Much like an *inclusio*, the first three are at the beginning (1:1, 4, 9), and a fourth occurrence is at the end (22:8). Hence, we are led to conclude from this that he claims to have written all of it. Every one of the visions were seen by and written down by the hand of a single author.

The apostle John, author of the Gospel by his name, and First, Second, and Third John, is unquestionably the one meant by this attribution. Only an apostle of Christ could have written as authoritatively as this man did. The confusion of this simple issue by some scholars' reading of Eusebius' ancient reference to Papias, and his seeming mention of two Johns at Ephesus, in our view, borders upon the absurd. In the first place, there is no great certainty that Papias actually did refer to two separate Johns. This is, in itself, a matter of some considerable dispute. It is more of a conjecture than a fact, even though some writers address it as if it were a fact of history.

The sum of the evidence amounts to Eusebius' interpretation of one sentence in Papias and a much later traveler's tale of two tombs in Ephesus each said to be John's. Upon this flimsy foundation has been built the whole disreputable theory of a separate "John the presbyter." Having then presumed his existence on this very shoddy and highly questionable testimony, some scholars make the giant leap of faith to give this unknown and enigmatic character credit for five books of the New Testament! In point of fact, there is no good reason to rule out the apostle John as the author of this material. All of the available external and internal evidence points to him as the writer.

Two things are clear about this author from the beginning of the book. First, the writer considered himself, at least primarily and for the purpose of the writing of this book, in the role of a prophet. An anonymous or otherwise unknown figure would hardly meet such profound criteria! Moreover, he repeatedly calls his work a word of prophecy (cf. 1:3; 22:7, 10, 18, 19). In developing the material for the book he depends heavily on the efforts of many of the former Hebrew prophets. The writings of Moses, Isaiah, Jeremiah, Ezekiel, and Daniel are the models for the literature that he produces, and he works as if he has their writings in front of him, or at least in his memory from thorough acquaintance. He also, in the tradition of the old Hebrew prophets, disputed the claims of false prophets, whom he refers to as Jezebel and Balaam, once more borrowing from the Old Testament and its list of villains. And while the future orientation of many of the visions gets the majority of the notoriety for many who study it today, it is actually quite secondary to their prophetic intent. The visions service the prophecy; the prophecy is not determined by the visions. Prophets were primarily preachers, not forecasters. So, the present is also not overshadowed by the future. References to the future are meant to influence a person's behavior in the present. In a very real sense the book of Revelation follows in this mode. John, like them, is a preacher trying to form or else reform the behavior of his reading audience, not a prognosticator attempting to foretell the future. Therefore, the book's prophecies include divine precepts for living in the present, about which the readers must make a decision. This understanding of the essential nature of prophecy is entirely consistent with the Old Testament idea, which emphasizes revealed interpretation of the present together with the future, demanding ethical response for the present audience in their daily lives. John the apostle is therefore a perfect fit based on this first criterion.

A second consideration has to do with the writer's extremely heavy dependence on Hebrew biblical material. The Old Testament has been central to his theological upbringing, and even though he is now a Christian, it is still his chart and compass as regards his essential theology. His employment of such information implies that the John who penned this work was in all likelihood a Palestinian Jew who had come to the conclusion that Jesus was indeed the Messiah of Jewish promise and that he filled the role of the Lord's agent charged with ushering in God's reign over the earth.

He writes in a kind of Semiticized Greek that suggests a penman who is someone whose native language was not Classical or even Hellenistic Greek but the Aramaic spoken on the streets of the ancestral homeland by Palestinian Jews.

He also appears very knowledgeable about the topography of Jerusalem, the design and cultic practice of the old Jerusalem temple, even prior to its destruction in AD 70, and the broader landscape of Palestine itself (Blount, 7-8). Once again, the disciple of Jesus whom we know as the apostle John is a perfect fit in this regard. It is our opinion that this leaves little doubt that the writer of this document was indeed John, the son of Zebedee, who also wrote the Gospel that bears his name and the three small letters entitled, 1-3 John.

In modern thought all sorts of alternative theories have been propounded on this matter, but most of them have been given very little consideration by readers who are evangelical in their approach and at the same time serious about the evidence found in the book itself and in the early extra-biblical historical materials written in the first couple of centuries after the apostolic era. A number of scholars have thought that an unknown writer using the name "John" as a pseudonym or false name was the actual writer. As mentioned above, some have thought him to have been "John the Elder" or "Presbyter," an obscure figure who may not even have existed. We deem this conclusion to be without any scholarly merit. Certainly it has no biblical justification. And the extra-biblical evidence is sadly wanting as well.

As we have already noted, an allusion from the second-century figure named Papias of Hierapolis is said to be the source of this view which states that there were two men whose name was John in the early church, John the apostle, and then an elder from Ephesus whose name was also John. This view is taken from a passage out of Eusebius' *Church History*, where he quoted from Papias in this regard. This is the only evidence that such a person may have ever lived, and there is no proof at all in the traditions or writings of the early church that he was the author of anything, much less anything in the corpus of the Johannine writings.

This theory also falls afoul of the considerable internal evidence found in the book. It ought to be observed that if an unknown author were attempting to identify himself with a well-known Christian figure like the apostle John who played such an important role in the Gospels and the book of Acts, he would no doubt have called himself not just "John" but rather "John the apostle" in order to attempt a direct connection with that historically prominent figure, but the author of the Revelation does not do this. He introduces himself simply as "John." And although he uses this name several times he never makes any effort to associate himself with any other office than that of a "brother" and a fellow sufferer during this era of persecution of the church. A pretender would never have failed to take such an opportunity to make a solid case for the genuineness of this document and his identification with the apostle John. We would also expect that he would give much information about the original John in order to fortify this attempted correlation, but he does not do this either. Why not? Because he did not need to do so. This writer was well known by his audience and they recognized him to be John, the son of Zedebee, from the outset. He needed no extensive introduction.

Indeed, there is relatively little additional information given about the author in the book. He only calls himself a servant, a fellow believer in God and Christ, a witness for Jesus, and one who is suffering exile on the Island of Patmos on account of that association (1:1, 9-10). Would a pretender have left his self-description so thoroughly devoid of an impressive resumé? And, although it has been argued with some considerable acumen and enthusiasm by a few respected writers that pseudepigraphical writing was an accepted convention among Christians in that era of the church, the reality of the situation is quite the opposite. In fact it was no more acceptable to readers then than it is to us today. It was a disreputable practice which was rejected and shamed when it was discovered. So, this justification does not provide rhetorical and moral cover for the theory held by some modern divines that this writer may have been a well-intentioned fellow who obviously claimed to be the apostle John, but actually was not.

Therefore, the consensus of modern evangelical thought has rightly held that the name John used in the book is more than a sophisticated ruse, an attempt at recapturing the glory and authority of a bygone era by some skilful pretender posing as John the apostle in order to set forth the content found in this Apocalypse. It is rather a personal self-reference to the real

Introduction to John's Book of Revelation

John mentioned elsewhere so often in the New Testament. Comparable to this view in some ways is the popular notion that an anonymous writer representing a "Johannine school" of thought and writing was actually responsible for it. Differences in writing style, grammar, vocabulary, etc., from the Gospel that bears John's name as well as the three diminutive epistles from him, have been appealed to by those writers determined to prove this view. And there are of course some differences, just as any author displays when he writes a different book on a different subject at a different time in his life.

But it cannot be denied that differences of occasion, purpose, and most especially, the very distinctive apocalyptic-prophetic genre to which most of the content of the work is formally to be associated will explain most of such differences quite effortlessly. Moreover, many similarities exist between various thematic elements between the Gospel and the Revelation. The Exodus-Moses motif is present in both, as well as a very similar christology: Jesus as the Word, Lamb, and Son of Man as glorified even through death, themes such as Shepherd, manna, living water, and life and light.

Of course, the Revelation introduces additional and singularly important christological figures not found elsewhere in the Johannine corpus such as, especially, the Divine Warrior which is seen in the book as judging the worldly institutions which John saw as oppressing the church and committing injustice toward Christians generally. Christ comes to their rescue as a victorious Warrior riding a white horse and coming to the aid of His suffering people, "and in righteousness He judges and makes war" (19:11). The key element of the concept of Holy War in the Old Testament is related directly to the notion that the Lord, as the Divine Warrior, led Israel into battle against her enemies and won the victory for them. Exodus 15 extolled the Lord's victory over the people of Egypt. Again, at Jericho, the Lord caused the walls of the great city to fall down flat, a battle that was won through divine intervention on Israel's behalf. The intentional and seemingly suicidal reduction of the number of troops that Gideon took into the field was also an evident illustration of the power of the Almighty to wage war for His people against the Midianites. The Messiah of Israel was to be a rider upon the clouds of heaven (Psa. 18:9-15; 104:1-4; Dan. 7:13; see Rev. 1:7). Many texts in the prophets also point out that the Lord rides upon the clouds (as if on a war chariot) to the rescue of His people (Isa. 19:1; Nah. 1:2ff.; Psa. 68:4, 33; Deut. 33:26; Jer. 4:13ff.; etc.). Jesus also directly made reference to this important figure so common to the Old Testament, employing it in regard to Himself on more than one occasion (Matt. 24:29, 30; 26:64; Luke 21:27; and Rev. 1:7; cf. also, Isa. 13:10; Joel 3:14ff.).

Jesus Christ portrayed as the Divine Warrior is also contrasted with the demonic warrior of Revelation 13, the beast. This becomes clear at that moment in which the beast emerges from the sea. The beast is described as "having ten horns and seven heads and on his horns were ten diadems." These ten diadems may be compared with the many diadems on Christ's head. Further, right after the mention of His diadems it is stated that "He (Christ) has a name written upon Him which no one knows except Himself" (Rev. 19:12b), "His name is called the Word of God" (v. 13b), and lastly, "On His thigh He has a name written 'King of Kings and Lord of Lords'" (v. 16b). This contrasts with the hellish warriors in 13:1b on whose heads "were blasphemous names." There may also be a contrast between the beast and Christ in that the former has a number which conceals a name, and the latter has a name which conceals a number (Longman, 290-307).

In addition to the motifs which they share in common, there are also very many words and phrases that appear in both the Gospel and the Revelation, and even occasionally are seen in the epistles of John: Word, truth, keep the commandments, sign, witness, testimony, etc. These are all distinctly Johannine words and phrases and they bear witness not to the presence of a school of thought and writing, as some have unconvincingly averred, but of the hand of a single, simple-minded and inauspicious author who finds no good reason to depart from the style and thematic concepts that he has employed already in all of his written works, and exhibited throughout his career as a writer right down to this final exhibit of his simple-but-profound literary efforts (cf. Beale, 34, 35). John was just writing in this instance in the style and method that he had used throughout his life. John was just being John.

What Can We Say about the Place of Writing?

The tiny Isle of Patmos, one of the group of the southern Sporades off the southwest coast of Asia Minor (modern Turkey), is mentioned by John

Introduction to John's Book of Revelation

The Island of Patmos

as the site of his witnessing the visions which are contained in this book (1:9). Early tradition is unanimous (Irenaeus, Eusebius, Jerome, and others) that the apostle was exiled there during the fourteenth year of Domitian's reign (AD 95) and was released during the reign of Nerva (AD 96) about eighteen months later, after the death of the dreaded Domitian. Whether he actually wrote the book there or at Ephesus after his release from exile is a matter of conjecture. At all events, according to consistent and early Christian tradition John spent about eighteen months in exile on this particular island for his preaching in the name of Christ, but afterward was permitted to return to Ephesus, where he lived out the remainder of his long life. Certainly the island has been celebrated for the last two thousand years as the place where he received his revelation. So the geographical and historical details of that small island would certainly have some interest for the deliberate student of the book of Revelation.

Patmos itself is a barren, almost treeless, rocky and rugged island located 24 miles west of Asia Minor (modern Turkey) in the Aegean Sea, at 37° 20' N, 26° 34' E, and about 37 miles southwest of the coastal town of Miletus. In John's day it would have been approximately sixty miles from the city of Ephesus. The tiny land mass is around 7.5 miles (12 km) long and about six miles (10 km) broad along the northern coast, and contains an area of but 34.05 km (ca. 13.15 square miles). Situated between Leros and Ikaria, this mountainous island is cursed with rocky soil and blessed with an abundance of small coves. Today it belongs to Greece, and is one of the northernmost islands of the Dodecanese complex.

The Cave of the Apocalypse, which lies within a short walking distance of the villages of both Skala (1.5 km) and Hora (1.6 km) on the island, is said to mark the site where the visions were seen and John wrote the book.

The cave was converted into a place of worship by the monk Christodoulos Latrinós in the eleventh century. The Monastery of the Apocalypse (*Agios Ioannis Theologos*, "St. John the Theologian"), which stands on a high point above the grotto, was built as a castle in 1088 by that same monk.

It is visible from almost all places on the scenic little island. Buildings of different ages form the Monastery complex, comprising ten chapels and ninety-nine cells, cisterns and other spaces, as well as a library and museum of some of the most important ecclesiastical treasures of Greece, of some 890 handwritten codices and 13,000 documents about the history of the site. Its marvelous treasury of priceless objects contains Byzantine and post-Byzantine icons, sacred vessels, 9th century embroideries, parchment documents, illuminated manuscripts, and rare old books. In the chapel, frescoes can be seen which date to as early as 1210-1220.

The island is about forty miles distant from the larger island of Samos, which in the narrowest part of the strait is scarcely two miles from the continent. Ships arriving at the modern Patmos dock at the island's harbor, Skala. It is a lovely and lively place with its white houses, flowered courtyards, fish tavernas, hotels, restaurants, cafes, and small shops. North of Skala is the village of Kambos, set among trees and greenery and near it is what many today consider to be the island's finest beach. Patmos' indented coastline conceals a host of lovely beaches. Among the favorites for modern visitors are Grigos, Kallikatsou, Psili Ammos, and Diakofti. When John visited the place, however, it was nothing like it is today. It enjoyed none of these qualities as a haven for tourists. It was a place of isolation and exile, away from the culture and sophistication, conveniences and attractions, people and things of the great cities of Asia Minor. It was a prison island. A destination for exiles and political prisoners, not for tourists or vacationers.

Patmos is rarely, if ever, mentioned in Grecian history. After Ephesus became the seat of the Roman proconsular government, from its remote insular situation and extreme barrenness it provided a convenient place for the banishment of prisoners. John was sent into exile there in about AD 95. Exile (*exsilium*), or banishment involving prolonged absence from one's country was a means of punishment imposed by the Romans upon different criminals throughout their history. Earlier Greeks had used it chiefly in cases involving homicide. Such an offender became an outcast either permanently or temporarily and was thus deprived of the comfort and protection of his home and community. Originally it was self imposed as a means of avoiding the death penalty. It was thought to be a more fair match to some crimes of a less severe nature.

Later, degrees of exile were introduced, with or without the loss of citizenship and with or without the confiscation of personal property. Those from the higher classes of society were simply banished and lost their status in Roman society. Poorer people from the lower classes would have to endure forced labor. The Roman historian Tacitus (AD 56-120) in his *Annals* informs us that such small islands of the Aegean Sea were frequently utilized by the Roman authorities to banish political prisoners, or else to force them into exile at hard labor (3.68; 4.30; 15.71). They were employed in the mines and marble quarries of the isolated places. Patmos, a rocky, volcanic and sparsely populated isle, was an appropriate place to send some of those captives, especially the ones from the nearby Ephesus region. John tells his readers that he "was on the island called Patmos on account of the Word of God and the testimony of Jesus" (Rev. 1:9).

John had not gone there to preach. He was there on account of his preaching. By the time of the writing of the book of Revelation, preaching the gospel of Christ was tantamount to proclaiming a *religio illicita*, an illegal religion, one that was not sanctioned by the Roman state. He also remarked that he was experiencing this isolation and exile (and perhaps also hard labor, although his advanced age may have prevented this) as an aspect of "the tribulation and the kingdom and the patient endurance" (cf. also Rev. 6:3; 20:4 where "Word of God" and "witness" and "testimony" are all used with reference to those who were at the time involved in a persecution scenario). John's own personal experience with this hard reality is an important key to understanding the message of Revelation. As Robert W. Wall rightly observed with respect to John's remarks in Revelation 1:9:

> In a world where civil religion was considered the duty of every good citizen, the public proclamation of the Christian gospel would have been viewed as a political threat. John's own experience may help explain the interpretation of the surrounding sociopolitical order as anti-Christian and in conflict with

God's sovereign reign. Perhaps it is for this reason that he describes both his composition and his imprisonment as ingredients of the same reality: "the word of God and the testimony of Jesus" (cf. 1:2). In this sense, John's imprisonment for the Christian gospel is an "acted parable" of the message of Revelation that envisions the fundamental conflict between two kingdoms, one divine and the other demonic (Wall, 61).

Eusebius of Caesarea (*Church History* 3.18.1) is the ancient writer who informs us that John was banished to this penal colony to work in the mines by the Emperor Domitian in the fourteenth year of his reign, i.e. AD 95 (cf. also, Irenaeus, *Against Heresies* 5.30.3; Eusebius, *Church History* 3.18.3; 5.8.6). Hence, John's own experience of suffering banishment or forced exile on Patmos provides an important ingredient in the overall theme of the book, for it is clear that his own suffering places the oppression and mistreatment of other Asian Christians in the context of evil as opposed to good and of Satan in his opposition to God and those who serve him. John did not see it merely as being on the wrong side of unpredictable political fortune.

Moreover, the view and perspective from this tiny and isolated island of Patmos, with its rugged volcanic hills set in the midst of a turbulent ocean (cf. Pliny, *Natural History* 4.69), no doubt also enters into the final form that the Revelation takes (4:6; 8:8; 10:2, 8; 13:1; etc.). This is an observation that has been made often by those who read the book and are knowledgeable of the geological and geographical features of John's diminutive temporary home in the waters off the coast of Asia Minor, not too far distant from his adopted home at Ephesus.

If John had the freedom of the island during his tenure there, which is likely, he could have seen some wonderful panoramas from its heights. The greater part of the irregular island would have lain at his feet. Away to the north would have appeared the peaks of the island of Samos, home of the father of mathematics, Pythagoras, the astronomer Aristarchus, and the philospher Epicurus, as well as the promontory of Mycale, and to the south the island of Leros. To the southwest in the open expanse of the Aegean could have been seen Amorgas Island and the distant volcano of Santorini. Off to the northwest lay Icaria (modern Ikaria), and numerous other islands clustered on the horizon (cf. C. F. Pfeiffer and H. F. Vos, *The*

Introduction to John's Book of Revelation

Wycliff Historical Geography of Bible Lands, 402-403). There seems to be little doubt that the Apostle took all of this in while he was there, and John was certainly greatly influenced by his surroundings, its sights and sounds. Henry M. Field made the following helpful observation:

> And is it too much to say that the Book of Revelation is a different book, written on an island, on the seashore, from what it would have been if written, like the Book of Job, amid Arabian deserts? All its imagery is of the sea. As the Apostle walked along the shore of Patmos when the waters were still and reflected as in a mirror the blue of the heavens, they furnished a not unworthy symbol of "the sea of glass, like unto crystal, which was before the throne." Again he stood upon the cliff, his white hair streaming in the wind, and saw the clouds rolling up on the horizon, the flashes from which lighted up at once the dark heavens above and the angry sea below, and these were images to him of judgments that were coming on the earth. And when he speaks of One "whose voice was as the sound of many waters," the very expression is an echo of the deep (Field, 42).

What Do We Know of the Setting and Date of Its Composition?

The earliest evidence we have suggests that John "saw the revelation . . . at the close of Domitian's reign" (Irenaeus, *Against Heresies* 5.30.3; Eusebius, *Church History* 3.18). In many ways this unique period of time and its political situation had significant input into the literature of the book of Revelation. So, it is important that we have some general grasp of the reign of this ruler.

Domitian (Titus Flavius Domitianus) was emperor during the period AD 81-96. Born on October 24, AD 51 and ascending to the throne on September 14, 81, he proved to be an able administrator and, it has rightly been observed, that he did not ignore the welfare of his people as some of the emperors did. Moreover, he was not an emperor without accomplishments, even though he has sometimes been viewed so. He was responsible for a reform of the coinage, a massive building program (including restoration of the gutted ruins of many public buildings, including the Capitol which had burned in AD 80, built a new temple to Jupiter, a new stadium, a concert hall for musicians and poets, for himself a new Flavian Palace on Palatine Hill for official functions, and to the south he constructed the Domus Augustana where he held banquets and receptions), he was responsible for the development of an important "power set" within the administration, his (rather than Trajan's) admission of a substantial number of easterners into the senate, his efforts to come to terms with the various groups within the senate, etc.

Too, in spite of his own lack of moral values, he attempted to raise the standards of public morality by forbidding male castration, admonishing senators who practiced homosexuality, and censuring the Vestal Virgins for, among other indiscretions, incest. One offender was even buried alive, and her lover was also put to death. By those around him during the early part of his reign, he was seen as generous, possessing self-restraint, considerate of all of his friends, and conscientious when dispensing justice. Domitian especially enjoyed the public games, and in particular he favored the chariot races. In fact, he enjoyed public entertainments and attempted to satiate the people's appetite for them to a point that their enormous expense took a heavy toll on both his and the empire's finances. So, even though the bills did eventually come due, the people of Rome were very happy with his decisions in this realm of public life.

Thus, even though it was eventually engulfed in both fear and paranoia, his reign was generally one of peace and stability for the Empire. Earlier generations did not have a full enough grasp of these factors in his life's work, as shown by the meager material found in the biography of Stéphane Gsell in 1894. Since that time a mass of epigraphic and archaeological material has been uncovered and now provides for us a more solid basis for a broader and more detailed picture of the period of Roman history than what was given to us through the writings of the early historians alone (Jones, viiff.).

The writer Suetonius claimed that Domitian was raised in "poverty." Of course, "poverty" is a relative term subject to various shades of meaning. And in this instance the word is clearly used as an insult to the man and his family rather than as a definitive word expressing the nature of their true financial position in society. This point is used as damning evidence against him, as though he had brought the temporary misfortunes of the family upon them all. In fact, the family was quite wealthy, although between 51 and 59 it was out of favor with the leadership of the country. They owned several villas and estates. As well, when he fell into political disfavor, his father Vespasian was forced to engage in trade in order to keep up his position in society.

Introduction to John's Book of Revelation

The ancient historians reveal that Domitian was a well-educated man, able to converse elegantly and to produce memorable comments. He wrote poetry during his early years and had written and published a book on baldness (he was extremely vain and so very self-conscious of his being bald, so this subject was a preoccupation for him), but it is highly unlikely that he was interested in literature for its own sake. More probably he wished to make a name for himself among the aristocracy of Rome, and at various times to be seen as a man of letters rather than an ambitious politician, for it is noted that on his accession he abandoned his literary pretensions, limited his reading to Tiberius' commentaries, and devoted his attention to his own stern and rigid ideal of emperorship, re-establishing Augustan standards in money as well as in morals for the Empire. Both Tacitus and Suetonius are convinced of this proposition. They refer to his love of reading and writing poetry and interpret it as politically motivated, in order to deceive everyone that his pursuits were literary and innocuous. Most modern scholars share their view. The only seeming gestures in the direction of his previous interests during his administration were the construction of the concert hall in Rome and the expenditure of vast sums of money to restore fully the great library at Alexandria, even sending scribes to copy works that he was unable to purchase for the collection. But even this has been interpreted as being a part of the new imperial image of himself that he wished to put before the Roman people rather than a revelation of his true aspirations and interests.

It is evident from the foregoing that Domitian was not an evil man from the outset of his reign, but it is also clear from what follows that he became so over time. It has been suggested, perhaps rightly, that his personal greed and paranoia over the possibility of being assassinated was what made him so. Several other emperors had been murdered prior to his time, so the danger of this cannot be dismissed. Cassius Dio in the *Roman History* said that he was both bold and quick to anger, so this was already an aspect of his character and personality. But, over time he also proved to be treacherous and secretive, feeling no affection for anyone except for a few women in his life. As his reign progressed and the pressures of ruling mounted, along with the harsh realities of a profligate spending policy, paranoia seized him and he came to trust almost no one in his inner circle. In order to pay for his extravagances he tightened the Jewish tax enacted by his father and seized the fortunes of senators and wealthy Romans. His paranoia even extended to his wife, Domitia Longina. At one point he accused her of adultery (some accounts claimed she was actually guilty of the sin) and planned to put her to death, a common practice at the time. Domitia had been married to a senator, Aelius Lamia, but he was convinced to divorce her so she could marry Domitian. Domitian temporarily left his wife to live with his niece Julia, Titus' daughter by his second marriage (whom Domitian had earlier refused to marry), until he was convinced by others to return to his wife.

The emperor's extreme paranoia caused him to take extraordinary measures to protect himself. He employed informers and as a means to obtain information about possible plots against his person or rebellion, he ordered interrogators to cut off the hands or scorch the genitals of prisoners. He lined the gallery where he took his daily walks with highly-polished moonstone so that it reflected everything behind him and made it difficult for a potential assassin to approach him without his knowledge. In September of AD 87 a number of senators were involved in a conspiracy to kill him and were summarily executed. Also, the governor of Upper Germany, Lucius Antonius Saturninus, led a mutiny against him and this also was halted in AD 89. In the end, he was assassinated. He was murdered by a group of conspirators, led by a member of the imperial staff named Stephanus who had been accused of embezzlement and so feared for his own life. In the ensuing incident, he was stabbed at first by Stephanus and then hacked to death by a group of conspirators. So, his fears were not utterly unfounded!

One of the most objectionable aspects of his administration had to do with his own constitutional and ceremonial position in the government. He continued his father's policy of holding frequent consulates. In fact, he was consul *ordinarius* every year from 82 to 88. He became censor for life in 85, giving him control over senatorial membership and general behavior. He wore triumphal dress in the Senate, and he presided, wearing Greek dress and a golden crown, over four yearly games on the Greek model, with his fellow judges wearing crowns bearing his own effigy among effigies of the gods. According to the writer Suetonius his most serious offense to the traditional order was that he insisted on being addressed as *dominus et deus*

Introduction to John's Book of Revelation

("lord and god"). This was distasteful to the Roman people generally and to the Roman elite particularly, but a special insult to Jewish and Christian sensitivities. He claimed to be the son of Minerva, his own particular tutelary goddess. The Jews, of course, were generally considered a protected minority under Roman law, but the Christians did not enjoy this special status. For the people of Rome, even though it was an era of relative peace and tranquility strategically, this became a time of great fear and paranoia.

As his reign progressed and the pressures of ruling the Empire pressed down ever more heavily upon him, outrageous paranoia seized control of his already fragile personality. He alienated the Senate, stripping it almost entirely of its powers and making of himself an absolute ruler. Senators and imperial officers were executed for the most trivial of offences. As mentioned previously, his paranoia even extended to his own wife. She was accused of adultery and came near to being executed also. On this account, it is thought that she may have participated in the eventual plan that led to his murder, since she still feared for her life. He even renamed two months of the year after himself; Germanicus (September) and Domitianus (October). It was during this reign of terror that the church caught his attention. In particular, Dio reported that:

> Domitian slew, along with many others, Flavius Clemens the consul, although he was a cousin and married to Flavia Domitilla, who was also a relative of the emperor's. [It has been theorized that this person may have been Clement of Rome (*Clemens Romanus*), or that some slave or freedman from his family was that writer. A Clement is also mentioned in the *Shepherd of Hermas* (cf. Vis. 2.4, 3). He has also been identified with the Clement mentioned by Paul in Philippians 4:3]. The charge brought against them both was that of atheism *(atheotēs)*, a charge on which many others who drifted into Jewish ways were condemned. Some of these were put to death, and the rest were at least deprived of their property. Domitilla was merely banished to Pandateria (Cassius Dio, *Epitome* 67.4; cf. Ancient History Encyclopedia, "Domitian," Donald L. Wasson, www.ancient.eu/domitian/).

E. M. Smallwood and a few others have argued that the two individuals mentioned here were not Christians. Smallwood views them as "godfearers" living on the fringe of Judaism who followed Jewish customs to a sufficient extent to be subject to attack from Domitian. She regards the case for seeing them as Christians as resting on a flimsy foundation. But, her view should not be taken very seriously, since there is no evidence in either the Classical or Jewish writings that Domitian ever attacked Jews by race or that they suffered any at all for their religious preferences during his reign. The status of Judaism as a *religio licita* continued unaffected and there are no indications that Jews were forced to commit idolatry while he was the Emperor of Rome. Why, then, ought we to assume that god-fearers or proselytes were treated any differently than circumcised Jews and also regarded as "atheists"? The single instance that is quoted to support this notion (Apollonius Molon, an illustrious rhetorician who provided material for Apion; Josephus, *Against Apion* 11, 48) and where this appellation is employed to depict Jews, is taken from a first century BC reference and is not really relevant to the reign of Domitian. On the other hand, the fact that Christianity was not a *religio licita* at the time and its followers had the charge of 'atheism' commonly leveled against them would appear to support overwhelmingly the interpretation most commonly given to this passage (cf. Barnard, 259, n. 4; Smallwood, 1-13).

The state religion had not turned against Christians formally or legally before Domitian. Nero's raging against the Christians had nothing to do with the cult of the emperor. But, under Domitian, who according to Oriental pattern claimed divine worship for himself as emperor during his lifetime, persecution of Christians by the state on purely religious grounds took place for the first time. Moreover, in the province of Asia the cult of the emperor was promoted with special zeal, in fact, under Domitian Ephesus received a new temple to honor the emperor and the imperial cult. And so, precisely in the province of Asia, the classical land of the emperor cult, at the time of Domitian all prerequisites are given for the severe conflict between Christianity and the state religion which the Apocalypse delineates (Kümmel, 327-328).

Further, the testimony of the book itself favors an origin for this literature in the province of Asia when the Christians were severely oppressed, a time best conceivable under the repugnant character Domitian and not prior to his reign. The circumstances of John himself, as depicted in the book, testify to this general situation. The writer describes himself as one who in the later persecutions was termed a "confessor," i.e., when taken before the Roman authorities, he had not denied Jesus Christ and worshipped the emperor; instead, he had maintained "the Word

Introduction to John's Book of Revelation

of God" (1:9), the Christian message, and had given his "testimony," his personal confession or "witness," that he was indeed and in truth a Christian man.

Thankfully, history has provided for us a description of the procedure as it was followed at the time. Pliny the Younger, then governor of Bithynia in northern Asia Minor, in a letter to the Emperor Trajan (AD 96-117), written between 111 and 113, gives his own version of it. He had the images of the gods, including the emperor, placed in the courtroom. He asked suspected persons if they were Christians. He asked those who confessed that they were such a second and a third time, in order to ensure that they understood fully the question itself and the ramifications of a positive answer. If they still persisted with their confession, they were led away for execution. Others, including some who admitted that they had been Christians, when questioned, cursed Christ and worshipped the statues of the gods and that of the emperor, things which those who are "really Christians" quite simply would never do (Pliny, *Epistles* 10.96). Here is Pliny's inquiry, along with the emperor's response:

Pliny's Inquiry

It is my rule, Sire, to refer to you in matters where I am uncertain. For who can better direct my hesitation or instruct my ignorance? I was never present at any trial of Christians; therefore I do not know what are the customary penalties or investigations, and what limits are observed. I have hesitated a great deal on the question whether there should be any distinction of ages; whether the weak should have the same treatment as the more robust; whether those who recant should be pardoned, or whether a man who has ever been a Christian should gain nothing by ceasing to be such; whether the name itself, even if innocent of crime, should be punished, or only the crimes attaching to that name.

Meanwhile, this is the course that I have adopted in the case of those brought before me as Christians. I ask them if they are Christians. If they admit it I repeat the question a second and a third time, threatening capital punishment; if they persist I sentence them to death. For I do not doubt that, whatever kind of crime it may be to which they have confessed, their pertinacity and inflexible obstinacy should certainly be punished. There were others who displayed a like madness and whom I reserved to be sent to Rome, since they were Roman citizens.

Thereupon the usual result followed, the very fact of my dealing with the question led to a wider spread of the charge, and a great variety of cases were brought before me. An anonymous pamphlet was issued, containing many names. All who denied that they were or had been Christians I considered should be discharged, because they called upon the gods at my dictation and did reverence, with incense and wine, to your image which I had ordered to be brought forward for this purpose, together with the statues of the deities; and especially because they cursed Christ, a thing which, it is said, genuine Christians cannot be induced to do. Others named by the informer first said that they were Christians and then denied it; declaring that they had been but were so no longer, some having recanted three years or more before and one or two as long ago as twenty years. They all worshipped your image and the statues of the gods and cursed Christ. But they declared that the sum of their guilt or error had amounted only to this, that on an appointed day they had been accustomed to meet before daybreak, and to recite a hymn antiphonally to Christ, as to a god, and to bind themselves by an oath not for the commission of any crime, but to abstain from theft, robbery, adultery, and breach of faith, and not to deny a deposit when it was claimed. After the conclusion of this ceremony it was their custom to depart and meet again to take food; but it was ordinary and harmless food, and they had ceased this practice after my edict in which, in accordance with your orders, I had forbidden secret societies. I thought it the more necessary, therefore, to find out what truth there was in this by applying torture to two maidservants, who were called deaconesses. But I found nothing but a depraved and extravagant superstition, and I therefore postponed my examination and had recourse to you for consultation.

The matter seemed to me to justify my consulting you, especially on account of the number of those imperiled, for many persons of all ages and classes and of both sexes are being put in peril by accusation, and this will go on. The contagion of this superstition has spread not only in the cities, but in the villages and rural districts as well; yet it seems capable of being checked and set right. There is no shadow of doubt that the temples, which have been almost deserted, are beginning to be frequented once more, that the sacred rites which have been long neglected are being renewed, and that the sacrificial victims are for sale everywhere, whereas, till recently a buyer was rarely to be found. From this it is easy to imagine that a host of men could be set right, were they given a chance by recantation.

Introduction to John's Book of Revelation

Trajan's Response

You have taken the right line, my dear Pliny, in examining the cases of those denounced to you as Christians, for no hard and fast rule can be laid down, of universal application. They are not to be sought out; if they are informed against, and the charge is proven, they are to be punished, with this reservation—that if anyone denies that he is a Christian, and actually proves it, that is by worshipping our gods, he shall be pardoned as a result of his recantation, however suspect he may have been with respect to the past. Pamphlets published anonymously should carry no weight in any charge whatsoever. They constitute a very bad precedent, and are also out of keeping with this age (Bettenson, 5-7).

In all likelihood a similar process was used in the region where John was indicted and convicted (probably Ephesus). John, however, was not executed for his confession; instead, he was exiled to the island of Patmos, off the coast of Asia Minor and only about sixty miles southwest of Ephesus. According to the elder Pliny, it was used at times as a place for the banishment of persons who were not accorded the freedoms of ordinary Roman society for some reason or other (Eusebius, *Church History* 3.18.5). There is a cave or grotto on Patmos, now made into a chapel, which since the Middle Ages at least has been associated with the apostle John and his work on the Revelation. Later confessors, in the tradition of the apostle John, enjoyed great prestige and influence in the early church. Ignatius, a bishop from Antioch who suffered the supreme penalty in Rome ca. 110, is an excellent example of this. While en route from his home city of Antioch to Rome with his Roman guard he was received with great enthusiasm by the Christians of the cities through which he passed, and was listened to as an authority figure. This was not on account of his bishopric at Antioch, but was due to his courage and eagerness to make the confession of the name of Christ when it was so perilous to do so, and thus to die as a martyr (Rist, 373). Ignatius seemed eager to die for the cause of Christ. By his time, martyrdom had become a very desirable outcome for those who were intensely loyal to Jesus.

Plainly the atmosphere of the Revelation is similar to what we see and hear in the writings of Ignatius as well as of Pliny in his letter to Trajan. It was an era of persecution, governmental oppression, and of Christian martyrdom. In the diminutive open letters of the Apocalypse, persecutions are expected at the hands of the authorities (2:10); the blood of martyrs has already flowed (2:13; 6:9); frightful danger threatens all of Christendom (3:10); in fact, the outbreak of a general persecution of Christians by the Roman state seems imminent. In 17:6 John sees the harlot, Babylon-Rome, drunk with the blood of the saints of God and from the blood of the witnesses of Jesus (cf. 18:24; 19:2; 16:6; 6:10). In 20:4 participation in a thousand-year reign of Christ is promised to the martyrs, who for the sake of the testimony of Jesus and for the Word of God fell victim to the executioner's axe, and who did not worship the beast and its image and did not receive its mark on their foreheads and their hands, i.e., to those who refused divine worship to the emperor and his genius (13:4, 12ff.; 14:9, 11; 16:2; 19:20). It is grossly apparent that Christianity has run head on against the Roman state and the state's favored religion, the emperor cult. This corresponds precisely with the situation under Domitian and the era afterward, but once again, *not prior to his time.*

Therefore, we must conclude that not only was this book written during the period of the domination of the world by Imperial Rome and that the beastly figure in charge at the time was indeed the Emperor Domitian, but that governmental power and its abusive ways are at the heart of the subject-matter of the Revelation. As in the Old Testament book of Daniel, which also deals with the relationship between the reign of God and the governments of men, these identical political realities are very much at the forefront of the author's attention (cf. Dan. 2:20-21, 44; 4:17, 25b, 32b, etc.). The hated tyrant Domitian had already begun his reign of terror at the time of its inception (ca. AD 96). His persecutions leveled against all who would not profess his divinity and worship him led to the death of many Christians and heralded an era of much more fierce persecution of the church by the Roman state (1:9; 2:10, 13; 6:9-11; 11:7-10; 13:15; 16:6; 17:6; 18:24; 20:4). Christians saw him as a resurrected Nero (13:3, 12), who in AD 64 had persecuted them on the false charge of burning the city of Rome. In fact, it was more likely Nero himself who set the city alight in order that he could rebuild it to greater glory (as many Romans believed when the city burned). But, at the time there existed a small element of society that had no political power at all. They were generally hated by the rest of the people. Others feared and distrusted them because they could not understand their strange ways. And, as unfortunate as it was for them,

Introduction to John's Book of Revelation

they became the perfect distraction! The Christians provided him with an easy and convenient means of taking attention away from himself. They were his "scapegoat" to divert the public's attention away from his own guilt in the conflagration that brought a portion of Rome to ruin.

Domitian, on the other hand, was the second great persecutor of the Christian faith. His actions against certain Christians, on account of their embrace of Christianity, are well-attested. Cassius Dio refers specifically to his putting to death his own cousin, Titus Flavius Clemens, and gives him responsibility for the banishment of Domitilla, Clemens' wife and Domitian's niece. She was sent away to Pandataria (Ventotene), one of the Pontine Islands in the Tyrrhenian Sea. "Atheism" or "sacrilege" (*atheotēs*) and "Jewish ways" were the formal charges that were leveled against them by the Roman state. A great many others were put to death or else deprived of their property on the same grounds, among them being one Acilius Glabrio, consul in AD 91, who had after his consulship been sent into exile (Cassius Dio, quoted in Ramsay, 260-261).

It is in this frightening environment, then, that the prophecies of the Revelation had their origin. Its concentration upon the subject of the persecution and oppression of the saints is fundamental to an appreciation of apocalyptic literature in general and the Revelation in particular. It is critical to understand that this type of material was born in the crucible of religious repression, social tyranny, totalitarian cruelty, and the hostility of the state toward pious believers who needed desperately to have something substantial to hold on to in the face of overwhelming coercive power being employed against them, in this instance by various officials of the Roman state. The corrupt and unjust Roman government was their oppressor, but the eternal and all-powerful God was their ever present ally. It is this complex of important religious, political and social realities which provides us with the real context of the Revelation theologically and historically.

We recognize, however, that there is another dating system which has been employed by other writers in their approach to the book. While we patently reject the view, it would not be advisable to go forward from this point without giving some attention to it. The position to which we refer identifies the "holy city" in the book with literal Jerusalem and the "beast" of chapter 13 with Nero, and therefore dates the Revelation in the reign of Nero (ca. AD 68). The following list of arguments have been set forth by those students of the work who hold tenaciously to this "early date" hypothesis for the book in spite of the overwhelming evidence to the contrary:

1. Mention of the Temple and the city of Jerusalem. Those references (particularly 11:1-2) within the book which allude to the old Jewish capital and its central shrine are seen literally by these expositors as still standing at the time of the author's writing of the document. It is claimed that these allusions make a date later than this untenable. On the other hand, this assumes a literal reading of one or more of the symbols of the book as they are presented in the midst of many other symbols which these scholars admit are to be taken as purely symbolic and not taken as literal. Why should these two symbols be isolated and read as literal when the others in these contexts are not so viewed? In fact, it is seldom noticed by them that the description and measurements of the temple as inscribed by John are *not* based on the Herodian temple which stood in Jesus' day, as is usually assumed by such readers, but on the eschatological portrait of the temple as depicted in Ezekiel 40-48. If John was alluding to the Herodian temple that stood in Jerusalem during the reign of the Emperor Nero, why did he not describe it as it stood? John had no doubt seen it many times. Why did he not picture what he had seen with his own eyes? Why did the measurements of his visionary temple not match with those of the Herodian structure? Could it be that he intentionally avoided both the description and the measurements of the temple of Herod in order to put the emphasis where it really belonged, namely upon Ezekiel's eschatological one?

In our view it is interesting to note that most of these same scholars believe that the temple to which the prophet Ezekiel made reference was not that of Herod. They readily admit that Ezekiel spoke as he did in order to envisage the church in the Church Age rather than the temple as built by Herod and destroyed by the Romans in AD 70. On this matter we deem them to be quite right in their interpretation. Moreover, these same students also believe the Messianic prophesies that picture the city of Jerusalem at several different points in the Old Testament also envisage the new covenant realities such as the church and the heavenly Jerusalem. Again, we consider their interpretation to be absolutely correct. So, once

Introduction to John's Book of Revelation

more, why in this former instance do they decide to depart from this consistent approach to the figure as it is employed in the prophetic Scriptures generally, unless it is to make a special point with this case, namely, to date the Revelation in the age of Nero? In our view this defies defensible logic and puts them in contradiction with themselves in regard to these other prophetical allusions.

2. Reference to "Babylon the Great." The passage which is central to this hypothesis is 11:8, which refers to the location "where their Lord was crucified." This reference is taken as proof positive by these writers that the literal city of Jerusalem was in the mind of the writer when he spoke so vehemently in regard to the judgment of God upon some great world capital. In that context the city in question is called "the great city" and in the chapters that follow "that great city" and "Babylon." However, seeing the metropolis in question as Jerusalem requires one to stretch the language of this text beyond its natural limits. The reference to the place of the Lord's crucifixion must be torn from its context in order to provide for such a reading. In point of fact, the whole of this is given a symbolic significance by the author himself, for he says that this is a municipality "which spiritually is called" and then identifies it with Sodom and Egypt, along with "Jerusalem . . . where their Lord was crucified." Hence, the force of the text itself is to say that the city in question is no more to be identified with literal Jerusalem than it is to be seen as literal Babylon, literal Sodom, or literal Egypt!

3. The coming of Christ in judgment (1:7). Some interpreters read Revelation 1:7 in terms of the Lord's return to judge the Jews for their rejection of Him, which employed the Roman army as the rod of God's judgment. This truth is certainly dealt with elsewhere in the Bible, and in language that is both powerful and frightening (cf. Matt. 24; Luke 17; and Mark 13). In the second part of the verse there is a citation of Zechariah 12:10 which describes those who mourn as "the house of David and the inhabitants of Jerusalem." Following this line of thought to its natural conclusion, those who are convinced that this is the proper approach to the text reflect that the "earth" in the passage means the land of Israel and the "tribes" of Zechariah 12:12 allude to the various clans of Israel.

The major problem with this approach to the question is the fact that the passage quoted from Zechariah does not refer to the judgment of Israel, but to her redemption. Now that is a major obstacle! Moreover, Daniel 7:13 is just as clearly being brought into the thought of the writer by his usage of the language of that text, and yet, once more, that text also relates not to the judgment of the Jewish people, but to their redemption. So, again, it frustrates the very purpose for which these interpreters envision John as having utilized the passage. This approach also ignores the common usage of the expression "tribes of the earth" *(pasai hai phulai tēs gēs)* elsewhere in Holy Scripture. Wherever this phrase (or something kin to it) is used in the Greek Old Testament it always relates to other clans and tribes of Gentile extraction, and never to the Twelve Tribes of Israel (cf. Gen. 12:3; 28:14; Psa. 71:17; Zech. 14:17; see also Rev. 5:9; 7:9). The mourning pictured on the part of those who see the Lord at His coming appears not to have to do with those who literally put Him to death, but those who have rejected Him and made of no effect the crucifixion and sacrificial offering inherent in His death. It pictures those who are alienated from His covenants, unwilling to own Him as their King, and so, simply put, the unsaved and unredeemed of all the earth!

4. The Seven Hills and the Seven Kings (17:9-10). It was well known at the time of writing that the city of Rome sat upon seven hills *(Septem montes Romae)* east of the river Tiber and that these seven hills (named as follows: Aventinus, Caelius, Capitolinus, Esquilinus, Palatinus, Quirinalis, Viminalis) formed the geographical heart of the city even as they do to this day. The Romans themselves referred to Rome as the "City of Seven Hills." So this was clearly a not-so-subtle hint to the reader regarding the identification of the city in question. Jerusalem was also founded on seven eminences, even though she is not very frequently referred to this way, and certainly not often enough to be identified as such (Mount of Olives, Nob, "Mount of Corruption" or "Mount of Offence" (2 Kings 23:13), Mount Zion, Ophel Hill, Fort Antonia, and the southwest hill that in the time of Simon the Hasmonean was called "the new Mount Zion"). The only reference to Jerusalem as a city of seven hills that we know about is found in the *Pirke-de-Rabbi Eliezer*, an eighth century midrashic narrative, stating that "Jerusalem is situated on seven hills" (cited in Bialik and Ravenitzky, *The*

Book of Legends, 371, para. 111). This may have been a well-known fact, but we doubt it. Certainly the proof of that is entirely lacking in literature generally. The greater likelihood is that Jews who had some knowledge of the Italian capital took the notion from allusions to Rome and identified various hills about the city with its foundation even though some of the hills were not inside the city at all. Some have also contended that ancient Babylon itself was set on seven hills, but this is a myth based on a misunderstanding of Revelation 17:9-10. Rome is the only city that has had an unquestioned association with seven hills throughout its history! This is a fact that is not subject to debate.

The notion of the seven kings is more difficult. Those who date the book in the age of Nero cannot identify the first of these "kings" (Roman rulers were not so described) as Augustus, the first official Roman emperor (which would be the most natural way to read the passage) since Nero falls in line at number five in that schema, but have to connect him with Julius Caesar, who first claimed the title of "Emperor" (*imperator*, originally only a military honorific), even though he is not normally numbered in the listing of the emperors. Thus they are able to identify the sixth ruler as Nero, while Servius Sulpicius Galba would be the seventh who is said to "continue only a short space" (he ruled for only seven months from 68-69, the first of four emperors who ruled in AD 69, which has come to be known as "the year of the four emperors"). The eighth in this numbering system who is described by the author as "the beast that was and is not" would be the little remembered figure Marcus Salvius Otho who reigned only three months from January 15 to April 16 of 69. There is nothing about him or his reign as Emperor that would make him important enough for this designation. So, even numbered in this most unnatural way the only advantage to this approach is to have Nero as the Roman emperor at the time of the writing of the book; the other identifications (seventh and eighth) have little significance at all.

On the other hand, those of us who have confidently dated the book in the reign of the emperor Domitian approach the list in a number of different ways. Some start the listing with Caligula, being that he was the first of the Roman rulers who served in office after the time of Christ and who shared some of the characteristics of Antiochus Epiphanes as a persecutor and oppressor of the worshippers of the true God (reflecting Daniel's prophecy in Daniel 9:26, 27 and Matthew 24:15).

Others begin the list with Tiberius, the Emperor under whom Jesus was executed by the Roman procurator and during whose rule the Jewish persecution of Christians was carried out. One may also begin with the great persecutor Nero, in which case the seventh ruler is Domitian. Still others begin with the emperor Augustus, proceeding through Tiberias, Caligula, Claudius, and Nero (the five fallen kings), then Vespasian (the "one" who "is") and Titus (the other one "who has not come"), though the eighth ruler (v. 11) is sometimes identified as Domitian. But this approach has the difficulty of excluding Galba, Otho, and Vitellius, who reigned only briefly and successively after Nero. Their temporary leadership is an argument for considering them illegitimate, even though some ancient writers saw them as belonging in the line of legitimate emperors (*Sibylline Oracles* and Josephus in his *Wars of the Jews*).

Clearly the theme of persecution and oppression of Christ and His church is the dominant thought considered in each of these approaches. It is worthwhile to note that the writer's intent was at the one and the same time to present a "revelation" of events and at the same time subtly to "conceal" the details of his methodology and technique. In both of these things he has been very successful. Certainly the prophecy of the "ten kings" which follows this one is even more elusive in regard to its precise meaning. In both instances, in our view, the author intends these listings to be only general in nature and not to be taken as precise historical markers. His choice of the two highly symbolic numbers to designate these listings are seven and ten, which should in and of themselves give the reader pause to reflect as to whether he might have meant them only to be figurative in the first place. If we are forced to come down at one place in our view of the string of leaders it would be with those who consider Nero to be the first and Domitian to be the seventh, for Nero was the first to marshal the power of the empire against the disciples of Christ, and Domitian was the seventh in order after him. The eighth, on the other hand, is probably a shadowy future leader, perhaps the last in the line of Roman emperors to persecute the church (Diocletian) or even the final governmental figure before the Lord's return. Whichever may be the case, it is certain that he

Introduction to John's Book of Revelation

will be no different than any one who has gone before him. He will be an evil man who will attempt to destroy the saints; he will endure for a short time; and then he will go to perdition. That is the thrust of the author's message to the seven churches of Asia, and that is his lesson for us today. Any man who assays to fight against the eternal purposes of God in the world, no matter his station, will be brought down to hell. The Lord will break in pieces his kingdom and will eternally judge him for his insolence and rebellion against his Creator.

5. *The Mysterious Number "666."* A good number of writers have contended that the number of the beast's name which is recorded in 13:18 as "666" has the numerical value of the title of *Nero(n) Kaisar* (Nero Caesar) in Hebrew transcription. This view is supported by the unlikely variant reading 616, which also yields the name of Nero when the Latinized spelling is followed. That is certainly one of the possible ways of interpreting this number. It has also been alleged that John was counting up an abbreviated form in Greek of the full Latin title of Domitian (*Imperator Caesar Domitianus Augustus Germanicus*), and that this is just as likely as the former. As well, some have argued that the number 616 (another possible reading of the Greek text of the verse) totals the Greek for *Gaios Kaisar* (the name of Caligula). Some others have the initials of all of the Roman emperors from Julius Caesar to Vespasian add up to 666, but to get to this number Otho and Vitellius must be excluded from the total. However, it must also be noted that early interpreters (less than one hundred years after John's writing) had different ways of viewing it. Irenaeus (*Against Heresies* 5.30), for example, identified this mysterious number as *Euanthas* (a name that is not identifiable to moderns) *Lateinos* (the Roman Empire), and *Teitan* (the Titans of Greek mythology who rebelled against the gods). Another early conjecture was *arnoume*, a form of the Greek word meaning "to deny" (R.H. Mounce, *NICNT: Revelation*, 264; W. G. Baines, "The Number of the Beast in Rev. 13:18," *Heythrop Journal* 16:195-196).

The main difficulty with reading it as "Nero Caesar" is that this solution asks us to calculate a Hebrew transliteration of the Greek form of a Latin name, and that with a defective spelling! At the same time, this defective form of the name (with a missing *yodh*) is attested in a Qumran document dated by reference to "Nero Caesar." On the other hand, a shift to Hebrew letters is unlikely in that Revelation is written in Greek and there is no indication in the text itself that the riddle is to be solved by transposing it into another language. How many of John's readers would have had an understanding of Hebrew or would have known the numerical equivalents of the letters of the Hebrew alphabet? This question may be difficult to answer definitively, but we would conjecture that in all probability the answer would be: "not many."

Furthermore, as already noted, the name of Nero was apparently never suggested by the ancient commentators even though his persecuting zeal was very well known and certainly would have been understood by them to be of such an iconic nature as to make of him a perfect foil for this "beast." Finally, the main problem for those who date the book early is the fact that this beast is not said to be the original persecutor of the church, but a resurrection of the same ("whose death wound was healed," 13:12). If the name "Nero Caesar" is really meant by the author to be the proper understanding of the beast's identification, then it is not Nero himself to which he alludes in this mysterious reference, but to his risen self in the form of another to which the writer directs the reader, i.e. the second great persecutor of the church, Domitian. It is as if he has come back from the grave to harass the people of God anew! That is certainly what John intimates in the other figures of the vision, whether the number 666 is meant to suggest that or not.

6. The church at Smyrna did not exist as early as the theory of the early date of Revelation would require. In Revelation 2:8-11 the apostle John addresses a letter to the saints who comprised the congregation in the city of Smyrna. There is one very significant problem with this fact which makes the early date of the Revelation virtually impossible. Not often considered at all by some students of the book, but singularly important, is the observation that according to the mid-second century churchman Polycarp that church did not exist at all in the days of the apostle Paul. For he says that in those days the congregation there had not yet been established (*Polycarp to the Philippians 11:3*, "we had not yet known him [i.e., the Lord]").

This is certainly what he asserts in his letter which was penned in the year of his martyrdom (AD 155). Although the precise year of Paul's letter to the Philippians is not known with certainty, assuming that the imprisonment spoken of there is the one at Caesarea, then the date would range from 56 to 58. This means that the congregation in Smyrna, first mentioned in Revelation 1:11; 2:8, could have been founded no earlier than ca. AD 52-55, and perhaps even as late as 60-64. Moreover, it is possible that during Paul's two-year stay at Ephesus (Acts 19:10) the Christian community at Smyrna saw its beginning (note especially Acts 19:26), though it must be recognized that nothing concrete is known about its actual starting-point.

Now it is generally accepted that Paul died in the year AD 67/68. John gives us the impression in the Revelation that when he wrote to them this church had already been tried for a long period of time. So, a pre-AD 70 date for the book simply would not be workable, unless the testimony of the Ante-Nicene father and bishop from Smyrna, the inimitable Polycarp, is to be rejected as unoriginal, unhistorical, or somehow mistaken. In our estimation this is a view which is utterly without justification and should not therefore be taken very seriously.

7. The church at Laodicea is depicted in the letter to them (3:17) as being rich and well situated. Historically, however, if we assume that the letter represented the circumstances of the city in the period prior to AD 70 there is a very considerable difficulty with this proposition. This absolutely could not have been the case in Laodicea during that time-frame. It is well known that the municipality was almost completely destroyed by a massive earthquake in AD 60/61. Even though the people of the town were well off enough financially to rebuild their devastated city without Imperial support, and wished to show themselves independent of any outside help to do so, it is nevertheless true that it would have taken several years for them to reconstruct its ruined buildings and repair or recreate its demolished infrastructure.

Too, it is also worth asking, why would John not have made some reference to this very recent and overwhelming tragedy, unless of course sufficient time would have passed when he wrote his book for it to have gradually faded from memory? And yet, there is no reference to it in any way in the little letter to them. In the mid-90's of the Common Era all of this would have occurred three and one-half decades previous, and so would have been finished long before and thus of no immediate concern. It would have been a distant memory and nothing more.

As a consequence, the late date for the letter to the Laodiceans and the book of Revelation generally suits the circumstances of the church at Laodicea much better than dating it in the 60's of the Common Era.

8. The literal city of Jerusalem in Palestine could not be the "holy city" of the Revelation. If the "holy city" is literal Jerusalem, then there are very serious problems which the prophecies of the Revelation predict. The book predicts the preservation of the "temple of God" and "the altar," and though it says Jerusalem will be trampled underfoot by the nations, it forecasts her ultimate preservation (Erdman, 18-19). History belies this position in regard to Jerusalem in the land of Palestine. Literal Jerusalem was in fact razed to the ground by Titus and his Roman legions.

If, on the other hand, the temple and city are interpreted in one part of the book to refer to the church, then surely it must be taken to mean the same thing in the rest of the document. The result of this would be that John is predicting the survival of the church in the face of terrible oppression and persecution, and this is of course something which proved accurate over the long term. God preserved His spiritual people and so made good on this important promise in the Revelation. And so, this dating of the work, held by a zealous, but very small minority of students and scholars even at the present time, is not only lacking in solid evidence to support it, but creates internal inconsistencies which make it almost impossible to justify.

On the other hand, the date for the Apocalypse which holds that it was written in the latter part of the reign of Domitian is consistent with almost all the evidence from the writings of the early churchmen. Several of these early writers provide solid testimony for its having been written near the end of the first century AD, namely Irenaeus, Clement of Alexandria, Victorinus, and Eusebius. Irenaeus is no doubt the most valuable of the witnesses among the ancient written sources, since he wrote very near to the time of the book and seems quite certain of his position on the date and circumstances of the composition. Writing about AD 180 he declared that the Apocalypse "was seen no long time ago, but almost in our own day, towards the end of Domitian's reign" (*Against Heresies* 5.30.3).

It is difficult to argue with such early evidence, especially given the writer's confidence in the historical accuracy of what he was saying. Being in a position to have to do so, as is the case with those who argue for the book having been written in the age of Nero, is a most unenviable position to be in. To posit that Irenaeus was simply wrong in his assessment of the situation, in spite of his apparent confidence in the matter and relative proximity in time to the events he describes, is a difficult position to defend, especially given the fact that so much of the additional evidence seems to fortify and bolster his viewpoint.

What Was the Original Destination of the Book? To Whom Was It Penned?

Revelation was written to seven churches located in Asia Minor (1:4, 11; 2-3), whose sites are found in western Turkey today. These were real churches with real problems. The book was penned to address their frightening situation. Any interpretation which does not take this into consideration must be rejected. The fanciful readings of dispensationalists, in particular, bear little resemblance to the legitimate analysis of the historic situation which any biblical text deserves. They read symbolism into the portraits of the seven churches given in the seven letters of Christ addressed to them, and literalize the visions which comprise the bulk of the work, in spite of their obvious symbolism and spectacular imagery. Thus, rational hermeneutical methodology is turned upside down in order to set forward a doctrinaire theological agenda! The results could not ever be desirable given such a wrong-headed starting point.

1. The province of Asia. Paul's letters have many references to "the province of Asia," and of course the "seven churches of Asia" are well known to all students of the New Testament. But, this word "Asia" is a bit confusing when used in this particular setting. In our minds we visualize Asia as the vast continent stretching from Turkey to the Aegean Sea eastward to China and Japan. Even some ancient writers like Josephus and the Greek historians often used this word in that sense. But, in the New Testament the term nearly always alludes to the Roman province located in the western part of what we now know as Turkey, earlier called Asia Minor or Anatolia. The seven churches of Revelation 2-3 were all located in this Roman province of Asia.

"I Saw the Heaven Opened"

When the Romans came into possession of this region they called it "Asia" because previously they had known the Attalid rulers as the "kings of Asia." Initially, Asia included all of the lands along the Aegean coast of Asia Minor and many of the Aegean islands including Rhodes and Patmos. In 116 BC, parts of Phrygia to the east were incorporated into Asia. Thus, by New Testament times the Roman province of Asia included all of the lands from the Aegean eastward to Galatia (250 miles), an area of about 56,000 square miles. The western part of Roman Asia had many important cities: Hierapolis, Colossae, Miletus, Aphrodisias, Priene, and others along with the seven great cities which are given special attention in the Revelation.

2. Roads to the Seven Churches. Sir William Ramsey, the 19th century British archaeologist who excavated in Asia Minor, was the first to observe that the letters to the seven churches in Revelation 2-3 are arranged precisely in the order that a messenger would have visited the seven cities, if he had been instructed to follow the circuit of the Roman roads used by most travelers of the day. So, if a disciple of John had been entrusted with delivering the letters, he would have set sail from Patmos to Ephesus, the largest and most important of these cities in New Testament times. From

Ephesus he would have journeyed about 100 miles north to Smyrna and Pergamum. He would have left Pergamum traveling southeast to Thyatira and Sardis, then he would have made his way on to Philadelphia and Laodicea, a distance of some 150 miles. From Laodicea it was another 100 miles west from there back to the coastal city of Ephesus. At this point the messenger's 350 mile triangle would have been complete.

3. *The predominant language and culture of the province.* At the time, the language and culture of Roman Asia were predominantly Greek. Some of the Greek cities along the Aegean coast had been there for 1000 years or more, so their history and culture was already quite ancient and certainly very well established. After Alexander the Great's conquests, all of Asia Minor became an integral part of the Hellenistic world and the rulers made deliberate efforts to Hellenize their territories. Philadelphia, for example, was the newest of the seven cities of Asia. It was founded by King Attalus II of Pergamum about 150 BC for the intended purpose of spreading the dominant Greek culture throughout this dominion. How successful this effort proved to be was impressive indeed! The Greek language and culture had become so dominant and pervasive by the time of the New Testament Era that in many instances the indigenous populations had virtually forgotten their own ancient languages. Greek had become the language of commerce and public policy, but it had also taken over on the streets as the common language (*koinè*) of the ordinary people of the territory.

4. *Ethnic makeup of the region.* Of course, it ought to be noted that Roman Asia was also home to many non-Greeks, even though great numbers of Greeks had settled there. The descendants of a variety of earlier races in the region, such as Lydians, Carians, Armenians, Hittites, and others, had been absorbed into the predominant Hellenistic culture that surrounded them. A significant Jewish population was also found in Asia. Asian Jews were in Jerusalem for Pentecost according to Luke's record of events after the crucifixion of Jesus (Acts 2:9), and it was Jews from Asia who disputed with Stephen (Acts 6:9).

Two of the seven letters, those to Smyrna and Philadelphia, reflect bitter hostility between the Jews and Christians of those cities. In Sardis, archaeologists have discovered and restored the largest ancient Jewish synagogue ever found. King Antiochus III (223-187 BC) had encouraged Jews to immigrate to Sardis from various countries. Moreover, Lucius Antonius, Roman proquestor during 50-49 BC had allowed the Jews there to have their own court system which did not involve the Roman juridical program (Josephus, *Antiquities of the Jews*, 14.10.17). Caius Norbanus Flaccus, a Roman proconsul later also upheld the rights of the Jews of Sardis freely to practice their religion (Ibid., 16.6.6). Likewise, the Jewish population at Ephesus had been given special permission to practice their observance of the Torah regulations without governmental interference by Marcus Julius Pomperus, son of Brutus (Ibid., 14.10.25). A similar decree was issued by the consul Caius Rubilius, on behalf of the Jewish community in the city of Laodicea (Ibid., 14.10.19).

So, it is evident that Jews had been there for many generations when the gospel swept through the province and in some areas, even though they still constituted a minority of the overall population, they were present in great enough profusion that they represented a formidable influence socially and politically.

5. Economic status of the realm. Asia may have been the wealthiest province in the Roman Empire in New Testament times. The valleys along the rivers were fertile, and Asia produced cereal grains in abundance, along with grapes, fruit, and nuts. The region was rich in building materials including timber, and fine marble along with other building stone. Although the gold and silver of earlier centuries had been depleted by this time, lead and other minerals were still being mined there. The area around Laodicea in particular was noted for its fine black sheep and the luxurious wool clothing produced from them.

6. Trade routes and the principality. The province was a natural land bridge between the Aegean world and the Mesopotamian world to the east. The Asian cities that stood astride those trade routes—Ephesus, Smyrna and Laodicea—grew rich from the considerable trade that crossed back and forth. The Roman statesman Cicero wrote of Asia's wealth thus: "In the richness of its soil, in the variety of its products, in the extent of its pastures, and in the number of its exports, it surpasses all other lands" (*De imperio Cn. Pompei ad quirites* 14).

7. Religious setting in John's time. The religions of the province showed a broad spectrum of beliefs and superstitions growing out of the ancient cultures intermixed with the newer ones which were taking root and making their influence felt in the sector. The Jews who had become acclimated to the region were quite Hellenized in their language and culture, though they held on with their usual tenacity during this era to the essential elements of the ancient Abrahamic faith.

A broad pantheon of Greco-Roman deities was worshipped by the other peoples of the area. An Asian fertility goddess, often represented as a many-breasted image, had been venerated in the region of Ephesus from very early times. When the Greeks came, this ancient faith was assimilated into the worship of Artemis (known as the Roman goddess Diana). The Temple of Apollo at Didyma, where the oracle spoke, rivaled the one at Delphi in Greece. The temple-hospital to Asclepias at Pergamum was second in magnitude only to the great sanctuary at Epidarus in Greece as well. Zeus and Athena also had famous temples at Pergamum.

8. Emperor worship in Roman Asia. Of greater consequence for our purposes, was the fact that Roman Asia was an important center for emperor worship. This was instituted in 29 BC when Rome granted permission to build a temple to the emperor at Pergamum. The city remained a center for emperor worship throughout New Testament times. In fact, emperor worship went on for many years after the Apostolic Era. Pergamum had a temple that was dedicated to Dionysus that was constructed in the second century BC. However, in the third century AD it was reconstructed and dedicated to the Emperor who reigned at the time, Caracalla. So, it was given over to the worship of the Roman sovereign long after the era of the apostle John. Furthermore, this proves that for nearly three hundred years Pergamum, the city where John said "Satan's throne is" (Rev. 2:13), continued to be the main center for Emperor worship in the region of Asia. Hence, John was describing a challenge for Asian Christians in his Revelation that persisted throughout a long period of painful and contentious years.

But, emperor worship was not limited to Pergamum alone. It was present throughout the Roman world, of course, but seemed to find a special place of respect and even admiration in Asia Minor. This religion spread rapidly throughout the province as other cities vied for the honor of building temples to the various emperors. People who already worshipped Zeus and the other Greek and Roman gods and goddesses found it easy to add an emperor or two to their long list of deities. But, for the Christians, emperor worship brought them into conflict with both the Roman state and local authorities who were set upon enforcing this worship as a means of unifying the Empire and assuring loyalty to the Roman state.

The ordinary provincial, in the days of John the apostle, had no necessary part in the emperor cult as such, but religion in many subtle ways was woven into the very fabric of his political and social life. He lived in an atmosphere permeated by the symbols and ancient rituals of the old fertility cults and of the deified state and its figurehead, the emperor, which were propagated by the temples and public buildings, by the law courts, by the theaters and gladiatorial games, and above all, by the coinage he handled to pay his everyday expenses.

To the average man it probably did not mean very much at all. Doubtless he thought little about it and would not have spent much time contemplating how it might affect others. It was a part of the culture. And, it was an aspect of the age-old patriotic idiom, rather like singing the national anthem in a sports stadium or taking an oath on the Bible in court would be to us today. But, for most Christians it made a difference. For them it was a constant reminder of how different they were from the surrounding culture and its mores. It was a reflection of the pagan nature of the Greco-Roman way of life and how steadfastly opposite it was from their own convictions and practices. Converted pagans, in their former lives, would have participated in many of these subtle reminders of the ever-present idolatry that infused every aspect of Hellenistic life in the city, but Jews had generally refused to do so with impunity on account of their unique status under Roman law. On the other hand, for Jewish Christians it represented the worst kind of sin; it was blasphemy, and they saw it as comparable to the idolatry of the Israelites when they reached the Promised Land and participated in the rituals and practices of the Canaanites who lived around them. Most believed that they had to take a stand against it, just as Elijah did when he struggled against Ahab, Jezebel, and the Baal cult in Israel. But, their Jewish immunity had been lost when they embraced the religion of Jesus Christ and abandoned the views of the establishment in Judaism, a point to which the leadership in Jerusalem and in the principal synagogues of Asia would have been quick to draw attention. The consequences of these two factors being brought together would have been disastrous and long-lasting for them, first in their daily lives in the communities and towns where they lived and then later in the law courts.

They could not, in good conscience, participate in any of the idolatrous practices of the community. Unfortunately, the whole culture was infused with it and it was virtually impossible to avoid it if one was to participate, in any fashion, in the public life of the society. This stand that they were forced to take did not, of course, endear them to most of their neighbors. Even though they did not take the religion that so permeated their culture all that seriously, they nevertheless resented its being insulted or ignored. Christian aloofness to it gave rise to strange but serious charges, like "atheism" and "hatred of the human race." Public religion, as opposed to private belief, was part of the fabric of what was considered normal existence, and their abstention from it was not only a strange aberration to which most of them were unaccustomed, but it was also thought to bring about all sorts of natural disasters upon the society as a whole. Events such as earthquakes, famines, plagues, or for that matter any natural disaster, were interpreted as happening as a result of the wrath of the ancestral gods. If the gods were displeased they would visit their displeasure upon the community through any sort of calamity or misfortune that might come their way. Thus, if something calamitous did happen, as inevitably it would over time, someone or something that was deemed to be neglectful or insulting to the gods was searched for within the common life of the people—and the Christians were the most ready target for suspicion and blame.

Hence, some Christians who came from a Greek background came to reject this intransigence on the part of those whose derivation was Jewish-Christian or were powerfully affected by this viewpoint. They wanted very much to participate fully in the culture and the social life of their cities. Freedom to do so was offered to them by the unique perspective placed on Christianity by those of a "gnostic" point of view (cf. Sweet, 31ff.). At first this was not the fully-formed Gnosticism of the second century which was an amalgam of sophisticated systems of thought and life, but rather, that which was represented in some of the patterns of thought and philosophical notions found in Greek congregations established by Paul and his close associates in the first century, and assuredly by those represented in the heterodoxy dealt with in the writings of John to the congregations in Asia Minor around the Ephesus area (1-3 John).

Gnostics tended to see matters having to do with the physical body as mostly "indifferent" to the spiritual state of the individuals involved. They also thought that such matters had no importance for the eternal life of the soul, and so they sometimes leaned towards "severity to the body" (Col. 2:2-23), but usually towards moral indifference, ending in various forms of licentiousness (cf. 1 Cor. 6:12-19). It makes sense then that this sort of attitude was probably behind the teaching of the Nicolaitans, who encouraged their Christian converts to "eat foods sacrificed to idols and commit fornication" (2:6, 14f., 20). Both of these practices were part of the ritual of paganism. From their point of view this would simply have represented a relative freedom to participate wholly in the social and religious life of the city. Of course, the word "fornication" was a regular metaphor for idolatry in the Old Testament, while at the same time in real terms pagan religion and sexual promiscuity were linked as in the time of ancient Balaam (cf. 2:14, 20). Furthermore, rites including cultic prostitution, both male and female, were a standard part of the various fertility cults of the time. The permissiveness of this type of gnostic thinking must have been terribly effective in drawing into its circle those who wanted not to be closed out of full participation in the religious and cultural features of the society.

Assuredly, involvement in the different required aspects of the emperor cult would have presented no problem at all for people who thought this way. To their minds, participation in all such things was a matter of indifference. This may help to explain the impressive growth of these gnostic groups in the second century. Among other things, they provided to their adherents a way out of the conundrum of having to resist forced compliance with cultural norms involving the ancestral Greek and Roman gods in general and the emperor cult in particular. To their way of thinking this was the best of all possible worlds! But, to the Lord their behavior represented compromise with evil and, even though they were able to justify this in

Introduction to John's Book of Revelation

their own minds, it was a defiance of God and His Word because it was participation in the practice of idolatry, pure and simple.

9. How were the seven churches founded? The seven churches of Asia had come to be on account of the preaching of the gospel at the first Pentecost after the resurrection of the Lord. Luke informs us that Peter's audience included Jews from Asia (Acts 2:9). Undoubtedly they were numbered also among the 3000 baptized into Christ that day. They returned home to be the first fruits of Asia. Later (ca. AD 51-52) Paul stopped briefly at Ephesus on his second missionary journey and left Priscilla and Aquila there, intending to return later if it proved to be the Lord's will (Acts 18:18-21). He did return there on his third journey and remained for three years (Acts 20:31). Priscilla and Aquila stayed there until late in 55 (cf. 1 Cor. 16:19). The presence of Paul and these other early disciples of Christ had a significant and lasting impact on the religious atmosphere of the region.

The New Testament does not say that Paul preached in any of the other cities of Asia, but without doubt the seven churches were mostly planted at that time, probably by various ones among Paul's associates, or even by Paul himself while he was based in the area during visits that are not mentioned in the historical record. A few years later (probably about 58, though some opt for sixty-three or so) while the apostle was imprisoned in Rome, he wrote a circular letter to the Ephesians which followed the Roman road as it circulated throughout the various cities of Asia Minor and wound up at Laodicea (see Col. 4:16). He urged the Colossians to read that letter and share theirs with Laodicea. Ephesians is almost certainly the "epistle from Laodicea" Paul refers to in that passage.

Toward the end of the first century of the Common Era, emperor worship was becoming a serious threat to the growing religious community that constituted Christianity. The faithful in Asia were being confronted with life-and-death choices. They would either have to confess that Caesar was Lord or be charged with treason against the Roman state. The Emperor Domitian (AD 81-96), who was worshipped as a god at a magnificent temple at Ephesus, exiled the elderly apostle John to the island of Patmos. This sets the stage for the writing of the Revelation. John was in the Spirit on the Lord's Day and heard a voice commissioning him to pen this work: "Write what you see in a book and send it to the seven churches" (Rev. 1:11). Thus, the historic occasion of this work of literature was the conflict between Christ and the emperor, the church and the Roman state.

What is this Strange and Mysterious Book?
A. The Type of Literature

Revelation is not like many of the other books of the Bible. Literarily speaking, it is certainly unique in the New Testament. Its form and substance are different in almost every conceivable way from what we encounter elsewhere. The Old Testament has some books like this, but this is the only one in the New. For this reason it must be read in a special way and interpreted in the light of these unique and very special circumstances. Thus, a number of considerations must be recognized in advance of the study of the material found here in order to comprehend its method and have any hope at all of appreciating its purpose and meaning.

First, it is apocalyptic in nature, that is, something is revealed heretofore unknown. The actual title of the book is its first word *apokalupsis*. This term is portentous for what lies ahead for the reader. These were dark days of uncertainty for the seven churches of Asia about what might happen in the future. It is this profound concern for a frightening future that is what sets the stage and effectively lays the groundwork for all apocalyptic writing. Therefore, in response to this need, apocalyptic literature in the mode and method of Revelation, and at least in broad and general terms, reveals what the future holds for those to whom the document is addressed. This helps us to appreciate what kind of writing we are dealing with in this case. Apocalyptic developed mainly out of Old Testament prophecy and wisdom literature in the postexilic period, even though some modicum of material exhibiting this style of literary composition appeared before the exile. Apocalyptic sections containing visions regarding "the last days" can be found in Isaiah (24-27), Zechariah (12-14), Ezekiel, Daniel, and Joel.

Another layer was eventually added to this biblical literature during a later era, however. Taking its impetus from the canonical Old Testament material, the great mass of apocalyptic-style literature arose between 150

Introduction to John's Book of Revelation

BC and AD 100. None of this material is inspired, but it became very popular as devotional reading for some people because it answered many questions that Jews were asking at the time and could not find an answer to in the Bible. To a certain degree it may be seen as resulting from the experience of the Jewish people of that era, who in the period following the loss of an independent nationhood were left totally at the mercy of great world powers. Israel was sandwiched between them, often being crushed in the midst of their fussing and feuding. She felt weak and alone. And she was troubled with many seemingly unanswerable questions. How would this all end? Was God concerned? Had he abandoned his people forever? Would God help the Jews or would he leave them to be perennial victims of these mighty powers? Were there some lessons to be gained from these unfolding events? Apocalyptic authors sought to supply an answer to all of these questions and many more.

The overarching question, of course, to which an answer is sought in this apocalyptic literature, is that of the goal that God has established for world history and the place that the endangered presence of Israel will occupy in the framework of God's plan for that history. The essential function all of the Jewish apocalypses serve, therefore, is to provide comfort and hope for a frustrated and puzzled people. It suggests in some way or another (which varies in the different apocalypses) that God intends to act on their behalf in order to save His people. He will not leave them without aid at the mercy of their powerful and pitiless enemies. So, given the special nature of their content, these writings make perseverance possible in the perilous present. That is their primary *raison d'être*.

The secondary function of this sort of literature is that of providing a reminder of the great biblical principles and warning about potential consequences of disobedience to God in the face of the present historical challenges. Their intention is always to show the pious that in their present critical situation everything depends on their own steadfastness. They will determine the outcome by their faithfulness, or lack thereof. The book of Revelation serves all of these purposes as well. It is perfectly consistent with the nature of the Jewish apocalyptic tradition, even though it departs sometimes rather radically from the type of material that appeared in the period between the Old and New Testaments.

In scholarly studies the apocalypse as such is seen as a genre or special type of literature because it can be viewed as a broad literary category that must be defined with reference to content and function as well as form. Dr. John J. Collins described this sort of material (on the basis of the International Colloquium on Apocalpticism guidelines) as follows:

> Apocalypse is a genre of revelatory literature with a narrative framework, in which a revelation is mediated by an otherworldly being to a human recipient, disclosing a transcendent reality which is both temporal, insofar as it envisages eschatological salvation, and spatial insofar as it involves another supernatural world, intended to interpret present earthly circumstances in light of the supernatural world and of the future, and to influence both the understanding and the behavior of the audience by means of divine authority ["Introduction: Towards the Morphology of a Genre," *Semeia* 14 (1979): 1-20; *Crisis and Catharsis: The Power of the Apocalypse* (Philadelphia: Westminster Press, 1984); "Introduction: Early Christian Apocalypticism," *Semeia* 36 (1986): 1-12].

The biblical book of Revelation fits this literary definition well. Most of the book consists of the author's narration of visions which he has received from a divine mediator, whether it be a particular angel (as in Rev. 1:1) or from Jesus Christ Himself (1:17-20). These revelations speak of eschatological or final salvation and judgment (20:11-15) and relate the coming of a new heaven and a new earth (chapter 21). In terms of overall function, the visions that are set forth in the Revelation encourage a persecuted Christian community (see 1:9; 21:3-4) to stand firm as God's people in anticipation of God's wrapping up of history, His mighty works wrought on their behalf in time and eternity, and of the ultimate realization of the new order of things.

Thus, this description of the genre is valuable in that it helps us to distinguish apocalypses from earlier Jewish prophetic literature, revelatory literary works in the Greco-Roman world generally, and even from other apocalyptic literature that may lack one or more of the essential characteristics given above. The definition also helps students of the genre become aware of variations found in apocalypses. For example, all apocalypses have a revelation mediated by an otherworldly being, in some cases the human recipient receives visions, whereas in others he is taken on an otherworldly journey.

Introduction to John's Book of Revelation

In the book of Revelation visions clearly predominate throughout, but there is a "heavenly journey" of sorts mentioned in 4:11ff. These observations help us to appreciate the very significant ways in which Revelation is like other apocalypses of that era, but it is so general that in other ways it provides little help in understanding the differences which also exist and cannot be minimized in making the comparisons (cf. J. L. Bailey and L. D. Vander Broek, *Literary Forms in the New Testament*, 201-202).

To the extent that Revelation shares features of other apocalypses, however, several necessary and important interpretative implications follow. Most importantly, we must recognize that John's Apocalypse employs highly symbolic and figurative imagery that we dare not attempt to interpret too literally. Virtually every reader recognizes this fact in the most obvious instances: as when John specifically explains that the seven stars are really seven angels (or messengers); that the seven lamp stands are actually churches (1:20); that the dragon is the Devil (12:9); that the bowls of incense are the prayers of the saints (5:8); that ten horns are ten kings (17:12); and that the great prostitute of which he speaks so dazzlingly is in fact a city that rules over the kings of the earth (17:18). In other words, she is not really a prostitute, she is actually a very powerful city.

In spite of all this, many readers still do not recognize that they should interpret the other images of the book as equally symbolic rather than literal in nature. Many still insist that the references to the temple (e.g., 11:1) must refer to a literal, rebuilt temple in Jerusalem, that the final earthly confrontation between the forces of good and evil in the world, i.e. the Battle of Armageddon (Hebrew for Mount Megiddo, 16:16) must occur at that specific geographical site in northern Israel, or that the mark of the beast (13:16-17) has to be some actual physical sign on the flesh that distinguishes unbelievers from believers, etc. An approach of this sort is counterintuitive from the outset. The symbols are intended to be representational, not literal.

A far more legitimate approach is to study each scene and each image in light of what Revelation itself tells the reader about them, taking into consideration the relevant Old Testament backgrounds and the similar images found there and what they meant for an earlier generation of readers of that testament, and in view of other historical information of which John's first-century audience would have been aware. In these terms, deciphering the imagery of Revelation then becomes much like interpreting an editorial cartoon in a contemporary newspaper. One interpreter offered the case of what a reader of an American paper in 1989 would have encountered, as a helpful explanatory instance. A newspaper published a cartoon depiction as follows: on the page there is a picture of a large bear extending an olive branch in his paw to a bald eagle. Taken out of its historical context this simple picture might have seemed very mysterious to an observer. For a contemporary reader it would have been quite different. The bear, the eagle and the olive branch would readily have been understood as symbols of something else other than what they appeared to be. That reader would immediately recognize the portrait of the Soviet Union's overtures of peace to the United States. People of a different time and set of circumstances might be challenged with these images. But those who lived during the era of the Cold War between the US and Russia would instantly understand what they were seeing.

That is precisely how these kinds of images work. They communicate certain ideas and conceptions to those who are "tuned in" and "in the know" with regard to current events and contemporary situations. People who live, as we do, two thousand years later, must interject some historical and cultural understanding into the process or else we will fail to appreciate the original intent of such pictures. If we make the extra effort necessary to put ourselves back into that historical moment when such images were fresh and new and were instantly recognizable, then we also will see their implications and read out of these portraits exactly what was intended by them. They are not a mystery at all. They are as simple as an editorial cartoon is for us when we read the daily newspaper.

Similarly, when we see in the thirteenth chapter of the Revelation the woman who flies off into the desert to escape the attacks of the serpent (who is also pictured as a dragon making war on her offspring) as the Church being protected by God even as individual believers are persecuted and sometimes martyred for their faith by Satan and those on earth who serve him (13:13-17), we recognize instantly the meaning of this simple portraiture. No doubt the early Christians did so just as readily. Many of the other portraits that are more difficult for us were no doubt much simpler

Introduction to John's Book of Revelation

for them. They probably understood most of them instantly. Time and circumstances are important, however. Our time is quite different and our circumstances are certainly different. Being that we are not contemporaries with them, therefore, at times it is much more challenging for us to see the message intended. But, it can be understood if we make the effort to place ourselves in their historical situation and read the symbols in the light of their particular historical predicament (cf. Klein, 371-372). Injecting our own historical situation into the picture will only confuse us, however. It was written to them originally, and to us only secondarily. It ought to mean to us what it meant for them. It was never meant to be read differently by every reader or even every generation of readers.

While the preceding points regarding the apocalyptic nature of John's material are important and certainly valid in every sense of the word, it should also be noted that there are also many differences between John's Apocalypse and the typical works in the collection of literary apocalypses which have come down to us. For example, in the Revelation there are regular references to the book itself as being prophetic in nature. Too, there are typically prophetic warnings and calls for repentance as well. This is not typical of the other apocalyptic literature. It is more in line with prophecy than with apocalyptic. Additionally, the pseudonymity which characterizes so many works in this class of materials is conspicuously absent in the Revelation. The author does not hide his identity behind an ancient figure from the Old Testament literature. Nor does he claim to be someone from the New Testament era who has already passed over. He uses his own name. He is that John who was well known to the churches of Asia at the time and who could simply tell the readers that he was "John" and they would all know without any further explanation who the writer was. Hence, the apostle John was the penman and he declares himself the writer from the very beginning.

Also, there is in evidence an optimistic worldview in John's work which is not present in these other bodies of literature that are classed as apocalyptic. They tend to be pessimistic as regards the future and what it might hold. John also fails to indulge in the retracing of past history in the guise of prophetic utterance as do so many others. Realized eschatology, the notion that the end time has already begun with the first appearance of Christ and the establishment of His kingdom in the institution of the church, is something that characterizes the writing of John and which is also absent in these others. Along with this there is the attendant idea that the Messiah has already physically appeared and spiritually redeemed Israel, i.e. made atonement for His people through His death on the cross. This is unique to the Revelation. John has this, but the others do not. Of course, the Revelation is very much an intrinsic part of the New Testament and the others are thoroughly Jewish, and not at all Christian in their orientation.

Finally, John spends little time interpreting the offices and facilities of the angels that he mentions in his visions, whereas many of the others put forth considerable effort speculating on such things. Thus, even though John clearly intends to utilize the basic approach of this type of literary artifice, he does not do so robotically, and so in many ways departs from some of the more expected and customary strategies of the paradigm (cf. Morris, 25-27). In large measure we may account for these differences by certain distinctive aspects of Christian rather than Jewish theology and by the fact that John's Revelation is prophetic as well as apocalyptic in nature. This brings us to our next point.

Second, it is limited prophetic. This is a point that is not nearly often enough realized by interpreters of the Revelation. As a result of this they frequently fail to appreciate the need for understanding the historical context of John's visions and lose sight of how anchored he is in that historical moment when he penned the letters to the churches and appended to them the visions he had experienced. In this work events of *their immediate future* are foretold to first-century Christians. In 1:1 John tells his readers that the purpose of his writing is to show them "things which must shortly come to pass" or "what is bound to happen soon." In v. 3 of the first chapter he concludes the verse by saying, "for the time is at hand" or "the crisis is near" (Caird, 9). Likewise, in 22:6 the author explains that the angel of God had been commissioned to show to him things "which must shortly come to pass." Then, in an even more significant clue to the nature of his material, at 22:10 he makes a very transparent reference to the well-known passage in Daniel where that visionary prophet was told that his visions

Introduction to John's Book of Revelation

were not intended to deal with the immediate future, but to a far-distant one: "Conceal these words and seal up the book until the time of the end" (Dan.12:4). Only for the Revelation to these churches of Asia, John says the angel told him to do precisely the opposite: "Do not seal up the words of the prophecy of this book, for the time is near." The prophecies of Daniel were for several hundreds of years in the future. But the playing out of the visionary drama of the Revelation was to come to pass immediately. The churches were already engaged in this life-and-death struggle with evil forces in the world of their day, and the intent of this author is to show the readers that God had not abandoned His church and that in the end He would deliver them and punish those who harassed and persecuted them.

This may seem like a small point for some readers, for it turns on just a few words in the introduction and at the conclusion of the book, but appreciating the force of what he has said is extremely critical. If we read past these texts and do not digest his meaning, we will have missed out on one of the most important clues to understanding the book that John provides for the reader. The intention of this work is not to foretell the end of the world as such, even though it to some extent deals with the conclusion of the Church Age. That is not its main goal, however. Such a statement may shock some people. It certainly represents a radical departure from the perspective of the book as understood by many evangelical authors. But, a close reading of these passages just cited will show that the keen interest of Revelation is not the distant future, but in those things that must "shortly come to pass." That is where the emphasis lies, and we must not fail to take careful note of this and keep it in mind throughout the study of this literature.

References to the ultimate end, the consummation of the age, are not the main thrust of the Apocalypse. They only serve to demonstrate the final conclusion of the battle between those forces locked in mortal combat at the time of writing. They inform us about how the story will finally end. But, once more, for it cannot be emphasized often enough, this book is primarily about the *near future* not the end-time! This is where many students of the work fail to understand its intentionality and go off into wasted speculation about the end of the world. Its purpose was not about the end of the world, it was intended for the "there and then," i.e. the end of the first century when the churches of Asia were threatened by an overbearing government which was fixated on getting them to conform to the contemporary civil order by worshipping the emperor and paying homage to the massive and powerful Roman state.

Third, the book is primarily symbolic. The angel of the Lord "signified" it to his servant John (1:1). So says the writer, and this picturesque language is not accidental. It gets at the very sum and substance of what this book is. Revelation makes use of imagery and signification common to the apocalyptic literature of the Old Testament (Daniel, Ezekiel, Zechariah) and imitated in apocryphal materials penned between the two testaments, as we noted in more detail above. Much of its language is metaphorical. The powers and events of history are described in vivid symbolic images that are borrowed both from Old Testament tradition and from ancient Oriental literary art. So, for example contemporary world powers are pictured in imagery as dangerous animals (Daniel 7; *1 Enoch* 85-86; *4 Ezra* 11), or as powerful trees (*2 Apocalypse of Baruch* 36).

This is a mode of expression much used in the prophets generally. The book says this about itself in the very first verse of the first chapter: "and he sent and *signified it* by His angel unto His servant John." The verb translated "signified" is *sēmainō* which derives from *sēma* (*seimeion*), "a sign." This word indicates the nature of the material. Symbolical representation is suggested. The Septuagint used the term *sēmainen* to express a great sign of a great thing (cf. Ezekiel 33:3). In the New Testament this verb is found only in a few places (John 12:33; 18:32; 21:19; Acts 11:28; 25:27; and Rev. 1:1). John favors this term, not using either *dēloō* or *emphanizō*, other words which express a kindred concept.

At any rate, this word is entirely appropriate to the symbolic character of the Revelation, and thus when in John 12:33 Christ predicted the mode of His death in a figure, He used this same wording. Some scholars have questioned whether it is appropriate to make this point too strongly, given this usage of the term and the heavy presence in the book of so many signs and symbols, saying that in some of these other instances we have cited the usage does not seem to warrant such a meaning. They opt instead for the sense of "signifying something by word, but not necessarily in a symbol." While there is some relative merit to this argument, for there are occasions

Introduction to John's Book of Revelation

where a less emphatic approach is justified, it is not necessarily capable of pushing this other more cogent meaning aside, especially as the term is used in Revelation. The Liddell-Scott Jones *Greek-English Lexicon* in fact lists its very first meaning as to "show by a sign, indicate, point out" (1592). It also states that when the verb is used absolutely (without an object) it means to "give signs." This is precisely how Revelation 1:1 employs the term. Being aware of this, and giving due respect to its force in that passage will preserve the reader from the error of mistaking these signs for literal events and personages, as well as a host of comparable interpretive misjudgments. As Edward A. McDowell observed: "The author implies that the message he has received is being given to his readers under signs and symbols. Attention to this fact should save us from crass literalism in interpreting the message of the book" (McDowell, 24).

Now, it is obviously harder to analyze and comprehend material of this type than it is to read and understand simple narratives. Perhaps more than anywhere else in our work of Bible interpretation then, interpreting the meaning of these symbols requires serious thought and sometimes a little careful research in order to find the appropriate background information that is necessary to bring these historical images back to life for the understanding of a modern age. We must comprehend the language and images of the Old Testament prophets, and have some grasp of the historical period when John wrote. If we do not have both of these elements at our disposal, then the symbols will have expressed meaning to those first readers, but it will be utterly lost to us. Our reading glasses will be insufficient because they are myopic. We see what is near at hand for us in our time, but fail to appreciate these images for the audience of John's time.

Thus, we are not trying to be overly simplistic in our approach or make it seem as if missing the meaning of these symbolic pictures is something that only the ignorant and perverse could do. That is not the case, and this is not what we are attempting to say at all. Some of these symbols are at first very difficult to understand. We appreciate that fact and honor that hard reality. Those picture portraits he employs that fall into this category require some serious thought and sometimes will need for us to dig into some background information in order to make them come back to life for our own generation, but they are symbols. There is no mistaking that fact.

That is what John says they are, and symbols always intend to communicate some idea other than the symbol itself. This concept is not difficult to comprehend, but it is so very important in appreciating the nature of these images.

Let us illustrate the point in the following simple way. If you were to drive to the edge of a town, say, Nashville, Tennessee, you would see there a sign standing beside the road. The sign would say, "Nashville." You would not pull to the side of the road, get out of your automobile and walk over to that sign and say, "Nashville! I was expecting more than just this little piece of metal with letters on it!" In other words, you would never mistake the sign for the city. The sign is not the city. The sign points the passerby to the city. Sadly, this is precisely what many expositors do with the signs in the book of Revelation. They fail to comprehend that the sign is only that. It is a sign and nothing more. The meaning is tied up in the sign, but is never identical with the sign.

Let us say it once more in different terms: the symbol is the vehicle of thought that the vision is trying to communicate. So in every instance there is behind that symbolic portrait an idea that John was trying to express for his audience, and diligent study today will uncover that meaning in every case if sufficient consideration and effort is spent on making the discovery. Students of history and culture over the years have supplied us with a treasure-trove of important material to enlighten us as we approach these symbols, so their researches are very helpful in our investigation of John's symbols. To ignore their work would be unsatisfactory and would starve the reader of much that is beneficial. For this reason, in the chapters that follow we intend to quote from these scholars quite extensively and, hopefully, assist the modern interpreter with those tools essential for a full appreciation of the rich images the apostle employs.

Fourth, Revelation is sequential, that is, it moves in cycles as it reveals future events. The consequence of this approach is that the same thing may be prophesied in several different visions under varying symbols. Thus, the righteous are similarly rewarded in 7:15-17 at the end of the Seal Cycle and again at the end of the book (21:14; 22:1-5). The Great Day of God's Wrath is portrayed at the opening of the Sixth Seal (6:12-17) and again toward the end of the book (20:11-15). Many of the earthly judgments

Introduction to John's Book of Revelation

described in the separate cycles are also repetitions of one another in dissimilar forms. This is not meaningless repetition. It is merely a result of the approach taken by the author.

This observation is not at all new. In fact, it was noticed by the earliest of expositors of the Apocalypse. The earliest surviving complete commentary on the book is the work of a Greek martyr bishop writing in Latin about the year 300. Victorinus of Pettau wrote a work which is often described as "inelegant in style and pedestrian in particulars," but which attempted to give a coherent reading of the whole book, and uncovered what has come to be recognized as one of the fundamental principles still used for dealing with its structure, the notion of recapitulation. "Do not regard the order of what is said," he wrote, "because the sevenfold Holy Spirit, when He has run through matters down to the last moment of time and the end, returns again to the same times and completes what He has left unsaid" (Victorinus, 8.2-3).

The idea that the structure of Revelation is recapitulative rather than linear or progressive has remained a major option for readers ever since. Moreover, since its revival half a century ago, it has been increasingly influential in historical-critical studies of the book as well (McGinn, 530). We deem this observation to be critical for a full understanding of John's method. Missing this point leads to interpretive chaos. Those who have failed to appreciate this notion have delivered to readers a badly mistaken impression of John's meaning. They have postulated that human history will be punctuated with multiple resurrections, as well as several judgments, when in fact John is only speaking of the same general resurrection and judgment in different settings using language distinctive to each particular vision.

Fifth, it is visionary. This means that in the Apocalypse of John pictorial accounts of visions are a significant element of the author's presentation. The phrase "I saw" or "I looked" runs throughout the whole book as a primary motif (1:12; 4:1; 5:1, 6, 11; 6:1, 12; 7:1-2, 9). However, it is noteworthy that the pattern of initially obscure vision and subsequently interpreted meaning, which is found in many of the other apocalyptic writings, is almost completely absent in the Revelation. Not only are the visual images and symbols not puzzling for the Seer, but the assumption is that their meanings were immediately clear and sensible to the readers of the book as well.

The only exceptions to this general rule are found in 7:13-17 and 17:7-18. But even here the words of the angel offer no real interpretation of the preceding vision, rather they provide merely a stylistic means of highlighting the attention of the readers (cf. 7:13) and also of introducing thematically related material (17:7). The composition of Revelation thus does not aim at highlighting the moment of tension of revealing hidden secrets; it makes no effort to captivate the reader by that which could be called the "keyhole effect" of the various apocalypses from between the two testaments. Those literary documents are of a different sort, even though they do share some things in common. John is less dramatic and much more accessible than those authors. As a result his apocalypse is more transparent and understandable than theirs. He does not seek for mystery, but for transparency. He does not aim at secrecy as most of them seem to do, but for full disclosure. John has written a "revelation" for his audience, just as the name of his book implies.

Sixth, the literature makes use of special and meaningful numbers. Among ancient Oriental writers it was commonplace to set forth moral and spiritual truths under the symbolism of various numbers. In those times when language was much more limited than it is today, and vocabularies were insufficient to communicate many ideas otherwise, men very often fell back upon the use of different numbers for the expression of a whole host of ideas. A specific number would suggest a definite concept. Numbers thus became the symbols of ideas, and employing that particular number brought forth the idea that it represented. Such numbers, obviously cannot be read with the same literal exactitude with which we employ and interpret mathematical formulae.

For example, in ancient times the number one almost universally represented the idea of unity. It stood for that which was unique and alone; what is independent and self-existent; in another sense, the Alpha and the Omega. This is the notion presented in Hebrew thought regarding God. He is seen always as One (Deut. 6:4; Matt. 22:37; Mark 12:29, 30; Luke 10:27). He is therefore the unitary, the alone, the self-existent, the independent One. And even though the number one does not occur in the book of Revelation in this symbolic and theoretical sense, it is one of those that John could well have employed had he been minded to do so. Had he utilized it, readers would have caught his meaning immediately.

Related to this is the notion that the number three came to be viewed as the divine number. The biblical idea of the Trinity, found extensively in both Old Testament and New, but most especially in the New, was at the heart of this idea, although some have argued that in the notion of human family life there is also a hint of it. In the interplay of love and kindness and family affection in one's own household there was at work the paternal love of a father, the maternal love of a mother, and the filial love of children.

In Jewish traditional lore the number three was particularly important. It was said that three was used in the Torah to mediate between two opposing or contradictory values. The third value mediates, reconciles, and connects the two. Hence, three was viewed as the number of *truth*. Time was divided into three portions. The past, the present and the future. The position in time that was considered the most expressive of the non-physical was the present, because it is so fleeting. The function of the present is as connector between past and future. Thus, the number three expressed a sense of *connection*.

Also, according to Jewish law, once something was performed three times it was considered a permanent thing. This is called *chazakah* (the *halachic* status of permanence). Hence, many actions were performed three times in Jewish ritual, since that was thought to add strength to these activities. The *Amida* was repeated three times. There were three people standing when a *sefer Torah* was read. The minimum number of verses read by a single reader was three. And the minimum number of readers was three. The number three therefore represented *permanence* as well. Additionally, according to *Mishnah Abhot* 1:2, "the world stands on three things: Torah (Law), *abhodah* (service of God), and acts of kindness." There were three patriarchs: Abraham, Isaac, and Jacob. There were three *mitzvot* (commanded things) in the *seder* (Passover ritual): the lamb, *matzah* (unleavened bread), and *maror* (bitter herbs). The *Tanak* (Bible) was divided up into three sections: Torah (Law), Nebhi'im (Prophets), and the Kethubhim (Writings). The Zohar pointed out that the Torah was given in the third month of the biblical year, to a threefold people (priests, Levites, Israelites), through a third-born man

(Moses), who was the third child in his family (after Miriam and Aaron). There are many more of such instances. Three is one of the most important numbers in Hebrew symbolism. What most of these seem to indicate is the concept of *unity* and *fullness* when that particular numeral is expressed. For example, it is noted in the thirteenth rule of Ishmael ben Elisha (a second century rabbi) regarding hermeneutics, that in order to understand the Torah you must compare three verses. If two verses seem to conflict with one another, a third verse is brought into the discussion in order to show how they may be reconciled. The result is *harmony*.

In later Christian understanding, the most divine aspect of human life was also represented with the number three, explaining in real terms the origin of physical life in this world. On the divine side of creation there is God the Father, God the Son, and God the Holy Spirit. In one of the catacombs there is a marble figure of Saint Cecilia, patroness of music, who is said to have suffered martyrdom in the third Christian century because of her refusal to sacrifice to idols. On the one hand of the recumbent figure three fingers are stretched out, testifying in the hour of her death to her faith in the threefold nature of Deity. She believed in the Holy Trinity. Again, this is not a notion that is employed by John, its main outlines being drawn together into a more fully developed and idiosyncratically defined theological notion after the era of that apostle, but it was already rich with meaning, and if he had chosen to use it, it was there for him.

What this shows, however, is that the range of numbers which could have been employed is larger even than what we do experience when we study the literature of John's Apocalypse. He uses numbers extensively and meaningfully, but he only "touches the hem of the garment" when it comes to numerology and its potential at the time. It also tells us that John was using a method which would have been very familiar to his original audience of readers. They knew and understood the concept behind this approach and comprehended well the ideas that were being communicated by the numbers he chose with such care.

Hence, certain numbers, such as 4, 7, 10, and 12, which are occasionally associated with a definite symbolic content, play a significant role in the Revelation. It is easy to see how some of these numerals would have

Introduction to John's Book of Revelation

entered the world of apocalyptic thought as having special meaning and even at times symbolic implications. For example, the number ten is one of the favorite numbers found in the Revelation. It has been suggested that our decimal system originated with man's study of his fingers and toes, just as the baby begins its earliest study of itself. In primitive times it was often the case that there were men who through accident or warfare had lost one or more of their fingers or toes. Missing these digits, they would have been viewed as crippled and incomplete.

On the other hand, the fellow who was fortunate enough to have all fingers on each hand and all five toes on each foot would have been considered a well-rounded and complete individual. His members were all present. And thus the number five, doubled to ten, as on the intact hands and feet, came to symbolize human *completeness*. The whole duty of the naturally complete man is summed up in Ten Commandments in the Old Testament. In the Revelation, the dragon and the first beast (chapters 12-13) are both pictured as having ten horns; and so also is the scarlet beast (chapter 17), whose horns are interpreted as representing ten kings. The ten horns are the symbol of complete power in government. As a multiple, ten occurs also in most of the higher numbers of the book as well. John speaks of the number of the angels about the throne of God as being "ten thousand times ten thousand" (5:11); the number of the armies of the horsemen of chapter nine was "twice ten thousand times ten thousand" (9:16). John also speaks of the church at Smyrna suffering persecution for only "ten days" (2:10). Thus, a brief but complete period of time was described in terms of the number ten. The church was to suffer, but only for an endurable span of earthly time.

Ancients also tended to utilize multiples of these important numbers as well. Ten, with its meaning of human completeness, when multiplied twice—as in ten times ten, times ten, equates to the number one thousand. This sometimes represented ultimate completeness. So, one thousand years was indicative of a long, protracted period of time. One thousand years is like one single day to God, says Peter (2 Pet. 3:8). And for John this period represents the long era during which the martyrs would reign with Christ their Lord in victory over their persecutors (20:4). This is not to say that they were to reign over their murderers for exactly one thousand times three hundred and sixty-five days, five hours, forty-eight minutes, forty-five and a fraction seconds. It merely points to a protracted period of time stretching over untold generations of unknown length. They suffered only briefly, but they would reign as conquerors for a very long time.

Four is customarily seen in the ancient world as the cosmic number. Primitive man had no conception of the universe as we know it, especially in scientific terms. To him the earth itself had four natural boundaries, north, south, east and west. His house in all likelihood had four sides to it. The city he lived in probably had four walls built around it. There were four winds coming from the four corners of the earth, and they were often conceived of as being controlled by four guardian spirits or angels. On account of all this, the number four became the symbol of the world in which he lived. So, in the book of Revelation we find four living creatures, representing all of nature, all creaturehood; four angels stand at the four corners of the earth, controlling the four winds of heaven; four angels are bound at the Euphrates River until the moment comes for their work of slaughter to begin. There are, of course, four horsemen in the Apocalypse, representing the destructive forces that go forth to accomplish the divine will. The earth on which man lived and labored and eventually also died was symbolized by the number four. It generally stood for the visible, material creation (Richardson, 18ff.).

The number twelve is also very important in the book. It stands next in frequency to the number seven. The Old Testament has the Twelve Tribes of Israel, and the New Testament of course has the twelve apostles of Jesus. Here in the Revelation the mother of the Messiah is crowned with twelve stars. There are also twelve gates to the holy city, New Jerusalem. Indeed, the city also has twelve foundation stones, on which are engraved the names of the twelve apostles. As well, the tree of life bears twelve manner of fruits.

In point of fact, the number seven is the most important of these cryptic numerals used in the book. It is found some fifty-four times in all. The number seven is particularly important, since it represented perfection, fullness or completeness, not just in the Bible, but throughout the ancient world. Perhaps for this reason most ancient civilizations considered seven to be a lucky number.

Introduction to John's Book of Revelation

For instance, the ancient astronomers had discovered seven moving planets in the sky (including the sun and moon), and this suggested to them a kind of astrological perfection. The musical scale, which figured prominently in Pythagorean and Platonic speculation about the nature of the universe, had precisely seven notes. Jewish thought, outside the Bible, frequently used the number seventy (7 times 10), ten being the number of human completeness and seven representing divine perfection. This produced an intensified numerical symbol for completeness. There were seventy members in the high Jewish court. The Jews believed that there were seventy nations outside of Israel, with seventy languages, and they were under the care of seventy angels. Jesus, perhaps using this significant number for symbolic reasons, chose and sent forth seventy disciples to preach during the days of the "limited commission" to the "lost sheep of the house of Israel" (Luke 10:1). In His teaching, when He wished to express the idea of unlimited forgiveness He took the number seven, representing perfection, and multiplied it by seventy ("seventy times seven"). This does not, of course, mean exactly four hundred and ninety times. That would ignore the symbolic force that the two numbers possessed. It meant unlimited forgiveness.

In the Bible itself, the creation of the world is said to have taken place in seven days, the last of which was made to be the day of rest after everything else had been completed. Therefore the Hebrews counted the passing of time in seven time units, the days of the week. In the law of Moses there were placed provisions for the setting aside of each seventh year as a time in which the soil of the land should be given a rest, old debts were settled, land was restored to its original and rightful owners, and the renewal of life celebrated in various ways.

Many important projects possessing religious significance are also reported as having been completed in seven time units, probably by intention. For example, the erection of the Tabernacle in the wilderness and the building of Solomon's Temple, were finished in seven time units. And very sacred events, such as a solemn oath (Gen. 21:28-32) or a religious ritual (Lev. 4:6), also involved the number seven. As previously noted, Jesus also stressed this symbolism when He sent out seventy disciples to preach His gospel to the sons of Israel (Luke 10:1, 17).

Both John and those first readers of the book of Revelation were very well acquainted with this common usage and the pregnant significance of this important number. And thus, employing it in such a prominent way, John obviously meant to communicate something that his ancient readers could grasp quite easily (but which at times may create some difficulty for those of us who are less experienced with these numbers and their intended meanings). In our view the first and most important reason for employing the number seven in this way was to alert his readers to the fact that this Revelation does not simply deal with a local and temporary problem, such as the persecution of the saints of Asia Minor in the first Christian century. John is saying, instead, that he wants to show how this problem of persecution and eventual divine deliverance is related to the whole future of the Kingdom of God on the earth in every century and in every culture and historical situation. He is taking the complete view, one which extends from Alpha to Omega, from the beginning of the church up to its end (Rev. 22:13). The problem is a universal one and is therefore pertinent in every age of the people of God, whether long ago or in the future (cf. Unjhem, 47-49).

Note for instance that the book itself is addressed to seven churches represented by seven lamp stands, while their angels are seven stars. Certainly there were more than just seven congregations of God's people in that region. That is not the implication of this usage in the book. In a sense these seven churches in Asia Minor are symbolic of all of the churches of Christ, and the seven letters that are penned to them are directed at all of the churches scattered throughout the earth at the time. They are merely representative of the whole body of Christ. There are seven Spirits of God, symbolized by seven lamps. The seven Spirits before the throne of God clearly stand for the perfection and completeness of divine power. The Book in the hand of God is sealed with seven seals; the Lamb before the throne has seven eyes and seven horns. Seven angels blow seven trumpet blasts (8:2–11:19); seven other angels pour out the contents of seven bowls (or vials, 15:1–16:21) full of the seven last plagues. Seven thunders utter voices which the Seer is bidden not to write. Seven thousand are killed in the great earthquake which follows the ascension of the Two Witnesses. The Dragon has seven heads, and upon them are seven diadems; the Wild Beast from the Sea has seven heads on which are "names of blasphemy"; the Scarlet Beast on

Introduction to John's Book of Revelation

which Babylon sits likewise possesses seven heads, variously interpreted by the writer as seven mountains, or seven kings. There is also a sequence of seven brief, but unnumbered visions that close out the book (19:11–21:8). There is no fortuitousness in any of this symbolism. In each case some sense of the representative meaning of the number seven is intended.

Thus these sequences of sevens are the most elemental aspect of the work, forming the framework of its recapitulative structure. And, interestingly, these sequences are made the more complex by such literary devices as inclusion, whereby one sequence can be seen as part of the final act of its predecessor (for example, the relation of the seven trumpets to the seventh seal in 8:1-2), and the method of "intercalation" in which two episodes that belong together are interrupted by another incident (for example, 8:2-6, in which the angels with the trumpets are introduced, but a heavenly liturgy intervenes before they begin to blow). Nor is it always perfectly clear to the reader how these series of sevens relate to the general structural principles of the work, such as that discerned in the cases of the two great books: the "closed book" with the seven seals (5:1), which can be taken as containing what is revealed in chapters 6–11; and the "open book" that the "mighty angel" gives John to eat in chapter 10, which can be seen as the message of the second half (cf. Bernard McGinn, "Revelation," 525).

At any rate, each series of seven is complete in itself, and each suggests the perfection which belongs to the divine, or else that which is falsely claimed by God's adversaries. Interestingly, half of the number seven takes on a special meaning of its own. So, the number three and one-half also appears frequently in the Book of Revelation. Since seven is the ultimate symbol of perfection, three and a half, one half of seven, is the ultimate symbol for imperfection or incompleteness. This broken seven is a symbol of the interruption of the divine order of things by the devices of Satan and the malice of evil men. It stands for restless longings unfulfilled, aspirations unrealized, and hopes deferred. In John's Revelation the Two Witnesses to the truth of God testify for three and a half years (11:3); the outer courts of the temple are trampled down by the ungodly for three and a half years (11:2); the witnesses dead bodies lie in the streets of the city unburied for three and a half days (11:9); the spirit of life enters into them and they rise again after three and a half days (11:11). The saints of God are persecuted for three and a half years (13:5); and the church was in the wilderness for three and a half years (12:6, 14).

To attempt to calculate the precise time period so described is to waste one's efforts. In the book of Revelation it simply signifies the age of persecution, of frustration, of unrealized hopes, whatever the actual length of time may eventually prove to be. As C. F. Wishart said: "(It) stood for the restless, the dissatisfied, the incomplete, for truth on the scaffold and wrong on the throne, for patient waiting until the dawning of the day-star in the eastern sky" (*The Book of Day: A Study of the Revelation of St. John*; quoted in D. W. Richardson, *Revelation of Jesus Christ*, 22).

Now, just as seven was seen as a very lucky number, there were numbers in the vocabulary of the ancient world that had dark overtones as well. In our modern culture the number thirteen is considered unfortunate and even sinister. Many buildings do not have a thirteenth floor. Many hotels refuse to number one of the rooms thirteen. Some people have even refused to sit down at a table with thirteen guests seated at the same dinner. It is considered a mystic number with sinister significance. Likewise, in the ancient world the number six was thought to be a digit possessing a similarly dark meaning. Seven, as we have noted, was the number of perfection, so this one falls just shy of the perfect number.

Consequently, in a sense six always fails and thus signifies the inability to reach the sacred height. For the Jews the numeral six had in it the very sound of doom about it. It spelled adversity, misfortune, calamity, and disaster. Triple the six, and you have tripled the foreboding. That is what John did in giving his evil "beast" a number. Six hundred and sixty-six is forever identified with "the number of the beast" (13:18) whom many have identified with "the Antichrist." In doing so John did not mean to be understood as having in mind one particular individual who was to appear in human history, but instead to picture every single human leader who has opposed the divine plan and attempted to assume divine prerogatives. Many such satanic figures have appeared on the horizon of history over the millennia who have fit John's description in the book, and John may even have had one individual in mind at the time (most probably the hateful Domitian who brought down the full weight of the Roman political structure upon the church, and sent John into exile on the Island of Patmos).

Introduction to John's Book of Revelation

But, John's portraiture is larger than just one mere man. It is a picture of evil incarnate and personified—and tripled! At the same time, there is a hopeful note in all of this, and it exists within the very nature of the number itself. Six always falls short of the sacred seven. Failure to reach the best is six, and so it represents sin. After all, in the final analysis, is sin not simply the ultimate illustration of failure? Certainly it never attains that end to which it aspires. The number six therefore fitly represents the perennial failure of sin to reach the goal of completeness toward which it aims and strives. In the symbolism of numbers it is therefore comforting to recognize that six is indeed the number for sin and that sin is symbolic of failure.

When we appreciate the fact that there have often been times when the specter of dark foreboding has cast its shadow over the history of humankind and it seems as though the power of evil has come to sit permanently ensconced upon the throne of earthly power, it is helpful to know that such an era of wickedness cannot be of unbroken duration. Evil wears upon its own dark brow the mark of imperfection and defeat. Its doom is already prefigured in the number that it wears. Seven will always equal victory, whereas six will always add up to eventual defeat. Sin may multiply itself to the highest level of six, but it can never reach seven. Hence, John's bestial figure is marked forever with the number of its eventual doom and its inevitable demise.

The number twelve is second in importance, found ten times in the book to picture various symbolic values. Multiples of twelve also are common: 12,000, 144, and 144,000. The numeral ten is also found ten times in the book. This is sufficient to illustrate our point. Both ten and twelve are numerals that signify completeness and unity. Man has ten fingers and ten toes. Israel had twelve tribes, and Jesus chose precisely twelve apostles. When Judas hanged himself the group chose one to take his place and round the number back to its original twelve. Obviously the number carried with it a spiritual significance as well as a symbolic value. Eleven would not have been sufficient!

Mainly these freighted numerals serve the purpose of uniting the visions of the book into groupings linked variously by similarity of structure. Hence, there are precisely seven seals which must be opened in order to reveal the divine purpose. There are also seven trumpets which must be given their time to sound, each in its own turn. Seven bowls of the wrath of God must be poured out as well. Such groupings of visions, in turn, express the central thought of apocalyptic writers generally: the course of world history and the concluding events of the same follow a definite schema of periods that is determined in God's plan from the very beginning. This schema must work itself out and nothing that the dark powers in the universe may do in the meanwhile is able to alter the final outcome. God and His people will be victorious. God's power is irresistible and His plan is unalterable, and so in the end those who stand with Him will prevail also.

The thesis behind this approach is therefore quite simple but unfailingly profound. It informs the reader in no uncertain terms that, among other things, nothing surprises God. He is well ahead of the horizon of history. He is in control at every moment, even when it seems that this just could not be true, and everything that happens somehow or other works into His eternal design. Even when the whole appears utterly opaque and incomprehensible to human eyes this is nevertheless true. God is the Master of history even as He is the Master of man. Nothing is beyond His power. He has a Master Plan for the ages, and that Plan will be worked out despite all of the might of the infernal powers being allied in their malevolent purpose to frustrate it. The God of the Bible is God in the truest and most comprehensive sense of the word. He is God Almighty, God without limits, and God without borders.

Seventh, the literature speaks to a particular historical situation. John's Apocalypse was penned to address real people and their very real problems. This critical circumstance, to which the Revelation alludes with repeated clarity (cf. 13:11-18; 17:8-14), can be described fairly accurately, even though it is clothed in imagery by the author: "All who dwell on the earth will worship him . . . And he makes the earth and those who dwell in it worship the first beast . . . telling those who dwell on the earth to make an image to the beast . . . and cause as many as refuse to worship the image of the beast to be killed." The writer of the Revelation sees the storm clouds of trouble brewing in the growing religious claim of the Roman state that it holds complete sovereignty over every aspect of the lives of its citizens and will exercise that sovereignty through imposition of the imperial cult of the Caesar on the peoples of the whole Empire. Augustus had already supported the divine veneration of the deceased Caesar because in it he saw a cultic-religious bond for the Empire that would override all of the local cults and deities and create a unifying force throughout the hundreds of disparate factions of the variegated governmental and socio-economic domain. It represented a unifying force in a complex, multi-faceted, multi-ethnic Empire. It had the potential of bringing the many into one, and so it had to be imposed upon the population, even by force if necessary. The overall goal appeared to be worthy of the cost to individuals who might object to it.

Among his successors it was particularly Caligula and Claudius who went beyond venerating dead men and demanded divine glory for themselves while they still lived. However, it was not until the last years of Domitian's reign (AD 81-96) that there was a systematic propagation of the cult of the Caesar that spanned the entire Empire. He had conferred upon himself the official title "our Lord and God" (Suetonius, *Domitian* 13). In the years AD 92-96, Asia Minor, a region in which the ruler cult already had a long-standing tradition going back to pre-Roman times, became a center of religious worship of the Caesar. Excavations of Ephesus, the major metropolitan center of the province at that time, have unearthed remains of a temple to Domitian and an enormous statue of the emperor that had been violently destroyed after his death. Therefore, Christians who refused to offer the divine worship the emperor demanded for himself, placed themselves outside of regular society and indeed, by making such a choice, had to reckon with suffering and persecution.

That Christians were considered strangers and outsiders who were distrusted in many ways was nothing new. Peter noted that this was a reality that had to be dealt with whether they liked it or not (1 Pet. 2:12; 3:16). The first major experience of this formal and very public societal rejection occurred in the so-called Neronian persecution (AD 64) in Rome. Tacitus (*Annals* 15.44) gives the account thus: "Accordingly, an arrest was made of all who pleaded guilty; then, upon their information, an immense multitude was convicted, not so much for the crime of firing the city, as of hatred against mankind. Mockery of every sort was added to their deaths. Covered with the skins of beasts, they were torn by dogs and perished, or were nailed to crosses, or were doomed to the flames and burnt, to serve as a nightly illumination, when daylight had expired."

The horrible excesses and punitive measures taken against the Christians at that time were horrendous enough; fortunately they were relatively localized and mostly remained confined to isolated places, rather than being Empire-wide. Too, they were fairly short-lived. After the reign of Domitian it seems that the flood-gates had been opened and the concerted power of the Roman government was turned against this strange and powerless minority. It has been noted both persistently and accurately that between the period AD 30 to 311, a period in which fifty-four emperors ruled the Empire, only about a dozen made a formal effort to harass the Christians, but that harassment was cruel and memorable. This confrontation, which was only in its infancy, was playing itself out at the time of the writing of the Revelation, for it is reflected in one way or another at every turn in the book. At this juncture in the history of the frightful altercation between Christianity and the Roman state, only in detached and far-flung places had the persecution become a matter of public concern (2:13). Certainly it could not be said that it was "generalized" throughout the Empire, but this was only the onset, and it represented the beginning of a new era for all concerned. Worse was coming. John was certain of this. The thrust of his symbol-shrouded prophecy leaves no doubt about it. And he was exactly right in his assessment of where things were headed.

In his dramatic images John not only announces an imminent, external intensification of the conflict, but also makes visible its true essence: the Christians of Asia Minor, in particular, needed to know that encountering them in the totalitarian religious claim to power by the Roman state was more than mere political mistreatment or societal rejection. It was more than the State vs. the Church. It represented the manifestation of the dark and foreboding powers of the infernal regions opposing God Himself. Satan is at work here, along with his enthusiastic minions. John predicts that in the end they will engage in a final futile battle against the lordship of Jesus Christ. When the entire bloody drama has played itself out, they will lose the conflict, but much harm will be done in the process.

For John, in this conflict between the Church and the Empire there cannot be any compromise. The way of the Church can only be that of passive resistance to the power of the State and thus of obedience to the Lord. At the time, what John offers God's people is comfort and hope. They must come to know that the powers opposing God will soon have exhausted themselves and that the ultimate victory of God, which is already inscribed upon the pages of heaven's sealed book, will soon be manifest to all those "who dwell on the earth."

B. The Purpose of the Book

The Revelation is written to comfort the persecuted Christians of Asia Minor with two significant facts: (1) Rome will ultimately be judged and destroyed; and, (2) Although Christians must endure a fiery trial for the present, the church will ultimately be victorious.

Nowhere may this dual message of the book be seen more clearly than in the Fifth Seal Vision of 6:9-11. This is a startling picture that is significant to an understanding of the Apocalypse. It must not be ignored. The reader would do well to fix it in his or her mind throughout the course of studying the book, for in a sense it is the guiding star of the document:

> And when he opened the fifth seal, I saw underneath the altar the souls of those who had been slain for the Word of God, and for the testimony which they held: and they cried with a great voice, saying, How long, O Lord, holy and true, do You not judge and avenge our blood on those who dwell on the earth? And each one was given a white robe; and it was said to them, that they should rest yet for a little while, until their fellow-servants also and their brethren, who should be killed even as they were, should have fulfilled their course.

Thus, given what this vision says, the purpose of Revelation is not to tell those oppressed Christians that the persecution would quickly end. That, of course, would have been a most welcome message for them to hear. In fact, however, the reverse was true! It was intended to say to them that they must be patient in the face of their suffering (1:9; 2:2, 3, 19; 3:10; 13:10; 14:12), even though it might last a very long time and be exceedingly cruel. At the same time, it informed them that God had some ultimate good in mind in what they were enduring, and that in the end both they and their righteous cause would be victorious (they will "sit on thrones," 20:4). On their part, they must remain faithful until death, whatever came their way (Rev. 2:10).

"I Saw the Heaven Opened"

How to Read This Book of Symbols: The Writer's Method

We must attempt to understand the book in precisely the same way the first Christians did, or else we will not comprehend it at all. We need, in a figure, to read the book through "first century glasses." It is the failure to do this which is the chief cause of confusion in the interpretation and understanding of the Apocalypse. While the code is sometimes difficult to break, because it is frequently alien to us in our own particular place and time, it is never impossible. Most importantly, we should try always to keep in view the broader picture, the larger lesson that John and the Spirit are trying to communicate to the reader. Smaller details must not obscure the true message of what John saw! This is another reason that many students of the book fail to comprehend its meaning. They get caught up in a maze of incidental details and lose track of the larger message.

Donald Richardson illustrated this point with his definition of a violin solo: he said that it was "the noise made by scraping the hairs of a horse's tail across the dried entrails of a dead cat." Viewed from the vantage point of the actual laws of physical science this picture is entirely accurate, but surely it is more than merely this! Is there not some art there along with the science? Is the beautiful music produced by this physical activity not the most important aspect of what is happening? If we consider it only in the light of the physical action occurring, have we not missed the art and the music and therefore lost out on what the whole process was about after all?

The book of Revelation is a document filled with intricate symbolism. Images flash before the eyes of the reader in rapid succession. Great dramas play out in the visions of the work. All of this is variegated as well as fast moving. As a result, the reader may be moved to become fascinated by one or more of the symbols, like the mark of the beast, the battle at Armageddon, the one thousand year reign, or the New Jerusalem. That would be a mistake, however. And many people have fallen victim to this temptation. For one or more of the symbols were not meant to be seen as such. Each in its own turn was planned to play a part in the larger whole and to serve as one piece of the fuller and more complete puzzle that the document as a whole was intended to communicate. And, surely the book of Revelation is more than merely the individual symbols which comprise the various visions of the book. Certainly it is also more; in point of fact it is indeed much more. The thematic structure is much more significant to an understanding of and appreciation for what the book is about than any one or more of the individual symbols. So, let us spend a few paragraphs on the important themes which make up the content of the literature of the Revelation.

Great Themes in the Book of Revelation

The Apocalypse, or Revelation, of John is in our view the most intriguing book of the New Testament. However, since books filled with symbolism and meaning-laden imagery lend themselves rather naturally to the speculations and extreme ruminations of those who enjoy that sort of thing, Revelation has proven to be a rich target for conjecture and speculative prognostication since the very earliest days of its existence. This has meant that for a certain class of people the book's reputation has been sullied, and they will have no part in its study. They feel, unfortunately, that it is somehow beyond them. They are confused by the many zany theories that have proliferated about it and so have come to believe that the maze of possible meanings creates a virtual slough of confusion, destined to bog them down in a swamp of despair. So they stay clear of it.

This is not actually the case with the material that is contained in it; it is actually quite meaningful and fairly simple to understand. But they have most assuredly started out on the wrong foot, so they need to be taught to approach the work from a different perspective. It would not hurt to begin by noticing some of the magnificent themes of the work. Everyone can understand these simple motifs which are so predominant throughout that it is difficult not to notice them and certainly important to comprehend them if we are to have some appreciation for the "big picture" of the book. And the "big picture" is indeed the best place to start.

In point of fact, for serious students of the Apocalypse, great lessons abound within its pages, and several marvelous themes are treated through the medium of its images and symbols. Revelation's themes cover a broad range of subjects, but always it is God's dealings with and on behalf of a persecuted and "beaten down" people which take center stage in this book. This is so in Revelation as it is with all works of an apocalyptic nature in the Bible, as well as in the extra-biblical literature written after the Old Testament. It will not be surprising, therefore that each of the major themes of this book somehow or other center around this idea and put forward the narrative that God yet loves His people and will eventually save them from their hateful enemies and deliver them from their cruel tormentors.

A. The Relationship between Church and State

When John wrote his letters to the seven churches of Asia Minor, and its attendant book of prophecies, the time was about AD 96. In the long sweep of human history, Rome had existed for some eight hundred and fifty years, and was about to embark upon some of her most glorious days as an Empire. Trajan, Hadrian, Antoninus Pius, and Marcus Aurelius were yet to come to power, and history tells us that these men brought Rome through the most prosperous and successful days of her sovereignty over the nations of the then-known world.

The church had begun its life in the Roman Empire, seen from the Roman legal perspective, as a sect of the Jewish faith, believing as it did in a Jewish Messiah figure and accepting the legitimacy of all the writings of the Jewish lawgiver Moses and of her other insightful prophets. For some thirty years Rome was favorably disposed toward Christians because Judaism was a recognized religion (Acts 18:12). The reign of Nero (54-68) had changed all this. Their seeming intolerance toward their pagan neighbors and their strange new religious practices irritated those who were themselves quite uncaring about what others did or did not do—as long as they paid homage to the ancestral traditions and gave proper respect to the cultural mores of the prevailing societal norms. This group's religious convictions, though, would not permit them to yield to such pressures. So, as time went by, Christianity came to be seen by the Roman government as an unauthorized and therefore illegitimate religion.

This situation was to hold true until the fourth century when the emperor Constantine (306-337) gave the church official status through the Edict of Toleration in 311 and the later and even more permissive Edict of Milan in 313. Constantine's political agreement with Licinius in 313 effectively established religious toleration for the church in February of that year. Up until that time the Christian religion was considered a *religio illicita* under Roman law. Under this rubric Christians were considered enemies of the

Introduction to John's Book of Revelation

Roman state and therefore were subject to prosecution for crimes against the state.

The persecution of Christians under Nero and then Domitian in the year 95 represented a foretaste of a long, arduous, and very painful journey for the church. John was suffering as an exiled prisoner on the island of Patmos when he wrote the book of Revelation (1:9): "I John, your brother and partaker with you in the tribulation and kingdom and patience which are in Jesus, was in the isle that is called Patmos, for the Word of God and the testimony of Jesus" He was a Christian in a pagan-dominated world. Hence, he was a prisoner of conscience, like so many after him would also be.

His visions from Patmos revealed a dark and foreboding future for the church during what would otherwise be halcyon days of military and economic success for the Roman Empire. The church was commencing a long and bitter struggle with the Roman state as the weaker and smaller of the two combatants in this life and death conflict. The heart of the book, chapters 12, 13, 14, 17, and 18, would make abundantly clear what was only hinted at in the earlier part of the work, namely that the Roman political and economic war machine would oppose the church with a power that only Christ could overcome:

> These shall war against the Lamb, and the Lamb shall overcome them, for He is Lord of lords and King of kings; and they also shall overcome that are with Him, called and chosen and faithful (17:14).

John makes his identification of the world power known, not only in cryptic terminology like "Mystery, Babylon the Great" (17:5), but also in more transparent language like that of 17:18: "And the woman whom you saw is the great city, that reigns over the kings of the earth." The emperor is also unquestionably referred to in the book in rather unambiguous nomenclature: ". . . and there was given to him authority over every tribe and people and tongue and nation" (13:7). Rome was ruling over all of the earth at the time of the writing of this book, no matter what date is assigned to it by modern writers, so there can be no debate as to what great world power he meant when he wrote these words. Imperial Rome was intended.

This clash between the people of God and the world-power in the form of the political state is already well known to us from our study of the book of Daniel. King Nebuchadnezzar and Belshazzar in the empire of the Babylonians were taught the same lesson by harsh experience, i.e. that "the Most High rules in the kingdom of men, and that He sets up over it whomsoever He will" (4:25; 5:21). God is in control of world events, world rulers, and political states. Moreover, He uses them to accomplish His ends in human history. They may fight against His purposes, but they will only frustrate themselves in the process, and in the end He will have His way. This is what Daniel teaches us, and it is also one of the great themes in the book of Revelation.

B. Martyrdom and Persecution

Just as the book of Daniel had made reference to the "abomination of desolation," i.e. the sacrilege which brings ruin (8:13; 9:12; 11:14; 12:12), symbolically suggesting the desecration of the temple by Antiochus and the persecution and murder of the Jews of Jerusalem by the Syrian Greeks, and perhaps also in a secondary fulfillment in the plundering of the temple by Titus and his legions at a still later time (cf. Matt. 24:15), so John addresses the martyrdom of Christians under the hand of the emperors of Rome. Both are apocalyptic works, and Matthew 24 with its parallels (Mark 13 and Luke 21) represent a "little apocalypse" in the Gospel (as it is sometimes described), and so deal with essentially similar subject-matter.

Martyrdom in the Revelation is a constant and recurring theme. Christ warns the Christians at Smyrna that they are about to undergo persecution, and may even be confronted with martyrdom (2:10). They must be faithful "unto death." He reminds the people of Pergamum of Antipas, his faithful martyr, who was killed among them (2:13). To those of Philadelphia He speaks of the "hour of trial, that hour which is to come upon the whole world, to try them that dwell upon the earth" (3:10). He repeatedly instructs those in the churches that they must not fail their Lord, but must instead overcome through His power: "He who overcomes, I will . . ." (2:7, 11, 17, 26; 3:5, 12, 21), then portrays the Lion of the tribe of Judah as one who "has overcome to open the book . . ." (5:5), since He "has been slain" (5:12) and thus is worthy of honor and power. He is therefore pictured as a "martyr" for His own cause.

But, undoubtedly, the greatest moment in the treatment of this theme is in the vision of the opening of the fifth seal (6:9-11), the importance

Introduction to John's Book of Revelation

of which we have already underscored. Here martyred saints are pictured groveling at the base of the altar of God, crying out for justice. The only message they are given is that they must wait until more of their brothers have died as they did. Clearly then, John's Revelation is a prophecy of still more martyrdom, not of a quick end to this horrible parade of martyrdoms. And, of course, this is precisely how history played itself out as the years rolled by. There was no quick end to it. It would be over two hundred years before the age of the martyrs would draw to a close. Nevertheless, later generations would see the divine logic in this terrible experience for the church. Tertullian observed that "the blood of the martyrs is the seed of the church." The church grew on account of it, for the pagans tended to inquire as to what the justification of such willingness on their part to die for this cause might be:

> But pursue your course, excellent governors, and you will be more popular with the multitude if you sacrifice the Christians to their wishes. Crucify, torture, condemn, crush us. For the proof of our innocence is found in your injustice. It is on this account that God suffers us to suffer this. Yet no cruelty of yours, though each were to exceed the last in its exquisite refinement, profits you in the least; but forms rather an attraction to our sect. We spring up in greater numbers as often as we are mown down by you: the blood of the Christians is a source of new life. Many amongst yourselves have exhorted to the endurance of pain and death, as for example Cicero in the 'Tusculan Disputations,' Seneca in his book 'On Chances,' Diogenes, Pyrrho, and Callinicus. Yet they by their words secured not so many disciples as the Christians have gained by their practical example. That very obstinacy which you assail as a teacher. For who is not aroused by the sight of it to enquire what the inward motive can be? Who, when he has enquired, does not adopt it? And who, when he has adopted it, does not choose to suffer, in order that he may acquire the whole grace of God, and also obtain all pardon from Him by the yielding up of his blood? For all sins are pardoned by this act. Hence it is that, at the moment of your sentencing us, we give thanks: and since there is an antagonism between divine and human beings, when we are condemned by you, we stand acquitted by God (Tertullian, *Apologeticus pro Christianis* 50).

Chapter 11 of the Revelation features two martyr-witnesses (balancing the double meaning of the Greek word *martus*), whose duty it is to preach for a time. After they had completed their testimony, they were killed and their dead bodies left in the streets of the "great city" (11:7). The horrible beast of chapter 13, who as we have previously suggested, is the Emperor of the Roman state, has as his mission "to make war with the saints, and to overcome them . . ." (13:7). The mysterious city of Babylon, pictured in chapter 17, Rome herself, is "drunken with the blood of the saints, and with the blood of the martyrs of Jesus" (17:6). When she is cast down, God tells His people: "Rejoice over her, thou heaven, and ye saints, and ye apostles, and ye prophets; for God hath judged your judgment on her" (18:20), because "in her was found the blood of prophets and of saints, and of all that have been slain upon the earth" (18:24). The judgment which she receives comes because God "has avenged the blood of His servants at her hand" (19:2). At the conclusion of the book the souls of these martyred saints are at last seated on thrones, victoriously reigning with their Lord (20:4). In the light of these frequent references it is difficult to deny that Revelation is a book about martyrs and martyrdom. John is clearly preparing all of his readership for the potential of martyrdom, and in that particular historical setting, that prospect was very real indeed.

C. Warfare and Victory

As Homer Hailey expressed it in his commentary on the Revelation, "The grand theme of Revelation is that of war and conflict between good and evil resulting in victory for the righteous and defeat for the wicked" (Hailey, 51). Words like *polemeō* ("to make war, to fight") and *polemos* ("war, battle, conflict") are found many times in the book of Revelation, but very seldom throughout the remainder of the New Testament. The visions of this book picture a gargantuan struggle between the forces of good and those which set forward the purposes and practices of evil, and thus between God and Satan. The armies of the Evil One will make war with the saints of God and they will defeat them (13:7). This is a key theme in John's book of prophecy. The mere mention of this depressing reality must have been extremely hard for the first readers of the Revelation to take in, but in their situation no other message would have been appropriate. The earthly power of Imperial Rome was irresistible. The church, on the other hand, was a small and powerless group of very dedicated people, but in no sense were they a match for the political and military power of the Romans. So, the Roman state was poised to crush this tiny religious minority. Armed resistance would have proven futile (Matt. 5:39; Jas. 5:6), but

Introduction to John's Book of Revelation

passive resistance to their threats was another matter altogether. It would prove very successful over time. For now, they must suffer and bleed and die. That is their immediate future, and that is the thrust of John's message to the seven churches.

And yet, the prophet was not finished with his revelation when he told his audience this heavy and distressing news. He went on to say that eventually God would cause them to enjoy the victory, for He would fight the battle for them behind the scenes of history, just as He did so effectively for the Israelites in the Old Testament. But they must hold on and not give up. For all of the good things of the book, the predictions and promises, await those who "overcome." As John says: "He that overcomes shall inherit these things; and I will be His God, and he shall be My son" (21:7). The word here for "overcome" is *nikaō*, "to gain the victory." That is really what the book is all about. It is a general accounting of the war, not of a single battle which may be won or lost, but of the war itself. The end result is the victory of the saints. They would undergo many hardships, there would be many casualties, and frequently during the course of the action the future would look very dim and uninviting, but in the end they would see victory.

What is the overall plan, the eventual outcome of the many struggles and battles small and great, fought and lost as well as fought and won, the exasperation and exhilaration, the sweat and the toil, the agony and the ecstasy, the blood and the gore? The goal of the book is to give the reader a quick preview of the war's terminus. It provides a picture of things at the cessation of hostilities. And so, what we have in essence is a prophetic preview of coming attractions, in the sense that, at the outset of the war, in order to encourage His warriors, God contributed through this grand "Revelation" a portrait of the war's end, and of its final outcome. The message is edifying, and the news is good. The saints will indeed be victorious. They may endure hardship and stress, persecution and tribulation, torture and even death. Their reward will be without end. It will last throughout eternity. The enemies of God, on the other hand, will win in the short run, but in the end they will be thwarted and frustrated, and eventually will be punished harshly. Moreover, their punishment also will be without end. It will last throughout eternity as well. And so, the last phase of the battle is written on stone; the Lord has spoken it, and it will come to pass. Nothing is left to the imagination. God's people will see the victory. They will win and pagan Imperial Rome will lose.

The final chapter, the last scene, will inevitably be the conquest over evil by the saints. They will not do this under their own power. God will give them the mastery. It is by His power and might that they will win. All of this has already been decided. The Lord has by His sovereign will and by His divinely inspired Word declared the eventual but inevitable conclusion to this earthly struggle. The heroes of the conflict will be the martyrs. They gave their lives for the cause, and they will not be forgotten. Their reward is waiting for them. When the contest is over they will reign with Christ in perpetual victory over their enemies. They also will enjoy an eternal reward with Him in the celestial city, the New Jerusalem. They will live and reign for ever and ever. This is the quintessence of the message of this great book and the prevailing theme throughout.

Approaches to the Interpretation of Revelation

Given the very different method John utilized in setting forth the important truths that are found in his book of New Testament prophecy, it is not at all surprising that throughout the years since its writing different methods have been employed to attempt to draw out meaning from the symbols found in the document. In this case, methodology is everything. Various approaches to the material have yielded very different results as to what the magnificent symbols intend for the reader to know and understand. In point of fact, there is no book of the Bible where the approach we choose as we attempt to understand the meaning is so critical as in the case of the Revelation. It is quite amazing how starkly dissimilar have been the results that have been brought forth on account of their different starting points. All of these perspectives on the book cannot possibly be true all at once. Their conclusions are too disparate from one another, and the view of both history and future events is too widely separated. Consider for a moment how different will be the result if a wayfarer were to change his direction only a few degrees on the compass. The distance that would separate him from his true destination would prove to be incalculable over many miles that he would travel. Too, the further he would travel, the farther away from his desired end he would be. Beginning points for interpreters are very similar to the traveler who employs a compass. Therefore, the inter-

Introduction to John's Book of Revelation

preter must choose wisely, for the ultimate outcome cannot favor the lazy in this process. The end result is too important for one simply to take up his approach to the material too carelessly. He may well end up far wide of the mark of understanding the author's real meaning for the symbols used in the Revelation.

The following summarizations represent the major lines of approach to the material that have been utilized by interpreters throughout the history of the book's interpretation. Each one appears in numerous commentaries and books whose intent it is to draw out the meaning of the author's rich symbology (the art of expression by means of symbols). Once more, let the reader choose wisely between them, for the resultant end-points are vastly different and very difficult to reconcile:

1. The Futuristic Approach. In Protestant evangelical circles, this is the most popular way of attacking the meaning of Revelation today. It views the book as almost completely eschatological, that is, having to do with the events of the "end times." According to writers who look at the work from this perspective, the cryptic symbols reveal the end of the age, the coming of the Lord, a millennial reign with the saints on earth, the loosing of Satan, the second resurrection, and the Final Judgment. It is seen primarily as a book of unfulfilled prophecy. The majority of the book's contents—from chapter 4 to chapter 22—are to be fulfilled in the future. They hold also that the events recorded in chaps. 4-19 are to be fulfilled in the brief span of seven years. This period of tribulation is said to answer to the seventieth week of Daniel's prophecy of the Seventy Weeks (cf. Dan. 9:24-27). In that series of prophecies they delineate a separation (nonexistent in the prophecy itself) which they suppose divides the seventieth week from the other sixty-nine, and which they propose to come at the close of the Christian era.

One of the major beliefs of futurists is their conviction that a personal Antichrist will appear on the stage of history at the end of time. They interpret the great beast of Revelation to represent a wicked secular or ecclesiastic figure who will come to power in the final days of world history. He is frequently associated in their thinking with Paul's "man of sin" in 2 Thessalonians, chapter 2.

Essentially they are also millenarian in their approach. When the Lord comes again, they argue, the judgment will not take place at once. Rather, they propose a period of 1000 years of earthly reign for Christ in Jerusalem. However, all of this is inconsistent with other plain texts from the New Testament which are found in literal contexts, where their meaning is undeniable. Futurists are forced to twist and strain the meaning of these literal passages in order to make them fit with their interpretation of the figures of the Revelation. This is not an acceptable methodology. The reverse is proper in the discipline of interpretation: symbols ought to be read in terms of the passages that appear in literal contexts. That is a common-sense approach.

Futurists frequently claim that they are literalists. In point of fact, they are not. They very often stray from a literal approach to what they read, because it does not coincide with what they believe about the future. Their treatment of Israel in the 12th chapter is perfectly illustrative. The symbolism obviously refers to the birth of Christ as a past event (which is a problem for a futurist), and Old Testament Israel and the New Testament Israel (the church) as represented by the figure of the woman who gives birth to this babe. This, however, is inconsistent with their overall approach.

Hence, they tend to argue that the aspect of a symbol in the Revelation which does not support their general view of future events is to be taken as "symbolism" whereas the symbol itself is to be seen as literal. This is obviously arbitrary. Buried in the symbolism of the book there may be a few references that could be viewed literally, but it is certain that John's own words must be taken seriously as to the nature of the material. It is virtually pure symbolism, so many of the main visions of the book are inconsistent with a futuristic approach.

One of the gravest dangers of futurism is summed up in the following observation made by Ray Summers in his marvelous little book *Worthy is the Lamb*:

> . . . The futurist method is associated with a materialistic philosophy of the kingdom of God and a basis of triumph for the cause of righteousness which appears to be unscriptural throughout. Any approach which turns from the purpose of grace and the cross of Christ to methods of victory of any other

description becomes repulsive to the sincere Christian mind. Futurism does this very thing, whether it will admit it or not (Summers, 34).

Futurism also leaves the Apocalypse of John entirely out of relation to the needs of the seven churches of Asia to which it was originally addressed. Imagine this now: someone pens a letter to you which has almost nothing whatsoever to do with you. In fact, it addresses the circumstances of people two thousand or more years after your time. "It could never happen," you would probably say, and you would be correct in your analysis of the matter. It would not and could not happen, but the futurist believes it did. Revelation, they inform us, was written to those churches *but not for them or about them*. The very first purpose of every biblical book was to instruct, to warn, and to comfort those to whom and for whom it was written. There is not a single exception to this rule in the letters collected in the canonical New Testament. Why should the Revelation be seen any differently?

2. *The Continuous History Approach.* This view is sometimes described as the "historicist" perspective on the Revelation. Many Reformation scholars held that the book is to be seen as a forecast, in symbolic form, of the history of the church. Once more, though, this viewpoint puts the Revelation out of sync with the needs of the churches to which it was originally written. The rise of Romanism in the church, which is the main thrust of this perspective on the document, would have provided little comfort to the suffering saints who strained under the yoke of Imperial Rome at the time. Most events of the history itself would have been impossible for these saints in the seven churches to understand because they are only viewed as they are today on account of the fact that this is the way the ecclesiastical history has played out over time. Thus, they are interpreted "after the fact" in this fashion. History is made to conform to the figures and the figures are made to fit the history.

The majority of the commentators who are wed to this approach have understood the seals, trumpets, and bowls as unfolding successive events of history in general chronological order. Christ's final coming is usually seen by them as very imminent. Typically this approach sees parts of the Apocalypse as prophecies of the invasions of the Christianized Roman Empire by the Goths and the Muslims. Further, the corruptions of the medieval papacy, the reign of Charlemagne, the Protestant Reformation, and the destruction wrought by Napoleon Bonaparte and Adolph Hitler have been seen as predicted by John in this work.

This view tries in vain to identify historical movements too specifically and limits the prophecies of the Apocalypse to western church history, leaving aside the larger historical portrait of the worldwide church. Proponents of this view living at different periods of church history cannot agree with one another, since they limit the meaning of the symbols only to specific historical interests contemporary with their own times (Beale, 46). This dictates that in every instance their interpretations are out-of-date within a generation or two. This has been their unfortunate lot as time has passed. Their work is quickly dated and rendered practically useless by the simple passage of time.

Moreover, this method has frequently lead to calculations of times and periods which have constantly been falsified by the events and which have done much harm to the cause of truth on that account. Like the calculations set forth by the futurists in their speculative interpretations, the method which states that a day in prophecy is the equivalent of a thousand years, proves far too much and cannot be recognized as a valid interpretational principle.

Thus, the beast which is to have power for forty-two months is really said to have power for 1,260 years. The irascible problem with this is that the papacy (which is interpreted as the evil Beast) has already lasted much longer than this, and seems not to be losing steam yet! Most of the older commentaries take this approach to the book. Unfortunately, it makes them almost entirely useless as aids to the study of this part of Scripture. Again, though, the chief criticism that we could aim at this perspective on the Revelation is that this approach to the meaning of the symbols of the book would have had little useful relevance to the first-century readers of this material. How would all of this have been helpful to those initial readers?

3. The Philosophy of History Approach. Sometimes this approach is referred to as the "idealist" perspective. It sees Revelation as a symbolic portrayal of the eternal struggle between good and evil. As per this view, the Revelation is seen as an expression of God's government over the affairs of men and that these general principles may be observed in every age. The

Introduction to John's Book of Revelation

most radical form of this view holds that the book is a timeless depiction of this ever-present struggle. So, symbols are understood to refer to forces or tendencies and may thus be fulfilled over and over as these forces or tendencies are repeated in human history. As a consequence, the evil Beast is to be seen as an expression of those secular powers antagonistic to the true church in every age. The second beast with horns like a lamb but a voice like a dragon represents corrupt religious power in league with corrupt secular power to bring injury to the Lord's people. One of the major problems with this alternative as an approach to the Johannine visions is that it holds that Revelation does not depict any consummation in real human history, whether in God's final victory or in a final judgment of the realm of evil. In our view this is a perspective on the work which is not "idealist" enough for our way of thinking. If Revelation says anything at all, it says that God will eternally judge the enemies of the church, and any view that fails to recognize this cannot be given much legitimacy.

Once more, as well, this methodology evinces a similar tendency to remove the work too far from the situation of the original readers. How would this approach, if the first readers would have read the visions and symbols this way, have been helpful to them? We need always to make this inquiry as we approach the material in our studies. Too, if this is the only message of the book, then these things are taught quite plainly in most, if not all, of the prophetic writings of the Old Testament. How is this new? What is John's contribution to prophetic theology and thought? What has John added in the Revelation to what was already available before he penned it? Quite frankly, it is nil, if this approach is correct.

4. The Preterist or Contemporary-historical Approach. Taken from the Latin word *praeter*, which means "past," this refers to a way of reading Revelation which sees it entirely in the past, a part of ancient history, so to say. This is precisely the opposite of the approach taken by the futurists who see everything in the book as applicable to the end times. This viewpoint has many things which commend it, although it is sometimes taken to an unreasonable degree. Some scholars are driven to see practically no usefulness of this book for the present. All of it was for the people of the time. This is of course true to the background and setting of the book itself, and is assuredly a point which may be made in its favor.

At the same time, while we certainly wish to place the first emphasis upon the generation for which the document was originally intended (and we ought always to try to do this before we make other possible or potential applications), still there is clearly an enormous amount of applicability to our own time and for our present circumstances, no matter the age of the reader.

But again, the one very positive thing that may be said for this approach, as stated so well by Baylor University scholar Ray Summers is this point:

> This system yields an interpretation which is consistent with scriptural teachings throughout the New Testament. One can follow this method and not have to believe that God's purpose in the cross of Christ will fail and that He will have to resort to the sword to bring in His kingdom. The same truths and principles which are observed in the teachings of Jesus and the preaching and writing of the apostles are observed in Revelation if one follows this method of interpretation (Summers, 45).

Preterist interpreters fall into one of two types, those who hold that the major prophecies of the book were fulfilled in the fall of Jerusalem in AD 70 (which represent a very small minority), and those who see the work realized in the fall of the Roman Empire (AD 476). The primary evidence against the opinion which states that it has to do with the fall of the city of Jerusalem in AD 70 is found in the book itself, since it predicts the fall of a mighty city which at the time of writing "was ruling over the kings of the earth" (17:18); the city of Jerusalem was a minor capital of an enslaved people, under the iron fist of that city which actually did rule over the kings of the earth, mighty Rome, the epicenter and capital of the Roman Empire. A host of other references in the book point to the same identification and away from Jerusalem. The body of secondary evidence against this view is made up of those historical references to the time of writing, to which we have made reference elsewhere in this work, and which with a single voice attest to the inauguration of the Apocalypse decades after the fall of the Jewish capital, near to the end of John's life, and during the era of the second great persecutor of the church (Domitian) rather than the first (Nero); see Revelation 13:12.

5. The Historical Background Approach. Although this way of seeing and interpreting the book borrows many things from the Preterist Approach, it is also different in a number of important ways. Obviously the reader who adopts this perspective will also place the emphasis on seeing the book as written by the author primarily for the encouragement and edification of the Christians of his own time, particularly the seven churches of Asia near the end of the first century AD

Therefore, a close study of the church at the time of writing and of its historical circumstance is relevant as a key to full and accurate appreciation of the various areas of investigation for understanding the actual social, cultural, and historical matrix of that time. Secondary lessons must be drawn after these are researched. They have the priority for very obvious reasons. This is called, in theological terms, Historical-Cultural and Contextual Analysis. It is combined with Lexical-Syntactical Analysis and it is applied to the literature of the Bible generally today in order to derive the original meaning of a passage, so as to be able to make secondary applications as they are required.

All of this may sound complex, but in reality it is very simple. All it really means is that we take any passage or book of the Bible in its complete context and through word and grammatical study of the original language we learn what it originally meant to the first readers. Then we make a secondary application to ourselves and to our own circumstances which is perfectly consistent with the message to that first generation of readers. Now, isn't that simple? Does this not apply the various rules of what we might describe as "educated common sense"?

H. B. Swete is correct in his estimation of the importance of the historical moment when the work was penned by John and how it must be honored when one reads the book:

> The Apocalypse is cast in the form of a letter to certain Christian societies, and it opens with a detailed account of their conditions and circumstances. . . . The book starts with a well defined and historical situation, to which reference is made again at the end, and the intermediate visions, which form the body of the work, cannot on any reasonable theory be dissociated from their historical setting (Swete, ccxii).

Thus, the primary message was not to the twenty-first century, or to any other subsequent century for that matter, other than the first century when pen was put to paper by the apostle John. What these Christians needed to know was that the church had a future and that it would not be wiped out entirely by the powerful hand of a persecuting government.

Understanding "dispensations" (as some futurists suggest) or the continuous history of the church from then to the end of the world, or even the great principles of divine governance of human affairs, would have been of little or no help at all to these suffering Christians at the time. They needed to know that God was involved in the world contemporary with them and that He would eventually make their righteous cause victorious over their heavy-handed persecutors. He had not forgotten them and was not intending to give them over to the tender mercies of their enemies for all time. He was working out his ultimate plan for them and for the church of all ages behind the scenes of then-current world history. That is what they needed to know and understand, and this is precisely what the book provides when read in those terms.

Therefore, the purpose of the book was to strengthen the courage and faith of the Christians by visualizing in shocking symbols the ultimate downfall of the church's mortal enemy, the Roman Empire, and to picture the final victory of the kingdom of God and of the Lord's Christ. Even though things looked hopeless for these humble saints at the time of writing, in reality they were not. God can be counted on. He will always fight for His people. And He will always win in the end, and His faithful people will share with Him His glorious final victory. Present difficulties are only temporary. Their seemingly invincible enemies are mere mortals. Even the great Satan is doomed over the course of time. When the final scene has played itself out, He will be cast into the lake of fire and brimstone with all of the enemies of God (20:10).

It should be evident to the reader then, that the present writer embraces this latter view of the book. The Preterist approach is good, as far as it goes. But, in our estimation the view which emphasizes the historical background and then applies the lessons learned to our own present-day situation is by far the best. This is the only approach that honors fully the original historical setting of the symbols of the Apocalypse while at the same time making the book contemporary by applying its message to our own time. Studying it in the light of ancient history may be interesting, but if taken

Introduction to John's Book of Revelation

in that sense alone it would not be much superior to studying the life of George Washington or Abraham Lincoln. Their lives and the events that surrounded them might be intriguing to the student of American history, but they possess no lasting spiritual benefits for contemporary men and women.

Likewise, the Revelation is a message that is framed historically by the dark events of the late first century of the Common Era, but it is far more than merely that. It is a message from Jesus Christ to those churches telling them to hold out and not to lose their faith in the face of impending persecution at the hands of the Roman Imperial power that held such frightening leverage over them all. Hence, it delivers to Christians of every age the message that God will reward our faithfulness with eternal life and the marvels of the age to come, if only we will persevere and not deny our faith no matter what evils betide us.

CHAPTER ONE

The Letters to the Seven Churches of Asia (Part 1)

A. The Introduction (1:1-3)

> *The Revelation of Jesus Christ, which God gave Him to show to His servants, even the things which must shortly come to pass: and He sent and signified it by His angel to His servant John; who bare witness of the Word of God, and of the testimony of Jesus Christ, even of all things he saw. Blessed is he who reads, and those who hear the words of the prophecy, and keep the things which are written therein: for the time is at hand (Rev. 1:1-3).*

Before the initial vision of 1:9-20, John provides a superscription (1:1-3) and a formal greeting which is set forth in the light of an important theological summary (1:4-8). The first three verses of this book are particularly important for a variety of reasons. To begin with, they form a sort of epistolary greeting and superscription. Beyond even this however, they are especially important and must be read with particular care, for they represent an important prologue to all that follows.

Many who read the Revelation seem to ignore the implications of what John says here in such clear language. These verses tell us how and for what purpose the book of Revelation was given, and pronounce a blessing on both the reader and the obedient listener as he studies what is set before him. Some have maintained that it was added after the completion of the writing, but there is no real evidence for this unhelpful speculation. It calls itself an "apocalypse" or "unveiling," claims divine origin through Jesus Christ, states that the things predicted must come to pass "shortly" *(en tachei)* as in 22:7, 12, and 20, and explains its methodology as employing symbolism. Ignoring the implications of these weighty statements is a dangerous oversight to any approach to this material.

The Letters to the Seven Churches of Asia (Part 1)   *1:1-3*

Those who speculate that the book intends only to address the concerns of those who live in the final generation before the Lord's eventual coming cannot explain John's words in these passages. This book is not about the end of the world, and it was not penned for the sake of the last generation just prior to the end of world history. The visions of the Revelation were intended to speak to the needs and concerns of those first Christians who read this book as it circulated from congregation to congregation throughout the region of the seven churches of Asia Minor at the end of the first century AD. That is the force of this important declaration. "Shortly" cannot be made to imply the passage of thousands of years. If anything at all, it is a powerful antioxidant which has the force of destroying the very prevalent mythology which suggests that this book was meant to speak to the final generation. The words of Professor G. B. Caird of Oxford University are both intelligent and salutary, and it would be wise for us to give due heed to them:

> What then was it that John expected to happen "soon"? There is a general agreement that he expected persecution of the church by the Roman Empire. But like the other apocalyptic writers he has set this threat against a background of world history, and his prophecy carries us from a vision of God the Creator at one extreme to a vision of the Last Judgment and the eternal city of God at the other. We cannot, however, do justice to this very plain opening statement (cf. 1:3; 4:1; 12:10) by saying that he foresaw a long series of events covering centuries, which could be described as imminent because they were to *begin* shortly. Whatever earthly realities correspond to John's symbols, he expected them to be accomplished quickly *in their entirety*. We must choose between two answers to our question. The one answer, which would have the support of a majority of modern scholars, is that John expected the End, the final crisis of world history, the return of Christ in victory and judgment and that everything else in his vision, the last plagues, the emergence of Antichrist, the great martyrdom of the church, and the fall of Babylon, are only premonitory signs heralding the great day of God. The other answer, which I believe to be the true one, is that John's coming "crisis" was simply the persecution of the church, and that all the varied imagery of his book has no other purpose than this, to disclose to the prospective martyrs the real nature of their sufferings and its place in the eternal purpose of God. . . (Caird, 12).

The Greek verb used here in the prologue (1:1, the verb translated "signified," *esēmanen*) is also significant, and the force of it should not be ignored.

It carries embedded within it the idea of a figurative representation and, strictly speaking, means to make known by some sort of sign or symbol. The root word *sēmainō* may at times overlap with the more general and abstract idea of "make known" in the sense of "to indicate," "declare," "be manifest." But its more concrete and at least equally common sense in the original language is "to show by a sign," "give (or make) signs (or signals)," or "signify." It typically has this idea of symbolic communication when it is not used in the general sense of "make known" (Liddell, 592). Both the abstract and concrete senses are found in the Greek version of the Old Testament (LXX). Of its five other occurrences in the New Testament, two have the meaning "to make known" (Acts 11:28; 25:27), though one (Acts 12:28) may have the nuance of symbolic information, if it is parallel with the prophetic mode of symbolic revelation by the same prophet in Acts 21:10-11. Three others appear in John's Gospel where it summarizes Jesus' pictorial description of crucifixion (12:33; 18:32; 21:19). The Gospel writers use the cognate noun *sēmeion* repeatedly to refer to Jesus' miracles as outward "signs" or "symbols" of His attributes and mission. Assuredly, however, it is the symbolic use of *sēmainō* in Daniel 2 which defines the use of the term here in Revelation 1:1 as referring to symbolic communication and not mere general conveyance of information (cf. Beale, 51).

An unmistakable implication of these words which introduce the book is that God is the source of all spiritual revelation. All that is revealed to man about Deity is revealed to him by God Himself. So, God is the One who reveals secrets and makes known what is to come to pass in the future, as Daniel declared to Nebuchadnezzar in his pronouncements to that Babylonian king (cf. Dan. 2:28, 29, 45) long before John's introduction to his Revelation. In fact, the words of John in this instance are very similar to those of Daniel in that earlier case (cf. Rev. 1:1; Dan. 2:28).

Further, according to John's formulation, this disclosure is mediated by Jesus Christ Himself (1:1), and this is very much in keeping with what we know from what we discover elsewhere. In the Fourth Gospel, for example, John had already revealed that the role of taking the things of God and showing them to man is often assigned to Christ (John 1:18; 5:19-23; 12:49; 17:8; cf. Matt. 11:27). He is in fact God's ultimate messenger. As in previous instances in the Old Testament, the word that was delivered to

The Letters to the Seven Churches of Asia (Part 1)   1:1-3

the prophets and through them to the people was inevitably a statement of God's intentions, combined with a demand for human cooperation in that plan. "Surely the Lord God does nothing without revealing His secret plan to His servants the prophets" (Amos 3:7). It is just such a plan which John has seen dramatically disclosed to him in his heavenly visions. And how God saw this purpose to be related to the immediate crisis of the seven churches is to be seen in the narrative as it unfolds in the visions as they are further pictured for the benefit of the churches.

Furthermore, the express purpose of God in giving the Revelation is "to show to His servants the things which must shortly come to pass." This informs the reader that the nature of the material is plainly prophetic and revelatory. Thus, history is not to be viewed as a haphazard sequence of unrelated and unconnected events, but instead as a divinely decreed ordering of that which must come to pass on account of God's manipulation of and maneuvering of historical happenings in terms of his own goals. There is a divine plan being worked out in history, and it is steadily moving toward its eventual culmination. That is a logical necessity arising from the nature of the Omniscience of God Himself and the subsequent revelation of His purpose in creation and redemption (Mounce, 64).

At the time of the revelation to John, the Apostle was on the island of Patmos, probably isolated there as a prisoner to work in the mines or else, if he was already too old for hard labor, banished to that lonely place by the authorities on account of his faith. Certainly he would have been considered by the authorities as a major figure in the churches of Asia Minor, and thus a perfect target for government removal from the larger community in order to assist in the remediation of this group of passive resistors. It was a crime to be a Christian in those days. It was a violation of the law that frequently was ignored by the government during the early days. But as time went by the numbers of this hated sect had grown to a point where it had become an irritant, and so needed to be dealt with in order to discourage its further proliferation. John was a victim of the repression that resulted.

The first vision of the book comprises chapters 1-3. The scene is easy to visualize. It was the Lord's Day as the Seer stood upon the shore of the tiny island, all alone with his thoughts and prayers, but happily also, he was in the presence of his God. In his mind no doubt he was yearning to be reunited with his brethren across the sea in Ephesus and the other churches of Asia. He had been cruelly separated from them because of his defense of the gospel. It may even have been at the very time that the brethren were assembling for their worship. Oh, how he wished he could be with them!

No doubt he stared off longingly into the distance, perhaps in the direction of Asia. The billows were booming against the rocky shoreline, and the hills off in the distance were dimly silhouetted against the sky, but his heart was far away, beyond all of this material beauty and the roar of the ocean. His heart was with the saints of God as they prayed and sang the praises of God. Then suddenly it seems as if the distant horizon recedes and as if the ground gives way beneath his feet. He is completely liberated from all that is earthly and material in nature. He sees, but not with physical eyes. He hears, but not with his ears of flesh. John is now in the Spirit, and his soul is in direct communication with God. He has assumed the ancient role of a Seer after the model of Daniel, Ezekiel, and Zechariah. He hears a voice speaking to him, and it says, "What you see, write in a book and send it to the seven churches" (1:11). Thus the book of Revelation came to be. It is the series of visions John saw that day as he communed with God and the Lord showed him what was to be.

B. The Formal Greeting and Opening Address (1:4-8)

John to the seven churches that are in Asia: Grace to you and peace, from Him who is and who was and who is to come; and from the seven Spirits that are before His throne; and from Jesus Christ, who is the faithful witness, the firstborn of the dead, and the ruler of the kings of the earth. To Him who loved us, and loosed us from our sins by His blood; and made us to be a kingdom, to be priests to His God and Father; to Him be the glory and the dominion for ever and ever. Amen. Behold, He comes with the clouds; and every eye shall see Him, and they that pierced Him; and all the tribes of the earth shall mourn over Him. Even so, Amen. "I am the Alpha and the Omega," says the Lord God, "who is and who was and who is to come, the Almighty" (Rev. 1:4-8).

At this juncture the author identifies those who are to be the principal readers of the book. He begins with a reference to them as "servants" earlier (1:1), and then narrows his focus to "the seven churches that are in Asia" (1:4). Later he will identify those congregations specifically (1:11). In v. 4 he also repeats his own name once more, and in doing so, he does it simply

The Letters to the Seven Churches of Asia (Part 1)   1:4-8

and without any other portfolio or identifier to accompany it. He is John. That is all he needed to say. In so saying, he clearly identifies himself with that John who was the fisherman son of Zebedee, one of the disciples of Jesus, and so, that disciple "whom Jesus loved." He is the same one who was responsible for the Gospel of John and the three small Johannine epistles. The churches of that region knew him well on account of his recent association with the city of Ephesus. It was likely there that he was arrested and sentenced to exile on Patmos.

As is the case with the first verses of the letter to the Hebrews, an impressive amount of profound theology is packed into these particular opening lines of the book. The writer informs us that God is eternal and is about to intrude onto the scene of human history. The language he employs here is interesting. He says that God is He, "who is, and who was, and who is to come." Some scholars have argued that the grammatical construction of this phrase violates conventional Greek grammar, but in fact it is quite intentional that it does. The writer wishes precisely to replicate the Hebraism which lies behind the Greek expression. R. H. Charles says that, "the Seer has deliberately violated the rules of grammar to preserve the divine name inviolate from the change it would necessarily have undergone if declined" (Charles, 1:10; cf. also Patterson, 58, n. 2).

Christ is further pictured as a "faithful witness" *(ho martus ho pistos)* or "martyr" whose suffering can give the readers considerable comfort in the face of their own trials; He is the first person to have risen from the dead; and He has power over all human rulers. The last two characteristics are seen as being the fulfillment of the Psalmist's words about the Davidic Messiah: "I will make Him the firstborn, the highest of the kings of the earth" (Psalm 89:27).

The writer further reminds his readers that through His love (see Psa. 89:28), Christ forgave their sins and made them "priests of God." With this last expression (see also Exod. 19:6; 1 Pet. 2:9), the author shares the view of some of the other New Testament authors that Christians are to be seen as the new people of God. Christ will return again as He promised, and at that time those who mistreated and crucified Him (Zech. 12:10; John 19:37) will lament for what they did. It is hard to say whether his reference to the fact that they will "wail on account of Him" means that this has to do with those who were specifically guilty of the crime of rejecting and crucifying God's Messiah or simply that all who have rejected the Christian faith will be judged accordingly, but for all intents and purposes this matters little, since this particular passage does not stand alone in teaching either truth.

C. The Vision of Christ among the Churches (1:9-20)

I John, your brother and partaker with you in tribulation and kingdom and patience which are in Jesus, was in the isle that is called Patmos, for the Word of God and the testimony of Jesus. I was in the Spirit on the Lord's Day, and I heard behind me a great voice, as of a trumpet saying, "What you see, write in a book and send it to the seven churches: to Ephesus, and to Smyrna, and to Pergamum, and to Thyatira, and to Sardis, and to Philadelphia, and to Laodicea."

And I turned to see the voice that spoke with me. And having turned I saw seven golden lampstands; and in the midst of the lampstands one like a Son of Man, clothed with a garment down to the foot, and girt about at the breasts with a golden girdle. And His head and His hair were white as white wool, white as snow; and His eyes were as a flame of fire; and His feet were like burnished brass, as if it had been refined in a furnace; and His voice was like the voice of many waters. And He had in His right hand seven stars: and out of His mouth proceeded a sharp two-edged sword: and His countenance was as the sun shining in its strength. And when I saw Him, I fell at his feet as one dead.

And He laid His right hand upon me, saying, "Fear not; I am the first and the last, and the Living one; and I was dead, and behold, I am alive for evermore, and I have the keys of death and of Hades. Write therefore the things which you saw, and the things which are, and the things which shall come to pass hereafter; the mystery of the seven stars which you saw in My right hand, and the seven golden lampstands. The seven stars are the angels of the seven churches: and the seven lampstands are seven churches" (Rev. 1:9-20).

For the third time, now, in just nine verses, the writer mentions his own name. Once again, he does so without any other associations or titles to distinguish himself. He is simply John. He will not do so again until once more in 22:8 as he gives a solemn affirmation of the things contained in the document as genuine. And so, after a prologue and greeting (1:1-8), John is presented with a spectacular vision of the Christ among the churches (1:9-20). Here the apostle is given the command to write down that which he sees (v. 11). What he sees first is a vision of Christ, and here He is pictured as majestic and powerful, lovely beyond all description. John had laid his head on the Lord's bosom at the Last Supper, and yet now what he beholds is something and someone from beyond the world of the ordinary. He is a heavenly being mighty in prospect, possessing the keys of death and of Hades. He had himself been victorious over death in His personal resurrection, and His promise was that He would call all of the dead from their graves and reward the believing with everlasting life (v. 18; cf. John 6:39, 40, 44).

But before he tells his audience about what he saw, he identifies himself with the readers as their "brother" and a "sharer in the tribulation and the kingdom and the patient endurance." The term "tribulation" may include a whole host of different related things: pressures ranging from ridicule, slander, social ostracism, and harassment, to poverty, violence, imprisonment, and even possible martyrdom. John informs his audience that he is their partner in such tribulation because he is presently enduring personal exile away from society, family and friends as a prisoner of the Roman state on the island of Patmos.

Patient endurance was essential in the face of such abuse by those in a position to mete out punitive measures against those who refused to conform to society's norms. That was the fate of many Christians in a pagan environment, and John saw it as his lot in life and theirs also. Endurance was praised as a virtue among the Greeks, and defined as the stamina that does not give up in the face of adversity. For Christians it has special importance attached to it, for it carries them through to the reward that awaits the faithful (cf. Rev. 2:2, 3, 19; 3:10; 13:10; 14:10). Later on we are made to understand that endurance also involves waiting for Jesus' eventual coming (3:10-11) and keeping the commandments of God under duress (14:12). Finally, it is only if they persevere in their faithfulness that they will reign with Christ when it is all over. All of this is true because they enjoy the privilege of being members of a higher "kingdom" than the Roman one that they were presently living in. The kingdom of God and of His Christ is their true citizenship and so they must not take too seriously the fact that the power and prestige of the Roman Empire at this point was being leveled against them, misusing and abusing them. Such understanding creates a mindset that permits the Christian to hold on and remain steadfast in spite of very undesirable circumstances.

John also explains that he "was on the island called Patmos on account of the Word of God and the testimony of Jesus." In so saying he uses the past tense "was" possibly suggesting that by the time that the book was actually set down in writing he had already left the island for freedom on the mainland. But the usage of the past tense may also be taken simply as a way to narrate what he had already seen on days previous, so that he may still have been on the island when he wrote the book. Too, in the light of similar phraseology using the Greek preposition "for" *(dia)* elsewhere in the book (6:9; 20:4) to describe punitive measures against Christians, it is fair to conclude that John was on Patmos because he was being punished for something that had to do with his proclamation of the gospel. His preaching led to his exile. Exile is not a modern concept since such punishment is no longer used to chasten or discipline offenders. So it is important for us to understand this ancient penalty for offenses against the state.

It is interesting to note that Roman law made a distinction between two types of exile. There was lifelong exile *(deportatio)* and temporary exile *(relagatio)*, and which of the two was the punishment for John we are not certain about. The Roman lawyer Tertullian, however, advanced the notion that it was temporary exile, even though under normal circumstances *relagatio* was only employed against citizens who were persons of rank in Roman society (Krodel, 92-93). But John did not fit that scenario. We deem it more likely that John was banished for life, but when Domitian was replaced those whom he had exiled for religious reasons were permitted to return home. Under both Nero and Domitian there were many in Roman society who considered such trivial matters not worthy of being punished, in spite of the emperor's zeal for the ancestral gods and his own personal divinity. Therefore, when Domitian was assassinated and the pressure was eased, if only temporarily, prisoners of conscience like John were probably released and permitted to go back to their former lives.

The thoughtful words of Professor Seiss in his lectures on the Revelation purport to explain the logic of John's being on the island of Patmos thus:

> He had been banished to this inhospitable place by the persecuting Roman government, not for crimes, but "for the word of God, and for the testimony

of Jesus Christ." He was the acknowledged head of the witnesses of Jesus, and the great promulgator and defender of the truth as it is in Jesus, and for his zeal and prominence in this, he was dealt with as a felon and an outlaw. The unconverted heart always has been, is now, and always will be, at enmity with God, and hence at disagreement with God's truth and people. It cannot endure what is not conformed to its views and tastes, and is full of malice, resentment, and revenge towards everything which holds with God and with Christ. And if the world is at any time at peace, and on good terms with the Church, it is because the Church itself has become debauched, and has descended to a compromise to be at one with the wicked. The nominal Christian and the formalist the world cannot hate, for they are of it, and it will love its own; but the Johns and Pauls must go into banishment, or give their necks to the stateblock (Seiss, 36).

When John says here, "I was in the Spirit on the Lord's Day," he does not mean to suggest that his soul went on a heavenly journey to another realm (4:1-2; 2 Cor. 12:1-3), but simply that on a Sunday, the day of the Savior's resurrection, when the Christians were worshipping together on the mainland, his heart longingly turned in worship and prayerfulness to thoughts that pertained to God. And then in the midst of those serene meditations, in the Spirit of the Lord, he heard a booming voice, and thus began the narration of the Apocalypse. In that circumstance he was carried away into the realm of the heavenly.

At this point he says, "and I heard behind me a great voice, as of a trumpet saying, 'What you see, write in a book and send it to the seven churches.'" As regards its form, this scene is often traced to Old Testament accounts of calls of the various prophets (e.g., Isa. 6; Jer. 1; Ezek. 1-3), but this is not justified by the content that we have before us. As Jürgen Roloff observed, "One does not find here a series of similarities in terms of motifs. For example, the exposition with reference to time and place (vv. 9-10) corresponds to Isaiah 6:1; Jeremiah 1:2-3; Ezekiel 1:1-13. Also, John's reaction to the vision (v. 17) is reminiscent of Ezekiel 1:28. However, absent is the moment of initiation—constitutive for the calling of prophets—to a new vocation that is defined by God's commission and that indicates a change in the life of the one who is called. John is already on Patmos for the Word of God and the testimony of Jesus (v. 9). The commission he received did not signify the initiation to a new ministry; rather, it addresses him concerning his ministry as witness to the word in which he is already engaged" (Roloff, 31). Thus, the vision we have before us here can most appropriately be characterized as a commissioning vision, in the sense that John was being commissioned to receive and transmit the visions he is about to experience. It's nearest parallel is found in Daniel 10. And that chapter provides many very close similarities if not downright affinities, both as to form and substance. In this particular case, however, the Lord charges John to see the coming revelation and transmit its contents, i.e. to write it down and send it to the seven churches specified in the Lord's instructions to the Seer.

The placement of this particular vision at the beginning of the book is significant. The Christians were a pitiably small remnant, persecuted by mighty foes. To all outward appearances their situation was hopeless. It is only as these people can see their Lord in His true Majesty that they can be sustained through the tribulation that lies ahead. That is what this first vision attempts to do. In vv. 17-18 Jesus makes three very powerful claims for Himself: 1) He says that He is the eternal God; 2) He says that He is the living Savior; and, 3) He states that He is the universal Sovereign. He is not to be viewed as a mere martyred rabbi from Galilee in the land of the Jews. John sees Him as He truly is. He is the mighty spiritual entity of Christian theology, a heavenly personage. He is no longer the humble carpenter from Nazareth. He is the King of kings and the Lord of all Lords, and thus He appears in His vision to John.

D.   The Letters to the Seven Churches of Asia Minor

1. General Overview. In chapters 2:1–3:22 specific messages are communicated to the seven churches in Asia Minor. Each of the churches is addressed in the order that a circular letter would take as it moved along the Roman roadway from the port at Ephesus to Laodicea, a distance of about 250 miles. No doubt this was exactly the route that the letters took as they moved from city to city. The seven brief epistles are full of biblical symbolism and colorful local references even though they are written in an epistolary style and format, characteristic of the personal correspondences of that day (as proven by the many letters discovered among the ancient papyri which have survived to our own time and have been deciphered for modern readers to analyze).

The Letters to the Seven Churches of Asia (Part 1) 1:9-20

Ephesus is an old, well established church which has lost its first zeal for Christ. This first letter is really about the challenge of false apostles and charlatan teachers described as Nicolaitans, along with the church's need to repent of their loss of their original spiritual enthusiasm. In fact, the central theme of the letters as a group is complacency and compromise, propagated by influential leaders, along with the need to repent and be restored to their original zeal for the Lord. Smyrna is singled out as a suffering congregation, persecuted at the hands of a powerful Jewish synagogue. Pergamum was the headquarters of the veneration of the emperors in Asia Minor ("where Satan's throne is"), and the church of the city was beset by the doctrine of Balaam, an attitude of compromise with this powerful evil influence in the town. Thyatira had become the refuge of a modern-day Jezebel, a woman who urged upon church people various flirtations with idolatry. Sardis was home to a dead church, which had only a few members who had not defiled their garments with sin. Philadelphia stands apart in that it is commended in Christ's missive and not reprimanded in any way, a church with little strength left, but which had wavered not at all in the face of fierce opposition. The city of Laodicea, the main commercial metropolis of the region, endowed with wealth and all the marks of earthly success, had produced a church which has become through the ages synonymous with "lukewarmness" and religion that is devoid of fervor.

It is important to observe that Christ is portrayed in the vision as walking in the midst of the seven golden lampstands (2:1), representing the seven churches of Asia. The message of this is obvious: the presence and power of the risen Lord is not limited to any one church of the group, rather He is there in the midst of them all. He observes first hand their faith and obedience, and He judges their weaknesses and occasional malfeasance. He is not far removed from them, but rather with them. He is their ever present guest. It will be remembered that He had promised the Twelve, "I will be with you always, even to the end of the age" (Matt. 28:20). He had promised them that He would be with them where two or three of them were gathered together in His name (Matt. 18:20), "There am I in the midst," He had said. So here He represents Himself as very present with them in the midst of their fears and apprehensions, their sufferings and difficulties in Greco-Roman Asia Minor. The ultimate message for us, then, is that in all of our terrors and struggles He is right there with us every moment. He is never very far from us, and we can know that His heart is invested fully in our concerns, just as it was in theirs.

2. The Letter to the church at Ephesus (2:1-7).

> *To the messenger of the church in Ephesus write: "These things says He who holds the seven stars in His right hand, He who walks in the midst of the seven golden lampstands: I know your works, and your toil and patience, and that you cannot bear evil men, and you tested those who call themselves apostles, and they are not, and found them false; and you have had patience and persevered for My name's sake, and have not grown weary. But I have this against you: that you have left your first love. Remember therefore whence you have fallen, and repent and do the first works; or else I will come to you, and will move your lampstand out of its place, unless you repent. But this you have, that you hate the works of the Nicolaitans, which I also hate. He who has an ear, let him hear what the Spirit says to the churches. To him who overcomes, to him will I give to eat of the tree of life, which is in the Paradise of God"* (Rev. 2:1-7).

Near the modern Turkish town of Selçuk lies what remains of the chief city of that part of the world in the days of Paul and John. Ephesus was a city of the greatest significance, religiously and otherwise. The place is especially important for the modern Bible student on account of Paul's extensive ministry there (two years and three months; Acts 19:8, 10), and the fact that it was from this city center that he and his companions ultimately evangelized much of Asia. Too, it became the headquarters of the apostle John during the latter years of his long life. The reason for both of these important men making this place the focal point of their work in Asia is very clear. It was one of the greatest cities of the Mediterranean world during New Testament times. Reliable historians and archaeologists have estimated its peak population during the second century to have been in the range of 200,000 to 500,000.

Serious archaeological work began at the site in 1863. An English architect, John T. Wood under the auspices of the British Museum, began his long search for the Temple of Diana in that year. He finally came upon the ruins of the Temple on December 31, 1869. Over the next five years he worked diligently to uncover what remained of that important ancient monument. Next, D. G. Hogarth worked at the same location during the

The Letters to the Seven Churches of Asia (Part 1)   2:1-7

years 1904-1905. The Austrian Archaeological Institute began excavations in 1895 under Otto Benndorf and their work has continued unabated (except for the two world wars) up to the present time. Since 1954, excavations and restorations have been carried out not only by the Austrian Institute, but also by workers from the Ephesus Museum. Even after an entire century and more of labor at the site, it is estimated that only about ten percent of the ancient city of Ephesus has been unearthed.

Three material facts caused the population to swell during that era. Politically, the Roman governor had his residence there and so for all practical purposes Ephesus was the capital of all of Asia. Its economic prowess lay in the fact that Ephesus stood on the great north-south road of western Asia Minor and controlled the flow of trade into the interior of the country along the Maeander and Lycus river valleys. The city was located four miles from the Aegean and possessed a fine inland harbor connected with the Cayster River. The harbor was kept deep enough and large enough by a constant process of dredging. The need for this process to be ongoing ultimately spelt the doom of the city, for after the decline of the Empire in the third century the harbor began to silt up and by the tenth century the city was completely deserted and is now swallowed up by marshes (Pfeiffer, 229).

Ephesus was also the religious center of the region for reasons just as obvious. The supreme glory of Ephesus near the close of the first century was, of course, the Temple of Artemis (or Diana) which played a role in the story told by Luke of Paul's tenure there. Investigators concluded that the Temple had passed through five distinctive phases of construction. The earliest phase was from the period ca. 600 BC. However, the edifice that Paul and John would have encountered was begun about 350 BC.

The origins of the worship of this goddess in the city had been lost in the mists of hoary antiquity by the time John wrote the Revelation at the end of the first century of the Christian Era. Croesis, the famous wealthy king of Lydia, had built the second temple to honor the goddess. It burned down the night Alexander the Great was born. The third temple, which was standing when John wrote his Apocalypse, was considered one of the seven wonders of the ancient world. It was a grand and awe-inspiring place. Visitors made pilgrimages from all over the world to see it. Antipater of Sidon observed as he compiled his list of the Seven Wonders:

I have set my eyes on the wall of lofty Babylon on which is the road for chariots, and the statue of Zeus by the Alpheus, and the Hanging Gardens, and the colossus of the Sun, and the huge labor of the high pyramids, and the vast tomb of Mausolus; but when I saw the house of Artemis that mounted the clouds, those other marvels lost their brilliancy, and I said, "Lo, apart from Olympus, the Sun never looked on aught so grand" (*Greek Anthology* 9.58).

The Temple itself was 180 feet wide and 377 feet long, standing on a platform that was 239 feet wide and 418 feet long. It covered an area that was 130 by 60 yards total, massively large for that ancient era. That meant that it was approximately four times larger than the Parthenon in Athens, Greece. Pillars stood in the great edifice, 127 Ionic columns in number, and each of them was 60 feet tall and represented the gift of a particular king. All were six feet in diameter and were carved from glittering Parian marble, and thirty-six of them were richly overlaid with gold and jewels, intricate carving and life-size figures. The holy of holies was apparently open to the sky. In this inner shrine stood the great altar, twenty feet square, carved by the greatest of the Greek sculptors, Paxiteles, behind which were velvet curtains. Hidden behind the curtains was the mysterious image of the goddess Diana or Artemis, described by the ancients as the loveliest of the goddesses, "huntress chaste and fair." The figure itself, however, was repulsive in appearance: a dark, squat, figure with many breasts, which was the symbol of her fertility. She clutched a club in one hand and a trident in the other. At the base of the figure were signs and symbols that no one could read. It was believed that it had fallen from heaven. The goddess was equated with the Cybele of Asia Minor, the mother goddess. As worshipped at Ephesus she was a considerably Orientalized fertility deity. During the Artemision (March-April), a month dedicated to the worship of the goddess, devotees came from many other provinces to participate in religious festivals.

This great Temple was a repository of the world's riches and of the precious things and valuables of business men and ordinary individuals. People from all over came there to store them for safe keeping. It was comparable to a modern central bank. Temples on account of their perceived holiness were only rarely looted or even violated. No term was more reprehensible than the expression "temple robber" (*hierosulos,* cf. Rom. 2:22; Matt. 21:13), since it was considered a place that was sacrosanct and inviolate. This was viewed even by pagans as the most exaggerated form of sacrilege; in fact, the word itself stood as the very definition for a "sacrilegious person."

Within a bowshot of the Temple dwelt all manner of criminals who had taken refuge, fugitives from the law, low-life individuals, dangerous as well as petty criminals, escapees, and so forth. All who wished to seek out protection from proximity to the sacred precincts were found there. Wonderful and terrible it was, at the one and the same time. The dregs of society mingled with the highly superstitious who came there to venerate the goddess. The city therefore became known for its detestable population of fickle, superstitious, and highly immoral people. Heraclitus, a renowned philosopher from the city, opined that the morals of the temple were worse than the morals of beasts, for, as he observed, "even promiscuous dogs do not mutilate themselves as these worshippers" did. He said that the inhabitants of Ephesus were fit only to be drowned and that the reason why he could never laugh or smile was because he lived amidst such terrible uncleanness (Barclay, *Letters to the Seven Churches*, 6-7). Is it not interesting to observe that it was in precisely this climate that the apostle Paul lived and worked during the period of his ministry at Ephesus (Acts 18:19; 19:1–20:1), and that in this same reprehensible city a faithful group of Christian disciples thrived in spite of all this? They were yet active and strong in their faith toward the close of the first century as the small epistle written to that church in Revelation 2:1-7 attests, even though like most of the other congregations addressed in that series of epistles they had some serious challenges and noteworthy problems that were unique to their particular situation.

In his search for the Temple of Artemis, John Wood uncovered the theater at Ephesus which was associated with the ministry of the apostle Paul (Acts 19:31). The structure was located on the western slope of Mount Pion. It measured about 495 feet in diameter and held about 25,000 spectators. The seating arrangement was divided into three bands with twenty-two rows of seats in each. Other archaeological efforts since that time have found that in apostolic times a street 1735 feet long led from the theater to the harbor. This was greatly enhanced during the second century. To the north of this street the Roman agora was built between the days of Paul and John. Further, during John's day the emperor Domitian built baths and gymnasia in the same area. At the southwest corner of the theater lay the older Hellenistic agora, the main center of the city in apostolic times. A total of 360 feet square, it was lined with porticoes behind which were a number of small shops. Interestingly, F. Milner of the Austrian Archaeological Institute found there the shops of silversmiths, perhaps the same ones who so troubled Paul in his labors (Pfeiffer, 230).

Furthermore, in 1984 a 3.5 foot tall monument was discovered on the street, known in antiquity as the Plateia in Coressus, that connects the theater and stadium in Ephesus. Presently this monument is on display in the Ephesus Museum in Selçuk, Turkey. It contains a 16-line Greek inscription that provides important background information for both Acts 19 and the second chapter of the Revelation of John. It reads as follows:

> Good Fortune! The silversmiths of the first and greatest metropolis of Asia, the thrice honored temple guardian of the venerable Ephesians, erected (this monument to) Valerius Festus, the flower of his ancestors, creator of many works in both Asia and Ephesus, according to the heroic Antonines, who improved the harbor (of the Artemisium). (Festus) has made himself savior and in all things a benefactor.

The reference to the Antonine emperors (who ruled in the second century: Antoninus Pius, 138-161; Marcus Aurelius, 161-180; and Commodus, 180-192) reasonably dates the inscription to the late second or early third century. So, a full century after Paul was in Ephesus, the guild of the silversmiths still flourished in the city, and a certain Valerius Festus was "the flower of his ancestors," one of a long line of such silversmiths, who apparently was endowed with such wealth as to be able to be a contributor to certain expensive public works. The titles ascribed to Festus at the climax of the inscription, "savior" (*sōtēr*) and "benefactor" (*euergetēs*), are common in Greek inscriptions for those who made large donations to various public works. The Greek word *kroisos*, which is rendered as "harbor" in the translation given above, refers to the outer colonnade of the Artemisium that bordered the harbor. It is unclear whether Festus improved the harbor itself, which during the Roman period needed regular dredging from silt deposited by the Cayster River, or expanded and improved the famous Artemisium adjacent to the harbor (Edwards, 26-27).

Ephesus was called the *neokoros* or "temple-sweeper" of the goddess Diana. To be so described was a very high honor for any pagan city. On the other hand, most ancient cities in those days were associated with some god or goddess very prominently. In fact, from the Hellenistic Period onwards we have an increasing number of divine patrons of civic communities which are designated with similar high-sounding epithets, *e.g.,* Apollo Archegetes in Kos, Artemis was called Archegetis in Ephesus, Athena Archegetis in Athens, Dionysos Archegetis and Prokathegetes in Teos, Eleuthera Archegetis in Myra and Kyanai, Gortys Archegetes in Gortyn, Hem Archegetis in Samos, Aphrodite Kathegetis, Kathegemon, Prokathemene, and Proestosa tes poleos in Aphrodisias, Dionysos Kathegemon and Prokathegemon in Pergamon, Asklepios Prokathegemon in Kos, Athena Prokathezomene Theos in Sicle, Hera and Zeus Patrioi kai Proestotes tes Poleos in Amastris, etc. Hence, all events that were fortunate and about which the people of the city could rejoice were attributed to the benefactions (*euergēsiai*) of those gods or of the special patron deity (*prokathegēmon*) whose particular responsibility it was to oversee and care for their city.

At various times in the history of the different cities in the Greco-Roman Era important decrees were issued by elite members of the town councils which were intended to honor these patron gods with special celebrations. Angelos Chaniotis made a study of a number of these declarations in such cities as Ephesus and observed that they had very clear and purposeful usages in the cultural communal life of the towns involved. One such benefactor was Longus of Kremna a wealthy citizen who supervised and probably sponsored the construction of the city forum. He is said to have dedicated a basilica to Hadrian, the divinised Caesar Trajan, the imperial household, and the city. He served as priest of Fortuna/Tyche and as *duovir* (one of the chief magistrates of the town, elected yearly). Clearly he was a member of the civic elite with a typical role in his community. He served in public offices; he excelled in benefactions; he was involved in religious activities, both in the emperor cult and in the cult of the Fortuna; and he made a dedication to a patron god associated with divination. All of these civic roles melded into one. Longus is therefore perfectly illustrative of the ideal civic man in Roman provincial culture.

Probably Erastus of Corinth referred to by Paul in his letter from that city to the Romans (16:23), prior to his conversion of course, was involved in comparable responsibilities for his own city. Paul describes him as *oikonomos tēs poleōs*, "treasurer" of that metropolis, a term that is probably the equivalent of the term *agoranomos* used elsewhere and in Latin the titles *aedile* and *quaestor* (usually a more junior position in the government, and customarily translated as *tamias* in Greek). It will be recalled that an inscription discovered at Corinth originally of bronze and written in Latin, documents his rank and one of his benefactions for the city: "[*praenome nomen*] Erastus for his aedileship laid (the pavement) at his own expense." Most biblical scholars today consider these two men to be the same individual, although some object to the conclusion. It appears clear to us that Paul was emphasizing the important governmental role played by Erastus at Corinth precisely in order to stress to the Roman Christians that it was indeed possible for a Christian to hold lofty office in government and maintain his spiritual integrity. But of course, in many instances there were challenges of the highest order of magnitude on account of the admixture of civic life with paganism in most cities of the Roman world. Political responsibility and religious life were wrapped up together in the person of one man in many of these offices of civic duty and benefaction. And this was precisely what was expected of anyone who filled a similar position in the culture of Asia Minor in the days of John's Revelation.

Chaniotis therefore concluded that we may "sum up with the words remembrance, performance, and guidance: remembrance of the past services of the gods, performance of an aesthetically pleasing celebration; and guidance—the assumption of a leading role in the moral education of the fellow citizens, and, more importantly, in the education and the acculturation of the youth" ["Negotiating Religion in the Cities of the Eastern Roman Empire," *Kernos* 16 (2003): 177-190]. One particular metrical oracle found at ancient Ephesus had to do with the city of Maionia (Koloe or Sardis) which at the time was suffering under a severe pestilence (ca. AD 165), and recommended the erection of a statue of Artemis in the town:

> Her form bring in from Ephesus, brilliant with gold. Put her up in a temple, full of joy; she will provide deliverance from your affliction and will dissolve the poison (or magic) of pestilence, which destroys men, and will melt down with her flame-bearing torches in nightly fire the kneaded works of wax, the signs of the evil art of a sorcerer. But when you have performed for the goddess my decrees, worship with hymns the shooter of arrows, the irresistible, straight shooting one, and with sacrifices, her, the renowned

Temple of Domitian in Ephesus

and vigilant virgin [translated and quoted in F. Graf, "An Oracle Against Pestilence from a Western Anatolian Town," *Zeitschrift für Papyrologie und Epigraphik* 92 (1992): 267-279].

But Ephesus in particular was more than merely the home of Artemis, religiously speaking, it was also a home to the Roman veneration of the Emperor cult and of their gladiatorial games. This was the city in which Paul stayed longer than any place else in his travels and where John wrapped up the closing years of his ministry. And it was the place where one of the seven churches of Asia worshipped and served God. So, it was obviously an important location, central in many ways to the efforts to share the gospel of Jesus with the world, and especially critical in regard to the Roman province of Asia and its place in the newly emerging Christian influence throughout the entire region. Therefore, the first letter penned to any of the churches of that geographical segment of humanity was directed toward the city of Ephesus and its mature congregation of believers.

Several things are evident from the little missive written to the Christians at Ephesus:

Their energy level was once impressive, but now it has eroded and become small. In v. 2 Jesus addresses the pressing need of this once great congregation: "I know your works, and your labor, and your patience." This church has been around for a long time, according to the standard that then applied. It was several decades old and it had an enviable record among the people of God during the early years of the apostolic era. But, as is so often the case, with the passing of time, the changing of personnel as one generation dies off and a new one takes its place, and the expenditure of considerable effort in battles fought, they had simply grown weary in their well doing (Gal. 6:9). Now they were tired of fighting the good fight of faith. Battle-weary and shell-shocked, they had lost their first love. They needed to be re-energized!

Ephesus is a "sound" church, one that stands foursquare in the doctrine of Christ, and stands against all doctrinal, theological, and ethical error and heterodoxy. This church was clear on where it stood doctrinally. This is evident from the fact that it even rejected the seemingly authoritative-sounding false apostles, and branded their teaching as untrue. Jesus had warned that the love of some of His disciples would eventually grow cold (Matt. 24:15). The church at Ephesus had fallen into this trap. Ideological soundness is important, but it is not all that is necessary. The Lord's short letter to them made that evident.

The congregation is warned that if they do not repent their lampstand will be removed from it's place. Clearly, the notion of the lampstand, one among a series of seven, is a depiction of their place among the churches of Christ in that region of the world. That position is about to be lost unless they take decisive action toward their restoration to faithfulness. Now undoubtedly this is a very frightening scenario that is being described by the Lord relative to a group of Christians meeting to worship and serve God in their community. All that has gone before has suggested that they have a wonderful record in divine service. Their labors have been considerable, but time and its vicissitudes have wrought upon this collective of people a weariness of spirit that has robbed them of their zeal. And so, if they are not careful, their lack of spiritual energy may someday rob them of their ultimate reward.

It is important for any church to remain enthusiastic for all of the good things of God, but if they do not, then they need to know that the Lord will hold them accountable. We are surrounded on all sides by people who are lost in sin and will surely be lost if the gospel does not reach them. It is our responsibility, within the limitations of our ability, to take the message of the Savior to them. If we become so borne down by discouragement and disheartened by events beyond our control that we make little or no effort toward this end, then we will surely fail in this important endeavor. They will be lost without a warning, and we will be held responsible for our inactivity and ineffectiveness. The Lord gives the warning, "I will come to you and remove your lampstand from its place." Whatever outward circumstances may suggest to the contrary, such a church will be devoid of the presence and spirit of Jesus Christ, much as the temple in Jerusalem was missing the presence of God's glory when His judgment fell upon it (see Ezek. 11:22f). The temple appeared as it had before. The priests and Levites went about their tasks as previously. The sacrifices and offerings were still made, but it was all a sham and a pretense, because God was not present in any of it. So it will be in the case of a church which has lost its "original love," the spiritual stamina it had when it first began.

Hence, it will lose its place in the fellowship of the congregations of Christ's saints. This prospect was certainly one that must have gotten the attention of a church as noteworthy as the congregation at Ephesus, with its rich history of faith and works on the Lord's behalf. The good news is that at this juncture it was only a prospect and not yet a fact. It could still be remedied, and let us hope that it was. The advice which follows is the key to their restoration to faithfulness. They must remember the love that they have lost and reconstitute it so that this terrible possibility is not realized. Likewise, if we find ourselves in a similar situation we must recall where we came from and where we have been and do as they were counseled to do in order not to lose their place among the faithful servants of God.

The church is counseled to "remember therefore from whence you have fallen." The word "remember" is key here, for it takes the mind back to yesteryear, to the time when this church was first founded and these ex-pagans had abandoned their idolatry to serve the living and true God. It returns to the time when Paul had addressed his beautiful epistle about the church to them. It carries them back to the days when their elders were called to Miletus to hear a special address from Paul before he went to Jerusalem (Acts 20:17ff). They were a special congregation for so very many reasons, and yet their present condition bore little relation to their storied history.

Their proud past seems to have diminished over time; they were no longer what they once had been, and so, what they had come to embrace then is what they needed to recall now. When they heard the story of Jesus and of His incomparable love, they were motivated to love God and serve one another with a spirit of loyalty and dedication. Now that they have fought so many battles, their early enthusiasm had waned. They were crestfallen and defeated, even though in fact they had conquered in every instance. They had won the many battles over false doctrine, but over the course of time had lost their love for each other and their enthusiasm for the cause for which they had been striving. The lesson in this for all of us is that we must not permit the burdens of today to cause us to lose our zeal for the Lord tomorrow. Life is sometimes very hard on our faith, but we must not permit it to quench the fire of our spiritual enthusiasm.

The Ephesian Christians are advised to set their sights on the final victory. In a word-play that utilizes the common word *nikan* "to conquer" or "enjoy victory," John points these disciples toward heaven and the "tree of life" as the proper offset to the carnality of the this-worldly message of the Nicolaitans who evidently proffered the most recent alternative to sound doctrine and genuine Christian living. They had faced many challenges already, but this one was to represent their greatest one on account of their present weakness. They must not fail this final test, and we must not either. Satan will assault our defenses precisely at that moment and at that place when and where they are at their most vulnerable. We need to know that in advance and not allow it to surprise us when it happens. Afterward we must carry on with ardor, in spite of it all, right up to the final moment of life. This is what the Evil One was doing at Ephesus. He was attacking the war-weary soldiers of the cross at a time when they were frazzled and beaten down by their past conflicts. Never mind that they had always been victorious. This enemy is tireless. He never relents. He always comes back one more time. So, we must never relax our defenses. We must never let down our guard. We have to remain strong and fight to the final breath.

3. *The Letter to the church at Smyrna (2:8-11).*

And to the messenger of the church in Smyrna write: "These things says the first and the last, who was dead, and lived again: I know your tribulation, and your poverty (but you are rich), and the blasphemy of those who say they are Jews, and they are not, but are a synagogue of Satan. Fear not the things which you are about to suffer: behold, the Devil is about to cast some of you into prison, that you may be tested; and you shall have tribulation ten days. Be faithful unto death, and I will give you the crown of life. He who has an ear, let him hear what the Spirit says to the churches. He who overcomes shall not be hurt by the second death" (Rev. 2:8-11).

Ancient resources and archaeological finds from the excavation of the city wall in the Acropolis area indicate that the new city of Smyrna was resettled from its location in Bayrakli (Palaia Smyrna) to the new location on the north and west slopes of the Acropolis between Kadifekale (Acropolis of Smyrna) and the sea by the end of the fourth or the beginning of the third century BC. It was no doubt founded by the successors of Alexander the Great, namely Antigonos Monophthalmos and Lysimachos. The fact that Smyrna, like Rome and Athens, has been continuously inhabited for many centuries in the same location complicates our ability to study the history of the city in the Hellenistic Period and later.

Until recently, the sole visible part of the ancient city of Smyrna was the Agora, but ongoing studies and excavations have revealed many other parts and findings that provide insight into the long history of the location. Scholars are excited to know that the simple structures above the Theater of Smyrna are soon to be pulled down and opened for archaeological studies, and that another building that has been located is the stadium. In 2007 the Mosaic Building, the City Council Building, and the Roman Bath were discovered. During excavation works in Altinpark Archaeological Area and the Şifa Parcels, the first ancient residential buildings were encountered in the year 2008.

The Agora of Smyrna is built on the outskirts of Mount Pagos with a slight southeast to northwest slope. The excavated area of the central open space as of the time of this writing measures ca. 129m by 83m. The northern side of the agora is occupied by the basilica, which is now almost completely excavated. To the west, the western Stoa, 20m wide, is partially excavated. Currently measured at 83m in length, the stoa is expected to span over 100m long when it is fully revealed (Bagnall, 1-3).

The city of Smyrna claimed the title *to agalma tēs Asias*, "the glory of Asia." Coins described it as "first of Asia in beauty and size." It had a long and storied history. At the time of the writing of the Revelation it had approximately 250,000 inhabitants. It stood on a deep gulf some 35 miles north of Ephesus, possessed a magnificent harbor, and stood at the end of the road that served the valley of the river Hermus. The primary ruins of ancient Smyrna, including its massive city market (*agora*), once an enormous three story building filled with products from all over the ancient Mediterranean world, in fact, the largest one known in antiquity, and its surprisingly complex and modern-looking sanitation system with its vast underground tunnels, are located in the middle of the modern Turkish city of Izmir. On this account, precious little of what might be known of the place has actually been uncovered, since most of it still lies hidden beneath a sprawling and bustling modern city. This, of course, presents a tremendous challenge for the archaeologist, one that in many instances cannot be overcome.

Though admittedly frustrating, the situation has not been entirely without positive news. In 2003, for example, a rich collection of Greek graffiti dating to the 2nd-4th centuries AD was unearthed while working in the basement level of the basilica in the ancient agora. The excavation was under the direction of Mehmet Taşlialin. These graffiti represent the richest collection of such Greek inscriptions ever found. They include writing, paintings and carvings which depict many different figures and scenes, from trade ships to gladiators. There were also confessions. The texts associated with the graffiti also shed light on the daily life of the people of the Hellenistic and Roman periods, including the feelings, emotions and beliefs of those who would never have composed a formal piece of literary art, but who might be willing informally to scratch a message onto a wall or column for the passerby to see. One inscription, for example, says, "I love someone who does not love me." Another writes, "The god healed my eyes, this is why I dedicate an oil lamp to the gods." Interestingly, the graffiti also contain many riddles which have not yet been solved. Some of the inscriptions were even made by Christians, showing that they were steadily growing in their numbers in the city during that period (Bagnall, 1-52).

Trade flowed through the markets of Smyrna from all of the cities of the region and made its way to the rest of the world through Smyrna's harbor.

The Letters to the Seven Churches of Asia (Part 1)   2:8-11

Like Ephesus, it was a city that enjoyed great wealth and considerable commercial appeal. It was also an important traditional religious center for the area. Grand temples of the gods of the Greeks and Romans graced the streets of the place. There was a Temple dedicated to Cybele on "Golden Street" near the ocean, one to Apollo, another to Asklepios, and still another to Aphrodite. A Temple for Zeus stood at the point where the street met the foothills inland from the sea. The Christians of this city no doubt felt humbled by this grandiose center of worship of the chief gods of the pagans! Meeting as they did in humble surroundings, away from the fanfare, ostentation and bravura of the city center, they certainly saw themselves as inconsequential by comparison with the splendor of heathenism at its best. And it saw its best in Smyrna! B. K. Blount observed:

> In Roman occupied Asia Minor in the last decade of the first century, during the reign of the emperor Domitian, there existed a strong motivation to accommodate. In Rome's ideological infrastructure, religion and politics were quite intentionally mixed. Worship often mutated into politics; politics was often exercised through religion. Worship of Roman deities not only demonstrated a cultic devotion and communal piety; it also signaled loyalty to the Roman state, which was mythologically connected to and practically founded upon them. It is not surprising, then, that the mother goddess would favor the name Roma, or that the messianic hopes for the empire should be bound up in the person of the emperor. This blending of politics and worship was especially evident in Asia Minor, where John and his seven churches were located. There, particularly during the last decade of the first century, emperor worship flourished. "Under the Flavians, especially Domitian, the imperial cult was strongly represented in the Roman provinces. Domitian demanded that the populace acclaim him as 'Lord and God' and participate in his worship. The majority of the cities to which the prophetic messages of Revelation are addressed were dedicated to the promotion of the emperor cult" (Schüssler Fiorenza, *Justice*, 193).

Thyatira was an illustrative case in point. The city was caught up in the throes of idol and emperor worship. Here, in fact, cultic propaganda went so far as to declare the Roman emperor to be the incarnation of Apollo and therefore a son of Zeus. The religious-political alliance heightened the risk for persons who tried to opt out of the Greco-Roman cultic infrastructure; rejection of the gods implied resistance to the state. Complicating matters even further was the fact that Thyatira hosted a large number of trade guilds that had strong cultic affiliations. Especially important were industries of wool, textile, and the manufacture of purple dye (cf. Acts 16:14-15). Beale believes that "since the guilds had patron deities, Christian guild members would be expected to pay homage to pagan gods at official guild meetings, which were usually festive occasions often accompanied by immoral behavior. Nonparticipation would lead to economic ostracism" (Beale, 261). Socially, economically, and politically, then, Christians in Thyatira had every reason to accommodate themselves to the expectations and practices of Greco-Roman religion and culture (Blount, 8-9).

Especially important in this larger socio-religious and cultural equation is the fact that in 195 BC Smyrna had been the first city in the world to erect a temple to *Dea Roma*, the goddess of Rome. Later, in AD 23 Smyrna had striven with ten other cities in Asia Minor for the right to erect a temple to the godhead of Tiberius, the reigning emperor, and won. So, Smyrna had become an especially enthusiastic center for emperor worship. This made it a dangerous place for Christians to live. By this time burning a pinch of incense on the altar of the emperor, and declaring affirmatively that "Caesar is Lord" was quickly becoming a test of loyalty to the Empire that had brought peace and security to the entire known world (the *pax Romana*, as they labeled it). In the time of the emperor Domitian it was to become compulsory and over time required proof of loyalty to the state in the form of a material receipt, i.e. a certificate of worship. This became necessary in order to assure the authorities that the citizen in question was loyal to Rome.

A second threat to pious Christians was the sizeable and very zealous Jewish population in the city which was actively hostile toward them. One of the most famous martyrdoms in history occurred in the city of Smyrna as a result of the hatred the Jews had for these followers of Jesus. Polycarp, a bishop in the church at Smyrna was seized and taken before the court, probably in the year AD 155. He was tried before the local proconsul, Statius Quadratus. He gladly confessed to the officer of the court that he was a Christian. When asked to repudiate his faith by worshipping the godhead of Caesar, he sternly refused. The Jews were his accusers at his trial (even though they themselves would have refused to worship the Emperor as a god), and then gathered faggots for the fire to burn him (on the Sabbath day) when he was condemned. His famous speech has gained immortality: "Eighty and six years have I served Christ, and he has never done me any wrong. How can I blaspheme my King who saved me?" Threatened with burning he replied: "I fear not the fire that burns for a season and after a while is quenched. Why do you delay? Come, do your will." As the flames licked his body, he prayed thus: "I thank thee that thou hast graciously thought me worthy of this day and of this hour, that I may receive a portion in the number of the martyrs, in the cup of thy Christ." His death was monumental. It became the first recorded martyrdom in post-New Testament church history, said to have been set down in writing within a year of his death. The narrator of the terrible event concluded by saying that Polycarp's death was remembered by everyone, "he is even spoken of by the heathen in every place" (*The Martyrdom of Polycarp*).

The letter to the Christians of Smyrna puts emphasis on the following things:

Tribulation amidst festivity and celebration. This grand city of Greek and Roman celebratory worship and service to their many ancestral gods came to be a miserable place for these greatly troubled Christians. The first thing Jesus said to His suffering disciples was, "I know your tribulation." Sympathetic understanding is a powerful reality. The Lord knew and understood what they were going through. The word for tribulation is *thlipsis*, which describes "crushing pressure." To be able to have someone who genuinely understood their situation and wanted them to know that He fully appreciated and identified with their feelings was important for them then just as it is for us in our own time. And the concomitant of this for us is just as critical to the intentionality of the divinely-inspired writer as were the circumstances of those hurting Christians of ancient Smyrna. God experiences no joy when He sees His people hurting. We need to know it is just the opposite that is true. The Lord wants us to be aware that He sees our tears, feels our pain, and sympathizes with us when we are suffering! That is the message of these powerful words.

Grinding poverty amidst the affluence and prosperity of those around them. In the face of this ugly reality, the Lord said also, "I know your poverty." As wealthy as the city was, and it was very rich indeed, nevertheless, in the midst of all of the beautiful outward manifestations of wealth, the opulence and plenitude of material goods and of rich resources, the Christians suffered in relative silence. The choice that each of them had made, to live as a Christian in a pagan society, had many painful ramifications and some of them had their consequences in the area of financial matters. And yet, there was one consideration that gave them some small amount of solace: the Lord knew and understood their state. He identified with and sympathized with them and not with the rich pagans.

Why were the Christians so poor? The logic of it is fairly simple. Every society of human beings is a closely-knit web of relationships involving people who do business with one another on account of their affinities and associations which are developed over time. They involve friendship and trust, and where distrust exists, individuals will, quite naturally, draw back from those whom they consider strange or untrustworthy. Jews had built up relationships with other Jewish businessmen and patrons, and pagans had established ties with others who shared their interests and beliefs, but the Christians were basically sitting on the outside of all this looking in. They were neither Jewish nor pagan, and their "otherness" labeled them as an alien presence, perhaps to be feared, but certainly to be shunned.

This was precisely where the Christians found themselves in the Greco-Roman world. These humble nonconformists were shut out of many of the available ways for people to make a living, establish a career, or even simply make money there. This was true because a good number of the major aspects of city life were tied into the predominant idolatrous religions in one way or another. The fact that they were conspicuous for their absence at the great Roman and regional civic festivals would have led to a situation where they were viewed with suspicion and mistrust. They did not participate in the pagan sacrifices that were so much a part of the common life of the city, and avoided even the most patriotic celebrations of Roman community life. All of these things incorporated practices and beliefs that Christians eschewed, so they stayed away. They paid a terrible price for their absence from such integral events and their general lack of involvement in the common life of the community.

Miserable poverty was the natural outgrowth of the totality of these factors. How important "fitting in" is, and not being viewed as a threatening presence to the status quo can be enormously important for financial success. So they were very poor. But the Lord assured them that they were actually rich in His sight. What a blessed assurance that must have been!

The Letters to the Seven Churches of Asia (Part 1)   2:12-17

Jewish blasphemy against Christ and the church. The "synagogue of Satan," as Jesus called it, was actively hostile toward the Christians, at every turn looking for an occasion against them with the authorities. It made their lives miserable. The Lord branded these hypocrites with a label that would have shocked them. They would never have thought of themselves in these terms, but its accuracy is not to be disputed. They were doing the Devil's work. So they were truly a synagogue of Satan. There is an important lesson in this for all of us. If we find ourselves working on the side of the Devil and doing his bidding, even unintentionally or unconsciously, then we are opposing God and we are Satan's servants. Never mind that we are sincere in this. These Jews thought they were doing service to God, but in fact they were serving Satan. We must be sure that we never fall into this same type of hypocrisy.

Worse things were coming. Unfortunately, the news for them was not good in terms of the immediate future. They were to suffer more than they already had. Just "ten days," the Lord promised; in other words, this period of pain and suffering was not to last forever, but only for a very limited time. Albeit, the ramifications were not to be mild, in fact, some of them would be put into prison. Such a prospect must have been frightening! Some would even be tested unto death (literally, *achri thanatou*, "into death") but in the end the good news was that they would not be hurt by the "second death" which would ultimately destroy their fanatical enemies.

So for this church the promise of God was not for earthly deliverance in the here and now but for heavenly reward. It might appear for the time that they were going down in defeat. But over the long term their victory would be made evident with the return of their Lord and the final judgment of their merciless opponents. In these comforting words we have the essence of the Book of Revelation. This was why the book was written. It was intended to give these desperate disciples something to cling to in the midst of these dark days of violence and oppression. Systematic persecution over so many years as these early Christians were forced to endure, has a tendency to wear down the resistance, if there seems to be "no light at the end of the tunnel," so to speak.

What John provided them with in this tiny letter was a precious and enduring hope that would make it possible for them to hang on for one more day as they put one foot out in front of the other for whatever amount of time was required and for however long and arduous the journey would prove to be.

4. The Letter to the church at Pergamos (2:12-17).

> *And to the messenger of the church in Pergamum write: "These things says He who has the sharp two-edged sword: I know where you dwell, even where Satan's throne is; and you held fast to My name, and did not deny My faith, even in the days of Antipas My martyr, My faithful one, who was killed among you, where Satan dwells. But I have a few things against you, because you have there some who hold the teaching of Balaam, who taught Balak to cast a stumbling-block before the children of Israel, to eat things sacrificed to idols, and to commit fornication. So also you have some who hold the teaching of the Nicolaitans as well. Repent therefore; or else I will come to you suddenly, and I will make war against those people with the sword of My mouth. He who has an ear, let him hear what the Spirit says to the churches. To him who overcomes, to him will I give of the hidden manna, and I will give him a white stone, and upon the stone a new name written, which no one knows but he who receives it"* (Rev. 2:12-17).

The road north from Smyrna followed the coastline in a northeasterly direction up the valley of the Caicus River, and about 10 miles inland from the Aegean Sea stood the impressive capital city of Pergamos, or Pergamum as it was variously called. It was about sixty-five miles north of Smyrna. Pergamum dominated not only the Caicus valley, but also a highway into the interior of Asia Minor as well as the western coastal road. Her considerable wealth was derived from trade, agricultural surplus, stock breeding and the dependent industries of woolen textiles and parchment, along with the silver mines that were located there.

The Roman statesman and scholar Pliny the Elder (Gaius Plinius Secundus, AD 23-79) described it as "by far the most distinguished city in Asia" (*Natural History* 5.30). The main part of the city was poised on a cone-shaped hill a thousand feet in height. Consequently, the site dominated the surrounding valley of the Caicus. The Greek word *pergamon* means "citadel." It rose to prominence during the era of the Attalids in the third century BC, when it was named the capital of their kingdom. It was brought to the height of its prosperity by the Attalid dynasty during the third and second centuries BC. When Attalus III willed his kingdom to Rome at his death in 133 BC, it became the crown jewel of the Roman province of Asia and encompassed approximately the western third of Asia Minor. While the Attalids were not great founders of cities like the other Hellenistic kings, they made Pergamum one of the greatest and most beautiful of all the Greek cities. An excellent example of Hellenistic town-planning, the place was laid out in terraces on a hillside, culminating in the palace and fortifications of the acropolis. It became renowned for its school of sculpture (Pfeiffer, Vos, 393).

Pergamum was the political capital of the region from the beginning, but it gradually lost its position of prominence and power to the coastal city of Ephesus, which was more easily accessible to Roman governors by sea (Pfeiffer, 438). It boasted a library of over 200,000 volumes. The city was described as the "finest flower of Hellenistic civilization," and until Attalus III bequeathed his kingdom to the Romans in 133 BC the Pergamene kings continued as enthusiastic patrons of Hellenistic culture and language.

Pergamum is one of the most completely excavated of ancient sites. The modern city is called Bergama. Archaeology has produced much important evidence since the first early efforts at the location by the German architect Carl Humann in 1868. Since that time up to the present day the German Archaeology Institute has persisted in working at the site. Out of their researches there and elsewhere grew up the *Pergamonmuseum*, an archaeological museum complex located in the *Museumsinsel*, an island on the Spree river in central Berlin. It contains an impressive collection of artifacts, mostly derived from excavations made during the 19th century by German archaeologists in Greece, Jordan, Egypt, Mesopotamia, and Turkey.

The Collection of Classical Antiquities (*Antikensammlung*) is world-famous for the 110 meter long Hellenistic altar of Pergamon (the great altar of Zeus), from which the museum complex takes its name. Its discovery was the first major triumph of the German excavators. Probably built by King Eumenes (197-159 BC), it originally stood on foundations that measured 125 by 115 feet. The magnificent altar rested on a great horseshoe shaped plinth thirty feet high, approached by twenty-eight sixty foot steps on the western side. These steps led through an Ionic colonnade into a square court where the altar proper stood. The three outer sides of the monument were sculptured with scenes of struggles between gods and giants along with pictorials representing the defeat of the Gauls by Eumenes. Another frieze ran around the three inner sides of the altar court on the upper level and depicted events from the life of Telephus, son of Hercules, and supposed mythical ancestor of the Attalid dynasty. This splendid frieze (almost 400 feet long) is only slightly shorter than that of the Parthenon. Some have supposed that this extraordinary altar is what the apostle John had in mind when he spoke of "Satan's throne" at Pergamum (cf. Rev. 2:13; Pfeiffer, 438-439).

At the foot of the acropolis, Eumenes (apparently) built the lower agora, a paved court 210 by 110 feet surrounded by Doric porticoes giving entrance to the shops that were situated there. Just up the hill from the agora stood a gymnasium complex, one of the major social centers of Hellenistic society, on three terraces. Above the gymnasium in about the middle of the slope lay the upper agora, above and to the left of which was the magnificent Altar of Zeus. As one ascended the western side of the acropolis from the Altar, he came to the beautiful temple of Athena. This sacred space was surrounded on three sides by the two story library which at one time had been the second largest of the ancient world, possessing some 200,000 volumes (scrolls). In John's day, however, it was mostly empty because Antony had given the contents of Pergamum's library to Cleopatra and so most of the books had been carted off to the city of Alexandria in Egypt.

Over against the side of the acropolis adjacent to the temple of Athena lay the theater which was constructed in 170 BC and held approximately 15,000 spectators. Four other theaters have been found in the larger Pergamum metropolis. Founded by a man named Archias, and directed at one point by the renowned physician Galen (131-210 BC), the Asclepeion of Pergamum was perhaps the most famous medical center of the ancient world. A monumental way leads into the Asclepeion. This was once an active market street, with the acropolis of the city lying beautifully in the background to the east. It is west of the city center, about one mile north of the main street. As one enters the principal precinct of the Asclepeion there is a large marble column fragment bearing the dedicatory symbol of the place: two snakes facing each other across a wheel. This was the ancient symbol of Asclepius, the god of healing.

This healing center attained the height of its ascendancy in the second century AD and most of the structures excavated there date to that period of time. There the sick, who often traveled great distances to reach the resort, underwent treatment by suggestion, sun and water baths, music, prayer, and interpretation of dreams. A non-venomous snake was often used in the healing rituals; they were permitted to crawl around freely on the floor in dormitories where the sick and injured slept. Pilgrims flocked to such healing temples (Asclepieia) to be cured of their various ills. Ritual purification would be followed by offerings or sacrifices to the god (according to the means of the patients) and then the supplicant would spend the night in the holiest part of the sanctuary (the *abaton* or *adyton*). The following day any dreams or visions would be reported to a priest who would then prescribe the appropriate therapy by a process of interpretation. A few of the healing temples employed sacred dogs to lick the wounds of sick petitioners. While all of this may sound strange and unimpressive to the modern reader, it was very popular in ancient times among people from all strata of society. In fact, even Roman emperors like Hadrian, Marcus Aurelius, and Caracalla came to the Pergamene facility to receive treatment and care. During this era the famous orator and rhetorician Aelius Aristides (AD 117-181) lectured in its theater; his early success in his chosen profession was interrupted by a decades-long series of illnesses for which he sought relief by divine communion with the god Asclepius, effected (he claimed) by interpreting and obeying the dreams that came to him while sleeping in the sacred precinct of the deity; his experiences were set down in writing in a series of discourses called *Sacred Tales* or *Heiroi Logoi* (Pfeiffer, 439-440).

Greek religion also flourished at Pergamos. It was a center for worship of four of the most important pagan cults of the day: Zeus, Athene, Dionysos, and Asclepios. The shrine of Asclepius, the god of healing, who was designated by his followers as *sōtēr* or "savior," attracted people from all over the world, but of greatest importance for the Christians who lived there was the fact that it was also the official center in Asia for the imperial cult. It was the first city of Asia to receive permission to build a temple dedicated to the worship of a living ruler. In 29 BC Augustus had granted authorization for a temple to be erected there to the deity of Augustus and for the goddess Roma (*dea Roma*; Tacitus, *Annals* 4.37—"The divine Augustus did not forbid the founding of a temple at Pergamos to himself and to the city of Rome..."). She personified the city of Rome and the Roman state generally. Temples to her were established in many of the Roman colonies in order more fully to cement the relationship of the colony with the authority of the city of Rome.

It was on this account that of all of the seven cities singled out in Revelation, it is worth noting that Pergamum was certainly the most likely of all of them for Christians living there to clash directly and painfully with the imperial cult. The disciples of Jesus were in jeopardy throughout the region, but those of Pergamum were in the most danger of them all. Pergamos was a tinder-box waiting for a spark to kindle it!

The following points are keynotes to understanding the problems this church was experiencing and the counsel the Lord offered to help them along:

Jesus wields the "sharp two-edged sword" of authority over life and death. This was the opening to the letter that was addressed to them. It declares that the Lord wears the symbol of absolute authority and is invested with the power of life and death. This He proclaims in the face of the fact that the official capital of the province, the seat of authority in the ancient kingdom and in Roman administration, were all housed in this city. Its administrators were powerful men, but Christ is more powerful than they could ever hope to be. His power extends to the areas of life and death, and of what extends even beyond the reach of the physical sword.

Additionally, Jesus claims authority that is superior to Roman Imperial government. In Roman estimation the sword was the symbol of the highest order of official authority, with which the Proconsul of Asia was invested. The "right of the sword" *(jus gladii)*, was roughly equivalent to what we call the power of life and death. Governors of provinces were divided into a higher and a lower class, according as they were or were not invested with this power. John plays upon this notion to tell his audience that the Christ holds absolute power over life and death in spite of the fact that many people would not have recognized it or acknowledged it. It is His whether they like it or not, and, as it was then, so is it today. Whether that authority is recognized and acknowledged or not, the Christ of God has it and does wield it.

Sir William Ramsey highlighted this idea in the following insightful words: "When the divine Author addresses Pergamum in this character, his intention is patent, and would be caught immediately by all Asian readers of the Apocalypse. He wields that power of life and death, which people imagine to be vested in the Proconsul of the province" (Ramsey, *Letters*, 292-293). Earthly rulers are also the subjects of the King of kings!

They lived "*where Satan's throne is.*" What a frightening prospect! And yet, this reference is entirely appropriate. This suggests that in the state religion of the Empire, the worship of the divine emperors, organized on a regular system in Asia as in all of the other provinces, Satan himself found his home and exercised his power in opposition to God and His church. Pergamum, as being still the administrative capital of the province, was also the chief seat of the state religion. Here was built the first Asian temple of the divine Augustus, which for more than forty years was the one center of the Imperial religion for the whole province. A second Asian temple had afterwards been built at Smyrna, and a third at Ephesus, but they were always considered secondary to the original Augustan Temple which stood at Pergamum. There is no doubt that this explains the language employed by the Lord in His missive to these Christians.

The Christians of Pergamos had held fast to Christ and had not denied His name, even when threatened with martyrdom. The Lord praised this good church for its courageous stand for the truth in a city where the very throne of Satan was entrenched. One of their own, a man by the name of Antipas, had already suffered at the hands of their common enemies. Antipas is described in this reference as a *martus* or "martyr"; this freighted term appears in the Bible thirty-four times and is normally rendered as "witness" (29 times), but in two cases it appears as "record" and in three instances (Acts 22:20; Rev. 1:5; 2:13) more properly should be translated "martyr." This is one of those three cases.

Moreover, they are not assured that there will not be more of their number who will in their own turn join the ranks with him! How and under what circumstances he died we are not sure, but later writings say that he was appointed a bishop in the city by John and that he was roasted alive about the year AD 92 in a brazen bull at Pergamos. Whether he died at the hands of an angry pagan mob or as the result of a formal judicial decree is hard to tell. The former is the most likely scenario, even though given the antipathy toward Christianity at Pergamos which is so evident in the words of this small letter, a formal sentence of death by the court is not out of the realm of possibility. From Pliny's letter to Trajan (*Epistulae* 10.96) and from the story of the martyrdom of Polycarp we deduce that in the early second century it was a part of customary court procedure that those who were accused of being Christians should be invited to exculpate themselves by cursing Christ, especially in cases where anonymous accusations were at the root of the investigation. So, his confession in court may be what this text refers to. The stories that surround his life seem to suggest that he at first may have served as a dentist among the medical professionals of the city who treated the maladies of the people and at times performed miracles to relieve the sufferings of some. Later Catholic lore saw him as the saint to whom people ought to pray who suffer from dental issues.

Yet now their faithfulness was being threatened by a spirit of compromise with immorality. People have the capacity to be very faithful in one area of life while at the same time showing weakness in another. That was apparently the case in this instance. The reference in v. 14 is to Numbers 31:16. Balaamites were among them! Teachers who were false to the gospel of Christ were leading some of them off into licentiousness. They were urging them to eat things sacrificed to idols and commit fornication, apparently suggesting that this represented an innocuous activity that posed no threat to their souls and that it would make them appear more "normal" in the society of that day. In truth, it represented compromise with sin!

Christians in Pergamum had every reason to accommodate themselves to the expectations and practices of the Greco-Roman religion and culture that surrounded them on all sides. Because they clearly did not believe in the reality or lordship of the pagan deities, their participation at the cultic festivals and other social gatherings where elaborate meals and rituals were prepared to honor those deities was socially, economically, and politically motivated. Their complicity in artisan, trade, and funeral associations allowed for upward social and economic mobility. Apparently they passed themselves off as Roman cultic devotees in order to avail themselves of Roman resources and enjoy the numerous benefits of full participation in Roman society. Unlike the true believers in Smyrna, who apparently opted out of such accommodating activities and thereby found themselves impoverished and persecuted as a result, many conciliatory Pergamum Christians simply blended in and therefore moved up socially, politically, and economically. They had bought in to the philosophy of the ancient prophet Balaam (Blount, 9). Compromise made life so much easier in a pagan city!

The Old Testament book called Numbers devotes an extended section to the incidents which have to do with the prophet whose name is Balaam and king Balak, covering chapters 22-24 and portions of chapter 31. The nation of Moab was fear-stricken at the thought of Israel's intrusion in the region, especially given her previous successes against the powerful Amorites. Balak, the country's ruler, was concerned that it would not be possible for Moab to fight Israel on her own terms.

Balaam was a famed prophet of the time, whose reputation reached far and wide. So famous was he, in fact, that an inscription about him was discovered by a Dutch archaeological expedition from Leiden University at Deir 'Alla in Jordan in the year 1967. Dated between 880-770 BC, the inscription was found in a many chambered structure that was destroyed by an earthquake. The writing was on a fragment of plaster which had once covered a column. It was written primarily in black but also had some red ink. The script was similar to that which was found on the Mesha inscription of the 8th century BC, and the language or dialect has been characterized as Ammonite or Gileadite (Jonas C. Greenfield). 119 fragments were found at the site. It speaks about "Balaam bar Beor, the man who was a seer of the gods. . . ." The segment of the larger inscription that has been reconstructed and translated, tells the story of one of Balaam's visions from the *Shaddayin* (a word related to the biblical term *El Shaddai*).

Balak decided that he would purchase the services of this supposed prophet to place a curse on Israel, and so he called for him to come. In a long and strange story of mysterious happenings, it is indicated clearly by God to Balaam that he would not be able to curse Israel, for the Lord favored her and blessed her future. His attempted violation of the divine mandate placed him in grave jeopardy with God, and so he was confronted by an angel planning to kill him, but his donkey saved him from death.

Being made aware of his dangerous situation by the talking donkey, Balaam made his way to his meeting with the king of Moab, in spite of the divine warning he had been given. When he reached the overlook which allowed him to see the extensive camp of Israel stretched out before his eyes, God repeatedly forced a blessing from his mouth rather than a curse. He finally explained to Balak that if God had made up his mind to bless Israel, it would be impossible for him to curse the one whom God intended to bless. With that, the two parted ways and Balaam went back home.

Apparently before he left for home, however, he gave Balak advice which would lead to Israel's doom if it was followed. Moses later explained that the women of Moab followed the advice of Balaam and caused Israel to sin at Peor, leading to a destructive plague, amounting to God cursing His people on His own terms (Num. 31:15-16). So in the end, at least to some extent, Balak was able to achieve the desired result he was after, even though to the extent that he wished it, God would not permit his desire to be realized.

Paige Patterson offers the following incisive follow-up to the biblical narrative:

> This incident in the history of Israel had come to represent, along with Aaron and the golden calf, the two most despicable moments in the history of the exodus and subsequent wanderings. Every child growing up in a Jewish home was introduced to the failure of the Jewish people in this incident and the danger of being seduced by Balaamite teachers. Interestingly, cases in post-Christian Jewish literature are substantiated where Jesus of Nazareth is compared to Balaam with the insinuation that the teachings of Jesus are the teachings of Balaam. Such could even have been taking place in the city of Pergamum. If so, John's reference to the teachings of Balaam would be even more explicit than other wise (Patterson, 105).

Where an attempted prophet's curse had failed to hurt them, the temptation to unchastity had prevailed against God's people. John worried that it might win out again in the church of Christ at Pergamum.

It has been said, and the ancient writings of the various pagan authors seem to bear this out, that chastity was the one completely new virtue which Christianity introduced into the ancient world. Judaism taught the identical principle, but was never a very evangelical religion, and thus sought to impose it upon none except its own community. The Christian system hoped to get everyone to live by this perfect standard of moral purity. Paul wrote: "Flee sexual immorality (*porneia*) and pursue self-control" (1 Thess. 4:1-8). Assuredly it may be observed, and frequently has been, that in the world of the New Testament sexual morals were extremely loose, and generally speaking, intimate relationships outside of marriage were entirely accepted and produced no stigma in society whatsoever. Christianity, however, was attempting to change the world by its stance.

So, liberal attitudes and loose moral practices could not be accepted in the fellowship of the Christian believers. Such compromise with evil could not and would not be tolerated. Even though it was the norm among most of the religiously minded pagans, as well as with almost all of the non-religious people who surrounded them, those who followed Christ could not adopt this way of thinking or living. Thus, in this letter Jesus promised those who stood firm in the face of such moral challenges that they would enjoy the "hidden manna" the spiritual "bread of heaven," in a word, the food of the angels. Because they are willing to give up earthly pleasure in the here and now, they would enjoy heavenly blessing in the world to come. That was the worthwhile trade-off that they were expected to make in their daily walk with Christ.

CHAPTER TWO

The Letters to the Seven Churches of Asia (Part 2)

1. The Letter to the church at Thyatira (2:18-29).

And to the messenger of the church in Thyatira write: "These things says the Son of God, who has eyes like a flame of fire, and His feet are like burnished brass: I know your works, and your love and faith and ministry and patience, and that your last works are more than the first. But I have this against you, that you tolerate that woman Jezebel, who calls herself a prophetess; and she teaches and seduces my servants to commit fornication, and to eat things sacrificed to idols. And I gave her time that she should repent; but she refused to repent of her fornication. Behold, I will cast her into a bed, and those who commit adultery with her into great tribulation, unless they repent of her works. And I will strike her children with death; and all the churches shall know that I am He who searches the minds and hearts: and I will give to each one of you according to your works. But to you I say, to the rest who are in Thyatira, as many as have not embraced this teaching, who know not the deep things of Satan, as they are wont to say: I will place on you no other burden. Nevertheless that which you have, hold fast until I come. And he who overcomes, and he who keeps My works to the end, to him will I give authority over the nations; and he shall rule them with a rod of iron, as the vessels of the potter are broken in pieces; as I also have received of My Father: and I will give him the morning star. He who has an ear, let him hear what the Spirit says to the churches" (Rev. 2:18-29).

It is interesting to note that the longest of the letters to the churches of Asia was written to a congregation in the smallest and most insignificant town of the seven. It was penned to the Christians of Thyatira, a completely unremarkable and utterly forgettable place. The city was situated at the mouth of a long vale which connected the two val-

The Letters to the Seven Churches of Asia (Part 2)   2:18-29

leys of the Hermus and the Caicus rivers, on the Lycus river, a little to the south of Hyllus, at the northern end of the valley between Mount Tmolus and the southern ridge of Tetanus. Great trade routes traversed the valley, most notably the one that ran from Syria to Pergamos, but none of those trade routes ran directly through Thyatira. It lay upon the lesser road that ran between Sardis and Pergamos, and stood just twenty-seven miles from the former. In fact, the roads which passed through its valley brought the trade of half the world to its doors, but only indirectly on account of the misfortune that it was situated in the Lycus river valley, and not the Hermus or the Caicus.

Furthermore, early history of the place is not well known. It had been called Pelopia, Euhippa, and Semiramus during various times in its earlier life. Until it was refounded by Seleucus Nicator (301-281 BC) it was a small and insignificant town. Standing almost on the dividing line between Mysia and Ionia, it was sometimes reckoned a part of one and sometimes a part of the other. At first a Seleucid outpost against Macedonia, Thyatira became a Pergemene outpost after the defeat of Antiochus at Magnesia in 190. When the Pergamene kingdom became the Roman province of Asia in AD 133, Thyatira passed directly under the control of Rome. It never proved to be of any significance militarily, therefore. Its chief problem as a military outpost was that it was not fortified sufficiently to hold out as such for a very long time. It lay in an open valley on a fertile plain at the east bank of the river, and there was no height that could be fortified, and so all that it could ever hope to do was to fight a delaying action until Pergamos could prepare to meet the invaders.

Historically its claim to fame was that it was the gateway to the impressive city of Pergamos, and so a mere sentinel town. But, over time this "off the beaten path" backwater became quite rich and prosperous on account of its proximity to these other strategic places and because of an accident of fate, the fact that madder root grew there in great abundance. Dyeing (manufacture of purple cloth) apparently formed an important part of the industrial activity of the city, just as it did that of Colossae and Laodicea. The height of its prosperity was during the Roman Era in the first century AD; so John wrote his letter to them precisely at the peak of their financial and commercial success.

Thyatira was not a center of either Caesar worship or of religious significance for the traditional Greek gods and goddesses. It possessed temples dedicated to Artemis and Apollo, as well as an Oriental mystical sibyl called the *Sambathē* where many sought guidance at her shrine. Some scholars have thought that the "prophetess" named Jezebel to which the letter alludes (2:20) was in fact this *Sambathē*, since her powerful influence could easily have led many astray from the truth and into heretical beliefs and practices. In our view the greater likelihood is that this woman whom he alludes to as "Jezebel" was a Christian convert who claimed prophetical powers but encouraged Christian men to make concessions to the pagan practices of their neighbors, especially in regard to indulgence in sexual immorality and enjoyment of pagan feasts which included eating sacrificial food offered to idols. The theory held by some writers which states that she was the wife of a Christian bishop has no evidence behind it.

Its tutelary deity originally was a sun god called Tyrimnos, depicted apparently as a hero, but merged in the divine nature as Apollo Tyrimnaios. A goddess associated with him was Boreatene, a deity of lesser importance. Upon the early coins of Thyatira this Asiatic god is represented often as a horseman with a double-edged battle-axe on his shoulder (similar to those represented on the sculptures of the earlier Hittites), an appropriate deity for a military colony, as the city was originally formed to be. Before the time of Nicator the place was regarded as a holy city on account of its association with Tyrimnos, and games were held in his honor there. But none of these religious shrines were particularly famous or important. Unfortunately, on the other hand, we know very little about this city, since historians and ancient writers rarely ever alluded to it. Moreover, the inscriptions that have been discovered and published throw very little light on the letter directed to the church in the Revelation. Religious persecution was evidently not a significant issue at Thyatira like it was in some of the other churches of Asia Minor.

It was the commercial importance of Thyatira that put it on the map. Bronze work from the guilds of Thyatira were considered to be of the finest quality found anywhere. As noted above, the city was also a great center of the wool trade and of the dyeing industry. Purple dye was extremely expensive and one of the sources of this dye was the madder root which grew plentifully around Thyatira. Lydia of Thyatira was a "seller of purple" (Acts 16:14). This woman was no doubt a merchant princess, a woman of great wealth, dealing as she did in one of the most costly substances in the ancient world. Thyatira was her home. The color obtained by the use of this dye in modern times is called "Turkish red."

The city of Thyatira was specially noted for the trade guilds which were probably more completely organized there than in any other ancient city. Every artisan belonged to a guild, and every guild, which was an incorporated organization, possessed property in its own name, made contracts for great constructions, and wielded tremendous influence in the city. Especially powerful among them was the guild of the coppersmiths; another was the guild of the dyers, who, made use of the madder root instead of shell-fish for making purple dyestuffs. Lydia may have been a member of this guild. But there were also guilds of workers in wool, leather, linen, bronze, pottery, bakers, makers of outer garments, and even slave-dealers. Most of the guilds were closely connected with the Asiatic religion so predominant in the region. Pagan feasts, with which many immoral practices were associated, were held by these tradesmen in their meetings and extracurricular activities, and so opposition to Christianity began to be obvious from the earliest days of their conflict with one another (cf. Banks, 2977, 2978). One of Paul's most rabid enemies was from the guild of the coppersmiths (2 Tim. 4:14, 15).

Unsurprisingly, given their relative proximity and close relationship as the only two Mysian cities of the seven, the letters to Thyatira and Pergamos bear considerable resemblance to one another. In addition, they were the only two of the seven cities which were strongly affected by the Nicolaitan teaching and both letters are dominated by the considerable hatred from the Lord for that particular heresy.

Little else is known about the city in ancient or medieval times. No excavation of it has been undertaken to date, and almost no ruins are obvious in the vicinity. The modern town of Akhisar ("white castle") in far western Turkey, which occupies the site, makes exploration or excavation there very difficult. For this reason not nearly so much can be said of the ancient city, how it was laid out and the main features of the place, as can be regarding those towns of the seven churches that have been extensively explored by archaeologists.

Here are the primary points underscored in the letter.

The Lord addresses Himself to the church as "the Son of God." Only here in the book of Revelation is Jesus so described, although this is intimated by two other texts (cf. 2:27; 3:5). Psalm 2:7 may be the inspiration of this usage, since it is quoted later in this same letter (v. 27). This stands in strong contrast to the local worship of Apollo Tyrimnos, which was merged with veneration of the emperor, so that they were both acclaimed as sons of Zeus. Christ is pictured here as having eyes like flames of fire and feet like burnished brass. Both descriptions are found in the initial vision in chapter 1 (cf. vv. 14-15). In Daniel's great vision of the last days the celestial being who appeared to him also had "eyes like flaming torches" and "legs that gleam of burnished bronze" (10:6). So, what John intends to underscore for his reading audience is that Jesus is the one and only Son of God. Others, even the emperor himself, are mere pretenders to the name. With eyes like flames of fire, nothing escapes his notice. He searches the hearts and minds of all men (v. 23). On this account He knows the circumstances of the church and its members. Nothing eludes His notice.

Christ is well aware of the church's record of love, faith, service, and patience. Because He is about to criticize them for their lack of fortitude in the face of temptation, He first lets them know that He has not forgotten the much good that they have done throughout the preceding years. The Lord is never remiss about such things (Heb. 6:10). Even though human memory is sometimes quite flawed, God remembers both evil and good with perfect recollection.

"That Jezebel of a woman" had led some of the believers in Thyatira into fatal compromise with their secular environment. In a city whose economic life was dominated by powerful trade guilds in which pagan religious practices had become essential criteria for membership, the Christian converts were confronted with bleak choices. They could make some compromises with paganism and accommodate the unions with their idolatrous rituals, or else stand steadfast against their ways and suffer for their lack of flexibility. A very clever female had stepped in to assure them that idolatry meant nothing and their compromises with their heathen neighbors were unimportant. This was a very appealing approach, but it was dead wrong. Their Christian convictions would be meaningless if this were followed. So this particular woman whoever she may have been, is accursed, and the doctrine of compromise with evil is forever given the tarnished name of Jezebel by the Lord's very direct message to her and those who were her followers. Her doctrines, moreover, are described as "the deep things of Satan." They are satanic in nature, and not at all divine.

To the faithful at Thyatira "none other burden" is given, but a promise is bestowed that if they will remain true they will someday enjoy "authority over the nations." Apparently the temptation to compromise was substantial. Jezebel was a smooth-tongued temptress. In all likelihood she was also a very beautiful woman in her appearance, and highly intelligent as well. Her words carried much weight at Thyatira. Certainly she claimed for herself prophetic powers, so she was a formidable opponent of truth in every respect. To those who are strong enough to resist her wiles, the Savior gives an interesting invitation. It is a simple promise to extend His power over the nations to His faithful disciples (vv. 25-27). Christ will rule, and they will in some sense share His rule with him.

It is popularly said of Satan that he preferred to rule in hell than to serve in heaven. Christ promises to those who serve Him faithfully on earth, that they will share His rule in heaven. Like so many other promises of God, we cannot fully appreciate the ultimate fulfillment of such divine blessings, nor comprehend their meaning with exactitude, but just the sound of them is so sweet that we shall leave it to the Almighty to explain them and work them out when the time comes! The persecuted Christians of Thyatira must have thought similarly as they first heard these encouraging and blessed words.

2. The Letter to the church at Sardis (3:1-6).

And to the messenger of the church in Sardis write: "These things says He who has the seven Spirits of God, and the seven stars: I know your works, that you have a reputation of being alive, but you are dead. Be watchful, and establish the things that remain, which are about to die: for I have found no works of yours perfected before My God. Remember therefore what you have received and heard; and keep it, and repent. If therefore you do not watch, I will come as a thief, and you will not know what hour I will come upon you. But you have a few names in Sardis who have not defiled their garments: and they shall walk with Me in white; for they are worthy. He who overcomes shall thus be arrayed in white garments; and I will never blot his name out of the book of life, and I will confess his name before My Father, and before His angels. He who has an ear, let him hear what the Spirit says to the churches" (Rev. 3:1-6).

Sardis was about 35 miles to the southeast of Thyatira, and it was one of the oldest and most important cities of Asia Minor. The Pactolus River, which flows in a general north-south direction through the city, empties into the Hermus about two and a half miles south. It was built at the base of Mt. Tmolus, with the acropolis on Mt. Tmolus, high above the city proper. Its location commanded the Hermus valley. A modern paved road, the Salihli Highway, passes in a northwest-southwest direction through the ruins of the ancient city. Rich fields of grape vines, figs, and tobacco surround the modern site.

Sardis is thought by some scholars (after W. M. Ramsay) to be the ancient city of Hyde, the primitive capital of the Hermus Valley, as identified by Homer. If this is correct, then the beginning of the city may trace back as far as about 1200 BC The name Sardis can be followed back through the Greek literature from the time of Aeschylus (ca. 525-456 BC) and Thucydides (460-400 BC) and onward. At any rate, until 549 BC it was the capital of the kingdom of Lydia, home to the wealthy and powerful king Croesus. It is here that the earliest evidence for the usage of minted coins has been found.

It appeared to be an impregnable fortress, and Croesus thought it so. The acropolis stood 950 feet high with triple walls surrounding it (which survive to the present day). Through the failure to watch, however, the acropolis had been successfully scaled in 549 BC by a single Median soldier, and again in 218 BC by a Cretan. On both occasions the invader had come by stealth, like a thief in the night, and the defenders had not known the hour of his coming. "If therefore you do not watch, I will come as a thief, and you will not know what hour I will come upon you" (v. 3). So, these memorable words from their Lord would have burned like a hot knife through the memories of the Christian inhabitants of the city. They knew well the frightening history of the place and certainly would not have wanted for it to become a feature of their own history as a church.

In 334 BC the city had been surrendered to Alexander the Great who on account of its graciousness granted it relative independence. But, a mere twelve years later it was taken by Antigonus after the death of the great conqueror. In 301 BC it became the possession of the Seleucidan kings who made it the residence of their governor. Under the Romans it was destroyed by an earthquake in AD 17, but Tiberius remitted the taxes of the people and quickly rebuilt the city.

The ancient metropolis was noted for its fruits and wool. Gold and silver were mined in the area, and coins were first struck there from the local product. A major landmark of the city was its temple of the goddess Cybele, whose worship closely resembled that of Diana in Ephesus. It was wild, frenzied, and hysterical as religions go, but apparently offered little opposition to Christianity. The Asiatic Cybele had been identified by the Greeks either with Persephone or, more often, with Demeter (Mother Earth). From 1958 forward, both Harvard University and Cornell have sponsored annual archaeological expeditions to the ruins of ancient Sardis. Their work uncovered what has come to be recognized as the most impressive synagogue in the western diaspora discovered from antiquity.

This building contained very elaborate mosaic pavings, geometrical floor designs, in spite of the fact that the Jews typically avoided representations of people and animals in their art work due to the second of the Ten Commandments (Exod. 20:4). Pieces of floral designs and representations of a camel, birds, and fish were found by the archaeologists. There are also colored stone wall decorations and numerous inscriptions, some in Hebrew. Interestingly, many spolia (reused sculptures and blocks) were found in the digging. Apparently a good number of pieces were salvaged from the sanctuary of Cybele (the indigenous Lydian goddess) and employed in one of the reconstructions of the Jewish place of worship. Inscriptions from as early as 213 BC and identifying the source as "in the sanctuary of the Mother," positively identifying the source of the blocks as the most famous temple of the ancient Lydian Sardis, that of Cybele.

The remains of marble slabs and pillars and massive doorways point to a structure of major importance and of grand proportions. Huge stone piers supported the roof of the main hall at a height of about fourteen meters above the floor. A surrounding pool was originally paved with flat stones, probably marble. The main hall of assembly was over fifty meters long and large enough to accommodate nearly a thousand people. It was originally constructed in the 200's AD and subsequently remodeled in the fourth, fifth, and sixth centuries. The size of this structure would attest to the existence of a very substantial Jewish community during the early Christian era. Donors whose names appear on the walls of the place held the honorary title of "citizens of Sardis," and several of them are identified as city councilors or holders of other government offices [cf. D. G. Mitten, *The Ancient Synagogue of Sardis* (New York: Committee to Preserve the Ancient Synagogue of Sardis, 1965); and A. R. Seager, "The Building History of the Sardis Synagogue," *American Journal of Archaeology* 76 (1972): 425-435].

The abiding influence of the extravagantly wealthy Lydian King Croesus reached even into the later history of the town. The one noteworthy characteristic of the people of the city was that they were notoriously loose-living, as well as famously pleasure and luxury-loving. Even on pagan lips, the city's name was identified with contempt and decadence, slack and effeminate living. Life had been too easy, and it had grown flabby and had sunk into a state of lethargy. That was life in the city in general, and apparently it affected the church as well. The church was not menaced by any peril, but it was in serious danger of being ruined by its own lassitude and lethargy.

John's letter to them is silent about any pressure on this church from pagan religion. Here no outward signs betrayed the silent inner workings of Satan. Here there were no Jewish accusers, no apostolic imposters, no fraternizing Nicolaitans, and no "Jezebel" caught up in prophetic ecstasy to draw them away from the Lord. This was a church of which, apparently, almost everyone spoke well. It was the perfect model of inoffensive Christianity, but a congregation of people who could not distinguish between the peace of inoffensive well-being and the peace of spiritual death.

This church had the reputation of being alive. Things are not always what they seem. Occasionally there exists a congregation that has a good name, but reality belies the reputation. This was the case with the church that met in Sardis. From all outward appearances, everything was good. But this congregation was like a corpse that lies in state in a coffin at the funeral home. As far as appearances are concerned, everything looked attractive on the exterior. If you had checked for a pulse, however, it would be apparent that something was very, very wrong.

This church was dead. The Lord said so. We are not talking here about what people thought about it, or even how they were perceived by outsiders, nor yet how they perceived themselves. Jesus passed judgment on them and said that the church as a whole was dead. It was still above ground, but someone needed to preach its funeral and put it into the soil, because for all practical purposes it was deceased. No doubt, this is the most horrible judgment our Lord could have leveled against them. It would be difficult to conceive of a worse one. The lesson for the modern congregation of the Lord's people is that this is a possible scenario for any church, and it would be wise to avoid it at all costs. Whatever else may come our way, let us not fall into the trap of allowing ourselves to fall victim to any of the circumstances that prevailed with the congregation at Sardis!

This church was at peace. There is no warning here about false teachers or fractious trouble makers. This congregation apparently was at peace with itself and the world, but, as William Barclay in his *Letters to the Seven Churches* wrote, this peace can be altogether deceptive in nature:

> In any church there is nothing to be so much desired as peace; but in any church there is nothing to be so much feared as the peace which is the peace of death, the peace of languorous lethargy, the peace which had descended on Sardis and its church (Barclay, 72).

This church was living off yesterday's accomplishments. The Lord told them to remember how they had come into possession of the gospel, how they energetically embraced it, and kept its precepts at the first. Repentance was essential now to get them back on the track they first had followed. Churches cannot live in the past. They must press on toward higher and nobler things. The work goes on from one generation to the next, and God's people must respond to the new challenges that a new era brings. Concentrating too heavily on the rich history that any church may have had in its past may cause it to relax and drift off into oblivion, while life goes on and the world continues to turn, but we need to understand that the Lord notices and takes account of such a view on our part. What the brethren of another era accomplished may be impressive, but that has nothing to do with the people of the present time. They may have turned the world upside down, but this does not affect the world of our own day. We must each give an accounting for the deeds done here and now, for that is the only time we have. Others must answer for yesteryear, whether for good or ill. It is the same for churches.

This church had a few names that had not defiled their garments and they would walk with Christ in glory. This is a very encouraging thought, and it is helpful to appreciate the force of it. Even in the midst of so much that had been lost over time, so much wreckage, desolation, and ruin, we are glad to know that there were some people who had remained faithful to God through it all. The church was dead, but there were yet some alive in its midst. Jesus said He would reward them for their faithfulness: "they shall walk with Me in white; for they are worthy." What a breath of fresh air! This should give every lover of God hope to stay steadfast even as so many around us are caving in to the pressure and slipping into the lethargy of the people of Sardis. Fear not: you will not be lost in the crowd of those who have abandoned hope and given up. The Lord knows those who are His (2 Tim. 2:19), and He will not forsake those who have remained strong in spite of what was happening in the unsteady hearts and disloyal lives of those all around them. In the end, "every tub must sit on its own bottom," as the old saying goes. So even when others fall about us, we must continue on in faithful service until the Lord returns.

3. *The Letter to the church at Philadelphia (3:7-13).*

And to the messenger of the church in Philadelphia write: "These things says He who is holy, He who is true, He who has the key of David, He who opens and none shall close, and who closes and none is able to open: I know your works (behold, I have set before you a door opened, which no one can close), that you have very little strength, nevertheless you have kept My word, and did not deny My name. Behold, I will make those of the synagogue of Satan—of those who say that they are Jews, and they are not, but lie—behold, I will make them come and bow down at your feet, and to know that I have loved you. Because you kept the word of My patience, I also will keep you from the hour of trial, that hour which is to come upon the whole world, to try those who dwell on the earth. I

The Letters to the Seven Churches of Asia (Part 2) 3:7-13

come quickly: hold fast what you have, that no one take your crown. He who overcomes, I will make him a pillar in the temple of My God, and he shall go out of it no more; and I will write upon him the name of My God, and the name of the city of My God, the new Jerusalem, which comes down out of heaven from My God, and My own new name. He who has an ear, let him hear what the Spirit says to the churches" (Rev. 3:7-13).

Philadelphia was probably the youngest of the cities of the seven churches, founded between 189 and 138 BC. The location of ancient Philadelphia commanded the high ground on the south side of the river Cogamis, a tributary of the Hermus. It lay some twenty-seven miles (44 km) west-northwest of Sardis and forty-eight miles (77 km) from Laodicea. It was situated where the borders of Mysia, Lydia, and Phrygia came together. It was founded especially as a mission city to expand the Greek culture and language to Lydia and Phrygia. Eventually they were so successful in this endeavor that by AD 19 the Lydians had forgotten their own language and were all but Greeks in that sense.

The site of the ancient town is today to be found in the Kuzucay valley, near the bottom of Mount Bozdad, in modern Turkey's province of Manisa. Behind the city stand volcanic cliffs which the locals describe as "inkwells." The city was founded in about 189 BC by Pergamon King Eumenes and given its name in honor of the love that he had for his brother Attalus II (159-138 BC), who would be his successor on the throne. Attalus' loyalty earned him the nickname, "Philadelphos," literally meaning "one who loves his brother."

The place was also called Decapolis, on account of the fact that it was considered one of the ten cities of the plain. In the first century AD it was referred to as Neo-kaisaria. During the reign of Vespasian it was called Flavia. In addition to these alternative designations, it was sometimes referred to as "Little Athens" because of its many pagan temples and other public buildings which adorned it. Its modern name is Ala-shehir, perhaps a corruption of the Turkish words meaning "city of God." Attalus III Philometer, the last of the Attalid kings of Pergamum, lacked a royal heir for his throne at the time of his demise, so when he died his bequest was that his kingdom which included the city be given to the Roman Empire.

Hence, the province of Asia was created in 129 BC by bringing together Ionia and Attalus' former kingdom.

Philadelphia was of commercial importance because of its strategic location on the imperial post route from Rome via Troas. Moreover, trade routes from Mysia, Lydia, and Phrygia all passed directly through Philadelphia. It enjoyed considerable prosperity on this account, and because of its import as an agricultural and industrial center. A great volcanic plain lay to the north of the city. It was called by the Greeks *katakekaumenē*, the "burnt land." This made for excellent grape and wine country, but it also made the region the victim of many earthquakes and tremors. The most devastating of these occurred in AD 17 when twelve cities of Asia were leveled. Philadephia was probably the worst of the lot. When it was rebuilt with the assistance of the Roman government, in gratitude toward the emperor, the city changed its name to Neocaesarea, "the new town of Caesar." No doubt in reference to this recent occurrence, along with a more recent change back to her old name, the Lord promised His people at Philadephia, "I will write upon him My own new name" (3:12). Their town had so many different names over its history that it was difficult to keep up with them all. But the Lord intended to give the Christians of the city a name that they would be proud of and that they would be able to wear into eternity.

Many temples dotted the landscape of the city, but because it was located in the wine-growing region, the worship of Dionysus, the great Olympian god of fertility and wine, was its chief pagan cult. He was also called Bacchus by the Greeks and Romans. Orgiastic worship of this deity seems to have been first established in Thrace and to have spread throughout the world from that center. It sometimes even involved human sacrifices, but the most characteristic aspect was intoxication and drunkenness. Emperor worship did not come to this city as an aspect of the common life until the third century of the Common Era.

Due to a series of ancient earthquakes, there is not much left in modern times of the city of Philadelphia from the days of the apostle John and the Lord's letter to the church there. Archaeological work has been limited to the devastated foundation stones, a Roman-era city wall and a few Roman columns that still stand. It is indeed a sad testimony to what once stood so proudly at the site.

The letter to the church at Philadelphia emphasizes the following points:

Jesus portrays Himself to the church as holy and true, one who has the key of David to open where none can shut, and can shut so that no man can open. Since the principal adversary in this instance is a synagogue of Jews, the Lord appeals to the ancient Davidic promises as referring to Himself. David was the king of Israel whose dynasty was imposed upon the nation for perpetuity. A "key" symbolized the power to open and shut. This was the promise made to king Messiah: "And the key of the house of David will I lay upon His shoulder; and He shall open, and none shall shut; and He shall shut, and none shall open" (cf. Isa. 22:22). So this represents a clear claim to the place of Messiah for Himself in the face of the Jewish challenge and opposition. Notwithstanding the Jewish denial of His kingship, Christ declares His sovereignty over them and promises that He will judge them and vindicate the church and its members who are so readily dismissed by them.

Jesus declares that the door is open: opportunity awaits them. No doubt many of these Christians would have described their situation as almost hopeless; they deemed themselves outnumbered and seemingly powerless. The Lord informs them in this diminutive letter to them that they have mischaracterized their circumstance. He declares that they still have a "little power." Furthermore, He says that they have kept His word and have refused to deny His name. So, clearly all is not lost and they are not left hopeless. We must never give in to the perception that all is lost. The words of Christ to the church in Philadelphia teach us this important lesson. It is never actually hopeless in reality, even though it seems frequently so as we may perceive it at the time. God always has the potential to make for us a way of escape (1 Cor. 10:13), and it is incumbent upon us to look about for it until we find it. It is there, we just need to search until we find it. The only thing that is inescapable is the inevitable judgment of God on the wicked (Heb. 2:3; 12:25; 1 Tim. 5:3).

Jesus promises that He will eventually judge their enemies. He calls them a "synagogue of Satan," and says that their claims to be the true people of God are mere lies. The church is the true Israel of God today (Gal. 6:16). The Jewish people have, in the main, rejected the Lord's Christ.

In this instance, the Lord promises this humble church that eventually He will force their enemies to come and fall down at their feet. They will then know that the Lord loves the church and has genuinely given His life for its redemption. The Jewish synagogue in that city had become a tool of the Devil, in spite of their regular worship services, the preaching from the Hebrew Bible, and their pitiful platitudes. If we find ourselves in opposition to the Lord Jesus Christ and we use our powers to destroy what He has built, as did this satanic synagogue, we have become an enemy of the good, and in the end we shall be judged precisely as we have lived and died. The outcome of this will not be attractive.

Jesus promises them relief from the hour of trial which is coming upon the whole world, because they have already suffered enough at the hands of their Jewish foes. As previously mentioned, Philadelphia was mostly immune from the plague of emperor worship which so troubled the other cities of the region. Pagan religion was more interested in partying and enjoying a gay lifestyle rather than pushing a particular religious agenda on others who lived around them. The hate-filled Jews were their principle opponents in this town. Moreover, this church for now had endured a tremendous amount of persecution at the hands of their powerful Jewish enemies. So the Lord would show them mercy during the next round of oppression and not permit them to be tested above their ability to resist (1 Cor. 10:13). Is it not interesting to note that while others in adjacent cities were experiencing relative peace previously and the church in Philadelphia was suffering at the hands of hateful Jewish opponents, in the years ahead while several of the other congregations were suffering terribly on account of pagan dedication to the emperor cult, the saints of Philadelphia would enjoy relative peace since their city was not a center of emperor worship? And yet, this was the Lord's promise to them.

Jesus promises, "I will write upon him the name of My God, and the name of the city of My God, the new Jerusalem . . . and My own new name." The city of Philadelphia, as earlier noted, had much more experience than most with "new names." It was given at various times in its history a number of "new names" in order to honor those whom it found worthy of special recognition. If archaeological evidence were available for confirmation, it would not be surprising to find also that the pillars of the temples of the city had emblazoned upon them the names of special individuals whom it honored for their service to the city ("I will make him a pillar in the house of My God," v. 11). The Lord intended also to confer upon the faithful saints the divine names as proof of God's ownership and recognition of their special spiritual achievement. Faithfulness in desperate times is not something to be minimized. Rather, it must be recognized and rewarded!

Jesus tells them that their crown is within reach. He also urges them to hold fast to their crown, to see that no one takes it away from them. So far so good for this church; this is the message the Lord sends to them. There are no condemnations here. There are no false teachers who have made inroads among them. They have not lost their fervor. They have not given up, but it was still important for them to hold on till the end. They must wait patiently until the Lord's return. They have some strength left. And they need to remain strong in the face of whatever comes their way. They must not lose their grasp on that precious crown! That is the Lord's advice to them, and we would do well to heed that advice ourselves.

4. *The Letter to the church at Laodicea (3:14-22).*

And to the messenger of the church in Laodicea write: "These things says the Amen, the faithful and true martyr, the beginning of the creation of God: I know your works, that you are neither cold nor hot: I would that you were either cold or hot. So because you are lukewarm, and neither hot nor cold, I will vomit you out of My mouth. Because you say, I am rich, and have accumulated riches, and have need of nothing; and know not that you are wretched and miserable and poor and blind and naked: I counsel you to buy from Me gold refined by fire, that you may become truly rich; and white garments, that you may clothe yourself, and that the shame of your nakedness be not made evident; and eye-salve to anoint your eyes, that you may see. As many as I love, I reprove and chasten: be zealous therefore, and repent. Behold, I stand at the door and knock: if any man hears My voice and opens the door, I will come in to him, and will dine with him, and he with Me. He who overcomes, I will grant him the honor of sitting down with Me in My throne, as I also overcame, and sat down with My Father in His throne. He who has an ear, let him hear what the Spirit says to the churches" (Rev. 3:14-22).

Laodicea was one of the cities in the Valley of the Lycus River, a tributary of the Maeander. It was located in the extreme southwest of Phrygia, an ancient district in west-central Anatolia (modern Turkey). The region was named after a people whom the Greeks called Phryges and who had dominated that sector of Asia Minor between the collapse of the great Hittite Empire in the 12th century BC and the ascendancy of the Lydians in the seventh century BC. Herodotus of Halicarnassus noted that Phrygians were in fact Thracian Brygians who had once crossed the Hellespont and settled in the area (*Histories*, 7.73). And this seemed to have been confirmed by the fact that their language is related to those of the southern Balkan Peninsula. This migration appears to have occurred in about the ninth century, when Gordium was founded. It is possible, however, that the first Phrygians were already in Anatolia in the eleventh century, because the Assyrian king Tiglath-Pileser I (1114-1076 BC) refers to the "Muški" he defeated near the Euphrates, and this name was later applied to the Phrygians.

Of course, it is possible that the Assyrians used the same word to describe two quite distinct ethnic groups, but it is also feasible that early Phrygian raiders indeed reached the Euphrates. Some have contended that these early raiders may have been the inhabitants of the city of Troy (Ilion or Ilios; modern Turkish city of Hisarlik) during the VIIb time period (destroyed by fire ca. 1250-1200 BC). At any rate, by the eighth century BC, Phrygians had settled everywhere in Anatolia, one group moving inland as far as Tyana in Cappadocia, another establishing a kingdom near Gordium, and a third remaining near the Hellespont, and founding the city of Dascylium. The most famous king of the Phrygians was Midas, known from Greek legends and perhaps also from contemporary Assyrian sources, which refer to an Anatolian ruler whom they refer to as *Mit-ta-a*. In 696/695 king Midas committed suicide after he lost a major battle (Strabo, *Geography*, 1.3.21). The sudden and unexpected loss of such a monumental figure left the region in perplexity.

After a half century of political and societal confusion, in which small Phrygian principalities survived, western Turkey was reunited by the Lydians, whose first great king was Gyges (ca. 680-ca. 644 BC). By the time of Alyattes (ca. 600-560), Phrygia was no longer a political reality, but more of a geographical designation associated with whatever Empire into which it was subsumed in the later ages. Thus, it was conquered by Cyrus the Great (ca. 547) and became a satrapy of the Achaemenid Empire, and in 334 was captured by Parmenion the Macedonian for Alexander and subsequently ruled by the Seleucid kings of Asia. Still later it was taken over by the Attalid rulers of Pergamon, and eventually by the Romans.

Phrygia was the least Greek of all the regions of the province; it still spoke the local language and was relatively little affected by Greek ways. This was relatively rare in a world where Greek ways and culture, not to mention the ever present language, predominated. The site itself was an almost square plateau some one hundred feet above the valley floor. The flat hill of the city was protected by two smaller rivers, the ancient Asopus and the Caprus, both tributaries of the Lycus. To the south of the city lay the high mountains Salbacus and Cadmus.

It was located on the ancient highway leading up from Ephesus through the Maeander and Lycus valleys toward the east and ultimately to Syria. The city of Colossae was only ten miles to the east while Hierapolis was a mere six miles north (see Col. 2:1; 4:13-16). Laodicea was founded about 250 BC by Antiochus II who named it after his wife Laodice. Josephus tells us that Antiochus III transplanted 2000 Jewish families from Babylonia to Lydia and Phrygia. These families were led by former Jewish military leaders who had served Antiochus faithfully in Babylonia and Mesopotamia and were placed there to stabilize that region at a time when the loyalties of the Phrygian and Lydian people were unclear. For the most part Laodicea remained under the control of the Seleucids until the Battle of Magnesia in 189 BC, when the Romans and Pergamenes drove the Seleucids out of western Anatolia. With the treaty of Apameia in 188, the Romans handed over control of the territory to the Pergamon kingdom, where it remained until the death of Attalus III in 133. After 133 BC it became the property of the Roman Empire and was made the center of a judicial district *(conventus)* to which Hierapolis and Cibyra among other cities of the district belonged. Under Roman peace and protection it became a truly wealthy city.

Laodicea was prosperous because it served as a textile production center as well as a center for banking. Many wealthy merchants made their homes in the city. Also, important trade routes ran through Laodicea leading to Ephesus, Sardis, and Smyrna. The extent of its wealth is evidenced by the fact that when it was flattened by an earthquake in AD 60 it did not require help from the Romans for its reconstruction. It is also illustrated by an incident in 62 BC, when the proconsul Flaccus seized more than twenty pounds of gold that was being sent by Jews in Laodicea to the Temple in Jerusalem. This impressive amount not only reflects upon the size of the Jewish community of the city, but also their great wealth.

The place was noted for its particularly fertile soil and excellent grazing for sheep, whose raven-black wool made her famous throughout the world (Strabo 12.578). Special garments and carpets were woven in the city and guilds of craftsmen, especially fullers and cloak-makers, were active in the town. Extensive financial operations and banking enterprises also brought massive wealth to the city and its inhabitants. Laodicea even struck its own coins from the second century BC on, with iconographic references to the local river gods and their cults.

The most important pagan religion was veneration of Men Karou, worshipped as Zeus by the Greek inhabitants of the place. Pliny explains that the city was known as Diospolis, "the city of Zeus," during the Classical period, but little is known about it during that early era. Later the city was known as Rhoas. In connection with the temple of Zeus, there grew up a famous school of medicine. It followed the teachings of Herophilos (330-250 BC) who, on the principle that compound diseases require compound medicines, began using a strange mixture of elements to produce them in order to deal with various diseases. An ointment for the treatment of the ears and another containing a powder for the treatment of visual issues both had their origins at Laodicea's school of medicine. The physician Galen makes mention of both of these concoctions.

The Jewish community, on the other hand, even though it possessed fabulous wealth, was relatively weak and without much political influence in the city. They had fallen out of official favor in 62 BC when, as mentioned earlier, by order of the governor Flaccus, the annual contributions that were sent to Jerusalem were seized and sent to Rome instead. If they had possessed more political prestige, such a thing would never have happened. The fact that they fell victim to such a public humiliation and a very sensational robbery of their gifts is certainly an indication that they were virtually powerless to help themselves in the city of Laodicea.

As regards archaeological activity at the site of the ancient city, early surface surveys of the ruins of the city were conducted by the Italians in the mid-1990s, and preliminary work at the location followed. In 2002, however, the site was assigned to the Turkish authorities, and the head of the archaeology department at Pamukkale University, Celal Şimşek, directed the work thereafter. As M. R. Fairchild observed, "The remains that are being uncovered at Laodicea exhibit a city that was furnished with a level of opulence seldom seen outside of capital cities. For a mid-sized city, this was remarkable" (Fairchild, 35-36). Many of the ancient city's main streets were supplied with a subsurface drainage system and were flanked by colonnaded porticoes. The city was outfitted with at least five decorative fountains (*nymphaea*) and an elaborate water distribution system. It had four public bath complexes and five agoras. Laodicea had six city gates and two monumental gates, an *odeon* (a small theater) or *bouleuterion* (town council house), two theaters and the largest stadium in Anatolia. The city boasted several temples and as many as twenty churches and chapels. As Fairchild further summarized the discoveries, "In short, Laodicea was affluent and exceeded most cities of its size in terms of monumental structures and sumptuous assets" (Fairchild, 36).

The requirement for the citizenry to participate in the imperial cult was enforced mainly by local officials in the various cities and towns of the region. The large cities of Asia Minor were in competition with one another to act as chief proponents of the cult in order to enjoy the numerous imperial benefactions which were extended to them when they demonstrated commitment and loyalty to the emperors. Ultimately this would translate into funds for all sorts of civic improvements as well as prestigious distinctions that a grateful emperor had the authority to confer upon those cities that showed him sufficient approbation. One of the most significant of these recognitions was the honor of being designated a *neokoros* of the emperor. This honorific title ("temple-sweeper" or "keeper") meant that the city was made the special guardian of an imperial temple dedicated to worship of the divinity of the Roman emperor. As we have already observed, inscriptions from the large, prestigious cities of Asia, such as Ephesus, Smyrna, and Pergamon, have been found which boast of the many times they had been thus honored. Interestingly, coins minted in Laodicea indicate that this mid-sized city was also given the honor of an imperial temple for the emperor Domitian.

However, since Domitian was the first emperor to proclaim himself a living god, this act of defiance against traditional Roman belief and practice angered the Senate as well as many of the most influential citizens of the Empire. They saw him as an arrogant megalomaniac, and his actions in this regard as disreputable. Emperor worship was common in the Roman Empire prior to his reign, but it was commonly believed that the emperors became gods only at their death, a concept known as *apotheosis*. This was already a settled belief in Roman culture, but this particular ruler was not satisfied with it. Suetonius explained that Domitian went so far as to describe himself with divine epithets such as "Lord" and "God." And, of course, these were titles which Christians reserved for Jesus Christ and Him alone. Fortunately, because Domitian was so hated by the senate for his many serious vices, that grand body issued a decree of *memoriae damnatio* following his assassination. The effect of this decree was that his memory was to be forgotten. In essence, he was erased from the historical record of the nation. This was a formal state judgment that was passed at various times in the senate regarding traitors and other persons of ill repute who brought dishonor upon the Empire (Fairchild, 37). But his actions while he yet lived brought this issue to the fore and forced the Christian community to choose between Caesar and Christ. It also brought the church unneeded attention to its unique beliefs that was not especially wholesome in terms of its societal repercussions.

Apparently the church at Laodicea during this period of persecution and difficulty in the other cities of the region did not offer much resistance to the forces that attempted to pressure them into compliance with regulations and practices that gave other Christians pause for reflection and even for resistance. They were focused on their financial and social status, but mostly on their money. The Lord's letter to this church threatens them with utter rejection on account of their remarkable complacency and self-satisfaction:

Christ addresses them in powerful and definitive terminology. He calls himself the "Amen!" Jesus is the final affirmation, the one who has the last say about the condition of the human spirit. The Lord judges the church and gives His approval or withholds it whenever necessary. He also describes Himself as "the faithful and true witness" or "martyr." His testimony is decisive. His martyrdom proved that He was little concerned with this material world and what it had to offer. What others say may prove unimportant, but what He testifies concerning men and churches is momentous and substantive. Lastly, He says that He is "the beginning of the creation of God." Clearly this is meant to declare that He is the one who initiated creation. He is the Creator God. He owns all that is by divine right of creation. The entire cosmos is His invention, fabricated according to His design, manufactured by His expertise, and formed by His mighty hand. Men are His and churches are His. Thus, His judgment is all that matters. What they think about themselves is of little concern. What Jesus thinks about them should be their *only* concern!

Christ informs them that He is aware of their works, and judges them to be "neither cold nor hot." They are a tepid congregation. Lukewarm. They are not cold, but then again, they are not hot either. What a sad state of affairs! The Savior says that He would prefer them to be either cold or hot. Even cold was preferable, but they are neither. The figure that He uses to illustrate his point is transparent. We all like drinks that are either cold or hot. We usually like our coffee hot. And we prefer iced tea cold. But if the coffee has sat around too long before it is drunk, it will need to be warmed up again, or else thrown out and replaced. If the ice has melted from our tea and it has become lukewarm, we refuse to drink it. Tepid drinks are never our first choice. In the end, the Lord told the Christians of Laodicea that He would "spew them out" of His mouth like a tepid liquid that is repugnant to Him. They made Him sick! What a distasteful image to have to read about yourself. And yet there it is on the pages of the Word of God for all to see and know. We can only hope that these words shattered their self-image and caused them to reassess and do some serious reflection about their spiritual condition. Hopefully also, they did some course correcting.

The word of Christ to them is that their riches are their downfall. The Lord's judgment of this church is harsh. "Because you say, 'I am rich, I have prospered, and I need nothing,' when in fact you are wretched, pitiable, poor, blind, and naked" (v. 17). In all respects their physical needs were satisfied and they had need of nothing that the material world could supply, but their superfluity had bred in them a spirit of complacency, contentment, and ease. And this was a fatal spiritual condition. In reality they were more pitiable than the poorest of the poor. At least the poor know that they have needs that are not being met. This rich and refined church had unmet needs they did not know about, so their condition was far more dire. They were comparable to a patient with undiagnosed cancer. It is eating away at the vitals whilst the victim goes about his daily activities without a clue.

Christ will be their healing and deliverance, if they will but heed His advice. "I counsel you to buy from me gold that is refined by fire, so that you may be truly rich, and white garments so that you may clothe yourself and the shame of your nakedness may not be seen, and salve to anoint your eyes, so that you may see" (v. 18). Some of these Christians may have come by their riches through the sale of fine clothing or the local eye-salve for which this area was famous. The Lord informs them that He is the true source of that which provides for the spiritual health of men. They needed sorely to pay attention to His advice and seek a cure from Him.

This word from the Lord was hard to bear, so Jesus assures them of His continuing love: "as many as I love, I rebuke and chasten; be zealous therefore, and repent." One can only imagine how shaken these brethren would have been to have heard such painful words of judgment delivered to them from the hand of John the apostle at the mouth of Jesus Christ Himself. Still, it is better for them to hear it now than in the final Judgment Day! At the same time, it is indeed encouraging to know that the Lord had not lost His love for them in spite of their precarious spiritual condition. This surely ought to be an encouragement to us also. No matter how far we stray from Him, we always know that He loves us still and will never give up on us until our chances have all been exhausted. At that point, and only then, our choices become final. It should also be noted that Jesus urges them toward repentance. The Christian who sins must turn away from his sins, confess and abandon them, and ask God for forgiveness and blessing (see 1 John 1:6-9). There is no automatic process that removes sins from God's people. Some people place their trust in such a process, but that concept is not taught in the Bible. Forgiveness is preceded by repentance. There is no way around it. That is precisely why Jesus told the Christians at Laodicea to "be zealous therefore, and repent."

Christ pictured Himself as standing at the door, knocking, asking for entry into their hearts and lives. Apparently their lives were filled with all of the finest things that money could buy them and the world could give them, but the Lord was missing from their inventory. He stood outside the door, hoping they would let Him in. It is very difficult for us to imagine such a portrait of reality when we are describing a "church of Christ" and her members, but Jesus deemed it perfectly appropriate. He viewed Himself as an outsider in terms of this church, and stood without knocking and requesting plaintively that they would open the door to Him. We would not ever want such a characterization to be appropriate for us today. Jesus belonged inside the church and inside of the hearts of the members of that church, and yet, there He stood on the outside, asking to be invited inside!

Wealth is on the one hand a blessing from God, but sometimes it can prove to be the wrecking bar of Satan suited to destroy all that we hold dear! "And Jesus said to His disciples, 'Truly, I say to you, only with difficulty will a rich person enter the kingdom of heaven. Again I tell you, it is easier for a camel to go through the eye of a needle than for a rich person to enter the kingdom of God'" (Matt. 19:23-24).

How much superior to this sad state of affairs is the Lord's recommendation for them. He wants them rather to enjoy the pleasantries of the relationship described by Him here: sitting down to fellowship with Him in intimate fashion as good friends have an enjoyable meal together, converse pleasantly, smile and laugh together. When a believer becomes host to the risen Christ, he gives Him full access to the home of his soul. Our Lord, according to His promise, awaits only the response to His knock and an opened door to bestow upon us the blessing of His presence. Moreover, there is also repeated here the promise of the faithful believer sharing in Christ's reign as the Son who sits at the right hand of His Father. This reward was promised also in another form in the letter directed to the congregation at Thyatira.

Chapter Three

Cycle One: The Seal Sequence (4:1-8:1)

The astonishing drama which is to be gradually unfolded in a series of remarkable visions given to the prophet John now commences with the opening scene. The beginning is magnificent in its scope, conception, and execution. As the curtain is drawn aside, John permits us to gaze upon the incomparable glories of the supramundane world, into heaven itself, and to catch a glimpse of the majesty of God. Too, there is a portrait of the cosmic mystery of redemption. This opening scene sets the stage and adjusts the tone for the entirety of this grand drama. The clear purpose of the author is to set forth in the language of splendor and grandiosity the sovereignty of the God of heaven. All of the rest of the scenes to follow will be permeated with the spirit and power of this superlative vision and its message.

As the curtain comes up, the reader is made to see something of an important reality: *the things which are.* Not merely the things which are in this world, but the things which are in the eternal world. It will be recalled that the author, in describing his commission to write, had said that he had been told to "write therefore the things which you saw, and the things which are, and the things which shall come to pass hereafter" (cf. 1:19). Those things described in this scene have to do with timeless eternity. God is eternal. Christ is eternal, the Lamb pictured here is the Lamb slain from the foundation of the world. So, what is described in this vision is beyond time and space.

This opening scene, therefore, fixes the character of the Revelation as having to do with the unfolding of a cosmic drama, a timeless struggle, which belongs in part to history, but in fact is not limited to history. The author takes us up to a high mountain, as it were, and bids us peer into the mysteries of the infinite, into the realm of the divine. The division between time and eternity, space and infinity, fade into nothingness as the eyes of the Spirit are opened and the glories of the world of the Spirit are revealed. From this point on, the visions of the book will carry us back and forth seamlessly and effortlessly.

The Revelation is a book that showcases some of the great theological ideas that are taught in the Bible. Doctrinally they are scattered everywhere in Scripture, but here in the Apocalypse these are painted with broad brushstrokes on a visionary canvas which makes them difficult to avoid and hard to misunderstand. At once here we are confronted with God, Christ, and the plan for redeeming man. These ideas are not stated in abstract terms as Paul would have written them. Even so, they are no less theological and no less dogmatic or doctrinaire. They are presented as remarkable pictures and startling symbols. Instead of a statement to the effect that God is the great First Cause, Himself uncaused, and sovereign over the whole universe, we see Him pictured in majesty upon a throne receiving the homage of the twenty-four elders and the four living creatures who are in His presence in the court of heaven. The twenty-four elders represent mankind while the four "living creatures" represent all living things outside the realm of man. Together they stand for the entirety of the living creation. This group is pictured worshipping their Maker. There is no statement of the sublime doctrine of redemption given here, but there is a portrait of "a Lamb standing, as though it had been slain."

Hence, any study of the theology of the book of Revelation would show an absolute consistency and perfect harmony with the theological ideas which permeate the remainder of the New Testament, and yet it would be evident that this unveiling of these same truths is absolutely unique in its manner of presentation. This is particularly important because Revelation is the only apocalyptic work in the literature of the New Testament, and it is radically different in its style and presentation from all the rest of the writings found in the canon of inspired Scripture. At the same time, it does not depart from the major themes found throughout the rest of the Bible. It just employs a different way of communicating them.

A. The Throne Scene: A Vision of the Court of Heaven (4:1-11)

After these things I saw, and behold, a door opened in heaven, and the first voice that I heard, a voice like a trumpet speaking with me, saying,

> *"Come up here, and I will show you the things which must come to pass hereafter." Immediately I was in the Spirit: and behold, there was a throne set in heaven, and One sitting upon the throne; and He that sat was to look upon like a jasper stone and a carnelian: and there was a rainbow round about the throne, like an emerald to look upon. And round about the throne were twenty-four thrones: and on the thrones I saw twenty-four elders sitting, clothed in white garments; and on their heads there were crowns of gold. And out of the throne came forth lightning flashes and voices and thunders. And there were seven lamps of fire burning before the throne, which are the seven Spirits of God; and before the throne, as it were a sea of glass like a crystal; and in the midst of the throne, and round about the throne, there were four living creatures full of eyes in front and behind. And the first creature was like a lion, and the second creature like a calf, and the third creature had a face like that of a man, and the fourth creature was like a flying eagle. And the four living creatures, each one of them having six wings, are full of eyes round about and within: and they have no rest day or night, saying, "Holy, holy, holy, is the Lord God, the Almighty, who was and who is and who is to come." And whenever the living creatures give glory and honor and thanks to Him who sits on the throne, to Him who lives for ever and ever, the twenty-four elders fall down before Him who sits on the throne, and worship Him who lives for ever and ever, and cast their crowns before the throne, saying, "Worthy are You, our Lord and our God, to receive the glory and the honor and the power: for You created all things, and because of Your will they existed, and were created"* (Rev. 4:1-11).

John begins his depiction of this heavenly scene by saying that "a door was opened in heaven" (4:1) and that immediately he was in the Spirit (v. 2). The Revelation of John is precisely what these two verses describe. They are a portrait of heavenly things, revelations from God Himself through the agency of the Spirit for the comfort and solace of suffering Christians. What they need so desperately, heaven itself provides by means of these picturesque visions. John is told, "Come up here and I will show you what must happen after these things" (v. 1). The apostle was not the only one who was given the honor of peering into heaven. It will be recalled that in a dream the patriarch Jacob was shown a stairway reaching up to heaven, from whence the Lord Himself addressed him. Jacob observed, "This is none other than the house of God, this is the gate of heaven" (Gen. 28:7). In addition, the prophets Isaiah, Ezekiel, and Daniel were shown God's celestial throne (cf. Isa. 6:1; Ezek. 1:26; Dan. 7:9). So, such a vision is very much in keeping with the ancient prophetic tradition of the Old Testament.

What is the purpose of John seeing the vision? As a fitting introduction to the series of visions which are soon to follow, two very special visions, one of God and the other of Christ, in all of their heavenly majesty, splendor, and power, are depicted. At the time of writing, God and Christ may have seemed to be very far removed from the earth and its inhabitants, who during the present evil age are under the domination of Satan and his demonic forces, both supernatural and human. Suffering saints need reassurance and encouragement. Through these visions, the readers are assured that God and Christ are not unaware of their desperate plight, are not without deep concern about their sorrows and tribulations; nor are they powerless to rescue them from their enemies and to save them out of this age where evil seems to be so predominant. On the contrary, these two scenes portraying them as they do in all of their majestic might are a solemn pledge that very soon they will intervene in the affairs of this world, will defeat and overpower Satan and his followers, will finally terminate his dominion, and then will institute a new age "in which righteousness dwells" (2 Pet. 3:13).

John identifies a "voice" as being the speaker in both of these visions: "And the first voice which I had heard as a trumpet talking to me said. . . ." It is worthwhile to consider the fact that when John encounters the divine, he avoids identifying either God or Jesus by name. Thus, the report of his first meeting on the Lord's Day lacks the name of Jesus, even though the reader is absolutely certain who it is that he is picturing in the vision (1:10-20). In the present instance also he identifies Jesus by calling Him a voice like a trumpet. The reference to the trumpet is not only a connecting link for the two visions, but it has solemn connotations as well. A Jew would immediately react to this sound because it meant that something important was to be heard. The trumpet sounded at the giving of the Decalogue (Exod. 19:16, 19; 20:18), at the beginning of the New Year, and the onset of the Feast of Trumpets (Lev. 23:24). In addition, John was well aware that the trumpet sound was to introduce the coming of the Lord (Matt. 24:31; 1 Thess. 4:16). He knew when he heard "a voice like a trumpet" that he was about to receive a new revelation that was of divine origin (Kistemaker, 183).

And so, this cycle begins with a scene capturing the essence of the divine throne room (Chapters 4-5), wherein God is pictured on His throne surrounded by twenty-four elders on twenty-four thrones. Seven lamps of fire are burning, which are said to picture the seven spirits of God. Four living creatures full of eyes (lion, young bull, man, eagle) also appear, with six wings each, reminiscent of the vision in Isaiah 6:2.

The message of this vision is transparent. It is that the God of heaven, if He could only be seen with human eyes, seated as He is upon His heavenly throne, far surpasses the majesty and mystery of the Roman Caesar's court. Rome cannot compare with heaven. Caesar cannot compare with God Almighty. The elders pictured here are probably representative of the leaders of both dispensations. "Seven spirits" represent the perfect Spirit in revelation, inspiration, etc., that is, God in His fullness. The four living things represent God's impressive and vigilant heavenly court in the act of showing their benevolence and veneration of the divine majesty.

This scene is especially similar to one which appears in Ezekiel 2:9-10. In it is found a book written on both sides with lamentations, mourning, and woe. It is given to the prophet from the hand of God who is also pictured on His throne in that vision. The reader should note that what follows here is also a book that in this case is in the right hand of God. Its opening reveals what the future holds for the people of God.

B. Opening the Seals of the Closely Sealed Book (5:1-14)

And I saw in the right hand of Him who sat on the throne a book written within and on the back, closely sealed with seven seals. And I saw a mighty angel proclaiming with a great voice, "Who is worthy to open the book, and to loose its seals?" And no one in the heaven, or on the earth, or beneath the earth, was able to open the book, or to look thereon. And I wept much, because no one was found worthy to open the book, or to look thereon: and one of the elders said to me, "Weep not; behold, the Lion that is of the tribe of Judah, the Root of David, has overcome to open the book and its seven seals." And I saw in the midst of the throne and of the four living creatures, and in the midst of the elders, a Lamb standing, as though it had been slain, having seven horns, and seven eyes, which are the seven Spirits of God, sent forth into all the earth. And He came, and He took it out of the right hand of Him who sat on the throne. And when He had taken the book, the four living creatures and the twenty-four elders fell down before the Lamb, each one having a harp, and golden bowls full of incense, which are the prayers of the saints. And they sang a new song, saying, "Worthy are You to take the book, and to open its seals: for You were slain, and did purchase unto God with Your blood men of every tribe, and tongue, and people, and nation, and made them to be to our God a kingdom and priests; and they reign upon earth." And I saw, and I heard a voice of many angels round about the throne and the living creatures and the elders; and the number of them was ten thousand times ten thousand, and thousands of thousands; saying with a great voice, "Worthy is the Lamb who has been slain to receive the power, and riches, and wisdom, and might and honor, and glory, and blessing." And every created thing which is in the heaven, and on the earth, and beneath the earth, and on the sea, and all things that are in them, I heard saying, "To Him who sits on the throne, and to the Lamb, be the blessing, and the honor, and the glory, and the dominion, for ever and ever." And the four living creatures said, "Amen." And the elders fell down and worshipped (Rev. 5:1-14).

Here in chapter five John is shown a closely sealed Book of Destiny which resides in God's hand. No one is found in heaven or earth worthy to open it. So John weeps. One of the elders says, "The Root of David has overcome to open it." Then a Lamb appears. The Lamb has seven horns (representing perfect power), and seven eyes (representing the all-seeing nature of divinity). The Lamb takes the book in His hand, whereupon the Song of Redemption is sung. The living creatures, elders, angels, and all of creation, praise God and the Lamb. Christ is, of course, the Lamb of God (John 1:29), the only one worthy to disclose the contents of the Book of Destiny, that is, to tell what the future is to bring. His part in the scheme of redemption has made Him worthy to divulge these mysterious secrets.

This vision of this scroll, that so clearly intends to represent God's complete plan for the entire world throughout the ages from beginning to end, rather naturally brings to mind a number of significant questions. Does history have ultimate meaning? Is it headed somewhere? Is God actually involved in directing it toward some end or goal? Or, is it simply an inexplicable series of happenstances? According to Paul, in his Ephesian correspondence, God has indeed had such a plan from eternity, and it was revealed by Him in the fullness of time, at least in some measure (Eph. 1:9-11; 3:9-11). Peter also explained that this mystery of human salvation has been revealed in the gospel, and further observed that the curiosity of the angels themselves was piqued by its details (cf. 1 Pet. 1:10-12). This is not to suggest that the events of human history were revealed in all of their rich detail, but that the bare outlines of the overall scheme of human redemption were planned out by Him before the beginning of time and then worked out by the hand of the Almighty in the unique sacred history of the people of Israel and of the church of Christ, the spiritual Kingdom of God. Regarding this important reference, George Eldon Ladd commented incisively as follows:

> Here is a simple but profound biblical truth which cannot be overemphasized: apart from the person and redeeming work of Jesus Christ, history is an enigma. For centuries since Augustine and his *City of God,* a Christian view of history as having a divinely ordained goal which was inseparable from the redemptive word of Christ has colored western thought. Since the Enlightenment, many philosophers have rejected the Christian view of life, and for them history has become a problem. The evolutionary view of inevitable progress is hardly popular today. Some of our greatest minds have been prophets of doom who see nothing but darkness ahead. The problem of the meaning, purpose and goal of history has become one of the most disturbing and difficult questions of our time. The secularistic, pessimistic attitude even penetrates the thinking of Christian theologians, and one of them has written, "We cannot claim to know the end and goal of history. Therefore, the question of meaning in history has become meaningless" (Rudolf Bultmann, *History and Eschatology,* 120).
>
> In the face of this modern dilemma, the fact that the scroll is so tightly sealed that no human eye can read its contents is highly significant. Christ, and Christ alone, has the key to the true meaning of history. It is therefore not surprising that modern thinkers are pessimistic; apart from the victorious return of Christ, history is going nowhere.
>
> It is equally significant that the scroll rests "in the right hand of Him who was seated upon the throne" (vs. 1). The whole story of human history rests in the hand of God. What simpler or more sublime way of picturing God's ultimate sovereignty over all history could be found than this picture of the scroll resting in the hand of God? However strong evil becomes, however fierce be the satanic evils that assail God's people on earth, history still rests in God's hand (Ladd, 82-83).

In all of heaven and earth no one was found worthy to break the seals and open the scroll, and thus precipitate its frightening woes upon the earth.

When John began to weep one of the elders consoled him. He was told that the Lion of the tribe of Judah, the Root of Jesse (see Gen. 49:9; Rev. 3:7 and 22:16), was indeed worthy to break the seals and unroll the scroll to reveal its contents. Quickly He is also characterized as a victorious Lamb, two concepts that on the surface appear incongruous, but when taken in the light of Old Testament imagery, are in total harmony. Christ is both God's Lion and His Lamb. Also, the Lamb is both slain and victorious. Once more, these are seeming opposites, but, the resurrection holds the key to this exciting mystery! This Lamb possesses seven horns and seven eyes. This pictures His power (horns always symbolize this in prophetic imagery), and the many eyes suggest that He sees and thus knows all that happens. He has perfect knowledge of the things that His suffering saints are experiencing and He knows what the future holds for them as well as what is to befall their enemies.

C. The First Six Seals Opened (6:1-17)

Chapter six gives the revelation of the first six seals. In the case of the first four seals opening, there is a frightening similarity between them: in each case a horseman with a rider appears to the prophet. These have been popularly described as "the four horsemen of the Apocalypse." As regards the style and fashion of the writer's presentation, it should be noted that the first six seals are listed sequentially here in chapter six, and then the seventh (8:1) is intended to serve as a call to all creation to be silent in order to consider meditatively upon the judgment of the wicked by the Lord. Between the sixth and seventh seals, chapter seven of the book is intended to function as an interlude. It should not be missed that the author uses a similar approach to the seven trumpets. There he also inserts an interlude (cf. 10:1-11:14).

The chapter divides naturally into three parts. The first four seals form a single unit which utilize colored horses to picture the temporal judgments presented therein. The second segment presents a dramatic and heart-wrenching portrait of the souls of those who have died for their faith. The third part portrays the terror and chaos that ensues in the face of the judgment of God upon the wicked.

The present passage sets up an interesting tension between the notion of the New Testament's concept of a kind and benevolent Deity and the chaos and destruction associated with visions of the seals, trumpets and the bowls. At the same time there is an obvious continuity with the Old Testament notion of God as cosmic and historical Judge who acts most violently and destructively when fighting on behalf of His people. Here in this part of the Revelation, John sees the violent executors of the Lord's judgment in terms of Zechariah's presentation of patrolling, colored horses (Zech. 1:7-17; 6:1-8). However, in Zechariah the colors (red, sorrel, white, black) are different and they appear to have no particular significance. With John here in the Revelation they correspond to the character of the rider and symbolize conquest (white), bloodshed (red), scarcity (black), and death (pale). Also, in Zechariah they are sent out to patrol the earth, while here their release brings disasters to the earth. The four forces of sword, famine, wild animals and pestilence in Ezekiel likewise prefigure his presentation (Rev. 6:8; cf. Ezek. 14:12-23; especially v. 21). On account of the fact that God is consistently just in His dealings with men, the apostle sees Him as acting decisively and even harshly to punish those who mistreat and harm His covenant people (Blount, 121).

The segment begins with the "four horsemen":

1. First seal: John beholds one on a white horse conquering.

And I saw when the Lamb opened one of the seven seals, and I heard one of the four living creatures saying as with a voice of thunder, "Come!" And I saw, and behold, a white horse, and he that sat thereon had a bow; and there was given to him a crown: and he came forth conquering, and to conquer (Rev. 6:1-2).

Some have attempted to make the case that the rider on the white horse is Christ, and that the white horse represents the victorious progress of the gospel during the early years of the church's history. We do not deem this to be a proper way of viewing this vision. It is usually argued in order to justify this reading of the vision that in 19:11 we again encounter a rider on a white horse and in that instance it is clearly picturing the victorious Christ. It is then reasoned that the rider of the white horse in the two visions should bear some relation to one another. In that case, of course, the writer uses terminology that cannot fail to be understood as pointing to the Lord Jesus ("Word of God," "King of Kings and Lord of Lords"). But in this case the rider wears a victor's wreath and carries a bow, whereas in

19:11ff, He is crowned with "many diadems" and is armed with a sharp sword proceeding from His mouth. The context is also quite different. Here in 6:2 it is one of conquest ("he came forth conquering, and to conquer"), while that of 19:11 is righteous retribution. Too, this identification brackets the proclamation of the gospel with a series of devastating calamities following one another as the inevitable results of human sinfulness (war, scarcity, and death). It is also problematical that the Lord is seen as the one opening the seals and then, according to this interpretation, He is also the rider on the white horse, so that He is two entirely different figures in the identical scene. The most devastating blow to this view is the usage of the terminology "there was given to him a crown," which normally in the book of Revelation refers to the divine permission granted to evil powers to carry out their nefarious work, i.e. the denizens of the abyss (9:1, 3, 5), the beast (13:5, 7), and the false prophet (13:14, 15). These points make it impossible for us to accept the hypothesis that this rider is Jesus Christ (cf. Mounce, 153-154; Caird, 81).

This fellow who rides on the white horse has a crown on his head and a bow in his hand. Roman rulers never wore crowns, and their soldiers never carried bows. This is a picture of a barbarian, not a Roman. In this case it is a Parthian general, signifying military conquests wrought against the Empire by their dreaded barbarian enemies. John's hearers would at once have understood that the horseman with a bow was a Parthian. Rome had a long history of trouble with the Parthians, and often were humbled by them. They were a perpetual nemesis to them, threatening them on the eastern frontier in Asia Minor.

Parthian cavalry had inflicted a humiliating defeat on the Roman legions under Marcus Licinius Crassus at the Battle of Carrhae, Mesopotamia in 53 BC through the military genius of Spahbod Surena, a Parthian general. Then the mounted archers unfurled brilliantly colored banners of silk, imported from China, attacked with ruthlessness and skill ("the parting shot" was one of their specialties), dazzled and terrified the legionnaires, put them to flight, captured and executed the proconsul Crassus, who was a member of the triumvirate with Julius Caesar and Pompey. Less than twenty years later, in 35 BC, Mark Antony lost more than one-third of his army of 200,000 through Parthian attacks during his retreat through

Armenia. The Roman armies also had been summarily vanquished by the Parthian cavalry (from modern Armenia) in AD 62 in the Battle of Rhandeia, this time at the hands of the Parthian king Vologeses I. The conflict ended soon after the Rhandeia humiliation in an effective stalemate and a formal compromise (Krodel, 173).

Roman pride had been wounded severely by this series of defeats. The Roman military was not accustomed to losing battles, much less wars. So it is entirely appropriate for Parthian imagery to symbolize Roman defeat militarily. This interpretation fits in well with the other three riders and their horses. All four seem to refer to misfortunes of one kind or another that are to be visited upon the empire to bring it to its knees and humble it before God.

2. Second seal: Red horse and rider, signifying bloodshed and war.

And when He opened the second seal, I heard the second living creature saying, "Come!" And another horse came forth, a red horse: and to him who sat thereon it was given to take peace from the earth, and that they should slaughter one another: and there was given to him a great sword (Rev. 6:3-4).

Frightening and tragic events lay behind these first two visionary portraits. The Roman Empire historically had viewed warfare in terms of opportunity and prestige. Victory had often been hers throughout her history. Her enemies usually tasted the bitter fruits of war, however, while she enjoyed the spoils, territorial expansion, the slaves won from a captive population, etc. But, with the passing of time, her "chickens would come home to roost." She would eventually know what her enemies had experienced before her. War meant privation, suffering, death, sorrow, and grieving for lost legions of soldiers who would never be coming home.

The word *machaira*, "sword," has been taken in two different ways. Hendricksen, for example, sees it as a reference to a sacrificial knife and views it in terms of the red horse and rider having to do with religious persecution. This interpretation has the insurmountable difficulty that this word in the New Testament does not have that connotation generally. The more likely meaning is a reference to the Roman short sword, a powerful weapon, but not especially long. Sometimes referred to as the Gladius or *gladius Hispaniensis* (Spanish sword), it was 50-60 cm long (24 inches). This particular stabbing and slashing weapon was employed by Roman legionaries from the 3rd century BC and afterward. It is also important that he employs the word "slay" in a form that is not the usual or expected word for "kill." Instead, he selects a term that means "slaughter" or "massacre." It is far more threatening in its nuance.

The ill-fated Legio IX Hispania (the Spanish Ninth Legion), made up of approximately 5,400 men, is illustrative of this coming era of uncertainty and death which John has in mind in the vision. This legion had an enviable record as a fighting force as early as the Gallic Wars (58-51 BC) and as late as the Battle of Mons Graupius (in what is now called Scotland) in AD 83-84. Stationed in Britain after the Roman invasion of the area in 43 AD, the legion disappeared from recorded history after AD 120. No account has ever been found to establish with any reasonable certainty what happened to it. Many different theories have been propounded to attempt to provide an explanation for its disappearance, but none has ever proven to be altogether satisfactory and to account for all of the evidence. The last attested reference to a location associated with the Legion was at Noviomagus Batavorum on the Rhine (Nijmegen, Netherlands).

At any rate, by the time of the reign of Septimius Severus (193-211), it was no longer mentioned in the two lists that are available to historians of the thirty-three legions existing during that era. Apparently it was wiped off the face of the earth by some very formidable foe, and the humiliation associated with this embarrassing defeat led to historians conveniently "forgetting" all about it and its loss. Rome was to experience what her enemies had for so long undergone at her hands. She would be defeated and humbled by military opponents. This would be her eventual fate, visited upon her as punishment by God for her hateful persecution of her finest and most faithful citizens, the despised Christians.

3. *Third seal: Black horse and rider, picturing scarcity.*

> *And when He opened the third seal, I heard the third living creature saying, "Come!" And I saw, and behold, a black horse; and he that sat thereon had a balance in his hand. And I heard as it were a voice in the midst of the four living creatures saying, A quart of wheat for a denarius, and three quarts of barley for a denarius; and do no harm to the oil or the wine (Rev. 6:5-6).*

A measure of wheat was the daily ration for a man and the average daily wage for a single worker. The price that is represented here was approximately eight times the regular cost of wheat and 5.5 times the normal cost for barley. Clearly this represents scarcity. The message of this vision is that a time is coming when a man will work an entire day and barely procure enough food to stay alive. But what of his family? What about those who may be dependent upon him for their daily bread? What about his animals? He can only survive by purchasing a less desirable and palatable product: barley. Interestingly, three *choinikes* of barley were the equivalent of a day's ration for a man's horse or mule. It also represented a day's portion for a small family. And so, inflation and famine were to trouble the Empire as a means of humbling and punishing it.

The curious expression, "do no harm to the oil or the wine," has rightly been explained in terms of an ancient tradition (well known at the time) that in the year that stands under the sign of the constellation "the Scales" (once every twelve years) the grain harvest will be bad, but the olive and the wine will yield plentifully. This passage clearly evinces a concern for these latter commodities in a time of famine, whether for the sake of the wealthy, who are less likely to be affected by a shortage of food than by the poor, or simply for the more reckless of men who often do not have the wisdom to make good choices. There are those who will not be denied the right to self-indulgence, even during a time of famine! The Jewish Mishnah has two passages that sound remotely similar to this text, and make pretty much the same point (cf. *Sotah* 49a; *Sanhedrin* 97a; Beasley-Murray, 133).

In the year 92 there was a severe grain famine in Asia. That was but a few short years before John wrote the Revelation. Domitian had issued an edict that at least half of the vineyards of the province be cut down and no new ones planted. The action itself was intended to increase grain production for a hungry population, but it hurt Philadelphia particularly badly because no city of Asia was more dependent on the produce of the vine than it. A connection with Domitian's edict would be an interesting association indeed, for it would represent a direct correlation between John's symbolic narrative and an actual historical event. Brian Blount disagrees with the proposition that there is a direct connection between that event and John's symbols, but he makes the following worthwhile observation:

There would also be interesting literary implications. Domitian's edict was apparently rescinded only after the aristocracy bitterly complained. Since John does not mention that historical detail, it could well have been his narrative intent to demonstrate that the victorious opposition to the imperial command came from God. While the emperor demanded that half the vineyards be chopped down, God commanded that they not be touched. That would mean that at the singular moment when God's desire for judgment actually matched the goal of one of Caesar's edicts (i.e., massive destruction, in this case of vineyards), God changed course. The end result would have been a human emperor humiliated by a heavenly countermand of his orders. God would have vetoed Caesar's order at the one time when accommodating to Caesar's order would have furthered God's stated plan of judgment, as that plan was embodied in the work of the first, second, and third riders. . . . It is difficult and risky to attempt such a speculative connection between historical events and John's eschatological work unless one can find a specific literary link to that event. None exists (Bount, 129).

The most likely intent of this passage, whether the foregoing point is legitimate or not (and we think that it probably does have legitimacy), is to make a point of dramatic irony. It is to be the divine intent to spare luxuries like oil and wine while destroying such staples as wheat and barley. The rich are thriving while the poor are starving. This whole situation would have been viewed as a portent of worse developments on the horizon as God visited the Roman people with judgment for their many sins, but most of all for their rabid persecution of the saints.

4. Fourth seal: Pale horse and rider, signifying pestilence and death.

And when He opened the fourth seal, I heard the voice of the fourth living creature saying, "Come!" And I saw, and behold, a pale horse: and he who sat on him, his name was Death; and Hades followed with him. And there was given to them authority over one-fourth of the earth, to kill with sword, and with famine, and with death, and by the wild beasts of the earth (Rev. 6:7-8).

When the Lamb opened the fourth seal, the voice of the fourth living creature is heard by John. The voice of the creature which has the form of a flying eagle (4:7), says, "Come!" The creature has something that he wants to show the Seer. As is usual for the style of the writer, he follows this request with the words, "and I saw. . . ." What is described in this fourth aspect of the vision is a rider on a horse that is the color of an ashen, bloodless corpse. (In reality, the Greek has "pale green" which signifies sickness and decomposition.) The rider of this horse is identified as death, with Hades (the invisible realm where departed souls await the judgment) following him. This is the only one of the horsemen who is given a name. John explains that he has the power to kill with sword, with famine, with pestilence, and with wild beasts. Death and Hades are partners here as elsewhere in the Revelation (see also, 1:18 and 20:13-14). John employs the imperfect tense to indicate the continuous activity of Hades. When death claims a victim, Hades gathers an inhabitant. So, the work of the fourth rider is the consummation of the labors of the three horsemen who have preceded him. This particular tableau pictures the sickness, pestilence, and death which are the inevitable results of wars and famines. John's language in this passage is highly reminiscent of Ezekiel 14:21 where God announced that He would rally his "four dreadful judgments" against the city of Jerusalem: sword, famine, wild beasts, and plague.

5. Fifth seal: Martyred saints are pictured beneath the altar beseeching God to avenge their blood.

And when He opened the fifth seal, I saw underneath the altar the souls of them that had been slain for the Word of God, and for the testimony which they held: and they cried with a great voice, saying, How long, O Master, the holy and true, do You not judge and avenge our blood on those who dwell on the earth? And each one of them was given a white robe; and it was said to them, that they should rest yet for a little time, until their fellow-servants also and their brethren, who should be killed even as they were, should have fulfilled their course (Rev. 6:9-11).

This is one of the most important little snapshots of this section of the book. Here John sees the disembodied spirits of martyred saints. He has no concern at all at this point for their bodies. Their bodies have perished. It should be noted, however, that in spite of the fact that their bodies have died and they are separated from them, these saints are still quite conscious and aware of their circumstances. They exist as spiritual beings both prior to death and after death. This identical condition seems again to characterize the beheaded saints in 20:4 who reign with Christ. John did not believe either in "soul sleep" or "soul extinction." He was convinced of the conscious existence of the soul after death.

This passage is especially significant for an understanding of the book of Revelation, since it provides us with an informative glimpse into the mind of the author and his special purpose for the book. These victims of the horrendous crimes against Christians by the Romans are described as "the souls of those who had been slain for the Word of God, and for the testimony which they held." The altar pictured here is that which is before the throne of God in heaven. These victims of imperial torture and murder, who have died in the cause of Christ, plaintively cry out, "How long, O Master, the holy and true, do You not judge and avenge our blood on those who dwell on the earth?" No doubt this reminded the readers of similar prophetic calls for divine engagement from the Old Testament (cf. Zech. 1:12; Psa. 79:5; 94:3). But in those cases a contrite people, humbled by divine judgment, asked how long God would keep punishing them. This is a call for justice against those who had committed atrocities against the disciples of Christ. They are innocent of any wrong-doing. They are not being punished for their sins. They are martyrs in the cause of spreading the gospel to the world. Rather than asking for forgiveness and expiation for sins, these gentle souls have been grievously sinned against, and so are asking God to right the wrongs done to them.

As well, it is to be seen as a plea for mercy to the God of justice and retribution, who has himself declared, "Vengeance is mine; I will repay" (Deut. 32:35; Heb. 10:30). Faith looks on evil with hatred not unlike God's own. It also shares God's will that it shall not ultimately triumph and trusts in God that it will not, only without the fullness of God's counsels or wisdom. Who knows best how and when to overthrow it? God alone. So, the church on earth and departed saints cry alike to God to execute His own purpose, and bring the reign of evil to an end. What a splendid picture portrait of that concept!

Some modern critics have seen this passage as beneath the dignity of genuine Christian martyrs. Martin Kiddle, for example, intoned that: "The modern conscience is shocked at the passionate longing for vengeance breathed out by the martyrs, and indeed, it is beyond doubt lower in tone than the lofty spirit of forbearance which distinguishes the Christian church in its earliest days" (Kiddle, 119).

Quite frankly, we consider such remarks as elitist and judgmental. In fact, there are many others in contemporary literature like it, but that does not absolve such authors from the "ivory tower" perspective that is demonstrated in such attitudes. Plainly, it is easy for a contemporary man who lives in the safety and security of a modern democracy, where his rights and privileges are guaranteed by a government that is friendly to his religion, to pass harsh judgment on the feelings and sentiments of people who suffered horribly for their faith without any recourse whatever in this world. Their situation was different, and so their feelings about what was happening to them and what ought to happen to those who were abusing and misusing them were different as well. But beyond all this, there is a very basic misunderstanding at work in such remarks that begs to be clarified and elucidated in biblical terms.

The notion that it is somehow wrong for God's people to seek punishment for those who mistreat them is a misrepresentation of the Bible's clear and plain teaching. It is not sinful nor is it beneath the dignity of a suffering saint or a dying or dead martyr (as in this instance) to ask God to judge his persecutor(s) or murderers. There are some very obvious similarities in the language of the prayers of these martyrs in the present scene in Revelation with that found on occasion in the Psalms of Israel. For example, "How long, O Lord? Will you be angry forever? How long will your jealousy burn like fire? Pour out your wrath on the nations that do not acknowledge You, on the kingdoms that do not call on Your name; for they have devoured Jacob and destroyed his homeland" (Psa. 79:5-7); or, "Why should the nations say, 'Where is their God?' Before our eyes, make known among the nations that You avenge the outpoured blood of Your servants" (Psa. 79:10). These anguished pleas for justice from God's Old Testament people are sometimes compared unfavorably with the prayer of Jesus on the cross (Luke 23:34) or with the prayer of Steven at his martyrdom (Acts 7:60), both of whom prayed for the forgiveness of their tormentors.

It is not fair to say that Jews prayed for vengeance against their foes and Christianity always prayed for unlimited forgiveness for theirs. This is not a correct assessment either of Judaism or of Christianity. Certainly it leaves out the words of the text before us in this instance (6:10-11). Moreover, it ignores the teaching of Jesus elsewhere on certain other related matters:

"And will not God bring about justice (literally "retribution," or "revenge" *tēn ekdikēsin*) for His chosen ones, who cry out to Him day and night?" (Luke 18:7). This passage in Revelation appears to be a reflection of the very idea that Jesus presented in His question to the disciples in this verse. The cry of the martyrs is a cry for justice, and in certain instances, like the present one, there is no true justice until there has been retribution against those who have committed the deplorable offences involved (cf. J. R. Michaels, 107-108).

These individuals are not said to be taking personal vengeance against their enemies (Rom. 12:19), they are pleading for God to take His ultimate vengeance upon them for their crimes against humanity. For those who not only fail to repent of their evil deeds, but revel in them to the end and refuse to renounce them, there is only one end in sight. And that is God's retribution, His judgment and punishment of those who have sinned and have no plan ever to give up their wicked ways.

Was not Paul correct to observe, "Alexander the coppersmith did me much harm; the Lord will repay him according to his deeds" (2 Tim. 4:14)? Was he wrong to deliver over Hymenaeus and Alexander to Satan "so that they might be taught not to blaspheme" (1 Tim. 1:20)? Was he being too judgmental or vengeful when he struck Elymas the sorcerer with blindness and said to him: "You son of the Devil, you enemy of all righteousness, full of all deceit and villainy, will you not stop making crooked the straight paths of the Lord" (Acts 13:10)? Was he showing an improper spirit when he encouraged disciples of Christ to "heap burning coals upon the head" of their enemies by acting in a kindly fashion toward them (Rom. 12:20)? No he was not. In no case.

It is entirely right and proper for the people of the Lord to hope for a day of vengeance upon those who hate them and daily try to make their lives miserable simply because they are in a position to do so. Certainly they should pray for their repentance and for them to change their ways, just as did Jesus and Stephen (and make no mistake about it, neither Jesus nor Stephen were praying that God would forgive the sins of their enemies without their repentance and the changing of their spiritual direction).

This must have been a question that plagued the hearts and minds of suffering saints throughout the horrible period of their suffering in the early age of the church. Antipas, the faithful martyr of Pergamum was symbolized there among them. So were the Christians who were burned alive to serve as torches at the nightly festivals of Nero in his gardens. Many more would eventually join their ranks over a period of several centuries. This was called "the Age of Martyrs" for very good reason. What is the answer to their plight? Of course, recompense to their persecutors will come in God's due time. When it does, the altar of God will cry out, "Yes, Lord God the Almighty, true and just are your judgments" (16:7).

Until then they must wait patiently. And so, they are given white robes and told to wait until their brethren were killed as they had been. John emphasizes this concept with the term *pleroō*, a verb meaning "fulfill." There is much more to be done, and these coming martyrs, like the earlier generation of them, must complete their tasks and live out their lives to the end. Their lives will be sacrificed also, while they joyfully confess the Lordship of their Master, but they must also know that eventually victory over their enemies is coming. And in the wake of it, vengeance is also sure to follow. So, in 20:4 these same martyrs are pictured victoriously sitting on thrones with their risen and triumphant Savior. God will not forget their sacrifices, but will reward them according to their works (22:12). And the Lord will bring their persecutors to justice at the fall of their mighty empire and then when they are finally cast into the lake of fire, the second death (20:14, 15).

6. Sixth seal: Earthquake and judgment.

And I saw when He opened the sixth seal, and there was a great earthquake; and the sun became black as sackcloth, and the whole moon became as blood; and the stars of the heaven fell to the earth, as a fig tree casts its unripe figs when it is shaken by a great wind. And the heaven was removed as a scroll when it is rolled up; and every mountain and island were moved out of their places. And the kings of the earth, and the princes, and the chief captains, and the rich, and the strong, and every bondman and freeman, hid themselves in the caves and in the rocks of the mountains; and they say to the mountains and to the rocks, "Fall on us, and hide us from the face of Him who sits on the throne, and from the wrath of the Lamb: for the great day of their wrath is come; and who is able to stand?" (Rev. 6:12-17).

Massive and destructive earthquakes had taken place during the lifetimes of some of these church members in Sardis, Philadelphia, and Laodicea. This entire region had been troubled by them both historically and recently. Geographically and topographically the location of Philadelphia in particular, in close proximity as it was to the Catacecaumene, the volcanic Burnt Land, which stretched along the frontier between Lydia and Phrygia, left much to be desired as to safety and security in the matter of earth tremors. This entire region was particularly susceptible not only to volcanic eruption, but also to severe earthquake. The notable one that occurred in AD 17 had a devastating effect on that city just as it did on Sardis.

Strabo speaks of severe aftershocks, oftentimes almost on a daily basis, along with the persistent cracking of walls. There is even an allusion to the fact that for a time at least few people lived in the actual town itself, but the vast majority of the city's inhabitants were by choice farmers and made their home in the countryside where it was safer for them. Indeed, there is evidence that Philadelphia must have been the relative epicenter of the great earthquake of AD 17 and suffered tremors for years to come. A similar earthquake in Laodicea in AD 60 would have been a sober reminder to the inhabitants of Philadelphia and Sardis of the particularly dangerous region wherein they made their home. Strabo commented about Philadelphia:

> Incessantly the walls of the houses are cracked, different parts of the city being thus affected at different times. For this reason but few people live in the city, and most of them spend their lives as farmers in the country, since they have a fertile soil. Yet one may be surprised at the few, that they are so fond of the place when their dwellings are so insecure, and one might marvel still more at those who founded the city (*Geography* 6.181; quoted in P. Patterson, 125).

So the frightening effects of these earth tremors were well known to all of the people who made up the seven churches, even the ones that were not so directly and severely affected by them as were they in the towns of Philadelphia, Sardis, and Laodicea. But in this case the cosmic earthquake described (like everything else in John's vision) is employed as a symbol, a picture of something else altogether. In fact, the cosmic earthquake is one of the most regular features of the Jewish apocalyptic literature. It is found in numerous passages in the Old Testament to stand for the overthrow of a worldly political order organized in hostility to God. Jesus used some of this language to describe the fall of Jerusalem by the Roman armies (Luke 23:28-31; quoting Hosea 10:8). In fact, it is so prominent and identifiable as symbolic that the author of Hebrews tells his readers that the earthquake of Old Testament prophecy is a figure that signifies "the removal of all that can be shaken . . . in order that what cannot be shaken may remain" (Heb. 12:27). This particular passage is a composite of several Old Testament texts: see Isaiah 2:12-17; 24:21; 34:2-4; Hosea 10:1-8; Joel 2:28-3:3; and Malachi 3:2.

The one element of John's picture which is not drawn from the Old Testament or the apocalyptic tradition generally is what he calls "the wrath of the Lamb." This phrase is entirely distinctive. It represents a deliberate paradox by which John intends to goad his readers into spiritual alertness. Obviously, a lamb is by its very nature a creature which is almost harmless. It is so small and weak that it is no threat to anyone, but this lamb is very different from what we are accustomed to think of when we envision a sacrificial lamb. Christ as the Lamb of God in this instance has already served in His role as the sacrificial lamb offered for the sins of mankind. He has presently moved beyond that function in the drama of God's eternal plan. He has now assumed the character of God's angel of justice. He is the Judge of the wicked who have rejected His previous sacrifice on their behalf (Acts 17:31), and so He is now the one who delivers them over to their ultimate fate.

Thus, it is the Lamb who is now seen here breaking the seals of the scroll, so that in a sense He may be deemed to have accepted responsibility for the retributive justice of God which His action sets loose upon the world. Such retribution is a very natural and inevitable result of human rejection of the divine wisdom implicit in the gospel of Christ. Rebellious men cannot forever escape the results of their sins. A price must eventually be paid. As J. P. M. Swete observed regarding the larger context of this notion as it is to be viewed in terms of both the Old Testament and the New:

> In the Old Testament passages which John draws on, the prophets were declaring the punishment of human pride and folly, usually with reference to contemporary disasters, in terms of God undoing His work of creation: bringing back chaos, opening the windows of heaven to pour down the flood waters, quenching the lights of heaven and rolling up the sky. This, however, was not mere destruction, but clearing the decks for a new order. "Creation"

in biblical thought is the imposition of order on chaos, understood morally rather than physically. Human pride and refusal to acknowledge the Creator bring chaos back: therefore men must be made to recognize God before a new order is possible, and His appearance or "coming" is the climax of the picture.

It is equally important to grasp the New Testament understanding of the divine *wrath*. In the Old Testament there are two main strands: God's passionate indignation at man's sin, but also the more impersonal sense of the disastrous effects in history of man's sin. In both cases it is preeminently a feature of the End, when sin, at present apparently overlooked, reaps its reward. In the New Testament the second strand is dominant. God is never said to "be angry" (though often to be gracious, etc.), and "the wrath" often occurs on its own as a technical term for the recoil of sin upon the sinner, rather than as an emotion in God; the NEB often translates it by "retribution" or "vengeance." But the impersonal aspect must not be over-stressed: it is still God's wrath, not just Nemesis. When man is blinded and corrupted by his refusal to acknowledge God, it is God who hands him over to the effects of his refusal (cf. Rom. 1:14-28)—in order that he may repent (Rev. 9:10; 16:9-11). For ultimately man must face the God he has refused to acknowledge.

It is this final confirmation which John here depicts. But what of *the wrath of the Lamb?* To many commentators this phrase proves that *wrath*, at least in Revelation, stands squarely for the divine anger. Others see in it the same paradox as in the conjunction of "Lion" and "Lamb"; the irony lies in men's rejection of the gracious initiative of God which the slain Lamb symbolizes (cf. John 3:16-19, 36). This is the consummation of the moment of truth on Calvary; John evokes the crucifixion by his echo of Jesus' words to the women of Jerusalem, "The days are coming when . . . they will say to the mountains, 'Fall on us,' and to the hills 'Cover us'" (Luke 23:28-31). God must be experienced either as love or as wrath. In the present He may let men keep Him at arm's length, but in the last resort there can be no middle ground (J. P. M. Swete, 143-145).

Hence, these events introduce the question, "Who shall be able to stand?" Chapter seven answers this challenging query. Only the faithful of God will be able to stand in the Judgment. Indeed, eventually they will stand victoriously before the throne of God. They will know boldness on this final day, not on account of their own righteous deeds, but because of their trust in the efficacy of the Lamb's sacrifice along with the grace and mercy of God (1 John 2:28; 3:21; 4:17; 5:14). For the rest, John has absolutely no doubt of their culpability and of its ramifications and the terrifying consequences for their eternal souls. The "wrath of the Lamb" is all there is left for them.

The various horses (6:2-8) which are sent out in this chapter are foreboding symbols. They represent the agents of destruction which God would employ over time and throughout many different generations and circumstances to punish the Christian's tormentors, the Roman Empire and her servile minions. The pale horse and his rider are the most terrifying of the lot. "His name was Death; and Hades followed with him" (6:8). This frightening horse and his rider are firmly ensconced in the folklore of the nations since John's book was penned so long ago, but the message of this series of horses and riders is brought to fullness with the revelation of this concluding part of the vision. The last horse heralds the End and the dreadful conclusion to this series of judgments. The Final Judgment would signal the decisive act of justice and vengeance upon these avowed enemies of God and Christ. "The great day of their wrath" (an expression that is repeated by the writer to emphasize this fearsome reality) is no doubt the Day of Judgment (v. 17; cf. also Rom. 1:18; Heb. 3:11).

The author, as he speaks of these realities places emphasis first on the verb *has come*, because it stands first in the sentence, and then on the noun *day*, which is followed by the descriptive adjective *great*. The Judgment Day is properly depicted as "the great day" and in the Old Testament as "the day of the Lord" (cf. Isa. 13:9; Joel 2:11, 31; Zeph. 1:14, 15). The verb *has come* is a past tense with a present connotation that awaits future realization. John draws a picture of that day in the customary "prophetic perfect" even though the day is still to come. That is to say, all the terrible upheavals in nature and the universe usher in the great Day of Judgment, even though the fulfillment of this awesome portent must wait until the consummation (Kistemaker, 239).

Hence, the prayer of the martyred saints would be forever answered when God at last brings their sins to justice on the final day. It is therefore entirely fitting that this also is symbolized with another horse and yet another rider: Jesus is pictured in chapter 19 on a white horse (19:11, 19, 21). He is called there "Faithful and True" and is shown in His role as a Judge who "makes war" with those who have rejected Him and at the last cuts them asunder with His sword "which proceeds from His mouth."

D. Sealing of the 144,000, and the Innumerable Multitude (7:1-17)

In swift succession the six seals of the roll have been broken, and as they were unsealed John saw the dramatic presentation of history's pageant of human suffering. With superlative skill the author now pauses in the recital of these fantastic events before the mystery of the seventh seal is revealed.

Before the action unfolding the secrets of the roll is resumed, he considers the status of the people of God, and this is indeed a rather natural question to ask in the firestorm of these fabulous images. Where do they stand in all of this? Are they to be destroyed in the fall of the wicked, or has God made some special provision for their protection and care? What is their fate to be? This is the query we now face as we approach the "interlude" or "parenthesis" vision preliminary to the breaking of the seventh seal. Kistemaker is right to suggest that this passage is more of a pinnacle than a pause. To the question raised in the sixth seal when the writer speaks of the coming great day of the wrath of God and of the Lamb, "Who is able to stand?" (6:17), John provides the answer: the 144,000 and the countless multitude.

Those who are able to stand are not the people who cry out to the mountains and the rocks to cover them and hide them from the divine wrath, but the saints who are here pictured as standing before the throne. They are the ones who are sealed by God for their protection, washed in the blood of the Lamb for their deliverance, clothed in white robes for their purification and glorification, and holding palm branches in their hands in worship and praise of their Savior and Lord. The writer sees these people as the true Israel of God (vv. 4-9a; cf. Gal. 6:16). They figuratively celebrate the Feast of Tabernacles (vv. 9b-10; Lev. 23:40), while all of the inhabitants of heaven worship the Lord (vv. 11-12). In addition, the saints are portrayed as martyrs who are being gathered as a body until the end of earthly time (vv. 13-14). (The prospect of martyrdom is never very far from this writer's mind!) At the last, they are before the throne of God and of the Lamb throughout an endless eternity, rewarded for their service and sacrifice (vv. 15-17).

1. 144,000 sealed (7:1-8).

After this I saw four angels standing at the four corners of the earth, holding the four winds of the earth, that no wind should blow on the earth, or on the sea, or upon any tree. And I saw another angel ascend from the

> *rising of the sun, having the seal of the living God: and he cried with a great voice to the four angels to whom it was given to harm the earth and the sea, saying, "Hurt not the earth, neither the sea, nor the trees, until we shall have sealed the servants of our God on their foreheads." And I heard the number of those who were sealed: one hundred and forty-four thousand; sealed out of every tribe of the children of Israel: Of the tribe of Judah were sealed twelve thousand: Of the tribe of Reuben twelve thousand; Of the tribe of Gad twelve thousand; Of the tribe of Asher twelve thousand; Of the tribe of Naphtali twelve thousand; Of the tribe of Manasseh twelve thousand; Of the tribe of Simeon twelve thousand; Of the tribe of Levi twelve thousand; Of the tribe of Issachar twelve thousand; Of the tribe of Zebulun twelve thousand; Of the tribe of Joseph twelve thousand; Of the tribe of Benjamin were sealed twelve thousand (Rev. 7:1-8).*

In this beautiful vision one hundred forty-four thousand saints (virgin men of Israel) are sealed for preservation through the trial of the persecutions (cf. also 14:1-5). They are described as "the servants of our God." It will be noted that as this picture unfolds there are four angels standing at the four corners of the earth, holding the four winds of the earth, "that no wind should blow on the earth, or on the sea, or upon any tree." This picture is very evidently one of *restrained destructive power*. The message communicated is that before utter destruction is visited upon the earth, it must be seen to, that the people of God are kept safe in the midst of that judgment which is to be initiated soon. So an angel announces, "Hurt not the earth, neither the sea, nor the trees, till we shall have sealed the servants of our God on their foreheads."

If the sealing described in this passage is fairly to be compared with the sealing that took place in the story presented in Ezekiel 9:4-8, upon which 7:1-3 is assuredly based, then its function is to afford divine protection for those who are depicted in the text. In Ezekiel's account, God commissioned six executioners to slaughter the idolatrous inhabitants of Jerusalem. At just the moment the reader expected the bloodbath to begin, however, there was an intermission. Before commencing the killing, the Lord ordered that all those who grieved the abominable behavior of the unrighteous be branded with a mark upon their foreheads. When an executioner saw the mark, he was to pass by those people who bore it, leaving them unharmed. Precisely the same scenario plays itself out in this case also. God's fierce and final judgment awaits the Lamb's breaking of the seventh seal. At precisely the moment when the reader expects God to act, the fifth of God's agents calls for a momentary halting of the hostilities so that certain believers may be branded with a protective mark on their forehead. Later still, the locusts, who are obviously executing at least a portion of God's judgment upon the guilty, are commanded to harm only those who do not possess God's protective seal on their foreheads (cf. Rev. 9:4).

The seal itself identifies the branded persons as God's possessions. John calls them God's "slaves" or "servants." Later, when this select group of God's servants is again mentioned, John explains that the branding is with God's own name (14:1-5). Throughout historic time men have written their own name on their possessions in case of loss or theft. This custom is still practiced. Thus, to mark someone with one's name is clearly to identify and claim them as one's own personal possession (see 9:4; 13:16; 14:1, 9; 17:5; 20:4; 22:4). The combination of the notion of sealing or tattooing with this term (*douloi*) indicates that this metaphor is derived from the eastern practice of tattooing religious and secular slaves.

So, to be marked with the seal of God implied divine protection through this unique and picturesque medium. That is certainly the idea that is primary here. It is also illustrative to note that in Bible times placing a seal on a document or a container guaranteed the authenticity of the contents. They could not be altered or removed without breaking the seal. Thus, the contents were kept secure and it could be recognized immediately if the item had been tampered with or changed in any way (cf. B. K. Blount, 143; and Reddish, 143).

Those who are under consideration here are, designated quite simply as "the servants of our God." The figure which speaks of their virginity, their association with Israel, as well as their maleness, are all illustrative pictures depicting different aspects of their character. Each is a symbol representing something else. It is particularly interesting, is it not, that they are portrayed as the true remnant of old Israel, a concept frequently visited by the prophets of old? These one hundred and forty-four thousand (12,000 times 12, the number of the original tribes of Israel) represent the complete number of God's remaining people who serve Him on the earth. God has sealed every one of them for his protection and care. Their bodies may suffer, but their souls are kept for everlasting life. More bloodshed, violence, and death are coming upon the earth, but all those who suffer should know that God will deliver them at last and give them eternal life with the redeemed of all ages. That is the simple message of this brief vision. Unfortunately, it has stupefied and confused many interpreters, and given rise to a number of highly speculative theories throughout the long history of its interpretation, which have nothing at all to do with its original intent, but its message is really quite easy to understand if it is allowed to speak for itself.

2. The great multitude before the throne (7:9-17).

After these things I saw, and behold, a great multitude, which no man could number, out of every nation and of all tribes and peoples and tongues, standing before the throne and before the Lamb, arrayed in white robes, having palms in their hands; and they cried out with a loud voice, saying, "Salvation be to our God who sits on the throne, and to the Lamb." And all the angels were standing round about the throne, and about the elders and the four living creatures; and they fell before the throne to their faces, and worshipped God, saying, "Amen: Blessing, and glory, and wisdom, and thanksgiving, and honor, and power, and might, be to our God for ever and ever. Amen." And one of the elders answered, saying to me, "These who are arrayed in white robes, who are they, and where did they come from?" And I said to him, "My lord, you know." And he said to me, "These are they who have come through the great tribulation, and they have washed their robes, and made them white in the blood of the Lamb. Therefore they are before the throne of God; and they serve Him day and night in His temple: and He who sits on the throne shall spread His tabernacle over them. They shall hunger no more, neither thirst any more; neither shall the sun strike upon them, nor any heat: for the Lamb that is in the midst of the throne shall be their Shepherd, and shall guide them to fountains of waters of life: and God shall wipe away every tear from their eyes" (Rev. 7:9-17).

In this vision, the scene changes from earth to heaven. The innumerable multitude pictured here is the same group (the saved of all ages added to them) after the trials are over (note especially v. 14). These have been able to stand. These have successfully endured the trials and tribulations of life. They have weathered the storm and arrived at the safe harbor. They have made it to heaven. This was the question which introduced the present chapter at the close of the last one, and it is answered through the picturesque content that is presented here.

Cycle One: The Seal Sequence

Previously the 144,000 were given the assurance that their souls are safely beyond the power of the enemies of God to hurt or destroy them. They were sealed for divine protection. In this magnificent vision of all the redeemed gathered about the throne of God, they are granted additional assurance. The lesson of this vision is that the *eternal salvation of God's people is sure.* Nothing in this world can alter that rock-solid reality. The powers of this world may be able to hurt their bodies, but they cannot change the final destination of their souls. They may curse them with their wretched tongues, but their curses are meaningless with God. They may torture them and even kill them, but that will only send them into the presence of their Savior (Phil. 1:21, 23). Jesus had said, "And do not fear those who kill the body but cannot kill the soul. Rather fear Him who can destroy both soul and body in hell" (Matt. 10:28). John here visits the same notion, but in a positive light and with an illustrative vision of the final episode of the drama. The words of Christ are encapsulated and exemplified perfectly and shown to be absolutely accurate.

And so in a sense the writer draws aside for a brief moment in time the curtain of eternity to reveal the end product of God's plan for redeeming and preserving His faithful people. It is a view into God's throne room when all of His children are finally gathered about His throne to give Him praise for all of His mighty works and wonders and signs, most especially those that have brought about their own deliverance. By the aid of this vision the Christians who faced torture and death at the hands of the Romans and their often malicious and sometimes downright evil emperor might always keep before them this surpassingly beautiful reminder of their ultimate destiny with their heavenly Father. This is what the end looks like. It will be incomparably beautiful. So you do not want to miss out on it!

The great multitude before the throne sings this haunting song: "Salvation be to our God who sits on the throne, and to the Lamb." God is the source of our deliverance, and is our Savior through the blood of the Lamb. When John inquires as to the nature of this vast crowd of saved persons, the elder replies:

> These are they that come out of the great tribulation, and they washed their robes and made them white in the blood of the Lamb. Therefore are they before the throne of God; and they serve Him day and night in His temple;

and He who sits on the throne shall spread His tabernacle over them. They shall hunger no more, neither thirst any more; for the Lamb who is in the midst of the throne shall be their Shepherd, and shall guide them to fountains of water of life; and God shall wipe away every tear from their eyes (7:14-17).

Is it not interesting that in this passage there is a curious shifting of roles that occurs? The reader would have expected that John would have asked the question about the nature of this grand assembly of persons and the elder dutifully would have supplied the answer, but that is not what happens. A striking feature of Revelation is that John never asks a single question in the entire book, even though he is permitted to view a long series of visions with extremely curious occurrences and strange personages found in most every one of them. And yet, John never asked one question of his angelic patrons. In chapter 5 it was not John but the "mighty angel" who asked, "Who is worthy to break the seals and open the scroll?" (5:2). John then wept because no one was found worthy to do so (5:4). An elder then responded to the angelic question. This incident illustrates that same general format, even though it does so with a slight twist. Here the elder both asks and answers the crucial question, while John is passive (and unaware of the answer and so unable to supply it). The effect of the elder's initiative in the scene is to assure the apostle's readers that the elder's explanation comes from God and may be trusted on account of its trustworthy source (Michaels, 114).

E. The Seventh Seal: The Majestic Silence (8:1)

And when He opened the seventh seal, there followed a silence in heaven for around a half an hour (Rev. 8:1).

When the first seal was broken, a voice like thunder was heard, saying to the prophet, "Go!" It was the same at the opening of the three succeeding ones. At the breaking of the fifth, there was a great cry from beneath the altar. And when the sixth was broken, a fearful tremor ran through the whole warp and woof of nature, filling the earth with concerted consternation. But, at the opening of the seventh, not a single voice is heard; not a motion is anywhere seen; an awful pause follows, and then all of heaven itself falls silent. Shortly before, everything was ringing with triumphant exultation over the multitude which no man could number, but now an eerie silence has taken the place of the reverberating songs, and everything lies mute and motionless.

Cycle One: The Seal Sequence

But as Joseph A. Seiss observed in his *Lectures on The Apocalypse*, "this silence, nevertheless, has made a good deal of noise in the world, especially among commentators." He went on to say that "it would be difficult to find another point upon which there have been so many different and discordant voices":

> . . . Some take this silence as a full stop to the chain of apocalyptic predictions, and so treat what follows as a mere rehearsal, in another form, of what had preceded. Others regard it as a blank, leaving everything belonging to the seventh seal unrevealed, so that its action can only be known when we come to the immortal life. Some pronounce it a mere poetic invention to heighten the dramatic effect, but having no particular significance. Others treat it as a prophetic symbol of scenes and experiences in the earthly history of man; some, as the suspension of divine wrath in the destruction of Jerusalem; some, as the freedom granted to the Church under the reign of Constantine; some, as the interval of repose enjoyed by Christians between the persecutions by Diocletian and Galerius in AD 311, and the beginning of the civil wars toward the end of the same year; some, as the disappearance of human strivings against God and His Christ; others, as a lull in earthly revolt and persecution, equivalent to a jubilee for the truth among men; others, as a millennium of peace and righteousness to be induced by the triumphs of evangelic effort and the progress of liberty; and yet others, as the everlasting rest of the saints. And yet there is not a word in the record about the Church, nor about the earth. The whole thing is distinctly located "in heaven," and its duration is specifically limited to "about half an hour" (181).

Reality is far less exciting than all of this rabid speculation about which Seiss comments with such rhetorical flourish. All of us understand the concept of the "dramatic pause." We have seen it often in plays and movies, as well as in dramatic presentations of various kinds. This is precisely what we have here. When the final seal, number seven, is opened, a great hush settles over the worshipping hosts of heaven. This is not what we expect. With all that has gone before we expect a peal of heavenly thunder, perhaps a flash of lightning, the crash of sword against armor, or some such boisterous and climatic shift of the scenes. But all of the amazing things that we have heard and seen to this point in the drama are followed only with a pregnant pause, a quiet moment, and nothing else, only utter silence. That is it. But that is precisely what this author wishes to accomplish. The very stillness and hush of that moment has set the stage for what comes afterward. It is as if there is an expectant stillness; a calm before the storm. A hush before the scream.

So, in our view this clearly represents a device for deepening the suspense of the reader for what might be coming next. It is similar to what we will meet in two subsequent visions: the restraining of the four winds of destruction (7:1-3) and the sealing up of the utterance of the seven thunders (10:4). It is presented as a striking contrast between the heavenly hymns that went before and the deafening blast that follows with the sounding of the heavenly trumpets.

One cannot help but be reminded of the words of the prophet, "The Lord is in his holy temple, let all the earth keep silence before Him" (Hag. 2:20; cf. Zeph. 1:7-8; Zech. 2:13). The significance of half an hour as the duration of this hushed silence is difficult to determine, but even though it is a relatively short period of time, it forms an altogether impressive break in the rapidly moving drama of this section of the work. For John's part it is just what happened as he watched the unfolding of the scenes before him. John simply states the fact of it: for him there was a long pause in the rapid-fire series of events that were being unveiled before his eyes. Half an hour is more than a pregnant pause. It is a long and uncomfortable wait for what is about to happen next. One cannot imagine in the heart of an oration having a speaker who pauses in the middle of his points for even a single minute. Half an hour would seem an eternity!

At all events, it is beyond any doubt that it appears here for the purposes of the literary composition that the Revelation represents. This silence described by John is the dramatic transition to the next cycle of divine judgments. It is a suspense filled silence that presages the next part of this grand drama that is the Revelation. It is that and nothing more mysterious or meaningful than that. When the silence is finally broken it is by a tremendous amount of noise: by peals of thunder, rumblings, flashes of lightning, an earthquake, and by the mighty blasts from seven trumpets. Obviously this long silence is meant as a prelude to what is to come. As well, it functions as an "apocalyptic bridge," linking together the seal and trumpet judgments, as two parts of a single beautiful spiritual reality.

CHAPTER FOUR

Cycle Two: The Trumpet Sequence (8:2-11:19)

Now that all of the seven seals have been opened and a short pause has occurred in the action, a second round of judgments is pictured through seven angels who blow their consecutive trumpets. John has a wonderful ability to combine in a single symbol ideas drawn from many different sources in this case, as also he does elsewhere. These "trumpets" of which he speaks in the present vision enjoy a wealth of rich associations which the trumpet as an object and as a symbol had in the Old Testament and in the Jewish religious liturgy generally.

Although Hebrew had two words for "trumpet," *shophar* (the ram's horn) and *chashosherah*, the metal instrument, such as Moses made for ceremonial use (Num. 10:2), the Greek version of the Old Testament (LXX) translated both with a single word, *salpinx*, and in this case there is no reason to suggest that John had in mind one rather than the other of the two. Later rabbis discriminated carefully between the two in certain cases, but John seems not to be interested in the differences between them or in the issues that concerned them in the debates of the savants on the matter.

In the Old Testament there are three passages which speak of seven trumpeters who formed part of a ceremonial procession, and two of these include a mention of the Ark of the Covenant of the Lord (Josh. 6; 1 Chron. 15:24; Neh. 12:41). The earliest of them is the story of the fall of the mighty Canaanite city of Jericho. Joshua's army is said to have marched around the city every day for six consecutive days and then seven times on the seventh, led by seven priests with their trumpets. The priests were the escort for the holy ark. When the priests blew their final blast on the trumpets and the army shouted, the walls of the city fell down flat. So says the narrative in the book of Joshua.

John surely must have had this story in mind when he wrote about his vision of the seven trumpets in this section of the book of Revelation. He tells his readers that with the blowing of the seventh trumpet the sacred ark appeared in the scene (11:19), and also that one of the consequences of the trumpet blasts was that a tenth of the great city fell (11:13). So, just as with ancient Jericho, which at the time blocked the entry of Israel into the Promised Land, Babylon the Great must fall before God's people can enjoy their permanent home in the New Jerusalem of God's promise (cf. Jer. 51:27). As G. B. Caird wrote: "The typological parallel is clear, yet it is only a partial parallel; for only a tenth of the city is said to fall. There is something provisional about this blowing of trumpets, for which we need further explanation" (Caird, 108).

So, in order to get the full explanation of John's image here, we must look further. A trumpet blast was also blown during Old Testament history to proclaim the accession of a king (1 Kings. 1:34, 39; 2 Kings. 9:13), and came in the Jewish worship to be associated particularly with the kingship of God (Psa. 47:5; 98:6; Num. 23:21; Zech. 9:14). In like manner, John's seventh trumpet is the signal for the heavenly choir to sing their coronation anthem, praising God because He has assumed the sovereignty and has begun to reign (11:15). There are also passages in the Old Testament where the trumpet acted as an alarm signal, summoning Israel to national repentance in the face of imminent divine judgment (cf. Jer. 4:5; 6:1, 17; Ezek. 33:3ff.; Isa. 58:1; Joel 2:1, 15). John too saw the purpose of these trumpet blasts and the disasters that they heralded as a signal for men to repent of their sins, even though that purpose may never have been achieved in any genuine sense. He observes that, "The rest of mankind who survived these plagues still did not renounce the gods of their own making" (9:20; cf. Amos 4:6-11).

Like Jeremiah before him, John knew that men could be at times too far gone in their idolatry to give heed to the divine trumpet call for repentance: "I will appoint watchmen over you; listen for the trumpet call. But they said, 'We will not listen'" (Jer. 6:17). Finally in this regard, trumpets were sounded at all of the Jewish feasts, on the first day of each month, and at the daily sacrifice "for remembrance before your God" (Num. 10:10; Ecclus. 1:16). The sounding of the trumpets in these ritual applications had to do with expression of Israel's constant prayer that God would remember His people for pardon, protection, and vindication. In that sense the Feast of Trumpets was portrayed in the biblical narrative as a "remembrance day of trumpet blowing" (Lev. 23:24). Likewise, John who was no doubt quite well aware of all of these traditional religious connections in the worship system of ancient Judaism, saw these particular trumpet blasts and their attendant judgments as evidencing the Lord's recollection of His suffering people in the midst of their trials and tribulations (Ibid., 109).

It is clear, therefore, that this series of trumpet soundings represent another portrait of the same concept which is set forth through different but somewhat similar symbols elsewhere in the Revelation. The major point of our author is that the prayers of the suffering saints have not gone unheard. Those prayers and God's muscular response to them are to have a powerful effect upon those who have persecuted His people and are making their lives so difficult. God intends to visit painful judgment on them for the sake of His praying people.

A. Seven Angels and Seven Trumpets (8:2-6)

Then I saw the seven angels who stand before God, and seven trumpets were given to them. And another angel came and stood at the altar with a golden censer, and he was given much incense to offer with the prayers of all the saints on the golden altar before the throne, and the smoke of the incense, with the prayers of the saints, rose before God from the hand of the angel. Then the angel took the censer and filled it with fire from the altar and threw it on the earth, and there were peals of thunder, rumblings, flashes of lightning, and an earthquake. Now the seven angels who had the seven trumpets prepared to blow them (Rev. 8:2-6).

In chapter eight an angel mixes incense with the prayers of the saints on the golden altar and casts it to earth. The message of the symbol is simple and straightforward: the urgent pleas and prayers of the saints have not gone unheard (cf. 6:10). No doubt there were many times when the disciples of Jesus wondered whether the Lord was listening to them when they were praying during those times of unutterable wickedness and unspeakable suffering. It seemed that there was so much injustice and so little recognition of the true nature of it in this world. On the surface of things it appeared that God was not willing to take action to bring them relief or to judge those who hated and mistreated them. The present vision represents a response to that feeling of vain hope in the face of so much relentless evil and constant travail.

This vision told those who prayed so intensely for help in their distress that God was indeed listening all the while and that when He took action to bring justice for them and their cause, it would be their prayers that initiated divine judgment. In John's vision their anxious petitions return to the earth as the wrath of God. Vengeance is now to be meted out. What follows in the remainder of this vision is a picture portrait of the various aspects of the Lord's action steps against their enemies. They are highly figurative, but it is clear that they picture the form which this retribution is to take. It will be remembered that it was seven trumpets that were sounded to bring down the city of Jericho when it was destroyed by God and to begin the process of Israel's establishment and settlement in the land of promise (Josh. 6:4, 6, 8). So figuratively speaking, seven trumpet blasts are to signal the punitive measures brought against the Romans to signal their eventual demise.

The first group of woes is upon nature: land, sea, fresh water, and the heavenly bodies. The second is upon mankind. The final woe is in fact the Final Judgment itself. They are comparable in some ways to what happened to Egypt during the Ten Plagues in the time of the prophet Moses, but the Trumpet Plagues are not in and of themselves intended to be seen as final. They affect a significant portion, but not all of the earth or mankind. The designation "one-third" occurs twelve times in vv. 7-12. The meaning is therefore transparent: these are preliminary judgments. They do not represent the Final Judgment, only various temporal means used by God to warn of worse things that may come if important matters are not attended to.

The obvious association of these Trumpet Judgments with the Ten Plagues in Egypt is singularly important and must not be missed by the reader. As John makes this transparent connection he offers his readers a well-recognized biblical background by which to better understand how the vision of the Trumpets relates to their own situation. According to the original story in the Hebrew Bible regarding Israel's exodus from Egypt, the purpose of the plagues was to assert the lordship of the Hebrew God over the world's most powerful ruler, the Egyptian Pharaoh. The plagues were a concrete demonstration of divine authority that was intended to convince the Lord's people of God's desire to lead them from Egypt to a Promised Land of their own, even better than Egypt. The Christians of the seven churches were being led by God toward a Beulah land of their own, but they must not fail to appreciate that this is where they are headed, and must not in the mean time get caught up in the good things of their own Egypt. These are mere trappings of their old life which need to be abandoned and forgotten, or else they will rob them of their eventual inheritance in the Promised Land.

We should also recall from Revelation 2-3 that the unfaithfulness of John's audience is due in large measure to cultural and societal pressures, which molded and shaped God's new Israel into a people more like Egypt (i.e., Rome) than the kingdom of priests "made" by the Lamb (cf. Rev. 5:9-10). The biblical and societal contexts in which John's believing audiences lived, then, interpret the significance of these Trumpets: the various "Pharaohs" who rule over the anti-Christian kingdom in John's world stand condemned and judged by Almighty God, while the unresponsive believers found among the seven congregations, who lack devotion to God, are rebuked like the grumbling, unfaithful Israel of old (cf. Wall, 125, 126).

The purpose of these Trumpet Judgments, when they are examined in their own right, seems not so much to be retribution as to lead men to repentance. Indeed, the sounding of a trumpet had as its primary intention to give warning. Like the watchman and his trumpet in Ezekiel 33, they warn the people of impending danger. When Joel gave his warning to Israel about the coming locust plague, he spoke also of the coming of the day of the Lord: "Blow the trumpet in Zion! Sound the alarm on My holy mountain! Let all the inhabitants of the land tremble, for the day of the Lord is coming!" (Joel 2:1). In John's way of thinking, greater and more destructive judgments are on the horizon. So, the Trumpet Plagues are seen as directed against a world that is adamant in its hostility toward God. It should be noted also that there is an obvious progression in John's presentation: as the intensity of the judgments increases, so also does the vehemence with which evil men refuse to repent (cf. also 9:20-21; 16:9, 11, 21).

B. Woes upon Nature (8:7-13)
1. *First angel sounds.*

The first angel blew his trumpet, and there followed hail and fire, mixed with blood, and these were thrown down upon the earth. And one-third of the earth was burned up, and a third of the trees were consumed, and all of the green grass was burned (Rev. 8:7).

In the course of this judgment hail and fire mingled with blood is cast upon the earth. One third of earth is burnt up, along with one third of the trees and all grass. This judgment centers upon *the land*. This echoes some aspects of the seventh plague of Egypt (Exodus 9:13-34). There are, however, some major differences. In the Exodus account there is no mention of blood being mixed with the hail and fire, and the fire in that case is described as lightning (Exod. 9:24-26; and compare Ezek. 38:22). Hail and lightning, of course, are natural phenomena. They occur with some frequency on the earth in every age of man. We also know that they are capable of killing both animals and men, and in fact have often done so over the course of human history. When they maim and kill animals and men the blood of the dead and injured mingles with the hailstones covering the landscape.

Such a frightful storm occasionally ravages the countryside, and with its characteristic hail and lightning destroys everything in its path. Such events are frequently interpreted as divine judgments on humanity for real or perceived sins committed against heaven. Here the text adds the particular detail that "these were thrown down upon the earth," apparently from heaven. So there is no doubt that it is intended as a divine judgment with God as the agent behind it (compare Psa. 29:3-10, where the author of this psalm says that the "voice of the Lord is powerful," which is a transparent reference to the sound of pealing thunder, "thunders . . . breaks in pieces the cedars of Lebanon"). In this particular instance, the hail and fire being mingled with blood may suggest that the blood of the martyrs of Christ is being responded to on God's part. He does not ignore the shedding of the innocent blood of His people. The wicked who do them harm will eventually pay with their own blood.

At any rate, the effect is disastrous. Great devastation follows in the wake of this storm. It may be recalled that in Zechariah 13:8-9 two-thirds of the people on the land are to die and one-third are to be brought through the refiner's fire. In this text it is one-third of the land and its vegetation that is devastated by fire. The fraction alluded to in this instance once more indicates that although God is bringing punishment on the earth, it is not yet complete or final. Hence, the purpose of the judgment is to move men toward repentance by reminding them that the full wrath of God will attend the Final Judgment. This reminds us of the language of the Lord's warning about the fall of Jerusalem and the destruction of the Temple. He told His disciples that there would be signs in the heavens, distress upon the earth, and men fainting for fear of what is about to come upon the world (Luke 21:25-26).

2. Second angel sounds.

The second angel blew his trumpet, and an object like a great mountain, burning with fire, was thrown into the sea, and a third of the sea was turned into blood. A third of the living creatures in the sea died, and one-third of the ships were destroyed (Rev. 8:8-9).

When the second angel sounds his trumpet, a great burning mountain is cast into the sea. One third of the sea becomes blood; one third of sea-creatures die; one third of ships are destroyed in the ocean. So, this judgment centers upon *the sea*. This reminds the reader of the plague of water turning to blood in Egypt, the first of the Ten Plagues (Exodus 7:20-21). When that plague struck Egypt the waters of the Nile turned to blood and the fish in the river died and "there was much blood throughout the land of Egypt." In this instance, however, there is a very considerable difference as to causation. Here there is an object like a great mountain that burns with fire and falls into the sea, turning the sea into blood. Volcanic activity was well recognized in this area of the world and this may be what John has in mind. For example, among the volcanic islands of the Aegean, Thera (modern Santorini) was especially notable. It took place in the middle of the second millennium BC and altered the whole map of the ancient world, devastating not only the island itself, but in Crete the cities of Mallia, Gournia, Pseira, Zakro, and others. It virtually ended the civilization of the Minoans and scattered the "sea peoples" throughout the Mediterranean basin and even into Egypt and Palestine. No doubt this event was long remembered. As well, the Greek geographer Strabo reports the formation of a new island as the result of an eruption in 196 BC. So, such formative happenings were well recognized and understood at the time of John's writing.

It has often been observed that the language of this passage reminds the knowledgeable reader of the events that took place in AD 79 (August 24) during the eruption of Mt. Vesuvius which disrupted the whole of the Bay of Naples from Capri to Cumae and devastated the surrounding area. Debris from the exploding mountain fell into the bay making it impossible to land boats (Pliny, *Epistles* 6.6.11). Pompeii and Herculaneum were both destroyed and approximately 12,000-15,000 people lost their lives in the wake of the volcanic activity during that brief but violent week. The two cities along with several small villages were covered over by volcanic pumice and effectively disappeared from the earth until they were unearthed by archaeologists hundreds of years later.

This tragic event left a lasting impression upon the Roman population and the story was retold in detail by several contemporary historians (Tacitus, *Annals* 4:67; Josephus, *Antiquities of the Jews* 20.144; Suetonius, *Titus* 8.3-4), along with the eye-witness account of the eruption provided by Pliny the Younger (*Epistles* 6.16, 20). As well, an epitomized account is preserved in Dio 66.21-23. Dio claimed that the sound of trumpets was heard prior to the disaster (cf. 66.23.1). In addition, the apocalypticists were impressed with the events of that horrendous period, seeing it as a judgment from God and as a portent of worse things to come. This is evident from their usage of it in their writings. In the *Sibylline Oracles* (4.130-34), for example, that writer speaks of it as a "firebrand" that "will burn many cities and destroy men; much smoking ashes will fill the great sky, and showers will fall from heaven like red earth." 1 Enoch makes allusion to seven stars that are compared to "great burning mountains" (18.13; 21.3). And even though that writer does not refer directly to the Vesuvius volcanic event and does not refer to the burning mountains falling into the sea, it is clear that something similar is in his mind, and it is certainly arguable that he may have taken his precedent from that historic horror which took place less than twenty years prior.

At any rate, we agree with Dr. Theodor Zahn who posited as long ago as 1922 in his essay in the Adolf Schlatter *Festschrift* that John was in all likelihood making a very direct allusion to that particular relatively recent tragedy in order to make his very frightening point in the present vision. It is also certain that Jewish writers considered it as a divine judgment meted out against Rome for her having destroyed Jerusalem and burnt the Temple.

The devastation that occurred in its wake seems to be illustrative and perhaps even suggestive of God's judgment of the Romans for their many evils, according to the writer of Revelation. Dio said that the eruption "wrought much injury of various kinds, as chance befell, to men and farms and cattle, and in particular it destroyed all fish and birds." Pliny the Younger also observed that the sea level receded and many sea creatures were left stranded on the dry land (6.20.9; cf. Aune, 519-20). The experience of such destruction and chaos would be long remembered and widely interpreted, even by the pagans, as a sign of divine displeasure.

3. Third angel sounds.

And the third angel sounded, and there fell from heaven a great star, burning as a torch, and it fell on the third part of the rivers, and upon the springs of waters; and the name of the star is Wormwood: and a third of the waters became wormwood; and many people perished because of the waters, since they were made bitter (Rev. 8:10-11).

From the water of the sea the author's attention moves to the waters on the land. It will be recalled that the first plague in Egypt was upon the waters of the Nile River. When this angel blows his trumpet a great burning star falls upon one third of the rivers and fountains of water. The star (or meteorite) is called Wormwood. Wormwood is a bitter herb (Artemisia absinthium L.) with neurotoxic properties, and although it is not usually fatal, water that is contaminated with it can be poisonous if imbibed over an extended period of time. This is a substance that is known from the Old Testament and a few references there (cf. Jer. 9:15; 23:15; Lam. 3:19; Prov. 5:3-4), where it was associated with bitterness and sorrow and classed in the category with gall.

In John's vision this contamination results in one third of water becoming bitter and men die from drinking it. Therefore, this judgment is aimed at the various sources of *fresh water*. This echoes the grumbling of Israel at Marah where God made the bitter waters sweet and drinkable (Exod. 15:23). In this case the opposite is true, however. The imagery that is employed here is rather unique. It seems to have no parallels in the other Jewish apocalyptic literature. Moreover, outside of Revelation, Scripture does not provide any close parallels with this reference to a flaming meteorite falling from the sky (cf. also 6:13; 9:1). It has been observed that Isaiah 14:12 refers to a falling star of this sort, but is quite different in its details: "How you have fallen from heaven, O morning star, son of the dawn. You have been cast down to the earth." This passage in Revelation differs markedly in respect to the size of the star, its fiery appearance, the inland waters that are said to be polluted by it, as well as its name. Isaiah relates his reference to the king of Babylon (cf. 14:4). This writer clearly intends something quite different, although he is not nearly so plain in his remarks as was the prophet Isaiah. John may have in mind the worship by the pagans of the many different river gods and deities having to do with particular water sources like springs. This judgment suggests that all such divinities are subject to the true God and are impotent before Him. They cannot oppose Him or stop Him from bringing whatever judgment upon even those aspects of the human experience that they are traditionally seen as possessing sovereignty over.

With this third trumpet the judgment of famine appears to be continued. The misery that sets in as a result of foul, undrinkable water is implicit in this circumstance as it is depicted. Privation, wretchedness, despondency and ultimately starvation are the natural repercussions of such a situation.

4. Fourth angel sounds.

The fourth angel sounded his trumpet, and one-third of the sun was struck, and a third of the moon, and a third of the stars, so that a third of their light were darkened, and a third of the day might be kept from shining, and in like manner a third of the night. Then I looked, and I heard an eagle crying with a loud voice as it flew in mid heaven, "Woe, woe, woe to those who dwell on the earth, at the blasts of the other trumpets that the three angels are about to blow!" (Rev. 8:12-13).

In this instance, one-third of sun, moon, and stars are smitten. They do not shine for one third of day or night. Thus, this particular judgment is directed at the *heavenly bodies*. This reminds us of the plague of darkness sent upon the Egyptians in the days of Moses (Exod. 10:21ff), the ninth one that came before the final plague. It symbolized the Creator's judgment upon a "fallen creation" (see Gen. 1:3-5). In the beginning God had spoken into the darkness and called for light. Now on account of human transgression He calls for darkness in the place of the light. Is it not interesting to consider that the place of final punishment for the wicked is described as a realm of "outer darkness"? Many people are afraid of the darkness. There are many reasons for this. We do not know what or who might be lurking in the darkness to do us harm. So we are very careful about being out and about after dark. Our eyes cannot see well in darkness. Some animals, like the felines, enjoy marvelous night vision. But in the darkness human beings are often completely blind and frequently stumble and fall and may be seriously injured or even killed in such accidents. In the plague upon ancient Egypt, and then in this case also, God utilized darkness as an effective weapon against perpetrators of evil.

We can imagine this writer looking up transfixed at the heavenly goings-on. The first four of the seven trumpets have sounded and the elements are devastated on that account. Moreover, with all of the previous references to angels in this context, suddenly John now hears an eagle screeching loudly as it flies in mid-heaven. It announces three woes to those who dwell on the earth. However, this text contains a significant textual variant, namely, the word *aetou*, or "eagle," has been the choice of some translators, even though *aggelou*, or "angel," was the choice of the translators of King James. One manuscript even conflated the two into the expression *angelou hōs aetou*, which should be rendered as "an angel like an eagle." In all likelihood we may safely conclude that the conflation probably is a classic attempt at making sense of the word the copyist encountered in the text as he read it, but in the course of doing so only made matters more confusing.

Undoubtedly the word he saw before making his effort was the term "eagle," which in the present context appears out of place (with all of the angels found in this context). This, in point of fact, helps to explain the textual confusion. An early copyist expected to see the word "angel" but instead encountered the term "eagle," and thought this surely must be an error. So he made a "correction" in order to fix what he deemed to be a mistake. But, for purposes of the text itself, the burden of the evidence lies on the side of the word "eagle," being that it is supported by Codex Sinaiticus and Alexandrinus and most of the manuscripts classified as minuscules. In addition to the evidence of the supporting manuscripts, the argument could be made that John is utilizing an interesting and strong metaphor when he says this creature called out, *ouai, ouai, ouai,* or "Woe, woe, woe." This is true because the sound of this Greek word is very similar to the cry of an eagle as it flies and screams its calls from the heavens. One may easily imagine an eagle screeching these three terrifying words as it flew over so that they could readily have been associated with the dire announcement God wanted declared to his servant John. Thus, even though there is some manuscript evidence on the side of the reading "angel," we may confidently assert that what John saw was an "eagle" and not an "angel."

At any rate, these first four trumpet blasts and their associated visions are pictures of the *various natural calamities* used as agents of divine wrath against the empire. Contemporary historical records indicate that in fact many distressing natural calamities occurred during this period which weakened the Roman economy and shook the morale of the Roman people. As previously noted, many students of the Revelation find the raw material for this series of judgments in the volcanic action of the region, including especially the homeland of the Romans, the Italian peninsula itself. It is especially important to remember that less than twenty years before John wrote this book, the Vesuvius volcano had erupted and destroyed Pompeii and Herculaneum. The entire region around the Bay of Naples was disrupted for many years by this violent and unexpected incident. Scientists have estimated that the eruption in AD 79, which spewed out molten rock and pulverized pumice, ultimately released a hundred thousand times the thermal energy released by the Heroshima-Nagasaki bombings. This catastrophe was widely known and variously interpreted by the highly superstitious people of the day.

In addition, Mount Etna, located in Catania, was an active volcano on the nearby island of Sicily. It erupted violently in 396 BC, 122 BC, AD

300-450, 950-1060, and 1607-1669. The mountain sits at the boundary of the African plate subducting underneath the Eurasian plate, and combined with the fact that it sits underneath a hotspot or crustal break means that the volcano has had a frequent eruptive history. Mount Etna is still very active today and nearly 25% of Sicily's population lives on the slopes of the volcano. Certainly there are many important associations that connect very well with the language of these Trumpet Judgments of John.

The eagle at the end of this series announces that there are three woes yet to follow. This is especially noteworthy, because once again the judgments are divided into two blocks, the first composed of four and the second of three, precisely in the fashion of the seal judgments.

C. Woes upon Mankind (9:1-21)

The fifth and sixth trumpet visions have been compared to horror movies. As one writer remarked, "One could dismiss these visions as creations of a deranged mind that is fascinated with painting monstrosities, heaping the grotesque upon the ugly." Certainly it is correct to observe that John revealed the bizarre, spiritual dimension of the world, a dimension that is present, though still hidden to the eyes and perceptions of most people, beneath a thin veneer of culture and sophistication.

Notwithstanding, the message of trumpets five and six is quite simple and straightforward. With a heavy eschatological twist they visualize the profound but unrelenting truth that "a person is punished by the very things by which he or she sins" (*Wisdom of Solomon* 11:16). Too, both of these trumpet soundings presuppose the traditional view that idolatry is, in its essence, the worship of demons (cf. 1 Cor. 10:20; Deut. 32:17). What they reveal in a most dramatic way is the true nature of idolatry and immorality in all of their unappealing, unattractive, ghastly and hideous perversity (Krodel, 200). They are hurtful and destructive to the very people who most adore and pursue them.

1. The fifth angel sounds.

And the fifth angel sounded, and I saw a star from heaven fallen to the earth: and there was given to him the key of the pit of the abyss. And he opened the pit of the abyss; and there went up smoke out of the pit, as the smoke from a great furnace; and the sun and the atmosphere were darkened because of the smoke from the pit. And out of the smoke came forth locusts upon the earth; and power was given them, as the scorpions of the earth have power. And it was said to them that they should not hurt the grass of the earth, neither any green thing, neither any tree, but only such men as have not the seal of God on their foreheads. And it was given them that they should not kill them, but that they should be tormented for five months: and their torment was as the torment of a scorpion, when it strikes a man. And in those days men shall seek death, and shall in no wise find it; and they shall desire to die, and death will flee from them. And the shapes of the locusts were like horses prepared for war; and on their heads as it were crowns like gold, and their faces were like men's faces. And they had hair like the hair of women, and their teeth were like the teeth of lions. And they had breastplates, like breastplates of iron; and the sound of their wings was like the sound of chariots, of many horses rushing into battle. And they have tails like scorpions, and stings; and in their tails is their power to hurt men five months. They have over them as their king the angel of the abyss: his name in Hebrew is Abaddon, and in the Greek language he has the name Apollyon. The first Woe is past: behold, there are yet two Woes afterward (Rev. 9:1-12).

When this trumpet sounds, a huge star falls to earth and the abyss is opened with a key. Smoke billows forth, and out of this smoke come destructive locusts. Locust plagues represented an ancient and horrendous scourge to civilized men. They consumed everything and left humanity destitute in the wake of their seemingly innumerable hordes. But these locusts are only like the ones known from experience with them in the world of the ordinary. These creatures are quite different. They are not ordinary locusts that eat up all of the green herbage in their path. These have the power of scorpions to hurt men during a period of five months. Their king has a name. He is called "Destroyer" (see Prov. 15:11).

Clearly this leader is Satan. He is depicted in the Bible more than once as fallen to earth (cf. Luke 10:18; John 12:9), and here he seems to be seen as a heavenly luminary (a star, or meteorite) that has been brought down from his high station. The pit of the Abyss is just as clearly viewed as his dominion (see Matt. 10:25; 12:24). Although there is an exception in Romans 10:6-7 where Paul relates this language to the abode of the dead, generally speaking reference to the Abyss has to do with the place where the Devil and his demonic spirits remain for now. Fallen angels are said to reside there; it is their prison for the present, awaiting the Judgment Day (Luke 8:31; 2 Pet. 2:4; Jude 6). In this instance their leader is given permission for a time, just five months, to open up that hellish region and permit it to vomit out its disgusting inhabitants so that they might bring misery to those who deserve to experience torment on account of their evil ways.

Why the reference to "five months" as a limit to the torture wrought by these beings? Some commentators have pointed out that the typical life cycle of a locust, and thus the time of torment described, agrees naturally with the actual time that ordinary locusts would have lived, swarmed and wrought their destruction and chaos on the world. But John is seldom so literal or scientific as this, and so there is little reason to believe that in this instance he would have intended such a message by his symbol. The more likely reason for this is to put forth a round number that indicated a specified but limited time for the work of the locusts to deliver their stinging message to sinners. Believers could therefore know that an end would come and that it would come relatively soon. According to Mark 13:19-20 (cf. Matt. 24:21-22), if God had not cut short the calamities associated with the acts of judgment that prefaced the end of Jerusalem and of the Jewish economy, no one would have been able to endure it. Because of the faithful, who are apparently, as in John's account, caught up in the maelstroms associated with the decline of the Roman state and its economy, God does indeed cut the time short in this case also (cf. Blount, 176-177).

Throughout all of this description it needs to be recalled that God is seen as Sovereign over these evil beings, and even over their leader. God grants them permission to do certain things because they fulfill His will. These beings are never seen as autonomous. Their power is granted to them for a certain period of time and then it is taken away again. Even though they have considerable power over a portion of the human population, that leverage is both limited as to extent and restricted as to duration. There is only one true God, and He is altogether sovereign.

Once more, their place of origin is also very important to the meaning of John's symbolism. These destructive fellows come from the inside of the earth, "the abyss" as the author calls it. On one level, then, they represent the problem of internal decadence which blights society and brings about every sort of affliction to the lives of unregenerate men and women. Human sin itself brings misery and pain to the human family, and has done this since the Garden of Eden. This internal rottenness, politically and otherwise, is well known to historians and has often been blamed for the decline of the Roman state. It plagued the Roman Empire perpetually and finally aided in bringing about its demise. Edward Gibbon in his book *The History of the Decline and Fall of the Roman Empire* (1776) observed that the fall of the Empire was very gradual, but clearly began after the death of Marcus Aurelius and the ascent of Commodus (180-192).

At the close of his monumental history of the Empire he alludes to four principal causes of Rome's decline and fall: (1) The injuries of time and nature; devastating fires consumed huge swaths of the city at various times; also the city was subject to frequent inundations which destroyed buildings all around Rome many times in her history; over time huge quantities of silt washed down from the hills and poured into the plain and it was elevated over the years some 14-15 feet, covering most of the ancient city but protecting the modern city from flooding by the Tiber and the other rivers of the region to some extent; (2) The hostile attacks of the barbarians and the tendency toward passivism and away from the militarism of the past on the part of the Christians who had become a very substantial portion of the population doomed the city to eventual takeover; (3) The use and abuse of the materials of their ancient civilization; the Goths and Vandals spirited away on their wagons the grand treasures of their history and plundered the essence of what had once been known as the imperial city of Rome; and, (4) The domestic quarrels of the Romans among themselves; through these centuries old hatreds and smoldering resentments, the Romans became balkanized and divided, and thus no longer presented a unified Empire to their enemies.

But the brunt of his argument was that the Empire succumbed to barbarian invasions in large part due to the gradual loss of civic virtue among its citizens. It became weak over time because the citizenry outsourced their duty to defend their empire to barbarian mercenaries. The Romans became soft and lazy and unwilling to live the more difficult military lifestyle required for soldiers. Without their patriotic legions to protect them, they became a second-rate power. Ultimately, the barbarians turned against them.

In addition, continual foreign wars compelled leadership to the extreme of excessive taxation of the citizenry in order to fund these wars, breaking the morale of the people and impoverishing the Empire generally. All of these factors entered into the decline and eventual fall of the Empire, but at the heart of the matter was the loss of civic virtue, or *internal corruption and rottenness*, precisely the demonic curse that John underscores in this fifth trumpet vision.

And, as terrible as this whole portrait may seem, the reality is that social corruption of this sort, at least to some degree, is not restricted to the Roman Empire, but has been a bane to most every society, no matter how "civilized" or "advanced" it has been. As Gerhard Krodel commented:

> The locust-demons seem to reappear in new disguises and torment in forms such as alcohol and drug abuse, insatiable yearning for sexual promiscuity, sexually transmitted diseases, collective hysteria and subgroup temper tantrums, neurotic drives in diverse forms, driving passions for power, prestige, and wealth at the expense of one's own humanity, torments of psychic disorders, debilitating inability to maintain personal relationships, and other "locusts." One can only wish them to go away—and they do—after a while (five months, 9:10). In contrast to the demonic cavalry of the sixth trumpet, "the locusts" do not kill. Yet their torment is bad enough for people to wish they were dead (9:5-6). These "locusts" arise out of the abyss, which is the counterimage of the heavenly temple, the place of worship (Krodel, 200-201).

There follows after these things an announcement that there are two more woes yet to follow. In other words, as bad as all of this seems, still worse things are yet to come.

2. The sixth angel sounds.

And the sixth angel sounded, and I heard a voice from the horns of the golden altar which is before God, one saying to the sixth angel who had a trumpet, "Turn loose the four angels that are bound at the great River Euphrates." And the four angels were set loose, that had been prepared for the hour and day and month and year, that they should kill one-third of humanity. And the number of the armies of the horsemen was twice ten thousand times ten thousand: I heard the number of them. And thus I saw the horses in the vision, and those who sat on them, having breast-

plates like fire and hyacinth and brimstone: and the heads of lions; and out of their mouths proceeded fire and smoke and brimstone. By these three plagues one-third of men were killed, by the fire and the smoke and the brimstone, which proceeded out of their mouths. For the power of the horses is in their mouth, and in their tails: for their tails are like serpents, and have heads; and with them they do harm. And the rest of mankind, who were not killed with these plagues, repented not of the works of their hands, that they should not worship demons, even the idols of gold, and of silver, and of brass, and of stone, and of wood; which can neither see, nor hear, nor walk: but they repented not of their murders, nor of their sorceries, nor of their fornication, nor of their thefts (Rev. 9:13-21).

When the sixth of the angelic trumpeters sounds his instrument, a voice is heard from the golden incense altar that is before God granting permission, and then four angels are loosed from the River Euphrates to kill one third of men. The writer does not mention at this point that these are those who have not been sealed by God for their protection, but that is apparently assumed to be the case (cf. 9:4). All of this is said to be laid out in advance, minutely and immutably planned by God (cf. Wisd. 11:20). These four angels remind the reader of the four angels at the four corners of the earth mentioned earlier in the Revelation (7:1). In the Old Testament Israel was threatened by the Assyrians and then the Babylonians from beyond the River Euphrates. So the figure of a massive and dangerous army from across that ancient waterway was one that was well understood and in fact very familiar to the apostle's audience.

Their army numbers 200 million. Such a number would be almost beyond imagining. It would also be beyond any nation's capacity to repulse, even powerful Rome, but these troopers are not ordinary soldiers. They are not even men. Like the locust plague before them, they are demonic forces. These cavalrymen do not wear the typical clothing or armor of human soldiers, instead they are endowed with an unconventional protection, a breastplate that appeared to be the color of fire and hyacinth and brimstone. These are the colors of hell (fiery red, smoky blue, and sulfurous yellow). They also breathe out smoke and fire and brimstone (sulfur). Thus, their breath also has the look and smell of hell. None of this is accidental or merely fortuitous. They look and smell like the place from whence they have come. Like the locusts that came before them, even though the writer does not say so here, these demons have come from the Abyss of hell also.

Those who survive this onslaught, the remainder of mankind, refuse to repent of their wickedness and give up their idolatries, murders, sorceries, fornications and thefts (cf. Exod. 20:13ff. where the identical order is found). The purpose of God in sending various judgments on mankind is always to elicit repentance from those who suffer these painful indignities. This was the case with the locust-horses of Joel (2:12-14) and the demonic cavalry of Gog (Ezek. 38:4ff.), along with the locust swarm of Amos (7:1, 2). Repentance on the part of wicked men is always the object of God's judgment (cf. Rom. 2:4-5; 2 Pet. 3:15). Again in this context also, the author makes the customary association of idolatrous practices with the worship of demons (Deut. 32:17; Psa. 106:37; 1 Cor. 10:20). Moreover, "sorceries" are commonly linked with the worship of demons as well. The two go hand in hand. John, like Paul in his writings, saw the varied practices of pagan worship as springs of moral and spiritual corruption, and a prime reason for the wrath of God being poured out on guilty humanity (cf. Rom. 1:18ff.).

These massive cohorts represent the third instrument of destruction used by the Almighty against the empire to bring her down: *external invasion*. They symbolize Parthian cavalry, Rome's most dreaded military enemy. Parthians were celebrated horsemen. Most armies of that day fought on foot. Soldiers on horseback were much more agile and threatening. The horse itself represented a weapon of sorts. These enormous animals can kick at and trample upon ordinary men and kill them with their hooves, but this is not the point that John makes about them. He says that these horses are endowed with a different weapon. It is in their tails. The "sting" that John says is in the tails of these frightening horses is no doubt an allusion to the "Parthian shot" (or "parting shot") as it came to be called: a light horse military tactic customarily employed by them. Being the skilled horsemen that they were, they were expert in the use of this deceptive tactic. While in real or feigned retreat, their archers would turn their bodies back in full gallop to shoot at the pursuing enemy. Such methods were beyond the abilities of most ordinary horsemen. But the Parthians were well practiced in its effective use, and their horses were trained to expedite the tactic. There seems little doubt that this is what John alludes to in this elusive reference. Across the Euphrates the Parthian hordes were a constant threat to the Roman's eastern boundary. Their history with Parthian armies were legendary. The Romans were never able to bring the Parthians into subjection. At every turn they were harassed by them and humiliated by their unconventional tactics and renowned toughness.

Such armies of alien enemies, says John in this horrifying vision, eventually will be granted permission by God to invade Rome and bring her to heel. Hell itself will be behind these unstoppable legions, outnumbering and overwhelming the powerful legions of Rome. The images of the Parthian hordes is representative of the swarms of barbarians who, from a host of different places, would eventually throng across the borders and inundate the protective armies of the Romans. The storied bravery and tactical sophistication of Rome's many illustrious cohorts would prove to be no match for such otherworldly enemies. In the end, the mighty Roman military would be vanquished by throngs of brutish, vulgar, uncivilized, uncultured, and unsophisticated savages.

D. The Interlude Visions (10:1-11:2)
1. The Seven Thunders.

And I saw another strong angel coming down out of heaven, arrayed with a cloud; and the rainbow was upon his head, and his face was like the sun, and his feet like pillars of fire; and he had in his hand a little book open: and he set his right foot on the sea, and his left on the earth; and he cried with a loud voice, as a lion roars: and when he cried, the seven thunders uttered their voices. And when the seven thunders uttered their voices, I was about to write: and I heard a voice from heaven saying, "Seal up the things which the seven thunders uttered, and write them not." And the angel that I saw standing on the sea and on the earth lifted up his right hand to heaven, and swore by Him who lives for ever and ever, who created the heaven and the things that are in it, and the earth and the things that are in it, and the sea and the things that are in it, that there shall no more delay: but in the days of the voice of the seventh angel, when he is about to sound, then is finished the mystery of God, according to the good tidings which He declared to His servants the prophets (Rev. 10:1-7).

Once again we experience one of John's interlude visions, much like we saw in chapter 7. In the sequence of the sevens (seals, trumpets, and bowls) there is an interlude after the sixth seal and the sixth trumpet, but not after the sixth bowl. The sounding of the sixth trumpet pictured those who are visited with judgment after horrible judgment, and yet they still refuse to yield themselves to the divine will. They will not repent, entirely in the mode of Pharaoh and the Egyptians in the story of the Exodus of Israel from the land of Egypt. These unbelievers have been on the receiving end of a series of malevolent plagues (8:6–9:21) intended to bring them to remorsefulness and contrition, but making no headway with them. Before he proceeds with the seventh trumpet, the writer presents for the consideration of the reader the mission of believers to a lost and dying world. They are to proclaim the message of the gospel. Whatever else may transpire, they have work to do. The Word of God needs to be shared. They may not be able to make much difference in the unfolding drama of world history, but they may be able to make a significant difference in the lives of those few who will be inclined to listen to them and their message of "good tidings which He (God) declared to His servants the prophets" (v. 7).

Without any great attention to the matter, apparently the scene has changed as this next vision is unfolded. Throughout chapters 4 through 9 John is pictured in heaven seeing the scenes as they play out before him. In this instance he is on the earth, for the angel of light which he sees descends from heaven (v. 1) and it is from heaven that the mighty voice is heard (vv. 4, 8). At the beginning of this series of visions, John is shown a very powerful angel descending from heaven. Three different angels in the Revelation are described as "strong" or "mighty" angels (*angelon ischuron*; 5:2; 10:1; 18:21). This angel reminds us of the powerful angelic figure that Daniel saw in Daniel 12:5-7. His celestial glory is manifested in several ways. He is clothed about with a cloud, a rainbow surrounds his head, his face beams like the sun itself, and his feet appear as pillars of fire. In his hand is a small open book. He is so great that he places one foot upon the sea and the other on the land. When he speaks it sounds to John like the roar of a mighty lion. The sound of his voice shatters the heavens, reverberating across the sky. It is as if lighting has struck seven times over and peals of thunder follow. John tells us at this point that in this quaking of the skies God revealed to him some very special truths that were not to be shared with others.

Thus when he hears the sound of these seven thunder crashes God manifested to him certain specific secrets for his ears only. Apparently the apostle heard and understood precisely what was uttered and thus exactly what was revealed in the message of the seven thunders. But rather than being told to write it down as he was commanded to do on a number of other occasions, John is told to seal up the things the seven thunders uttered. He is not to disclose their content. The larger message of this secretive divine communication and the fact that John tells us about it, whetting our curiosity about it, but does not explain the content and so satisfy our curiosity, may be taken to suggest that there are many ineffable truths that heaven knows but retains for its own, but which man is not permitted to know. The secret councils of heaven are not always revealed to men (Deut. 29:29). In this case John, like Paul in a similar instance (2 Cor. 12:1-4), was made privy to a particular heavenly mystery, but was told not to write it down in the book that we have before us.

So, sometimes God reveals to His people the fullness of His will. On other occasions He only tells us what we need to know, and little else. This will, for example, at times leaves us to wonder as to what God is trying to accomplish in permitting certain evils to persist without being quickly vanquished and judged. Sometimes this may leave us frustrated and bereft of easy explanations. We may wonder about it and pray about it, but still find no answer to the mystery. The message of this vision is that God's will is sovereign and we must be satisfied to know what is revealed for us. And while this may be the case, in the meantime there is important work that needs to be done. The message of the gospel must be published abroad. The world in general may not heed its revelation of divine deliverance, but there are people who will, and so we must not spend our precious time in perpetual agitation over what we do not or cannot know. Howbeit, for now it is revealed only to the prophet that there is to be no more delay. One more trumpet is about to sound and that blast is to signal the eternal judgment of God (1 Thess. 4:14). Men must make preparation for that one, so we must preach the gospel while there is yet time.

2. The Little Book.

And the voice which I heard from heaven, I heard it again speaking with me, and saying, "Go, take the book that is open in the hand of the angel who stands upon the sea and upon the earth." And I went to the angel, saying to him that he should give me the little book. And he said to me, "Take it, and eat it up; and it shall make your belly bitter, but in your mouth it shall be as sweet as honey." And I took the little book out of the angel's hand, and ate it up; and it was in my mouth as sweet as honey: and when I had eaten it, my belly was made bitter. And they said to me, "You must prophesy again over many peoples and nations and tongues and kings" (Rev. 10:8-11).

The apostle is shown a little book. Once more we are reminded of Ezekiel's earlier vision (cf. Ezek. 2:1ff) that had to do with his call to a career of prophetic proclamation. In that much more elaborate vision, the prophet is commissioned to preach to the sons of Israel, "to a rebellious people who have rebelled against Me; they and their fathers have transgressed against Me to this very day. And I am sending you to them who are stubborn and obstinate children, and you shall say to them, 'Thus says the Lord God,' As for them, whether they listen to you or not—for they are a rebellious house—they will know that a prophet has been among them" (v. 3ff.). Whereupon, God commanded the prophet to "open your mouth and eat what I am giving you" (v. 8). He was then shown a hand with a scroll in it. When it was spread out before him, "it was written on the front and back, and written on it were lamentations and woe" (v. 10).

Ezekiel was then told to consume this scroll, "Son of Man, eat what you find, and go, speak to the house of Israel." So he opened his mouth and was fed the scroll that was in the hand of him who was speaking. God then commanded him, saying, "Son of Man, feed your stomach and fill your body with this scroll which I am giving you." When the prophet ate it, "it was sweet as honey in my mouth," he observed (3:3). The words of the Psalmist come immediately to mind when reading this text, as well: "How sweet are your words to my taste, sweeter than honey to my mouth" (Psa. 119:103). As well, the comments of the prophet Jeremiah: "Your words were found, and I ate them, and your words became to me a joy and the delight of my heart" (Jer. 15:16).

At this point Ezekiel was instructed to go to the house of Israel and speak the words of God to them. But He warned him, "the house of Israel will not be willing to listen to you, since they are not willing to listen to

Me" (v. 7). The Lord then prepared him for their resistance to His message by making his forehead "like emery harder than flint." Thus, in the end though the message was sweet in his mouth, it was bitter to him like it was for John, even though in the case of Ezekiel it is not expressly mentioned as it was with John.

This vision does not represent the commissioning of John as a prophet, as the vision of the scroll was for Ezekiel. This vision, and the impressive theophany that introduced it, marked the beginning of Ezekiel's work as a prophet. John was already a prophet. In fact, John was already an old man, most of whose life and career were already behind him. John's vision has a completely different intentionality, even though the messages are quite similar in the two visions. John is told to eat the book in order to assimilate its message of mourning, lamentation, and woe for its future proclamation (even though this particular aspect of his message is not directly mentioned, it is assumed by the clear reference to the work of the prophet Ezekiel, along with the nature of the visions that have come immediately before this one).

So John took the book from the angel's hand, just as he was instructed, and ate it. In his mouth it was as sweet as honey, but he also found it to be bitter when he consumed it. He was then informed that he had more preaching to do. Patmos would not represent his end. "Once again you must prophesy over many peoples and nations and tongues and kings." The little book, then, was the message of the gospel of Christ which John was commanded to preach to his generation of men and women. In that proclamation John saw a message of woe for those who would remain under the judgment of God because of their rejection of the counsel of God. But, it is also a message for the suffering saints of God, as Mounce so artfully observes:

> The sweet scroll which turns the stomach bitter is a message for the church. Before the final triumph believers are going to pass through a formidable ordeal. As the great scroll of chapter 5 outlined the destiny of all mankind, so the little scroll unveils the lot of the faithful in those last days of fierce satanic oppression. It tells of the two witnesses who, when they have finished their testimony, are destroyed by the beast out of the abyss (11:7). Like the crucified Lord their dead bodies are exposed for public contempt (11:8).

Erdman writes concerning the people of God faithfully bearing their testimony, that "they are delivered not *from* martyrdom and death, but *through* martyrdom and death to a glorious resurrection" (99). The prospect of no further delay in the fulfillment of God's purposes is sweet indeed. That it will involve a bitter prelude is hard to swallow (Mounce, 216).

3. *The Measuring of the Temple.*

Then there was given to me a reed like a measuring-rod: saying, "Arise, and measure the temple of God, and the altar, and those who worship in it. And the court which is outside of the temple leave alone, do not measure it; for it has been given over to the nations: and the holy city they shall tread under foot for forty-two months" (Rev. 11:1-2).

Long before John's Revelation, Ezekiel had a vision of an angel with a measuring-rod whose task it was to measure the temple, and the prophet Zechariah also saw an angel who measured the city of Jerusalem. Those Old Testament prophets in their prophecies, however, spoke of the restoration of the temple and of the city of Jerusalem to their former glory. Those prophetic utterances were realized in the temple construction of Zerubbabel and then Herod the Great. The Herodian temple, especially, was considered one of the most beautiful sights to see in the ancient world. In AD 70, however, that temple complex was brought to ruin. Here John speaks not of an earthly but of a heavenly temple. Additionally, this measuring of the temple has a different purpose. John is told to measure this temple in order to protect it, and of course by this time the physical temple in Jerusalem had been in ruins for almost a quarter of a century. In this vision the church is pictured figuratively, as it is elsewhere in the Bible, as the temple of God (1 Cor. 3:16-17; 6:19; 2 Cor. 6:16; Eph. 2:21).

In this vision it is measured for protection and preservation (Zech. 2:2-5) through the coming judgments upon mankind. This is the obvious force of the apostle's brief vision. John is told that the court which is outside the temple must be given over to the "nations" (i.e., the Gentiles, or heathen) and they will trample the holy city underfoot. Therefore, according to John's view of the future, the temple itself would not be given over to the pagans. It would be sustained and would survive this period of devastation.

It will be recalled that some scholars see the Revelation as written before the fall of Jerusalem and read some of these predictions as having to do with the literal city and the physical temple. If this were true then John was predicting the survival of the city of Jerusalem and the Jewish place of worship.

But this was not his intent. The physical temple in Jerusalem had no such future. The advocates of this position do not realize that if this view is taken as the proper intent of John's prophecy, then his prediction proved untrue. But that was not his meaning. He was saying that the Lord would protect His church, and He would surely preserve it throughout the frightening period of the persecutions and sufferings to come, and that it would survive even though some truly terrible things were ahead.

The time reference in this text regarding the trampling of the sacred city, "forty-two months," even though it appears enigmatic at first sight, is very important for John's understanding of the future of the church during these times of persecution. The forty-two months are the equivalent of three and a half years, which is the time of the beast's authority and of his war against the saints of God (13:1-7). It is also equivalent to the one thousand two hundred and sixty days that the witnesses are said to prophesy (11:3) and the woman is nourished in the wilderness (12:6). As three and one half years it represents the mysterious "three and a half times" of the book of Daniel (cf. 7:25; 12:7; cf. also Rev. 10:6; 12:14). This is the divinely limited period of oppression prior to final victory, which also lies behind the "three and one half days" of the earth dwellers' triumph over the dead witnesses (11:9) and the half-week of Jesus own eclipse, spent in the grave. Taken together, these time referents are very significant. They set forth an important notion which for many readers of the Revelation have gone unnoticed and unappreciated.

In employing this special symbolism, John is urging the church to see its whole life and work under the sign of "three and one-half." He is expressing symbolically what was set out historically in Jesus' own career, in His instruction to the twelve (Matt. 9:17-10:42) and the seventy (Luke 10:1-20), and in the stories in Acts of the Apostles regarding Stephen, Peter, James, Paul, and others. It was a pattern of intrepid witness, audacious opposition, virtual invulnerability and impressive success for a while, then defeat and death, but in the end, final vindication and triumph for the cause. His "three and a half" covers the time both of invulnerability

(11:3-6) and of eclipse (11:7-9; 13:5-7). His implication is that both of these aspects are part and parcel of the church's essence. There can be no period of time when the church is simply at peace in the world. There will be no time when the church is only triumphant, and there will be no era when the church is merely crushed and destroyed, defeated and despondent. Each of these realities is appropriate in every phase of the church's life and history (Sweet, 182, 183).

E. The Two Martyrs/Witnesses (11:3-14)

> *And I will give to My two witnesses, and they shall prophesy a thousand two hundred and threescore days, clothed in sackcloth. These are the two olive trees and the two candlesticks, standing before the Lord of the earth. And if any man desires to hurt them, fire proceeds out of their mouth and devours their enemies; and if any man shall desire to hurt them, in this manner must he be killed. These have the power to shut the heaven, that it rain not during the days of their prophecy: and they have power over the waters to turn them into blood, and to strike the earth with every plague, as often as they shall desire. And when they shall have finished their testimony, the beast that comes up out of the abyss shall make war with them, and overcome them, and kill them. And their dead bodies lie in the street of the great city, which spiritually is called Sodom and Egypt, where also their Lord was crucified. And from among the peoples and tribes and tongues and nations do men look upon their dead bodies three days and a half, and do not permit their dead bodies to be laid in a tomb. And those who dwell on the earth rejoice over them, and celebrate; and they shall send gifts to one another; because these two prophets tormented those who dwell on the earth. And after the three and a half days the breath of life from God entered into them, and they stood on their feet; and great fear fell on those who beheld them. And they heard a loud voice from heaven saying to them, "Come up here." And they went up into heaven in the cloud; and their enemies beheld them. And in that hour there was a great earthquake, and a tenth of the city fell; and there were killed in the earthquake seven thousand persons: and the rest were frightened, and gave glory to the God of heaven. The second Woe is past: behold, the third Woe is coming soon (Rev. 11:3-14).*

Two "witnesses" whose work it is to prophesy for 1,260 days appear next. John relates to his audience that these two figures he introduces at this point in the narrative are the two olive trees and the two lamps which stand before the Lord of the earth (v. 4). In the book of Zechariah these images stood for Zerubbabel and Joshua, the anointed ruler and the anointed priest of Israel during that Seer's day. Here they stand for the whole body of the church of Christ whose task it was to proclaim the gospel. Two is the minimum number of valid witnesses required in any legal situation (cf. Deut. 19:15; John 8:17). It will also be recalled that the seventy, like rabbinic delegates, were sent out in twos (Luke 10:1; cf. Acts 13:2; 15:39f.). The fact that they are said to wear sackcloth befits them because they are clearly intended to be seen as heralds of repentance in the fashion of Elijah (2 Kings 1:8) and John the Baptist (Mark 1:5).

Three stages are to be discerned in this vision as regards the activities of these two men: (1) The witnesses proclaim their message with great power and no one is able to harm them. (2) The beast comes up out of the abyss and kills the witnesses. (3) Finally, the witnesses are raised and taken to heaven. Each of these stages has profound meaning, but each in its own turn is easily understood and appreciated for the message that is contained within it.

Several interpretations have been offered by various interpreters regarding these two figures. Some see them as Moses and Elijah. Others as Enoch and Elijah. And still others as two unknown Christian believers whom God will call to be his witnesses in the end times. These three views ignore the obvious symbolism of the context and opt for a literalness in their approach to the passage that is not appropriate. Like the other symbols of the book, they are representational of something other than the symbol itself. That much is clear. In our view, the martyr/witnesses represent the church and her important task of preaching the gospel of Christ during a period of success and then of persecution and martyrdom (2:13). John says that they not only wear the miter of Joshua and the crown of Zerubbabel, but they also have access to the rod of Moses and the mantle of the prophet Elijah. They are heirs to all the power and prophetic preaching of the storied messengers of the Old Testament age.

Hence, as heirs to the great legacy of these Old Testament worthies, at first the church had preached successfully, relatively unhindered. Great signs and miracles attended those early days of amazing success. But all of that eventually changed. Peacetime gave place to a time of spiritual warfare. Satan was not happy with the progress of the gospel in the world. He was not content to allow the Lord's message free course among the nations who had served him for so long through the gods and goddesses whom he held up as divine beings when in fact they were merely stand-ins for his own willful rebellion against the true God. So the church had to be opposed and her representatives had to be destroyed. Thus began the period of persecution. During the time of the persecutions, many Christians were killed and their message was hindered. The last part of the vision, however, promised them a time when they would again be able to bear their witness to the Lord's mercy and salvation without successful opposition or violent protest. God would, by His sovereign power and might, make this possible in spite of terrifying odds which seemed at the moment to be so unassailable. In the end, the martyred heroes of the faith would be raised from death and called up to heavenly glory.

The writer's reference to "the great city, which spiritually is called Sodom and Egypt, where also their Lord was crucified" has proven confusing for some readers, but it ought not to be. If read closely and insightfully it is quite easy to understand. This series of geographical references are symbolical through and through. Here is the key to understanding them: Certain cities have come to have great events (whether good or bad) associated with them both historically and spiritually. If one mentions the city of Hiroshima, for example, the catastrophic atomic bomb explosion at that location is immediately associated with it in the mind of the hearer. That is so in spite of the fact that it is a thriving city today, and much time has passed since those dark days during the second great World War. Likewise, Nanking is associated with the slaughter of hundreds of thousands of Chinese soldiers and civilians during the Second Sino-Japanese War, along with the rape of women and children in the city. "The rape of Nanking" comes immediately to mind when the name is cited. Waterloo, Belgium will forever be connected with the events of June 18, 1815 and Napoleon Bonaparte. There he "met his Waterloo." Such historical bonds are impossible to break. Time and history cannot erase the tragic memories of yesteryear or divorce them from those events which made them infamous.

In like fashion, John's freighted references to Sodom, Egypt, Babylon and Jerusalem were heavy with readily identifiable meaning. In a sense it could be said that the apostle's city is not to be found in any one place on any particular map. In another, it is on every map of every place. To say, as some students of the book have done, that the words "where also their Lord was crucified" must be a reference to the physical Jerusalem of biblical fame is to misunderstand all of John's symbolic geography. John's unique form of geographical reference is different because it lies in the special realm of apocalyptic language and symbol. Jerusalem is indeed called "Sodom" by some of the prophets in their condemnations of the sins of the city (cf. Isa. 1:10; 3:9) and Sodom is likewise linked with Egypt occasionally in the ancient Jewish literature (cf. Wisd. 19:14), but it is clear from John's own description that he is speaking allegorically ("spiritually") and not literally.

Paul utilized a similar methodology when he spoke of the handling of divine secrets in his first letter to the Corinthians (2:6-16). In that language Christ was represented as crucified by "the rulers of this age" (1 Cor. 2:6-8), who at that moment in time were embodied in the persons of men like Caiaphas, Herod, and Pontius Pilate, and of course the deed was done in one particular great city, which was to be identified at that moment with Jerusalem. The city alluded to in the present context, however, represents not the city itself, a metropolitan assemblage of human beings living in close proximity to one another at a given spot on a map and at a certain time period, but the social and political embodiment of human self-sufficiency and angry rebellion against the sovereignty and majesty of Almighty God. That is the more complex and highly symbolic meaning of this text.

It's most powerful image is that of Babylon (16:19), which itself was intimately associated with the ironic account of the Tower of Babel in Genesis 11. Its present location, at the time of John's Revelation, was the Imperial city of Rome (chaps. 17 and 18), but it had been preceded by Sodom, various places in Egypt, and then Jerusalem (and has been followed by many comparable successors whose infamy has been recorded by history since that time). Each of these in its own turn had, in their arrogant vice and unholy oppression of God's faithful servants (the two angels of Genesis 19:1, and God's two witnesses, Moses and Aaron, and still later Jesus and Stephen) come to represent this concept theologically or "spiritually," in the language of John. Peter and Paul had also died at Rome in the later 60's of the Common Era. There is a very good case to be made that this oblique reference is an allusion to the two of them.

It is interesting to note also, that Jesus used language similar to this in his sending forth of his disciples into the cities of first-century Palestine, even likening them to sinful Sodom when some of those cities and towns turned a deaf ear to the gospel (Luke 10:10-12). Chorazin and Bethsaida, along with Capernaum, were given particular attention on account of their willful rejection of the Lord's message of repentance to them through the preaching of the seventy (Luke 10:13-16). So, such language as this is very familiar to the student of the Scriptures in both of the testaments.

As the writer wraps up this segment of the series of visions, he announces that the second of the woes has passed and that the third one is soon to come. These three woes are literary devices that serve as horizontal connections between the cycles of visions. As we have previously noted, the cycles describe different aspects of the same pattern of divine judgments against the wicked. The second woe connects the plagues of the trumpet visions (8:7-9:21) with the activity of the beast from the bottomless pit (11:7-10) as well as with the bitter taste of the small scroll (10:9-11). The events of the second woe are essentially twofold. First, they are directed at the godless world (8:7-9:21). And, second, they have repercussions which effect the faithful saints of God, and especially its prophetic preachers and martyrs. In similar fashion, the onslaught of the demonic powers is twofold. They plague godless humanity, but in the beast's hateful response to them, he seeks to destroy the church (Krodel, 228). So, once more the church is troubled and experiences suffering even though the Lord's people are innocent of any wrong-doing.

F. The Final Trumpet Blasts (11:15-18)

Then the seventh angel sounded; and there followed great voices in heaven, and they proclaimed, "The kingdom of the world is become the kingdom of our Lord, and of His Christ: and He shall reign for ever and ever." And the twenty-four elders, who sit before God on their thrones, fell upon their faces and worshipped God, saying, "We give You thanks, O Lord God, the Almighty, who is and who was; because You have taken Your great power, and have reigned. And the nations were angry, and Your wrath came, and the time of the dead to be judged, and the time to give their reward to Your servants the prophets, and to the saints, and to those who fear Your name, the small and the great; and to destroy those who destroy the earth" (Rev. 11:15-18).

At last, the *seventh angel sounds*. The previous six trumpets sounded an alarm, each in its own turn, calling for men to repent of their wicked works in the face of imminent judgment. As was the case with the seventh seal, this trumpet sounding represents the end. That is one aspect of John's style and method. It is called *recapitulation*. Of course, there is only one end, but it is marked out and elaborated upon repeatedly by the author at different junctures in the book. The writer is in no sense confused about the fact that there is but a single conclusion to earth history. When this occurs, this seventh trumpet is sounded, great voices are heard in heaven praising God. The time of *eternal judgment* is here; note esp. 11:15, 17, and 18. When the herald has sounded and this announcement is made, the twenty-four elders are seen paying homage to God in that they fall down before Him in worship. Their obeisance *(proskunēsis)* is described almost verbatim as it is pictured in 4:10. This is an indication that this is not a new kind of heavenly worship. It is the identical worship that takes place in heaven continuously. In this instance it has achieved a new dimension, however, in that these heavenly beings are offering thanks and praise to God for accomplishing the ultimate victory over His enemies.

One aspect of the angelic announcement is the proclamation concerning the enthronement of the King of Kings: "You have taken Your great power, and have reigned." And again, "The kingdom of the world is become the kingdom of our Lord, and of His Christ: and He shall reign for ever and ever." The "world" of this text is to be understood as the realm of humanity and of the nations of earth. Of course, the reign of God is in one sense eternal. It is the general world rule of its Creator. When He spoke it into existence and then established the rule of order in the midst of chaos in the primeval world, He entered upon His rule of the physical universe (cf. Psa. 93:1-4). He has subsequently ruled throughout human history by commanding men and angels to obey His laws and worship Him. "But," as Caird has rightly argued, "always up to this point He has reigned over a rebellious world. A king may be a king *de jure*, but he is not king *de facto* until the trumpet which announces his accession is answered by the acclamations of a loyal and obedient people" (Caird, 141). "When God in the end time assumes dominion, the whole world will be whole" (Roloff, 137). That is what is pictured here. God is finally recognized as the King He has always been and ever shall be.

Note that the language of the passage makes the definitive association of this trumpet blast with "the time of the dead to be judged, and the time to give their reward to Your servants the prophets, and to the saints, and to those who fear Your name, the small and the great." God's kingship will be most fully recognized when the Final Judgment has seen realization. Likewise, the King's true nature will not be fully appreciated until men have beheld it through the keenness and wisdom of His judgment of their lives and deeds. John says that heaven will ring with this recognition of His infinite being: "The sovereignty of the world has passed to our Lord and to His Christ, and He shall reign for ever and ever. We thank You, Lord God Omnipotent, who are and were, because You have assumed Your full power and entered on Your reign." The familiar designation of God in 1:4, 8; 4:8, "who is and who was and who is to come," is shortened in this instance, seemingly on account of its usage in a prayer associated with the concluding events of human history. The final aspect, that God "is to come," is omitted here because the last demonstration of divine power over history, not yet realized throughout most of the book but longed for by both John and the church, has now been realized. God is King and His reign is universal and has been universally recognized!

Interestingly, this trumpet is comparable to the Tenth Plague of Egypt only in the sense that it was final. It clearly brought the Egyptians to their knees and forced them at last to yield to the will of God, in spite of their reluctance to do so, and even in spite of their recalcitrance and stubbornness. In like fashion, this picture portrays the finality of God's judgment upon wicked humanity. Paul declares that "every knee shall bow . . . and every tongue confess that Jesus Christ is Lord, to the glory of God the Father" (Phil. 2:10, 11). Every spirit of human rebellion will be finally broken.

As a footnote to this section, it is worthwhile to notice that the introductory formula of the prayer of thanksgiving, "We give You thanks" *(eucharistoumen soi)* is the only phrase in the hymns of Revelation (of which there are many) for which a simultaneous use can, with certainty, be authenticated in primitive Christian worship. Among other places, it is found in the *Didache* 9:2, 3; 10:2, 4 (Roloff, 137).

G. The Vision of the Ark of the Covenant (11:19)

> *And the temple of God was opened in heaven; and there was seen in His temple the ark of His covenant; and there followed lightnings, and voices, and thunders, and an earthquake, and great hail (Rev. 11:19).*

What appears in this vision represents an impressive conclusion to this section of the book. With the sounding of the last trumpet, the temple of God is opened in heaven and the Ark of the Covenant is seen within. Here the apostle employs a passive construction in order to say that God has opened for human scrutiny the heavenly temple sanctuary (*naos*). This is in contrast with the earthly sanctuary mentioned earlier in the chapter (vv. 1-2). That sanctuary was clearly intended to picture the church on earth as the place of the divine-human encounter, much like the ancient temple was the central location for Israelite worship and service to Deity. In the wording of this passage John uses a clarifying attributive clause in order to specify that he has in mind the sanctuary located in heaven. Such a reference was absent in the depiction of vv. 1-2. At 15:5 when the author again narrates the opening of the heavenly temple, John sees seven angels with seven bowls filled with the wrath of God. What John sees in this vision, however, is a stunning spectacle: the lost Ark of the Covenant, the sign of the Lord's throne and of His presence, which had not been viewed by human eyes for many centuries. Mention of the Ark confirms the conclusion that John's visual object at that moment was in fact the temple sanctuary, and so, the most intimate and sacred aspect of the heavenly sanctuary.

It will be recalled that in the Old Testament after the construction of the Tabernacle, the holy Ark was confined to that sacred space except when the encampment moved from one location to a different place, and on rare occasions when it made an appearance among the people in order to raise their morale. Hence, under normal circumstances the Ark was hidden to the eyes of ordinary men and women behind the concealing curtains of the Tabernacle. The comforting presence of the Ark of the Lord with the armies of the nation of Israel was of great importance to the Lord's people because it represented not only a visitation by a sacred object, but the divine presence itself. It was the nearest thing on earth to a physical manifestation of Deity. The Lord "dwelt between the two cherubim" (the "mercy seat") and was said to commune with His people from that vantage point (Exod. 25:22; etc.). So even though God Himself in His very person is not pictured at this juncture in the Revelation, it is nevertheless clear that the figures set forth proclaim in boldest relief His presence in the turbulence and thunderous events pictured. The Old Testament symbol always suggested one indisputable fact: God is where the Ark is, and the Ark is where God is. The symbol was indicative of God's presence.

In earliest Old Testament times when the holy Ark appeared, especially on the battlefield, the people were encouraged and strengthened (1 Sam. 4:3-9). Moreover, the earthly ark had come eventually to stand in the Holy of holies of Solomon's temple as a result of the king's orders (1 Kings 8:1, 6; cf. Heb. 9:1-4). There it was shrouded in obscurity in the Most Holy Place where it had found its home from the days of the Tabernacle in the wilderness (Exod. 40:21; Lev. 16:2). There it was only visited once a year by the High Priest on the Day of Atonement.

When the holy Ark was taken by the Philistines during one of their frequent wars with Israel, and a child was born to the wife of Phinehas the priest, son of Eli, the child was named Ichabod (meaning, "No Glory"), saying, "The glory has departed from Israel" (1 Sam. 4:21). The Philistines sent the Ark home after a short while, on account of the misery it brought to their land (1 Sam. 6-7). Eventually this beautiful symbol of God's abiding presence with His people disappeared from the revelatory record. This happened with no fanfare, and with little direct explanation. Of course, there is little wonder as to why it occurred, for Israel had abandoned the Lord as a nation, and loss of the Ark represented a figurative abandonment of his disobedient, disloyal, ungrateful, and unfaithful people. They deserved to be abandoned by God!

But where did it go? There is much speculation on the matter, but little in the way of genuine information found in the Bible. If it had not previously been removed by Shishak (1 Kgs. 14:26) or Manasseh (2 Chron. 33:7), it was almost certainly destroyed along with the temple in 586 BC when Nebuzaradan razed Jerusalem and burned the sacred enclosure with all of its contents. It had disappeared from the earth, and earthly eyes would see it no more until John saw it in heaven in one of his visions in the Revelation. A later legend had it that Jeremiah removed the ark to safety in a cave on Mount Nebo (some interpret this text as referring to Mt. Sinai), where it would remain hidden until the final restoration of Israel (2 Macc. 2:4-8; cf. 2 Bar. 6:5-10; 80:2, which says the angels of the Most High hid the contents of the sanctuary, which would have included the holy Ark).

In 2 Maccabees 2:7 it is said, "The place shall be unknown until God gathers His people together again and shows His mercy. And then the Lord will disclose these things, and the glory of the Lord and the cloud will appear, as they were shown in the case of Moses, and as Solomon asked that the place should be specially consecrated." So, according to this view, the reappearance of the Ark would signal the last days and the final assemblage of the people of God. At any rate, the Second Temple (of Zerubbabel and then of Herod the renovator), was bereft of an Ark in the Most Holy Place from the day of its reconstruction (in 520-516 BC) to the time of its fall at the hands of the Romans in AD 70.

But John had no interest at all in the fate of the earthly Ark, even though as a Jewish person who all of his life had read from the Old Testament narratives about this important symbol of God's throne he must have been fixated and captivated by what he saw, being that no human being had laid eyes on that sacred object for so many years. The Ark was a priceless antiquity, central to Israelite religion from the time of its founding! Even though this was no doubt so, nevertheless, that is not what this aspect of John's vision or this particular reference is about. The writer is more interested in the spiritual significance and the symbolic value of this now missing ancient artifact and its meaning for his audience.

Here he sees in his vision the heavenly archetype of which the original physical ark was but a pathetic copy (Exod. 25:40; cf. Heb. 8:5). This is altogether appropriate, for the mysterious and mostly hidden Ark of the Covenant (not just a name for the Ark, but a potent aspect of what this sacred object represented in the midst of Israel), which originally had its place in the tent of meeting during the desert period, came over time to be associated with portrayals of theophany, or appearances of Deity for purposes of divine revelation that are readily apparent in some Old Testament passages (cf. Isa. 33:3, 10; Psa. 99:1). The classic elements that accompany a theophany in the literature—lightning, voices, thunder, earthquakes and hail—are found in this case also in John's brief vision of it (cf. Exod. 19:16-19; Pss. 18:13; 104:7; Isa. 30:30). Thus, it is this implication of *covenant* and *theophany* set forth in order to reveal the divine will that is intended by the figure in this context. The idea of covenant is particularly important since that is the most natural and significant association of the Ark conceptually, as William Barclay stressed in his comments of this text:

> Why the special reference to the Ark of the Covenant? This is to remind people of God's special covenant with His own people. Originally that covenant had been with the people Israel; but the new covenant is the covenant in Jesus Christ with all of every nation who love and believe in Jesus. This means that in the full display of God's glory, in the destruction of God's enemies, God will remember His covenant and God will be true to His own. Whatever the terror and whatever the destruction to come, God will not break the covenant that He made with His people and will not be false to His promises (Barclay, Vol. 2, 90).

And so, when the curtain is drawn aside to expose the inner sanctum of the temple, all of the congregation of God's people may see for themselves this great and meaningful symbol of God's comforting presence in their midst, assuring them that their sins are forgiven, that God's covenant with them stands firm and that they have not and will not be abandoned by the Lord, but will assuredly be cared for throughout the terrifying events that have been and are about to be depicted in these frightening revelatory visions.

Plainly then this snapshot of the "most holy" represents a beautiful message of assurance to the Christians in the seven churches. Even though the circumstances about them are difficult and even threatening, they must not misunderstand what is happening around them. They must not get the wrong impression or draw a misguided conclusion. The judgment spoken about here and elsewhere presents no direct threat to the Lord's faithful people, as long as they remain faithful, because of God's covenant of fidelity with them. The Lord has not forgotten His promises to His people. That He will never do.

Just as the precious Ark of the Covenant was a symbol to old Israel of God's abiding presence and a promise of ultimate victory over their enemies, God reveals heaven's priceless treasures to them to assure and strengthen them in the face of what is to come. The Lord is judging and punishing His enemies who deserve to be punished for their iniquities, not disciplining His faithful people. Thus this lovely little vision of heaven is intended to console and comfort, reassure and embolden the frightened Christians of Asia Minor in the face of the ominous coming judgments that are directed against the wicked in the chapters that are to follow.

Chapter Five

Cycle Three: The Beast Sequence (Chapters 12-14)

A. Seven Figures

At this point in the Revelation a new cycle of visions is inaugurated by the writer. In this instance the reader is confronted with seven personages who stand at the center of the drama presented. Even though the number seven is not even mentioned directly, its significance cannot be ignored. It is symbolic of the fullness of this mighty struggle which involves characters from both heaven and earth. And, although it could be said that the material that is covered here is duplicative, covering some of the same ground as has been the case in all of the visions, it also pictures a different side of the drama of human history. That is the case with each of these sequences. To be specific, Chapters 1-11 has given us a portrait of Christ as the ruler of the Church and controller of the world's destiny, whereas chapters 12-22 place the emphasis on the trials and triumphs of the Church. So, Christ is at the center of the first part of the book, while the Church is at the center of the second portion.

Here in chapters 12-14 of the Revelation, seven distinctive figures are involved in intense conflict and hostility toward one another. These personalities consist of (1) the radiant pregnant woman, (2) the man-child, (3) a Great Red Dragon, (4) the archangel Michael, (5) a beast that comes from out of the sea, (6) a beast emerging from out of the earth, and (7) the Lamb. When each of these personages is identified and its own unique part in the drama is seen in its true light, then the nature and sphere of this raging struggle for dominance in which they all are such an integral part will become apparent.

These visions compress a great amount of time and a tremendous amount of meaning into a brief moment and a very few words. For example, the birth of the child transmutes immediately into the moment of His being taken up into heaven. So, the birth of Jesus turns almost instantly into His resurrection and ascension. The Messiah, once born, becomes the crucified, risen and ascended Lamb. Only the ascension is actually mentioned in John's cursory portrait of the child's life, from birth to death and resurrection. All of that is condensed together in just a few words and in a single snapshot of the vision. The angry red dragon rages over his failure to consume the male child, and "makes war with the remainder of her offspring." So, the ferocious red dragon turns into Satan, the evil "accuser" of mankind and principal persecutor of the Church. In this subtle but artful way the local issues in the towns of Asia Minor in the last decade of the first century are set in the context of an eternal struggle, a world-shaking cosmic battle between good and evil. Michael and his angels are pictured as going out to fight with Satan and his minions. This is an age-lasting conflict, an encounter that has been raging since time began, and which will go on until time is no more.

B. The Vision of the Woman and the Dragon (12:1-17)

And a great sign was seen in heaven: a woman arrayed with the sun, and the moon was beneath her feet, and on her head there was a crown of twelve stars; and she was with child; and she cried out, travailing in birth, and in pain to be delivered. And there was seen another sign in heaven: and behold, there was a Great Red Dragon, that had seven heads and ten horns, and upon his heads there were seven diadems. And his tail drew one-third of the stars of heaven, and cast them to the earth: and the dragon stood before the woman who was about to be delivered, that when she had given birth, he could devour her child. And she gave birth to a Son, a male child, who is born to rule all the nations with a rod of iron: and her Child was ascended up into God's presence, and to His very throne. And the woman fled into the wilderness, where she had a place prepared for her by God, that there they might nourish her for one thousand two hundred and sixty days.

And there was war in heaven: Michael and his angels going forth to battle with the dragon; and the dragon fought along with his angels; But they did not prevail, neither was there any place found any longer in heaven. And the great dragon was cast down, the old serpent, he who is

Cycle Three: The Beast Sequence   12:1-17

called the Devil and Satan, the deceiver of the whole world; he was cast down to the earth, and his angels were thrown down with him. And I heard a great voice in heaven, saying, "Now is come the salvation, and the power, and the kingdom of our God, and the authority of His Christ: for the accuser of our brethren is cast down, who accuses them before our God day and night. And they overcame him because of the blood of the Lamb, and because of the word of their testimony; and they loved not their life even to death itself. Therefore, Rejoice, O heavens, and you who dwell in them! Woe to the earth and the sea: because the Devil is gone down to you, having great wrath, knowing that he has but a short time remaining.

And when the dragon saw that he had been thrown down to the earth, he persecuted the woman who had given birth to the male Child. And there were given to the woman two wings, like those of a great eagle, so that she might fly into the wilderness to her hiding-place, where she is to be nourished for a time, and times, and half a time, away from the face of the serpent. And the serpent belched forth out of his mouth after the woman, water like a river, in order to cause her to be carried away by the stream. But the earth assisted the woman, and the earth opened its mouth and swallowed up the river which the dragon had belched forth from his mouth. And the dragon became very angry with the woman, and went away to make war with the rest of her offspring, namely, those who keep the commandments of God, and hold the testimony of Jesus (Rev. 12:1-17).

Each new vision before this one has been announced by the words "after these things I saw," but this one is tellingly different. It is the first vision that is described as a wonder or sign that he sees in the heaven above him. This is language that is quite familiar to those who are conversant in biblical ideas and notions. In the New Testament a sign is a manifest token of God's presence or purpose. Both concepts are embraced within the present symbol.

At the beginning of this new cycle of visions a woman appears. This is the first appearance of a female figure in the Revelation, so she is certainly someone who is very special. She is a glorious figure: arrayed with the sun, the moon under her feet, and a twelve-star crown upon her head. In the Bible generally the sun, moon, and stars exhaust the biblical idea of the heavenly bodies that give light to the earth. Speaking of the apparel of the woman, John states that she is arrayed with light from head to foot. Clearly she represents the light of God's Word on the earth, and the number twelve assuredly associates her, at least figuratively, with the people of God.

But in spite of her incomparable glory, she is depicted as being in pain. Travailing in birth, she is about to be delivered. Mysteriously, a Great Red Dragon is seen with seven heads and ten horns, being crowned with seven diadems. The tail of the dragon draws one-third of the stars of heaven. This dragon is the Devil (12:9). His seven heads and ten horns symbolize that he has power and authority on the earth, even though in all of his efforts it is clear that he wishes only to frustrate the purposes of heaven. The dragon stands before the woman to devour her Child. In spite of the dragon's best efforts, she bears a healthy Son, destined to rule the nations. Finally, He is caught up to God's throne.

The woman, however, flees into the wilderness to hide for 1,260 days (42 months in 11:2; a time, and times, and half a time in 12:14; see also Dan 7:25; and 12:7; this is a figure used regularly in apocalyptic literature for an uncertain but limited span of time). Meanwhile, there is war in heaven between Michael and his angels and Satan and his angels. The dragon is cast to earth where he persecutes the woman and her children.

The woman pictured in the totality of this scene is clearly a composite figure. John sees her almost kaleidascopically, as an intricate complex of patterns and colors, a many-hued, variegated figure. She represents the people of God in continuity (note Gal. 6:16). At first she is Israel, God's chosen nation, the Lord's people who served him throughout the Old Testament revelation. However, as the scene changes she is now the Church, God's new chosen people. Always in Scripture the Church is depicted as a female figure: sometimes she is a bride (Rev. 22:17; Rom. 7:4; 2 Cor. 11:2); at other times she is a mother (cf. Gal. 4:26), and in still other instances she is seen as an elect lady (2 John 1). In yet another sense, this female figure is also Mary, the mother of God's anointed. The aspect that views her as the mother of Christ is obvious in the text, but gets lost in the overall portrait. Mary is, in her essence here, the representative Israelite mother of God's unique and only-begotten Son (Isa. 7:14).

So, in a sense this woman has three different significations at once. She is Mary, the mother of our Lord. She is Israel who is the mother of Israelite religion and the Mosaic way of life. And she is also the Church, the natural-born offspring of Israel, harassed and persecuted by the devilish powers that be.

Cycle Three: The Beast Sequence — 12:1-17

Her child is much less difficult to identify. He is Jesus. There is no doubt as to His identification. Nothing is left to guesswork here. But the series of events which follow His birth are slightly more difficult to discern as they unfold before the reader. At first the Devil attempts to swallow up this newly born child, but he is frustrated in his efforts. The reader will recall that Herod tried to slaughter all of the children of Bethlehem in order to destroy Him, but God gave Mary and Joseph warning and they fled to Egypt with their new-born until the danger had passed; Herod the Great died, and so the hunt for the Christ Child was ended (Exod. 4:22; Hos. 11:1; Matt. 2:14, 15). This series of events is assuredly in the background and perhaps also in the mind of the author as the scene plays out before him. The Devil is angry because the Child has escaped his grasp. He has missed his chance to stop the divine master plan while the Child is still in His infancy. It was his quickest route to victory, but God thwarted it. Hence, he is cast down to earth in defeat. The shrewd but cruel objectives of Satan have miscarried. This part of his scheme has failed and God's plan has gained the victory, but the war is not over. Satan has lost a battle, but the war rages on.

At this point the author turns his attention back to the female figure at the center of the vision. The woman goes into hiding amidst terrifying persecution. This is the very experience that the churches of Asia Minor and those throughout the Roman world were experiencing at that very moment when the book was being written. The Church is hereby pictured as in a period of horrible oppression wrought by none other than the Devil himself. He uses the power and authority of earthly rulers to affect his wicked plans and devices. Emperors, governors, magistrates, judges, tribunes, censors, consuls, praetors, proconsuls, etc. Thus, even though these other highly placed and often arrogant figures appear to be in control, they are not really. Satan is. He must always be seen as the evil culprit, the dark puppet master, behind the scenes pulling the strings and controlling events as they unfold on the earth. God has given him temporary license to test His people.

The message of all this would have been quite transparent to the Christians who were suffering at the hands of the Roman government at the time. They would have read this as an affirmation that they were not hurting because they were bad people, but quite the contrary. They were suffering precisely because they were good people. They loved God and were doing their best to serve Him, and on account of Satan's hatred for God and all that is good, they had become the unfortunate target of his evil designs.

So, until his final defeat he would be doing all that he could to damage and destroy them. Their suffering was not a sign of divine disdain, but rather of divine approval. Suffering has many causes in life, and it is not always an indication that God is displeased with us. Sometimes it is, of course, but not always. Bad behavior frequently leads on to terrible consequences to the perpetrator. We have all seen this play out before our own eyes. Therefore there is a natural tendency to see every bad event that happens to an otherwise good person as punishment for something about which we are unaware. We suppose them to be guilty of "secret sins."

It must be remembered that the suffering of Job in the Old Testament followed upon God's highly complimentary testimony to the life and works of that grand patriarch: "Have you considered my servant Job? For there is none like him in the earth, a perfect and upright man, who fears God and turns away from evil" (Job 1:8). Suffering may occur in the lives of the people of God precisely because they are righteous and their deeds are pleasing in the Lord's eyes! Like their predecessor Job, their loyalty to God has attracted the attention of Satan! We need to keep in mind that the Devil "is very angry because he knows that he has but a short time remaining." And, "the dragon became very angry with the woman, and went away to make war with the rest of her offspring, namely, those who keep the commandments of God, and hold the testimony of Jesus."

The twist that is given customarily to the circumstances of Job usually has to do with his sufferings testing and refining him, making of him an even better man than he was at the beginning of the narrative, and certainly one who was possessed of a more mature faith in God at the end of his difficult journey. In our own particular case it may be this or some other divine purpose or goal for our lives. At any rate, God assuredly knows why He has granted permission for our testing, and sometimes He may well be the only one who has either the wisdom or the intellect to understand it fully!

But let us resist the temptation to judge His ways and instead always leave Him to understand such matters and, in the mean time, simply do our best to serve Him faithfully in spite of whatever suffering or testing may come our way. As is the case with a good soldier: "Ours is not to reason why; ours is but to do and die." Our task is to finish our course faithfully, regardless of obstacles that Satan may place in our pathway. When we get to the finish line, it is then and only then, that we ought to stop for reflection. At that point we may pause to look back and reflect upon the "whys and the wherefores" of our lives. The Father may then determine to explain it all to us, but even if He decides not to do so, heaven will assuredly "be worth it all; worth all the sorrows that here befall."

C. The Vision of the First Beast (13:1-10)

And he stood upon the sand of the sea. And I saw a beast coming up out of the sea, having ten horns, and seven heads, and on his horns ten diadems, and on his heads there were names of blasphemy. And the beast that I saw was like a leopard, and his feet were like the feet of a bear, and his mouth as the mouth of a lion: and the dragon gave him his power, and his throne, and great authority. And I saw one of his heads as though it had been smitten unto death; and his death-stroke was healed: and the whole earth wondered after the beast; and they worshipped the dragon, because he gave his authority to the beast; and they worshipped the beast, saying, "Who is like the beast? And who is able to make war with him? And there was given to him a mouth speaking great boasts and blasphemies; and he was given authority to continue forty-two months. And he opened his mouth for blasphemies against God, to blaspheme his name, and his tabernacle, even those who dwell in heaven. And he was given the power to make war with the saints, and to overcome them: and he was given authority over every tribe and people and tongue and nation. And all those who dwell on the earth shall worship him, every one whose name has not been written from the foundation of the world in the book of life of the Lamb who has been slain. If any one has an ear, let him hear. If any one is for captivity, into captivity he must go: if any one shall kill with the sword, with the sword must he be killed. Here is the patience and the faith of the saints (Rev. 13:1-10).

This segment begins with the great dragon, the Devil, standing expectantly on the shore of the sea (actually 12:18). He seems to be waiting for something. It is not long before John sees what it is that he is waiting for. The ocean's waters begin to churn and are soon parted to reveal a "beast" arising out of the ocean depths. It is as if he looks proudly upon that which he has initiated and controls for his own wicked purposes. Assuredly that is the case here. Some of the older translations have "I stood" at the start of the chapter. But the best manuscripts are very strongly in favor of the reading "he stood" (*estathēn*). A third century papyrus (**P**[47]) is among them. Those manuscripts which favor "I stood" are of much more recent provenance. So it is the dragon who is standing on the seashore, not John.

The beast that comes up from the depths is, to some degree at least, the dragon's own mirror image. Like him, it also is said to have "seven heads and ten horns" (cf. 12:3). The author draws a distinction between the two however, in that he notes that the dragon has as a sign of its claim to dominion seven diadems that rest directly on its seven heads, whereas ten diadems rest on the horns of the beast. This seems to be explained by the fact that the horns are identified with earthly kings as is the case also in Daniel 7:24 (cf. also at 17:12). Undoubtedly, the blasphemous names that stand so conspicuously on the heads of this beast refer to the honorific titles bestowed on these rulers by those who venerate them.

Following the heads, the body of this mysterious beast becomes visible to the Seer. It is a strange hybrid creature that is part leopard, part bear, and part lion. Its body resembled a leopard, while its feet were those of a bear and its mouth was like that of a lion. The dragon beams with pride at what has now been fully revealed, and he shares his power and dominion with this horrid monster. Four times in this context we are informed that this beast "was given" or "was allowed" by the dragon (by either Satan or God) to do this or that. Satan is plainly the puppet master in the case of this terrible being, he is behind his evil deeds, but God also permits him to do his frightening work. He can only exist because the Lord allows him to live and breathe. He is not autonomous, and he is not even much more than human. "Even God's adversary can do nothing without God's tolerance and permission, which will someday come to an end. He may still display his power without restraint, but he nonetheless remains dependent on God's leaving him alone. And that means that he is subordinate to God in every respect" (Roloff, 157).

Interestingly, one of the heads of this hideous creature is said to have a mortal wound, but this wound has healed and he has not perished. This may be a parody of Christ, the Lamb of God who overcame death, triumphing over it (cf. 5:6). But this beast's survival is merely a ruse. Most interpreters see this reference as having to do with the well-known and very popular legend, which is said to have been widespread in Asia Minor at the end of the first century when John wrote the Revelation, of the survival and return of Nero. Some form of such a view lingered for a number of years after the death (under questionable circumstances) of another evil villain, Adolf Hitler. It seems that evil is always difficult to destroy, or at least it is a considerable challenge to get the general public to believe that it has actually been destroyed.

According to one version of this myth, this eccentric and dreadful emperor did not really commit suicide in AD 68, as it was rumored. Instead, it was believed that he fled unrecognized to the Far east in order to return from there in the near future at the head of the Parthian cavalry forces and retake his empire. In a sense this would be a combination of two of the worst nightmares of the Roman people. The dreaded Parthian invaders would be on the march against the empire and the hated Nero would still be alive. According to a different variant of the legend, Nero was thought to have truly died but was expected to return from the dead in the near future (cf. Suetonius, *Nero* 57.2-3; Dio Chrysostom, *Oratorio* 21.10; *Sibylline Oracles* 5:23-24; Roloff, 157). In whatever form, this fanciful belief came to be described as the *Nero redivivus* legend. In our view, John is using this well known public fantasy to depict Domitian as a resurrected Nero. The apostle is not employing this fiction in order to give it cogency, historical legitimacy, or to describe Domitian as a vivification of the actual Nero. He uses it to picture this new oppressor as a revival of the persecuting spirit in the life of the church. Both of them were persecutors of Christians who took special delight in trying to stamp out the church. They did so from different perspectives, Nero in order to redirect public anger away from himself on account of the great fire in Rome in 64, and Domitian in order to punish a tiny minority for their unwillingness to extend to him those divine honors which his egotistical mania demanded of them. But, of course, the result was practically the same. Clearly then, this terrible creature represents the line of Roman emperors who accepted worship from the people, and in some cases even demanded it of them.

The most critical aspect of John's description of this fellow is summed up in the simple line: "And all those who dwell on the earth shall worship him" (v. 8). This vision is clearly about one thing and one thing only: emperor worship. In fact, the next vision is also supportive of this idea, as v. 12ff indicate. The second beast in the following vision has one task to perform: "He makes the earth and those who dwell in it to worship the beast whose fatal wound was healed . . . telling those who dwell on the earth to make an image to the beast . . . and cause as many as do not worship the image of the beast to be killed." It represents the support structure of the emperor cult in Asia Minor. The job it must do is to use whatever means necessary to force upon the population, including the unbending Christians, the veneration of the Roman Emperor.

It is difficult for modern Christians, especially those who live in many of the western societies where religion is extended civil rights not heretofore seen in world history, to appreciate how extremely challenged these early disciples of Jesus found themselves. They were in an environment where their particular brand of religion was outlawed. They were caught between the proverbial "rock and a hard place." They loved and respected their heritage as Roman citizens, were proud of the many helpful things Roman civilization had brought to their way of life, and yet were being called upon to venerate a mere man (frequently manifestly flawed) as a god in order to satisfy the fanatical quirks of emperors who were often even deemed by much of the general population to be certifiably insane.

For many of these people, in their earlier life as pagans they would have simply shrugged and bent to the requirements of the civil state. They would have done what they were told to do without question, and certainly would have offered no resistance to these demands. Their love for their country and gratitude for the many special benefits it had afforded them would have caused them to do what was obviously absurd on the one hand, but plainly a pledge of loyalty to the state on the other. In that case, they would have been considered good citizens and would have drawn no attention to themselves.

However, after they embraced the tenets of Christianity and committed their hearts and lives in service to the one true God and His Son Jesus, this choice suddenly and rather startlingly took on an entirely different aspect. What they would have mindlessly yielded to in former days was no longer even a possibility for them. This placed them at a sort of spiritual crossroads going forward. They had a very difficult decision, religiously and culturally, to make with regard to how they should proceed, given the facts of the case. E. A. McDowell characterized the resultant "crisis of conscience" created by this dilemma thus:

> The crisis that confronted the churches was made more serious by the element of patriotism involved in the tradition of emperor worship. Rome had achieved great success in unifying the Mediterranean world and in bringing into one vast political organization many diverse nationalities and political units. The empire had brought peace and order and a measure of prosperity to a good portion of the civilized world. She fostered a measure of freedom and self-government among subjugated peoples. It was an honor to be a Roman citizen. The emperor had become the symbol of this vast unifying force. It was a mark of patriotism to do him honor. With the masses it was no cause for alarm that the emperors from time to time had asserted a claim to be descended from the gods. Doubtless many of the more educated members of the population put no faith in the truth of the claim, but they accepted the custom as a wholesome aid to patriotism and cheerfully entered into the performance of those rites demanded by it. At the same time they would look with quick suspicion upon those individuals who saw anything wrong with the custom or refused to perform the necessary rites. Such an attitude on the part of the many would make the lot of the Christians harder in those communities where emperor worship was made an issue (McDowell, 138).

It is in this superheated atmosphere of potentially divided loyalties that John sees these terrifying portents concerning these two frighteningly evil beasts. The visions he is shown make it plain that the matters involved represent more than issues of societal tranquility and unity. There are larger and more profound issues at stake. They have to do with the stark contrasts between evil and good, right and wrong, idolatry and true religion. Simple decisions made by Christians as they pondered their dangerous future and whether or not to conform to these political and social expectations were matters relating to eternal verities: of faithfulness to God or worship of idols, of yielding to satanic practices or staying true to Jesus Christ, and so ultimately, of heaven and of hell.

And so, in this context, these spiritual enemies of the Lord's people are pictured as frightening beasts in John's visions. Those persons whom these symbols represent may have appeared at the time as non-threatening entities in everyday life. They may have been (and no doubt in some instances were) idolized by the masses and looked upon as important and even vital to their national identity by many who thoughtlessly loved the special aspects of the culture at the time. But appearances can be and often are deceiving. And they assuredly were in this instance. In reality, John avers, they are like dangerous, wild animals, threatening, ravenous, consuming, and destructive of the souls of innocent and good men and women. Most people of the day would never have visualized them as such. They saw them through the lens of patriotism and love of country and in terms of the common culture of the Greco-Roman world which had been infused into their very thought processes from the time of their childhood. Their heroes were all great Roman generals and generous civil servants honored and even deified by the Roman state. But John depicts them in terms of their spiritual reality. He sees them in another light altogether. He views them as ferocious creatures making war with God and His saints.

Considering the particulars of John's depiction of these figures, the most critical aspect of this first beast is its place of origin. John says that it comes from the sea. At the time of writing of the Revelation, he is located not far across the ocean from the region of the seven churches. Also, this creature that he sees has ten horns and seven heads, representing the succession of emperors and their limitless power of life and death over those who are under their authority. Too, we are told that on these heads are written "names of blasphemy." These are suggestive of the ungodly titles used by the emperors and those who gave them religious veneration in their efforts to encourage the blasphemous notion that they were divine and deserving of worship. Emperors were accorded such titles as *divus* (divine one), *augustus* (exalted one), *dominus et deus* (Lord and God); *Caesar divi filius* (Son of the Eternal, Caesar; i.e., Son of God); etc. According to John's description, the Dragon (Satan) gives him his throne and great authority. One of his heads had been "smitten unto death," but his death-stroke had healed. Too, it is said that the whole earth worships this magnificent beast.

The identity of this strange beast is not difficult to discern. He is, of course, the emperor of Rome, then the presently serving sovereign, the tyrant whose name was Domitian, or more specifically, Titus Flavius Caesar Domitianus Augustus. He is a single representative of the long line of such men who take to themselves divine epithets and make outrageous claims of divinity. He is also here seen as the persecutor Nero revived (his "death-stroke" was healed). Historically this turned out to be an accurate depiction of that particular ruler. He did indeed viciously turn the vast power of Roman government against the weak and helpless Christians just as Nero before him had done so heartlessly and with such unimaginable cruelty. An evil beast is what he was, and this monstrous creature artfully but menacingly painted by the hand of John in the Revelation is an appropriate caricature for the grotesque figure that Domitian ultimately became. He was more than merely a ruthless but efficient autocrat. Spiritually he was a monster.

The Emperor at the time was worshipped throughout the world. He was commonly and thoughtlessly addressed with the special nomenclature of deity, divine epithets reserved for God alone, titles which John and other Christians would have considered repugnant, "names of blasphemy," denominations such as "Lord," "God," and "Savior." So, this whole proposition, to John's mind, represents much more than merely a test of fidelity to Rome or an aspect of patriotism or loyalty to one's country. John saw it in a completely different light. In his view, Christians needed to see this as the Devil's influence. In these strange goings-on Satan is himself using these wicked men to further his cause in drawing men and women away from faithfulness to the true God. It represented just another form of idolatry, pure and simple. Israel was destroyed by it, and the church had the potential to fall by it also.

Thus, to yield to it in whatever way was to do the Devil's bidding. How very easy it would have been to submit to this simple set of governmental demands! And yet, a simple pinch of incense offered at the altar of *Dea Roma* and for the sake of the divinity of the emperor represented so much more than what it seemed to be at the time that this seemingly harmless ritual was performed. In point of fact it had eternal consequences. It represented disloyalty to God and Christ. The echoes of it would resound into eternity itself. It could destroy the souls of men and cause them to be banished from heaven, robbed of eternal life, and cast into the lake of fire and brimstone.

D. The Vision of the Second Beast (13:11-18)

> *And I saw another beast coming up out of the earth; and he had two horns like a lamb, and he spoke like a dragon. And he exercises all the authority of the first beast in his sight. And he makes the earth and those who dwell therein to worship the first beast, whose death-stroke was healed. And he performs great signs, so that he should even make fire come down out of heaven onto the earth in the sight of men. And he deceives those who dwell on the earth on account of the signs which were given him to perform in the sight of the beast; saying to those who dwell on the earth, that they should make an image to the beast which has the stroke of the sword and lived. And it was given to him to give breath to it, even to the image of the beast, that the image of the beast should both speak, and cause that as many as refuse to worship the image of the beast should be killed. And he forces everyone, the small and the great, and the rich and the poor, and the free and the bond, that there be given them a mark on their right hand, or on their forehead; and that no one should be able to buy or sell, except the one who has the mark, even the name of the beast or the number of his name. Here is wisdom. He who has understanding, let him take notice of the number of the beast; for it is the number of a man: and his number is, Six hundred sixty-six (Rev. 13:11-18).*

Once more, as was the case in regard to the first beast, the important thing to notice about this terrible fellow who emerges to take center stage in John's vision, is where he comes from. John says that this beast comes from the earth (that is to say, from Asia Minor itself). Remember that the former beast arose from the sea. It is as if he was from far away. He derived from a location far across the ocean, removed from the scene of the action. This character is not. This being is a local monster. In this caricature John probably had in mind the people and infrastructure that institutionally embodied Asia Minor's commitment to the imperial cult. Rome, as the beast from the sea, is a foreign force. Land based, the false prophet has a more indigenous feel; he rises up out of the very soil on which John's hearers and readers have built their lives and homes. This beast is local. It represents the native traditions and institutions that nevertheless serve the bestial imperial cult. Rome exercised its rule through just such institutions. In Asia the imperial cult was in the hands of a body known as the *koinon* in Greek and the *commune* in Latin. The *commune Asia* was a provincial council that included representatives from the major towns. Such councils were often populated with priests or other political representatives who promoted the imperial cult. These priests of the imperial cult wore crowns that displayed the busts of the deified emperors and the gods whose cult they served. The Asiarchs of Acts 19:31 may well have been members of just such a *commune* (Blount, 257; Aune, 2:756).

So this figure is less mysterious and more in touch with the locals than that first creature who had arisen from the ocean depths. The Apostle observes that it has two horns and speaks much like the Dragon does, that is to say, it talks like the Devil, and (in the mode of the first beast) he possesses some of his authority. He creates an idol, or image, of the other beast. He deceives the earth and causes them to worship the first beast (the Emperor) through this idol. This is his chief task, his malevolent work in the world. He perpetrates and facilitates the worship of that first monster. He is said to have only two horns, like those of a lamb (a parody of Christ, the Lamb of God).

Therefore he is less fearsome than the first beast who was possessed of ten horns and seven heads as well. He also places a boycott against all those who do not worship the first beast. This is how he carries out his evil labor. And he even murders those who refuse to venerate and worship the first beast. Later this fellow will be described as "the false prophet" (16:13; 19:20; 20:10), and will be viewed as the constant companion of the first beast. In fact, only in the present context is he described as a "beast," his formal title and his dastardly work is associated with the term "false prophet." This prophet is by very definition "false" since worship belongs exclusively to God and this figure intends to see to it that the whole world worships the first beast instead of God. Moreover, he is a formidable figure, for he is possessed of "all the authority" of his predecessor. His dark and mysterious number is 666. All of this is critical to an understanding of who this "beast" is intended to represent.

John even makes allusion to his abilities as a "wonder worker" of sorts. He performs all sorts of fraudulent miracles to show that his religion and its strange practices are to be seen as genuine. These fake performances are its "proofs." Magic was quite common among first-century priesthoods as a means of impressing the gullible. Pagan religion used it extensively (Acts 13:6ff.; 16:16; 19:1ff.). So, this second beast performs his stunts (habitually, as per the author's choice of the present tense of the verb), portrayed as "great and miraculous signs." This noun is sometimes employed by John in his visions (cf. 12:1, 3; 15:1), but a number of times also for what are normally described as "miracles." In this sense it always denotes miracles worked by evil powers (here, v. 14; 16:14; 19:20), a sharp contrast with the Fourth Gospel where it is a characteristic word for the miracles of Jesus. This may be a further example of this evil creature's parodying of the good. The term indicates that the "miracles," so described, are not aimless wonders. They possess a deep significance and are a part of Satan's evil design to deceive the whole world (cf. Mark 13:22; 2 Thess. 2:9). "Those who dwell on the earth" is an idiom that is employed frequently in the Revelation to describe unregenerate men and women; these are the people who are taken in by the false prophet's deceptive tactics. An example of this type of trickery is him "making fire to come down out of heaven." It is not said that it was employed in order to destroy the enemies of the beast or anything of that sort. It is simply a magic trick intended to deceive and arouse the admiration of those who are sufficiently trusting to be exploitable (cf. Morris, 166).

This figure's task is clearly that of being the facilitator of pagan worship. Romans were very religious, dedicated to a pantheon of ancient traditional deities along with the newer emperor cult, and so Christianity (and any other rival devotion, for that matter) was viewed suspiciously at first and then later as an existential threat to their established religious system. Unlike members of some of the other religions, Christians in general flatly refused to sacrifice to the traditional Roman gods or to the emperor who was viewed as a god. Pagan Romans were not only offended by this, but also felt that their strange reticence threatened the very basis of society itself. They were convinced that Roman society was protected by what they called the *pax deorum*: i.e., the peace compact or unspoken agreement that the whole people had with the gods in every city and town of their empire. The people faithfully worshipped and served the gods, and in consequence, the gods dutifully protected the cities, towns, and the entire empire in exchange for this continuing service and sacrifice. In their view, this relationship must not be interfered with or disturbed in any way. The very safety of the community was at stake. If a substantial element of society failed to recognize the authority of the gods and refused to worship the gods, they would become angry at the whole society and bring all sorts of malevolent events to bear against them: floods, fires, earthquakes, destructive storms, etc. So, retaining and maintaining this friendly and happy relation with the gods was viewed as critical to a positive future for the nation.

Thus, in rich but transparent detail, the author depicts an institutional aspect of the society of the region. The beast of this vision rather obviously represents those in Asia Minor who are given the responsibility of enforcing worship of the divine-human Emperor in the provinces. Those who did not hold a certificate which proved they had worshipped the head of state were denied the right to engage in commerce (buy or sell). From the Decian persecution alone (ca. 250), some forty-six of such certificates (*libelli*) have survived from that era and have been published for historical purposes. These particular certificates were issued to those who satisfied the pagan commissioners during that dreadful persecution (June-July, AD 250). In particular, four of such *libelli* were found among the thousands of papyri at the archaeological site near Oxyrhynchus in Egypt (P. Oxy. 658, P. Oxy. 1464, P. Oxy. 2990 and P. Oxy. 3929).

Of course, participating in any sort of pagan sacrifice was considered a sin for a Christian, and by the time of the Emperor Decius it was formally punished by excommunication from the Church. As Barclay observed, "The mark of the beast may be the certificate of worship, which a Christian could only obtain at the cost of denying his faith and being false to his Lord. Once he had that certificate he was labeled as a worshipper of Caesar and a denier of Christ" (Barclay, 2.130). However, for one to refuse to participate could prove fatal. In that era participation was represented by the practice of pouring a libation and tasting the sacrificial meat. Refusal made one liable to arrest by the provincial or local authorities. Interestingly, a warrant for the arrest for a certain Christian (although the grounds of the arrest are not documented) also survived among the documents from that era (P. Oxy. 3035, dated ca. AD 256). Declination to sacrifice was often punished by being jailed, tortured, and even in the most extreme instances by execution.

According to John, the number 666 is the number of a man (v. 18). This strange numeral may perchance constitute a case of *gematria*, the ancient and well-attested practice which concerned the adding up of the equivalent numbers of some proper name. This was a common practice in the ancient world of John's day. In fact, from the eighth century BC the

Greeks used letters to signify numbers. This made it possible to replace a name (or another word) by a cryptic number representing the total of the numerical values of the letters making up the name.

This, for example, is frequently seen in the graffiti of the first century CE. On a wall in Pompeii it was scribbled: "I love her whose name is 545." The use of letters as numbers also made it possible to replace a word by another word with the identical numerical value. This left room for making fun with someone's name, and so this was frequently done in satirical epigrams. The numerical value of letters was also important in dream interpretation. In his well known *Oneirocritica* Artemidorus Daldianus (second century AD) recommends the use of the "principle of equal numerical value *(isopsēphois)* for interpretation of dreams: "For example, if a sick man sees an old woman, it is a symbol of death. For *graus* (old woman) and *hē ekphora* (the carrying out of a corpse for burial are 704" (4.24). Furthermore, in Jewish and Christian literature from the second century there are many occurrences of speculations based on the numerical value of letters, especially among the Gnostics. One of the most interesting examples is in the *Sibylline Oracles* (8.145ff.), likely written before ca. 180, where Rome's destiny is predicted on the basis of the numerical value of the city's name: "Thrice three hundred and forty eight/Years shalt thou fulfill, when upon thee shall come ill-fated/A destiny violent fulfilling thy name." A text which is also frequently quoted in this regard is from the *Epistle of Barnabas* 9:7-9 with the interpretation of Abraham's 318 men (Gen. 14:14). This text is of special interest to many on account of the fact that we encounter in this instance a similar interpretation of the same verse by the rabbis, who saw 318 as an allusion to Eliezer, the servant of Abraham (cf. Gen. 15:2). However, whether or not this intriguing passage can be described accurately as a definite case of *gematria*, has been disputed (Hvalvik, 276).

In this instance in the Revelation of John, it has been observed by some students of the work that the Hebrew letters produced are *Neron Caesar*. But to assume the audience of this document (mostly Gentiles from Asia Minor) would have had sufficient knowledge of Hebrew and of the numerical values of Hebrew letters and thus would have been aware of that fact is at least worth being suspicious about and inquiring into. We addressed the specifics of this view earlier in our Introduction, but for now in order not to be repetitious we will simply say that this rather complicated approach to the problem of these numbers has some considerable difficulties associated with it and should not be too quickly or injudiciously embraced. Whether or not this proposal is to be accepted, it is positive to note that at the very least those readers and students of the book who have tended to read the number in this way are definitely looking for its meaning in the right direction.

This curious numeral may also be much less mysterious than this elaborate view presupposes and represent just one number short of the perfect 777. If this simple interpretation is accepted, then this makes a further crucial point worthy of consideration, namely that each member of the "Satanic Trinity" of chapters 12-14 (the dragon and the two beasts) in a sense parodies the "Holy Trinity" by mimicking the crucifixion (13:3) and working signs and wonders (13:13), but always falling just short of that which is any part of the divine program, and so ultimately fails. If this is the intended meaning, it would thus present a clever parody of the common number for Jesus used in other apocalyptic literature, 888, which is one way to say that Christ is one number beyond that of absolute perfection. At all events it is in one way or another associated with veneration of the emperor of Rome.

E. The Triumphant Saints on Mount Zion (14:1-20)

And I saw, and behold, the Lamb was standing on Mount Zion, and with Him there were one hundred and forty-four thousand, having His name, and the name of His Father, written on their foreheads. And I heard a voice from heaven, as the voice of many waters, and as the voice of a great thunder: and the voice which I heard was as the voice of harpers playing upon their harps: and they sing as it were a new song before the throne, and before the four living creatures and the elders: and no man could learn the song except the hundred and forty-four thousand, even they that had been purchased out of the earth. These are they that were not defiled with women; for they are virgins. These are the ones who follow the Lamb wherever He goes. These were purchased from among men, to be the first-fruits unto God and unto the Lamb. And in their mouth was found no lie: they are without blemish.

And I saw another angel flying in mid heaven, having eternal good tidings to proclaim to those who dwell on the earth, and to every nation and tribe and tongue and people; and he said with a loud voice, "Fear God, and give Him glory; for the hour of His judgment is come: and worship Him who made the heaven and the earth and sea and springs of water." And another, a second angel, followed, saying, "Fallen, fallen is Babylon the great, that has made all the nations to drink of the wine of the wrath of her fornication."

And another angel, a third, followed them, saying with a loud voice, "If any man worships the beast and his image, and receives a mark on his forehead, or on his hand, he also shall drink of the wine of the wrath of God, which is prepared unmixed in the cup of his anger; and he shall be tormented with fire and brimstone in the presence of the holy angels, and in the presence of the Lamb: and the smoke of their torment will ascend upward for ever and ever; and they have no rest day or night, they that worship the beast and his image, and whoever receives the mark of his name. Here is the patience of the saints, they that keep the commandments of God, and the faith of Jesus."

And I heard the voice from heaven saying, "Write, 'Blessed are the dead who die in the Lord from henceforth: yes, says the Spirit, that they may rest from their labors; for their works follow with them.'" And I saw, and behold, a white cloud; and on the cloud I saw one sitting like a Son of Man, having on His head a golden crown, and in His hand a sharp sickle. And another angel came out from the temple, crying out with a loud voice to Him who sat on the cloud, "Send forth your sickle, and reap: for the hour for reaping has come; for the harvest of the earth is ripe." And He who sat on the cloud cast His sickle upon the earth; and the earth was reaped.

Another angel came out from the temple which is in heaven, he also having a sharp sickle. And another angel came out from the altar, he that has power over fire; and he called with a great voice to him who had the sharp sickle, saying, Send forth your sharp sickle, and gather the clusters of the vine of the earth; for her grapes are fully ripe. And the angel cast his sickle into the earth, and gathered the vintage of the earth, and threw it into the winepress, the great winepress, of the wrath of God. And the winepress was trodden outside of the city, and blood flowed from the winepress, as deep as the bridles of the horses, for one thousand six hundred stadia (Rev. 14:1-20).

The writer opens this segment with one of his favorite formulas for announcing a new vision, "Then I looked, and behold..." (*kai eidon, kai idou*; see also 5:1; 6:5, 8; 13:1, 11; 14:14; 19:11). At this point he introduces *the* Lamb to his audience. His usage of the definite article in reference to this particular Lamb tells us that John's hearers and readers were already quite familiar with this figure, it being an expression frequently associated with Christ Jesus. He has alluded to Him so (in that instance without use of the definite article) in 5:6, but in that special case He was named as a lamb who was also "*the* lion of the tribe of Judah," terminology which by itself was freighted with both significance and power.

In this passage the author intends to say something very important to his readers, and to do so by usage of the particular grammatical forms he chooses. And the message is this: that even these mighty and impressive beasts which were just shortly before portrayed as endowed with such power and might in the preceding vision, are not in any wise to be compared with the Lamb. Even though they obviously represent very powerful antagonists to the Kingdom of God and its Christ, they are nevertheless infinitely inferior to *the* Lamb. As Brian Blount insightfully observed, "Once again John allows his grammar to state his case before he presses it narratively" (*NT Library: Revelation*, 264). Thus, even the simple grammatical choices he makes as he constructs his sentences and assembles his larger narrative, are in and of themselves both profound and revelatory.

The two chapters which have preceded this one have set forth the three great enemies of the church of Christ. The first enemy was depicted as a Dragon and shown to be the source and root of all evil which the church suffers. The second enemy was the First Beast, the power of the world to which the Dragon has committed his authority on the earth, clearly intended to picture a powerful governmental figure. The third enemy was the Second Beast, the spirit of false religion on earth, a symbolic representation of religious error in some form and which opposed the spirit and nature of the true congregation of those who remain faithful to God. So, quite clearly their opposition to God and His saints is the predominant theme being portrayed by these colorful but terrifying images. The faithfulness of the church in the face of their antagonism and contradiction is set forth by what follows.

1. The Lamb and the Saints on Mount Zion (vv. 1-5). In this next vision the Lamb and his 144,000 reappear from chapter seven. This time they are seen standing on Mount Zion. In this case John employs actual physical geography to set forth his theological ideas. The name "Zion" originated as a title for the impressive fortress in the Jerusalem area prior to David's conquest of the region (cf. 2 Sam. 5:7; 1 Chron. 11:5; referred to as the "stronghold of Zion"). Later the name was given to the ridge that separates the Kidron and Tyropean valleys in Jerusalem. Solomon built his temple on the highest point of that ridge, which came to be known afterward as "Mount Zion." Eventually the term was generalized and came to be utilized as a descriptor for all of Jerusalem, and sometimes even euphemistically for the people of Israel. Central to all of these applications of the term was the understanding that Zion, whether as place, building, or people, was the location of God's presence and the central focus of God's rule over His people (1 Kings 8:1; 2 Chron. 5:2; Pss. 2:6; 9:11; 14:7; 50:2; 53:6; 84:7; 99:2; 125:1; etc.). In terms of eschatology, it was utilized broadly and figuratively as the gathering place where the Messiah would assemble the Lord's people and execute final judgment (Psa. 2:6-12; Isa. 24:23; Mic. 4:7; *Jubilees* 1.28; *4 Ezra* 13.25-52; *2 Baruch* 40).

So, this "Mount Zion" is not in fact a mountain in the environs of the Old Testament Jerusalem, but a figure taken from it. This is one of John's already familiar markers for the new City of God, of which the writer of the epistle to the Hebrews wrote so beautifully: "You have come to Mount Zion, and to the city of the living God, the heavenly Jerusalem, and to the innumerable hosts of angels, to the general assembly and church of the firstborn who are enrolled in heaven, and to God the judge of all, and to the spirits of just men made perfect, and to Jesus the mediator of the new covenant and to the blood of sprinkling that speaks better things than that of Abel" (Heb. 12:22).

The number 144,000 is, of course, no more literal than the fact that they were literally virgins (v. 4), literally only men (v. 4), and literally only of Israel (7:4). They are not the total number of the redeemed, but are merely representative of the first-fruits of the saved (v. 4; compare 7:9). Not one of these symbols may be taken in a literal sense. Each must be viewed in its context and interpreted as something else which bears an important relationship to the theme being portrayed. The fact that they are called "virgins" (*parthenoi*, employed in the masculine rather than in the more usual feminine gender grammatically) is certainly not meant as a disparagement or condemnation of marriage, an idea which is set forth nowhere in the New Testament. Jesus recognized the practice of abstinence only in the case where men were able to receive it (Matt. 9:12). Paul described it as a superior state to that of marriage, but explained His reasoning as having to do with being able to more fully and single-mindedly offer service to God. Instead, this must be understood in the same sense that Paul explicated in 2 Corinthians 11:2, "For I am jealous over you with a godly jealousy, for I espoused you to one Husband, that I might present you as a pure virgin to Christ." Indeed, it is in this sense only that this figure is intended.

The fact that these people are also described as "men of Israel" only borrows from Old Testament usage the general terminology regarding those who are considered to be the servants of the Lord as opposed to foreign nations who bear no allegiance at all to the true God. So, the intended meaning is that these persons so described are individuals who practice moral purity and are both formally and informally associated with God's chosen ones in the present spiritual dispensation. Quite simply, they are the disciples and followers of Jesus.

2. The Three Flying Angels (vv. 6-13). The scenes that now follow are to be considered the negative counterpart of the preceding. The victorious church has been pictured in communion with God, perfected in their holiness. But, what is to become of the rest of mankind? The remainder of this chapter in rapid succession by means of four quick portraits of the future answers this question. On the other hand, none of these word pictures is very fully developed. So we may be left with many questions if we are greatly interested in having all the details of the situation.

In the latter part of chapter fourteen, then, there appear three flying angels. Once again, these angels play a very important part in the scenes before the prophet, but little is said about them. This author has little interest in the angels themselves. Angelic speculation, which found a home in apocalyptic Judaism, is not important to John. The angels are merely to be viewed as "stage props" in the drama of the Revelation. They are present to assist in the revealing of the different scenes of the drama, but do not play an especially important role in the story itself. They are essential to the progress of the narrative, but they are not major players in the drama that unfolds before the eyes of the Seer.

The first angel declares, "Fear God and give Him the glory, for judgment is come." The second says that Babylon the Great is fallen. The message that is thus delivered is that God has brought judgment to the city that signifies hostility toward the true God. The language is reminiscent of the words of the prophets regarding the fall of the original Babylon (Isa. 21:9; Jer. 51:7-8; Dan. 4:27). Obviously, the name Babylon is being used as a pseudonym for Rome, not so much to disguise the reference as to reveal its true meaning. The capitol city of the New Babylonian Empire, Babylon, was understood, since the time of the exile, as the epitome of the satanic world power (cf. Isa. 13:1ff., and elsewhere). The designation of Rome as Babylon is very familiar to all students of Rabbinic Judaism (cf. Strack-Billerbeck, 3: 816; cf. also, *Sibylline Oracles* 5.143, 159; 2 *Apocalypse of Baruch* 67.7). This announcement is only a hint of what is to come in the chapters that follow. God's judgment brings destruction to the evil city which is at the heart of the suffering of the Christians of that time.

The third angel then warns, "If any worships the beast, he shall drink of the wrath of God." Afterward, there is heard a voice from heaven announcing, "Blessed are those who die in the Lord." Failing to venerate the beast will have its awful consequences for those who are unfortunate enough to live within the realm of his authority and be subject to his cruel whims!

3. *The Harvesting of the Earth (vv. 14-20).* Next, John sees the Son of Man on a cloud with a sharp sickle. This notion of the "son of man" is a somewhat familiar figure found elsewhere in the Bible (cf. Dan. 7:13-14; Matt. 16:13). It is a concept which attempts to communicate a rather simple notion, namely that the person being identified is the offspring of a human parent. The first interpreters of the New Testament (the patristic authors) universally said that when the expression was used to refer to Jesus, it meant that He was born of a human parent and that it was a straightforward reference to Jesus' humanity. Ignatius wrote that "you come together in one faith and in Jesus Christ, who was of the line of David according to the flesh, the Son of Man and Son of God" (*tō huiō anthrōpou kai huiō theou*; *To the Ephesians* 20.2; cf. also Justin Martyr, *Dialogue with Trypho* 6.709; and Isidore of Pelusium *Catena* at Matt. 16:13). With the ever present recognition in the New Testament that Jesus is in truth also the divine Son of God, this becomes a not-so-subtle hint at the fact of His incarnation. Thus, this unadorned language conceals within it a deep theological concept with profound spiritual overtones and stunning implications for those who are willing to give careful consideration to them.

When this figure appears, an angel from the temple announces that the time of reaping has come (cf. Matt. 3:12; 9:37; 13:30; 25:24, 26). It should therefore be recognized that in this passage several angels appear, and along with them is the Son of Man. Thus, Christ appears in the company of a group of angels, in the fashion of the prophecies of His second coming (Deut. 33:2; Matt. 25:31; 16:27; 26:64; Mark 8:38; 2 Thess. 1:7). And, although the scene is not described in the light of that concept, it is nevertheless clear that this time of reaping the harvest of the earth attends the Lord's return.

Two angels respond to this call to action that comes from the temple in heaven. One angel proceeds from out of the temple with a sharp sickle, another from the altar. The symbol of the sickle is a very obvious reminiscence of Joel 3:13 where that prophet said, "Put in the sickle, for the harvest is ripe. Go in, tread down, for the winepress is full. The vats overflow." The overflowing winepress, and the stomping down of the vintage, are also figures borrowed from that passage. The vintage of the earth is gathered, placed in the winepress of the wrath of God and crushed, but the author's picture is not of ripened grapes in the winepress, but wicked men. And so, it is a terrifying scene that John sees. A picture of carnage. The place is filled with horrid gore. The blood runs in the place like a scarlet river, as deep as the bridles of the horses. Evil is brought to heel. Judgment is meted out against the enemies of Jesus Christ. God has rectified all of the evil done since the foundation of the world. What has not been forgiven through the shed blood of Jesus on the cross, has now been punished with an everlasting punishment. "Multitudes, multitudes, in the valley of decision! For the day of the Lord is near in the valley of decision. The sun and the moon are darkened, and the stars withdraw their shining" (Joel 3:14, 15).

In essence, this little cluster of visions represents a rapid-fire summary picture of the things that are to come in the chapters that are to follow this one. They run quickly across the field of vision of the prophet, are given precious little time or detail, and then disappear from view. They prepare us for what is to follow. The reader must wait a while to see their full importance. The Revelation will deal with each and every one of them in greater detail as the successive chapters roll by.

Chapter Six

Cycle Four: The Bowl Sequence (15:1-16:21)

The theme of this section is "the seven last plagues through which the wrath of God is finished." This thread carries through all the way to chapter 22. They are obviously connected both thematically and substantially to the Trumpet Plagues of chapters 8-14. They signaled the self-destructive nature of idolatry. They were clearly modeled on the plagues of Egypt from the Old Testament book of Exodus and had a similar effect: even though they were intended to effect repentance, they only hardened men's hearts (9:20f.). No true conversion took place afterward. No change of attitude. Only stubborn resistance and obstinacy followed in their wake. In the Old Testament it will be recalled that even after the death of the firstborn, Pharaoh once more hardened his heart to the Word of God and resisted God's demands one last time. He hotly pursued Moses and the Israelites into the desert with his armies. This led to the miraculous deliverance by God of His people at the Red Sea, much like a new birth for the nation of Israel.

But, afterward Israel's wilderness journey was threatened by the worship of the golden calf and the seductions of Balaam and Balak. In the case of the trumpet blasts and their plagues, it should be noted that the sixth trumpet warns of death and is followed in chapter 12 by a new exodus, which is threatened in chapter 13 by the worship of the beast and the seductions of the false prophet. Finally, just as in chapter 7 the reader is provided with an anticipatory glimpse beyond the "great tribulation," so that after the "final woe," which corresponds to it, chapter 14 vaguely foreshadows the triumph of the Lamb and of His followers, the fate of the wicked city as well as the beast and his worshippers, and the final return of the Son of Man.

The Bowl sequence covers much of the same ground. It is also inspired by the Exodus narrative and its emphasis on God's resounding defeat of the

Cycle Four: The Bowl Sequence 15:1-8

nation of Egypt and its Pharaoh, but it is not merely a recapitulation of the Trumpet Plagues. It possesses an entirely new focus. The ultimate triumph over Satan, his work and his associates, is presented as the main emphasis. Satanic influence is viewed as having its embodiment in the harlot, called Babylon, and her enablers.

The final triumph of God's work, on the other hand, is seen as having its realization in the bride of the Lamb, the city which he calls "the New Jerusalem," and the purified and glorified population of that anticipated heavenly city. At the center of the portrait is the coming of the Son of Man (cf. 19:11ff.), the conquering Bridegroom, in whom is realized the consummation of all of the grandest prophetic promises of Sacred Scripture.

A. The Victorious Saints by the Fiery Sea and the Seven Angels with Their Seven Bowls (15:1-8)

And I saw another sign in heaven, great and marvelous, seven angels having seven plagues, which are the final ones, for in them the wrath of God is finished. And I saw as it were a sea of glass mingled with fire; and those who come off victorious from the beast, and from his image, and from the number of his name, standing by the sea of glass, having harps of God. And they sing the song of Moses the servant of God, and the song of the Lamb, saying, "Great and marvelous are Your works, O Lord God, the Almighty; righteous and true are Your ways, O King of the ages. Who shall not fear, O Lord, and glorify Your name? For You only are holy; for all the nations shall come and worship before You; for Your righteous acts have been made manifest."

And after these things I saw, and the temple of the tabernacle of the testimony in heaven was opened: and there came out from the temple the seven angels who had the seven plagues, arrayed with linen, pure and bright, and girt about their breasts with golden girdles. And one of the four living creatures gave to the seven angels seven golden bowls full of the wrath of God, who lives for ever and ever. And the temple was filled with smoke from the glory of God, and from His power; and none was able to enter into the temple, until the seven plagues of the seven angels were finished (Rev. 15:1-8).

Once again the symbols of this chapter bear a very close resemblance to the events that occurred at the time of the Exodus. John informs the reader that these seven angels bring "the seven last plagues." The word for "last" is *eschatos*. This is the word from which we derive our term *eschatology*. They are the last, the final ones, he says, because in them the wrath of God is complete. Thus, the bowls from which the wine of God's wrath is poured bear a close relation to the Ten Plagues that brought judgment upon the land of ancient Egypt. In these, according to John (15:1), the wrath of God is finished.

The opening scene of this revelation is stunningly beautiful. And it is astonishing. In fact, John describes it as such. He uses the words "great" and "marvelous" to depict what he sees. The term for "marvelous" is the Greek word *thaumastos*, which emphasizes the quality of astonishment wrought in his own heart by the scene. In this astonishing vision, a sea of fiery glass and the victorious saints appear before the eyes of the Seer. The sea of glass we have encountered previously (4:6), but the fact that it is now said to be mixed with fire adds another dimension to it. In the previous instance it was said that it was like crystal. This time it has a different meaning, since fire always has a certain sense of foreboding and danger about it. Here it seems to picture God's wrath against the wicked, since the "lake of fire and brimstone" is clearly the place of eternal residence for the Devil, his angels, and those who have served his cause and followed his lead in life. It is therefore the fire of God's holiness and justice (cf. 8:5).

The picture presented instantly brings to our minds memories from the Old Testament story of the Israelites on the shore of the Red Sea after their crossing of that body of water on dry land. The Egyptians were subsequently mired down and then swallowed up and drowned in the sea by God's mighty power. God had delivered His people from the awful power of Pharaoh there and then, and He would also deliver the saints from the frightening power of the emperor of Rome. Hence, we are naturally reminded of the Israelites as they stood in safety and looked across the Red Sea at their Egyptian pursuers as they were vanquished by God. The message of the vision is plain. Just like the Israelites were petrified at the sight of Pharaoh's charging army, the saints of John's day were greatly frightened by what threatened them in their own time.

But, God would ultimately deliver His people and give them the victory. The vision says that through these final judgments God will also spare His saints. They are therefore pictured as on the other side of the sea standing triumphant and having in their hands the harps of God. There they (like Moses and the children of Israel on the banks of the Red Sea in Exod. 15:1-21) sing the song of Moses and the Lamb, a hymn of praise to God for His judgments on their enemies and for their ultimate deliverance and victory over their enemies. The saved ones stand, as it were, on the shore of the fiery sea, victorious like the Israelites of old: "And they sing the song of Moses the servant of God, and the song of the Lamb." For them the danger is over. Like the Israelites who had been miraculously delivered from the Egyptian Pharaoh and his army, they have reached the other shore of the sea. They are safe. So, this vision represents yet another look at the great consummation, the saints of God gathered beyond the fiery sea singing the sweet song of victory.

The harps of this chapter (along with those in 5:8 and 14:2) are symbols like the temple, tabernacle, altar, and incense found throughout this book. They all have one thing in common. They are remembrances from the religion of the Old Testament. And they are intended as symbols to represent higher and more noble ideas than themselves. Symbols do not stand for themselves. Attempts at justifying the use of mechanical instrumental music in the worship of the church on the basis of these symbols in the heavenly realm are futile. What proves too much, proves nothing. In this case, if these harps justify the use of instruments such as organs and pianos in the church services, then these other symbols are just as probative. Construction of a temple or tabernacle would be justified. A physical altar like the one that appears throughout the Revelation could be constructed (the original purpose of which was to offer animal sacrifices), and incense could be employed during worship as well. Justification of religious practices on the basis of the symbolism found in the Apocalypse is a fool's errand.

It will be recalled that after the people of Israel had crossed the Red Sea, they came to Mount Sinai, where God gave them the law, and in front of that burning and smoking mountain they placed the precious tables of the law inside the holy ark within the Tent of Testimony. The next part of this vision reveals a heavenly "temple of the tabernacle of testimony" of which, of course, the earthly tent at Sinai was but a copy (Exod. 25:9, 40; Acts 7:44; Heb. 8:5). Hence, once more John is given a peek into the temple. It is opened and what he sees is not the ark as when he had previously seen it open (9:19), but instead it is the Testimony that he beholds. The glory of the Lord is manifest and smoke fills the temple in order to signify its frightening manifestation (cf. Exod. 40:34; 1 Kings 8:10; Isa. 6:4; Ezek. 44:4). The message is clearly that the time for mercy has now passed. God's law must now be brought to bear upon those who have ignored it. It is time for judgment to be meted out. And so, when this scene is revealed to him, he is shown seven angels also. These mighty messengers of God are given their bowls of wrath by one of the four living creatures. Smoke belches from the temple, manifesting God's power and glory in the form of these fearsome judgments. It is clear from this that John is always mindful of his audience: they need reassurance in the face of such frightening future prospects.

In this chapter, John looks to eternity and then back to time, to heaven and then back to earth. The Lord's people need to be reminded that He will care for them throughout these troublesome times and that He will see them through to the other side of all of this madness and mayhem. Like the Israelites of old, the apostle is telling these disciples that someday they will stand on the other shore of the sea of life and look back at all that they have endured and give God the praise for carrying them on His powerful wings to everlasting glory (Deut. 32:10, 11). Like the Israelites who sang and rejoiced on the banks of the Red Sea, the saved will one day jubilantly intone "the song of Moses the servant of God and of the Lamb" beside the crystal sea, their trials and tribulations all past.

This thought is the key to understanding this part of the vision. God remembers His covenant of love and provision for His faithful ones. Thus, this quiet moment of symbolic reflection prior to the unleashing of the bowls of divine wrath remind the Lord's precious people that He has not forgotten them or His covenant with them. The same law that brings wrath and cursing upon those who have spurned it is a hedge of protection and blessing for those who have respected and observed it. While God is bringing judgment and woe upon His feckless enemies, He has His arms of love wrapped about His faithful saints, protecting them from all this madness, maelstrom and mayhem, winging them steadily toward their heavenly home. They must never lose sight of this marvelous reality. It is for this reason that John provides many different images at different junctures in the Revelation that in one sense or another draw a rhetorical picture of this truth.

Cycle Four: The Bowl Sequence   16:1-21

B. The Bowls Are Poured Out (16:1-21)

And I heard a loud voice from out of the temple, saying to the seven angels, "Go forth, and pour out the seven bowls of the wrath of God upon the earth." And the first went, and poured out his bowl onto the earth; and it became a loathsome and grievous sore upon the men who had the mark of the beast, and worshipped his image.

And the second poured out his bowl into the sea; and it became blood as from a dead man; and every living soul died, even the things that were in the sea.

And the third poured out his bowl into the rivers and the fountains of the waters; and it became blood. And I heard the angel of the waters saying, "You are Righteous, who are and who was, O Holy One, because You have thus judged: for they poured out the blood of the saints and of the prophets and blood have You given them to drink: they are worthy." And I heard the altar saying, "Yes, O Lord God, the Almighty, true and righteous are Your judgments."

And the fourth poured out his bowl upon the sun; and it was given to it to scorch men with fire. And men were scorched with intense heat: and they blasphemed the name of God who has the power over these plagues; and they repented not and refused to give him glory."

And the fifth poured out his bowl upon the throne of the beast; and his kingdom was darkened; and they gnawed their tongues for pain, and they blasphemed the God of heaven because of their pains and their sores; and they repented not of their works.

And the sixth poured out his bowl upon the great river, the River Euphrates; and the water of it was dried up, in order that the way might by made ready for the kings who come from the sunrise. And I saw coming out of the mouth of the dragon, and out of the mouth of the beast, and out of the mouth of the false prophet, three unclean spirits, like frogs: for they are spirits of demons, working signs; which go forth to the kings of the whole world, to gather them together to the war of the great day of God, the Almighty. (Behold, I come as a thief. Blessed is he who watches, and keeps his garments, lest he walk naked, and they see his shame.) And they gathered them together to the place which is called in Hebrew Har-Magedon.

And the seventh poured out his bowl into the air; and there came forth a great voice out of the temple, from the throne, saying, "It is done": and there were bolts of lightning, and voices, and thunders; and there was a great earthquake, such as has not been since there were men on the earth, so great an earthquake, so mighty. And the great city was divided into three parts, and the cities of the nations fell: and Babylon the Great was remembered in the sight of God, to give to her the cup of the wine of the fierceness of His wrath. And every island fled away, and the mountains were not found. And great hail, every stone about the weight of a talent, came down out of heaven upon men: and men blasphemed God because of the plague of the hail; for the plague was very severe (Rev. 16:1-21).

The parallels between this group of judgments and the Trumpet Plagues (chaps. 8-11) are readily apparent. As G. R. Beasley-Murray observed: "The differences between these two series are but variations on common themes" (Beasley-Murray, 239). The distinctions between them are primarily a matter of intensity and severity. In each series the first four plagues are visited upon the earth, sea, inland waters, and heavenly bodies respectively. The fifth involves darkness and pain (compare 16:10 with 9:2, 5-6), and the sixth, enemy hordes from the vicinity of the Euphrates (compare 16:12 with 9:14ff). As we mentioned, and demonstrated with numerous illustrations in our treatment of the Trumpet Judgments, both of these series draw heavily for their imagery from the plagues of Egypt and their aftermath (Exod. 9:10ff; 7:17ff).

As such they are an attack upon the same four elements of the material world, and through them the world of human beings. These plagues target not only human kingdoms and the individuals who rule and populate them, but also the very four essences of the creation itself: earth, water, fire, and air. The turning of water into blood (8:8; 16:3, 4) parallels the first Egyptian plague in which Moses struck the waters of the Nile River, turning them into blood (Exod. 7:20). Too, the darkening of the sun (8:12; cf. 16:10) has as its counterpart the ninth of the Egyptian plagues, in which the book of Exodus records that thick darkness prevailed over the land for three days (Exod. 10:21-22). Close comparison shows that several other very obvious parallels are intended by the language and symbols of the two accounts as well.

One thing that is very clear about the differences between these two series of judgments, though, is that the Trumpet Plagues are intentionally described as being only partial in their effect (one-third of the earth is burned, one-third of the sea turns to blood, etc.), while the judgments associated with the bowls are seen as universal ("every living soul died," "every island fled

Cycle Four: The Bowl Sequence 16:1-21

away"). The trumpet judgments are intended to lead to repentance, whereas the bowls are seen as punitive in a final sense. It should also be noted that the bowls are poured out in rapid succession with the customary interlude between the sixth and seventh elements of the sequence missing in this case. This all suggests that the patience of God has worn thin and He no longer hopes for their repentance and correction. He has now set about seeing to their punishment. So, the author is making the case that the judgments described match measure for measure the crimes which have triggered them.

A great voice out of the temple instructs the seven angels to pour out their bowls of wrath upon the earth. The voice of God is thus portrayed as issuing forth from the heavenly temple. The temple origin of this voice reminds the reader of the vision of 15:5-8 picturing the tent of meeting in heaven as the beginning point of the seven angels. After the declaration in 15:8 that no one could enter the smoke-filled temple other than God during this period of judgments, God is clearly the one who is speaking.

John utilizes heavily freighted language in his selection of terms with which to describe what is going on in this passage. The verb *ekcheō* means "to pour out, or shed" in its usual employment. Interestingly, this is the only place in the book where he uses it. But he makes use of it repeatedly, and to the exclusion of any other comparable term (cf. vv. 1, 2, 3, 4, 6, 8, 10, 12, 17). This is indeed a word with very strong religious and cultic associations historically. It is employed many times elsewhere, as in this instance, in connection with libation bowls that contain liquid offerings. As Brian Blount noted, "John deploys the verb in a very calculated, balanced way. His mechanical 'pouring' narration occurs four times before and four times after its clarifying central use at 16:6. There John explains that God's enemies, working at the direction of the dragon and its beasts from the sea and land, have "shed" the blood of those who have faithfully witnessed to the lordship of God and the Lamb. The measure-for-measure punishment meted out against God's enemies begins right there. In a kind of apocalyptic *lex talionis*, God intends to 'shed' plagues of wrath upon the earth as an appropriate judicial response to the criminal shedding of human blood" (Blount, 294).

And so, the divine voice thunders forth from the temple, commissioning the seven angels to pour out the contents of their bowls upon the earth. It is heard with the following devastating result:

(1) First bowl: The first of these angels sets in motion his judgment, which is brought about in order to punish those who are guilty of idolatrous worship. It brings on grievous sores festering on those who worship the Beast. The Greek describes these sores ("ulcers" or "abscesses") as "bad and evil" (*kakon kai poneron*), meaning that they are "loathsome and malignant." This bowl's effect is based on the literal Egyptian plague of boils (this one being just as figurative as the "mark of the beast"; see 13:16-17; 7:2-3) (cf. Exod. 9:9-11), which is later summarized in Deuteronomy 28:27, 35 as an "evil sore" using the identical Greek words in the LXX version of the text as John employs in this context. It could be said therefore that in this instance the punishment very much suits the crime, since those who receive an idolatrous mark are chastised by a penal sign in their flesh. The "sores" of the Egyptians plague caused suffering for those who were stricken by them. The abscesses referred to here also represent some sort of physical and mental suffering, presumably like that which is referred to in the case of the spiritual and psychological "torment" (*basanismos*) of the fifth trumpet judgment (cf. 9:4-6, 10).

(2) Second bowl: When this bowl is spilled out, the sea becomes blood, and sea creatures perish. This is very much like the first plague in Egypt which struck the Nile River and turned it to blood (Exod. 7:20), and it is similar also to what was described when the second trumpet sounded (8:8-9). It will be recalled, however, that in the first instance only one-third of the sea became blood, and so it only killed one-third of the sea animals and destroyed only one-third of the ships at sea. It is paradoxical that in the ancient world blood was seen as having two absolutely opposite qualities. On the one hand it was acceptable as a means whereby human beings were made pure through the offering of sacrificial blood, both in the sacrifices of the people of Israel in their book of Leviticus and throughout the Old Testament, as well as among the various religions of the nations. The blood of Christ in the New Testament is also seen as the means by which men are brought into a spiritual relation with God and Christ (Acts 20:28; Rom. 3:25; 5:9; Eph. 1:7; 2:13; Col. 1:20; Heb. 9:12, 14; 10:19; 12:24; 13:12, 20; 1 Pet. 1:2, 19; 1 John 1:7; Rev. 1:5; 7:14; 12:11). At the same time it is also almost universally viewed as a serious source of pollution, practically, cultically, ceremonially (cf. Lev. 7:27; 15:11; 17:14; 20:18; Num. 35:33; Ezek. 36:17, 18; Psa. 106:38; etc.). In this case the writer describes the blood under consideration as being "like the blood of a corpse," which would naturally be perceived as being putrid and therefore unclean and a serious pollutant for either fresh or salt water.

(3) *Third bowl:* Rivers and fountains of water become blood. This judgment bowl resembles very closely the first plague against the Egyptians and is parallel to the third trumpet blast (8:11). It is especially interesting to note that in this instance the author goes on to comment that those who suffer this judgment "have shed the blood of saints and prophets," and so "you have given them blood to drink" (v. 6). Such references should not be ignored. They are an important key to understanding not only the moral intent of this particular judgment, but also to an appreciation for the reason for the book of Revelation in general. When John wrote this book the saints and prophets were suffering greatly at the hands of practitioners of idolatrous religion who enjoyed positions of authority within the Roman state. They were resolved that they would force the Christians to comply with their demands and conform to the state religion. John predicts that such people will ultimately be served a heavy dose of their own medicine. Why are they to be served this particular drink? Because, as the writer notes, "They deserve it" (NASB). Note also that as this bowl judgment is concluded, John tells us (literally) that he "heard the altar saying. . ." Of course, this involves the personification of the altar, because he has explained that on this altar are to be found the prayers of the saints and beneath this altar are the souls of the martyred saints crying out for vengeance. Moreover, what the altar says reflects almost precisely the content of the song of Moses and of the Lamb. God's judgments are true and righteous. There is nothing unfair or unreasonable about them.

(4) *Fourth bowl:* The fourth angel pours out his bowl upon the sun. This causes the sun to scorch men with fire. Instead of repentance following in the wake of this frightful judgment, which we would normally expect as the most reasonable outcome of such a terrible event, we are told that men "blasphemed the name of God . . . and they repented not to give Him glory" (v. 9). Once more, just as it is patently obvious that it is figurative for an angel to pour out a bowl upon the sun, it is likewise logical that this judgment is itself figurative in nature. It follows therefore that if the cause is figurative, then the effect is equally figurative. One thing is emphasized by the writer, however, and that is the divine cause of all of this human suffering that is being depicted. This is not a natural calamity. It is not a "man caused disaster," nor is it a phenomenon associated with weather patterns as they are altered by various aspects of a changing earthly ecosystem.

Rather, John tells us that God is the One "who has power over these plagues." These are divine judgments, all of them are. And even though they are not intended to depict actual details of terrible physical plagues like those that were brought upon the population of Pharaoh's Egypt, what is pictured here is intended to frighten the wicked away from persistence in their evil-doing, and to encourage the faithful in loyal service to their God, even in the face of oppression or an agonizing death. What they describe in their highly figurative way is the Lord of heaven's panoply of modes and methods suited for bringing the guilty to justice. The blameworthy will not walk away free. They will be held responsible for their crimes. And God will show Himself to be exceedingly creative in prosecuting the culpable for their evil deeds.

(5) *Fifth bowl:* This container is poured out upon the throne of the Beast. The result is that his kingdom is darkened. It will be recalled that this also was the ninth plague sent against the population of the land of Egypt in the days of Moses (Exod. 10:21-23; cf. Wis. 17:1-18:4). The whole country of Egypt was as black as night for three consecutive days. In their case this was particularly onerous because their chief god was Amun Ra, a solar creator god. Given the title "King of the gods" by Egyptians, most usually pictured in iconography as a man with the head of a hawk and a solar disk over his head with a coiled cobra around the disk. In this way another of the deities of the Egyptian pantheon was brought low in the opinion of the populace, and thus was raised the profile of the God of the Hebrews. He was obviously superior to them all.

It will also be recalled that during the fourth trumpet plague (8:12) the light of the sun, moon, and stars was partially darkened (which is a typical event found in various apocalyptic literary contexts: Isa. 13:10; Joel 2:10; 3:15; Amos 8:9; Hab. 3:11; *Sibylline Oracles* 5.344-49; Pseudo-Philo, *Biblical Antiquities* 19:13; *Testament of Moses* 10:5; Mark 13:24; Matt. 24:29; Acts 2:20). It is also especially noteworthy that this judgment is sent against "the throne (*thronon*) of the beast." The throne of the beast is only mentioned elsewhere in the book at 13:2, where it is explained that the dragon (Satan) gave his throne to the beast along with great authority.

So, the throne of the beast is actually the throne of the dragon. Most modern interpreters see this reference as a specific directional indicator pointed at the city of Rome where the seat of imperial power was centered. That power was so interconnected with various idolatrous rites and practices that there is little wonder that John saw it as being, in its very essence, a satanic menace to the Christian cause and those associated with it. It is therefore crucial to bear in mind that the dragon is in fact Satan personified (12:9).

Again, it is said that instead of contrition and repentance being the outcome of their misery, rather, "because of their pains and their sores" they blasphemed the God of heaven. The people who suffer through this plague are assumed to still be experiencing the painful boils and blisters on their skin during this period of darkness, and as a result they bite their tongues on account of the agony they are experiencing.

(6) *Sixth bowl:* In this part of the vision, the River Euphrates, historically a barrier to frequent invasion of Syria-Palestine by the Mesopotamian kings, is dried up and the kings of the East are free to cross over it and attack. In John's day that would imply a threatened invasion of the Roman Empire by the Parthian hordes who perennially threatened the Romans from their eastern flank. Certainly that would have been the first thought that would have come to the mind of the Roman who lived in the time of the Seven Churches. But that aspect is only introductory to this part of the vision. It only opens the mind of the reader to the concept of a massive and dreaded military conflict that would bring about much suffering, misery, bloodshed, and death. When introduced to this notion, that is the first thing that comes to mind, but this vision is not a warning to the Roman Empire of an invasion of its eastern flank. Rome is only a minor player in this larger-than-life conflict. It is a warning to the whole world that the Devil will not "go quietly into that good night," he will instead "rage against the dying of the light" (Dylan Thomas).

What John sees next is strange indeed. The dragon, the beast and false prophet produce three unclean spirits which have the horrid appearance of frogs. The plague of frogs in Egypt is brought to mind, quite naturally, although in this instance there is only this very slight resemblance to that plague. These fellows are quite different from the pests who worried the people of Egypt for a time in the days of the prophet Moses. They are portrayed as froglike leaders of the army. It is as if they are the generals, possessed by "unclean spirits like frogs," or "spirits of demons," marching their followers off to war. They gather the whole earth to the mountain of Megiddo to do battle. Satan is not content to allow God to have the final say without some response on his own part. He plans to attempt one last effort to destroy the influence of God in the world. And so he raises his army, appoints its leadership, imbues them with demonic spiritual energy, and marshals his troops in concert, "to gather them together for the war of the great day of God, the Almighty" (v. 14). And so to John's way of thinking this is no ordinary conflict. This is truly, "the war to end all wars."

The figures before us, of course, are not literal, but are rather symbolic of God's retributive wrath against Rome which God intended to use to bring about its eventual demise. But, once more, the struggle pictured is much larger and more general than just the earthly conflict that would eventually and inevitably end in the fall of Rome and its mighty empire. Evil and good were in perpetual struggle with one another. Even when the Roman military was no longer a threat to any other nation, the war would rage on through hosts of other bad actors on the stage of human history. Rome was only a symbol of a larger problem, much more complicated and considerably more violent and destructive than the swords and spears of Rome's proud and powerful legions. And the problem will only finally be solved, once and for all, when God brings about his final judgment of wickedness when time is no more.

The Battle of Armageddon is no more literal than the three frogs who lead the armies to this great skirmish. The mountain of Megiddo was a famous Hebrew battlefield: here Gideon defeated the Midianites, Deborah and Barak defeated Jabin, the Philistines defeated Saul, Jehu killed Ahaziah, and Pharaoh Necho killed Josiah. Why this particular location? It is a symbol. Great battles aplenty were fought there throughout the various eras of biblical history. The writer uses it specifically because of all these ancient historical connections. It is employed to represent the spiritual battleground where righteousness overwhelms evil, that is to say, where and when God defeats His enemies, in this case, cruel Rome. But beyond this, it also depicts the fall of all those who make of themselves enemies of God and of His Kingdom, the church of Christ.

Again, these visions of the bowls portray various judgments bringing about the end of the evil empire, the contemporary enemy of God's people. The author further underscores this truth with some important additional rhetorical flourishes. He tells the reader that the persecutors have spilt the blood of the saints of the Most High God, "they poured out the blood of the saints and of the prophets" (Rev. 16:6), and so He will have their blood in return! "He will give them blood to drink"! The blood of the righteous dead must be avenged (cf. Rev. 6:10; also Luke 11:50, 51).

Finally, a **(7) Seventh bowl** is poured out upon the air. Lightning, thunder, voices, and an earthquake follow in the wake of it. God's wrath falls upon the earth with such ferocity that the earthquake levels the mountains and submerges the islands, which are the imperial city's strongholds. Thereupon, the city is divided into three parts and remembered in the sight of God "to give unto her the cup of the wine of the fierceness of His wrath" (v. 19). A plague of hail is visited upon her (each stone weighing about 100 pounds). The city in question is the entity represented as the despicable Harlot of the following chapters. Her being "remembered" here is preparatory to her agonizing fall in the next section. This bowl is Prelude to that vision.

In this instance, as previously, the writer uses picturesque symbols to say that three weapons will be utilized by the Almighty to bring down the city of Rome along with her powerful allies in heaven and on earth: *natural calamity, internal rottenness, and external invasion*. In each and every case the bowl judgments pictured here fit one of these three destructive influences to the detriment of the mighty city that so viciously assaulted the saints of God and oppressed them for the better part of two full centuries. What God was telling His faithful, but hurting people here is that He would not forget the wicked deeds of Rome, even though they may have worried at the time and for a long time afterward, that it was taking so long for Him to react that they thought He somehow might have forgotten them. Rather, John says to them that God will ultimately visit her with wrath in many different forms in direct response to the sincere prayers of the wounded and bleeding saints.

Taken together, these seven frightening portraits are particularly horrid; they picture three foul spirits like frogs, demon spirits, the armies of earth being summoned to a place called Armageddon, the great city being split into thirds, and Babylon being forced to drink the wine cup of God's fury. All of this is intended to picture how truly hideous sin is when it is bared to the eye of the Spirit. But most of all it tells us that sin will not go unpunished. There will be a time of reckoning.

Chapter Seven

Cycle Five: The Judgment of the Harlot (17:1-19:21)

Chapters 17 and 18 portray the judgment of God upon the great Harlot, the anti-Christian city of Rome, which in those days represented a citadel of paganism and determined opposition to all that was righteous and good, and especially so in respect to the cause of Jesus Christ. From a literary perspective of the book of Revelation, these two chapters are quite unique. John does not want his readers to be lost in the symbolism of his book. He wants them to understand his method and message with absolute clarity. So He does something he has not done previously. He explains himself in great detail. In chapter 17, after the opening vision of this disgusting harlot seated upon the Scarlet Beast (vv. 1-6), the author turns to an extended interpretation of his symbols. This is very helpful to the reader, but it is not characteristic of the rest of the book. It is as if he says to his readers, "If you do not understand fully what I have said to you up to now, this part I do not want for you to miss."

The writer identifies the seven heads (vv. 9-10), the ten horns (v. 12), the waters upon which the harlot is seated (v. 15), and the woman herself (v. 18). As for the Beast upon which she sits, he is "of the seven" yet "is himself also an eighth" (v. 11). Anticipating some bewilderment on the part of the reader, the Seer adds, "Here is a problem for a profound mind" (v. 9). The seven kings are the first seven rulers of the Roman Empire: Augustus, Tiberius, Caligula, Claudius, Nero, Vespasian, and Titus. The beast is a ruler who has died and is to be resurrected in his role as persecutor. That person can only be Domitian. He is Nero resurrected to trouble the church again. (Three others ruled during the space of a single year, Galba, Otho, and Vitellius, but are considered of no importance at all by this writer, as they were also mostly ignored by the Romans themselves. None of these temporary occupants to the throne performed any great service on behalf of the Roman people or accomplished anything worthy of note. Their reigns were for mere months, and their influence was negligible. So they were generally forgotten men. John also treats them in this way.)

Chapter 18 is a dirge over the fallen city. Kings, merchants, and all seafaring men bewail her catastrophic destruction. Her fall creates repercussions that are felt worldwide. It has affected them as well. Echoes from the prophetic taunt songs found in Isaiah, Jeremiah, and Ezekiel reverberate across the centuries and find their influences salted throughout the entirety of the chapter (Isa. 14:3-23; 37:22-29; 47; Jer. 38:14-28; Ezek. 16; 23; Nah. 11-19; Hab. 2:6-20).

In response to the admonition of 18:20, "Rejoice over her, thou heaven," comes the "Hallelujah Chorus" of 19:1-2. Consequently, the first five verses of chapter 19 constitute a fitting climax for the lengthy section on the fall of Rome which began at 17:1. Heavenly jubilation breaks out at the judgment imposed on those who have brought pain and suffering to the church. This is in marked contrast to the solemn dirges of the kings, merchants, and seafarers, whose economic empires have also collapsed with the devastation of the mighty imperial capital. The series of three laments is then followed by the adulation and worship of a new grouping of three: the heavenly multitude (vv. 1-3), the twenty-four elders and four living creatures (v. 4), and a voice that echoes forth from the throne (v. 5).

Subsequently the great multitude in heaven praises God for His judgment of the harlot. At last heaven has granted justice to the martyred saints! Their blood has finally been avenged. The last part of the chapter announces the wedding of the Lamb to His bride the church. Those who are blessed of God are invited to come to the wedding supper of the Lamb (19:6-10). The last section of chapter 19 describes the appearance of the warrior-messiah on a white horse, followed by the armies of heaven (vv. 11-16). Overthrow of all who are the enemies of God follows His march of victory (vv. 17-21).

A. The Harlot Imagery

The certain doom of the wicked city which poses such a threat to the divine purpose and to God's suffering people has been pictured in vivid imagery already. In the visions of the pouring out of the bowls of divine wrath

Cycle Five: The Judgment of the Harlot 17:1-18

the clear message has been that God is not pleased and that he will swiftly take action to judge this evil metropolis. The drama has moved swiftly and climactically toward the ultimate expression of divine displeasure. Rome is here pictured as a disgusting harlot, and is also called "Babylon," the hated arch-enemy of old Israel, used of God as a destructive bludgeon to bring down His sinful people when they had displeased Him by their persistent forays into idolatry and iniquity.

It will be remembered that harlotry is one of the favorite depictions of the practice of idolatry in the Old Testaments by Israel's historians and prophets (Num. 25:1; Deut. 31:16; 1 Chron. 5:25; 2 Chron. 21:11, 13; Isa. 1:21; Jer. 2:20; 3:1, 6; etc.). In fact, it is the favorite accusation of God against His unfaithful people, i.e. "playing the harlot." So it is the perfect symbol with which to picture the foul practice of making statues of the emperors and forcing the people to worship these idols in order to prove one's loyalty to the Roman state.

Thus, the message is clear here also, even though the imagery is at times rather perplexing to the casual observer: the Lord will bring down this enemy of His faithful people, just as He brought down mighty Babylon of old. It remains now for the Seer of the Revelation to identify this hateful harlot, this spiteful Babylon, and to describe the fateful events leading up to her eventual fall and then to give an account of her final destruction. This is what the present segment of the book proposes to do and it does it with artful device.

B. Vision of the Mysterious Harlot (17:1-18)

And there came one of the seven angels that had the seven bowls, and spoke with me, saying, "Come here, I will show you the judgment of the Great Harlot who sits upon many waters; with whom the kings of the earth committed fornication, and they who dwell in the earth were made drunken with the wine of her fornication." And he carried me away in the Spirit into a wilderness: and I saw a woman sitting upon a scarlet-colored beast, full of names of blasphemy, having seven heads and ten horns. And the woman was clothed in purple and scarlet, and adorned with gold and precious stones and pearls, having in her hand a golden cup full of abominations, even the unclean things of her fornication, and on her forehead there was a name written, MYSTERY, BABYLON THE

GREAT, THE MOTHER OF THE HARLOTS AND OF THE ABOMINATIONS OF THE EARTH.

And I saw the woman drunk with the blood of the saints, and with the blood of the martyrs of Jesus. And when I saw her, I wondered with great wonder. And the angel said to me, "Why did you wonder? I will tell you the mystery of the woman, and of the beast that carries her, which has the seven heads and the ten horns. The beast that you saw was, and is not; and is about to come up out of the abyss, and to go into perdition. And those who dwell on the earth shall wonder, those whose names have not been written in the book of life from the foundation of the world, when they behold the beast, how that he was, and is not, and is to come. Here is the mind that has wisdom. The seven heads are seven mountains, on which the woman sits: and they are seven kings; the five are fallen, the one is, the other is not yet come; and when he comes, he must continue a little while.

"And the beast that was, and is not, is himself also an eighth, and is of the seven; and he will go into perdition. And the ten horns that you saw are ten kings, who have received no kingdom as yet; but they are to receive authority as kings, with the beast, for one hour. These have one mind, and they give their power and authority to the beast. These shall make war against the Lamb, and the Lamb shall overcome them, for He is Lord of lords, and King of kings; and they also shall overcome who are with Him, called and chosen and faithful." And he said to me, "The waters which you saw, where the harlot sits, are peoples, and multitudes, and nations, and tongues. And the ten horns which you saw, and the beast, these shall hate the harlot, and shall make her desolate and naked, and shall eat her flesh, and shall burn her completely with fire. For God put it into their hearts to do His mind, and to come to one mind, and to give their kingdom to the beast, until the words of God are accomplished. And the woman whom you saw is the great city, which reigns over the kings of the earth" (Rev. 17:1-18).

The angel (one of the seven who had the seven bowls) is the speaker in this scene, and he offers to show the Seer the judgment of the Great Harlot sitting upon many waters. It will be recalled that John's sevens represent his complete and panoramic views of the various divine judgments, and his unnumbered visions his close-up consideration of detail (as in 7:1-5). The seven trumpets and the judgments that they represent signified the second series of divine punitive measures that were to be taken against the kingdom of the beast; and the three following chapters (12-14) laid bare the true nature of the spiritual conflict unfolding before John's dazzled eyes. The seven bowls have led up to the announcement of the fall of Babylon, and the next two chapters will explain the nature and causes of her terrible fall.

In this instance John is carried off into the wilderness (*erēmon*; cf. also Rev. 12:6, 14). Why a "wilderness" or "desolate place"? We may suppose that it is because a wilderness is an entirely appropriate place for one to consider such a weighty matter as the one before the Seer. Wilderness places were frequently the haunts of monks and those who wished to escape away or retire from society and the common life of the community. The most important feature of such desolate and lonely places was that they were perfect as refuges from the cities and towns and offered the one who was motivated to find such a space the benefit of total solitude. One could be alone in such a place. The concomitant of this was that such quiet and solitude made fellowship with God easier, far from the noisy hustle and bustle of the cities and towns with all of their various kinds of distractions. Meditation and prayer, and sometimes fasting, could be engaged in. It will be recalled that John the Immerser went there (apparently to avoid the temptations and evils of society, to pray, meditate, and commune with God), and the people went out into the desolate regions of Judea in order to hear him preach (Matt. 3:1; Mark 1:3, 4; Luke 7:24; John 1:23). He was a man of the wilderness. Jesus went out into the wilderness as well, although only temporarily, to be tempted of the Devil. For him it was also a place of fasting and prayer (Matt. 4:1; Mark 1:12, 13).

From this perspective on the world, a despicable woman is seen by the prophet sitting on a scarlet beast with seven heads and ten horns, full of names of blasphemy. She is arrayed in costly raiment, with a golden cup full of the abominations that she has wrought. Upon her forehead is written, "Mystery, Babylon the Great, Mother of Harlots and Abominations of Earth." "Babylon" is an intriguing title for her to be given. Why was she so described? Babylon was the name of the powerful adversary of ancient Judah, a heathen city used by God to judge the idolatrous harlotries of the southern kingdom. To that city the exiled inhabitants of defeated Judah were sent to serve out the time of their separation from the homeland of the Jewish people. It will be noted that this name is written on her forehead, an interesting phenomenon, but entirely in keeping with the symbols of

John's Revelation. In this book names written on foreheads is already for us a familiar concept. We have come to know by now that they reveal the true character of people thus depicted, and their ultimate spiritual relationship, whether to God (7:3; 14:1; 22:4) or to Satan (13:16; 14:9; 20:4).

Likewise, the "name written on the forehead" of this particular harlot reveals her seductive and idolatrous character, which further identifies her as on the side of the beast. The depiction could possibly reflect the practice of some Roman prostitutes of John's day, who purportedly had their names written on bands across their foreheads, although the validity of the references attesting this have been disputed by some historians, except in the case of Seneca (cf. *Controversiae* 1.2.7). There is no need, though, to look beyond the general sense of the figure as employed in the book generally. For, the author goes on to suggest that those who corporately compose the bride of the Lamb and have "His name on their foreheads" (22:4) are particularly set in contrast to this audacious prostitute (cf. G. K. Beale, 858). Sometimes slaves had a metal collar riveted around the neck and such a collar was preserved in Rome and states in Latin, "I have run away. Catch me. If you take me back to my master Zoninus, you will be rewarded."

Roman law even permitted the branding of slaves on their faces until AD 319, when this abhorrent practice was banned and slaveholders were forced to brand them on their hands and legs. Clearly in the ancient world the name written on the forehead was also associated with and thus a sign of some form of slavery. For example, the ancient Romans branded runaway slaves with the letters FGV (for *fugitivus*). Also, the slave punishment for theft was to be branded on the forehead with the letters FUR, for the Latin word for thief (*fure*). Individualized brands and numberings were also used. The enslaved Athenians "when they were sold, were branded in the forehead with the mark of a horse" (Plutarch, *Life of Nicias* 29.1). And so, the facts of this matter are not subject to dispute. Obviously, the forehead was the most conspicuous part of the human body where a sign of some sort might be attached, or even tattooed. But in the OT it meant something else entirely, even though the forehead was once more the conspicuous location where a notification could be and so was inscribed. Thus, Aaron bore the motto, "Holiness to the Lord" engraved on a golden plate upon his forehead (Exod. 28:36-38). The present reference might have some connection with that usage, but we deem it far more likely that this instance has to do with the practice of marking slaves, and especially the labeling of slaves who were prostitutes, in Roman society at the time John wrote this book.

Again, why is this prostitute called "Babylon"? What is there about that particular appellation? The old Babylon from whence this woman derives her name was a place that was majestic in every way; at the height of its power during the Neo-Babylonian Period it was certainly so, and even beyond that historically speaking, from what we are able to ascertain. The massive city spanned the Euphrates River and was surrounded by an eleven mile long outer wall punctuated by eight massive gates, the most impressive of which was the famous Ishtar Gate, spectacularly decorated by the world-famous Hanging Gardens, and towered over by the 300 foot high ziggurat of Etemenanki and the temple of Esagila, dedicated to the patron god Marduk. It remained an important economic center and provincial capital during the rule of the Persians, and even into the time of the Greeks it was both influential and wealthy.

Herodotus, who visited the city in 460 BC, long after its heyday, could still remark that "it surpasses in splendor any city of the known world." Alexander the Great, conqueror of the Persian Empire, embarked on a program of rebuilding Babylon to its previous glory, but this was interrupted by his death in 323 BC. After the time of the inimitable Alexander, the city declined economically, but remained an important religious and cultural center for centuries, even until New Testament times. The site was deserted by AD 200. In Jewish thought, however, Babylon was more than just a prestigious and powerful ancient city. It had become to the Jewish people a religious symbol. It represented earthly power manifested for the intended purpose of frustrating the plans of God and bringing His people to ruin. That is what it had accomplished in the era of the Exile and beyond. And so, any mighty earthly metropolis that stood opposed to the true religion and persecuted those who clung to it was in a sense to be seen as a modern-day "Babylon."

In the Old Testament, Babylon was the city where the Jewish people were taken as they were carried off into captivity. Henceforth, in their literature it became identified with the place of exile away from their homeland (Psa. 137; Isa. 43:14, in context with 5-6). It was considered always as a wicked and arrogant place ruled by wicked and arrogant men (Isa. 13; Jer. 50-51; Dan. 5:17-31). Here in the Revelation it is a place particularly associated with persecution (Rev. 17:5-6; although this is also implied in some of the texts from the Hebrew Bible as well). Thus, Jewish savants employed the term with regularity to describe their new arch nemesis, Rome, especially after she brought Jerusalem to ruin in AD 70 (*4 Ezra* 15:43-48, Syriac *Apocalypse of Baruch*, and book five of the *Sibylline Oracles*). 2 Baruch (67:7) even says: "But the king of Babylon will arise *who has now destroyed Zion*, and he will boast over the people, and he will speak great things in his heart in the presence of the Most High."

This book was clearly written after the fall of Jerusalem in AD 70 at the hands of the Roman legions. The *Sibylline Oracles* even locate Babylon specifically in Italy: A "great star will come from heaven to the wondrous sea and will burn the deep sea and Babylon itself *and the land of Italy*, because of which many holy faithful Hebrews and a true people perished" (*Sib. Or.* 5:158-161; cf. also 143). These passages connect both the rulers of Rome (especially Nero) and the city itself with what we might describe as "Babylonish" ways and attitudes. In all likelihood, in line with this common Jewish manner of speaking, Peter also refers to Rome as "Babylon" in his first epistle (cf. 5:13), even prior to Jerusalem's decimation by the Romans. In neither case is the writer intending to use "code language" to confuse a potential government official, or someone else for that matter, even though that might have been an unintended result of this usage. Rather, it is a simple application of a recognizable symbol which has come to be commonly identified with Rome both in Jewish and Christian circles. Therefore, in keeping with Jewish usage, and Peter's own intriguing employment of the symbol, John also sees this as an appropriate name for such a formidable foe of God's people in the Church Age.

Why does John employ the image of a harlot to picture this great enemy of the church? Of course, the major reason in the present context of this book is on account of his intention to place this ugly and unattractive feminine figure over against the pristine and pure picture of the bride of Christ which he presents so beautifully later on in the book. The fall and death of this ghastly female removes her from the central place in the symbolism and permits the reader at long last to get a glimpse of the Wife

Cycle Five: The Judgment of the Harlot 17:1-18

of the Lamb. Furthermore, it is because this is a well-known idea from so many of the Old Testament prophetic discourses where it is used to symbolize religious apostasy. Isaiah lamented that the once faithful Jerusalem had become a harlot (Isa. 1:21). Jeremiah spoke of Israel's "adulteries and neighings" (elsewhere she is depicted as a wild ass in heat; Jer. 2:24) and of her "lewd harlotries" (Jer. 13:27; cf. Jer. 2:20-31; Ezek. 16:15ff; Hos. 2:5).

Since the harlot of the Apocalypse is plainly a pagan city (cf. 17:18), it is more likely that a passage like Nahum 3:4 or Isaiah 23:16, 17 supplies the immediate background. In the former case, the harlot was Nineveh, who betrayed nations with her harlotries and her charms (cf. Rev. 17:4). Isaiah, on the other hand, portrayed Tyre as a forgotten harlot. In the context of Revelation 17 and 18, though, the image is not that of religious profligacy but of the prostitution of all that is right and noble for the questionable ends of lust for power and enjoyment of luxury and extravagant wealth. As Robert H. Mounce so keenly observed, "Whether Jezebel or Cleopatra sat for the portrait John is now painting (Caird, 212-213) makes little difference. The harlot is Rome. Adorned in luxury and intoxicated with the blood of the saints, she stands for the dominant world system based on seduction for personal gain over against the righteous demands of a persecuted minority. John's images are timeless in that they portray the essential conflicts of mankind from the beginning of time until the end" (Mounce, 307-308).

The author notes that this nightmarish harlot is "drunk with the blood of the saints." This latter depiction is critical to John's purpose, for it shows her in her true light. She represents more than a tremendous economic and military monolith. Truly she is more than a mere super-power that wields unprecedented dominance on the world stage. Her overwhelming political strength and considerable international influence only hints at the ultimate sway she has over the lives of the people of the whole earth. She wields an almost irresistible jurisdiction in the realm of moral suasion, leaning toward injustice as she does, and crushing all who resist her protection of the ancestral Roman deities and of the Roman state. Hence, she is indeed a detrimental force in the world that is utilized mercilessly by Satan to persecute and murder God's people in order to put forward the practice of religious harlotry (idolatry) and discourage true religion. So her ultimate defeat and decisive downfall are imminently reasonable and completely just.

The angel in this case gives the interpretation of the vision, and in this he is helpful, but still somewhat elusive as to his meaning: The Beast that was, and is not; and is about to come out of the abyss and go into perdition is an earthly ruler. When the curtain is pulled away and the symbols are read in simple terms, this ghastly figure is the emperor Domitian as the persecutor Nero revived. Nero was the fifth important emperor while Domitian was the eighth. He stands in the place of all the later Roman emperors who would oppose the will of God and the church of Christ until they are finally brought to justice and eventually to eternal judgment. He is their figurehead. After him many others were to follow, cruel and hateful toward the Christians: Trajan, Hadrian, Marcus Aureius, Septimus Severus, Maximus the Thracian, Decius, Valerian, and Diocletian.

The seven heads are also said to stand for the seven ancient Palatine hills upon which the city of Rome sits. The waters are peoples and nations. The ten horns are ten kings, vassal kings in the provinces who will cooperate while they are forced to do so, but then eventually turn against mighty Rome to aid in the process of destroying her. The woman is the great city who reigned over the kings of the earth at that time (17:18). This particular text is a key verse of the book. It nails down the evil culprit whose decisive defeat this work is written in order to herald and celebrate. As Beasley-Murray acknowledged, "If verse 9 also be taken into account, there was one city only in the first century to which this description could refer, namely Rome, whose rule reached virtually to the limit of the world of western and mid-orient man. Rome, then, was the Babylon of her age" (260-61).

Especially intriguing to many students of this work is the reference to the seven kings, to which we have given some attention earlier in this book. The writer says tantalizingly, "Here is the mind that has wisdom. The seven heads are seven mountains, on which the woman sits: and they are seven kings; the five are fallen, the one is, the other is not yet come; and when he comes, he must continue a little while. And the beast that was, and is not, is himself also an eighth, and is of the seven; and he will go into perdition" (vv. 9-11).

The reference to the seven mountains (or hills; *oros* can mean either one) is transparent. From the time of her sixth king, Servius Tullius, Rome had been known as *urbs septicollis* ("the seven hilled city"), even though the plateau of the Esquiline hill now lies outside the Servian Wall, and Rome originally started within these walls and was probably built by Servius Tullius. The Aurelian Wall was built under the Emperors Aurelian and Probus (AD 271-275). Every year the festival of Septimontium was celebrated in December to commemorate the enclosure of the seven hills within her walls (cf. Suetonius, *Domitian* 4). Ancient Rome was frequently referred to in the literature as a "city of seven hills" (Virgil, *Aeneid* 6.782-83; *Georgics* 2.535; Martial, *Epigrams* 4.64; Cicero, *Ad Atticum* 6.5; *Sibylline Oracles* 2.18; 11.113-16; 13.45; 14.108)

But the matter of the seven kings is not nearly so simple to navigate. What is the writer's meaning here? Many different approaches have been taken to this text, but all of the ones which attempt to reconstruct a precise order of rulers have fallen upon internal inconsistencies and frustrated those students who have advocated for them. William Hendricksen, for example, suggested that these kings represent the line of pagan kingdoms which have at various times in history attempted to frustrate the purposes of God in the world and the kingdom of God in particular. William Milligan offered a reconstruction that is similar to this, but which departed from this approach in some particulars. Alfred Plummer offered an interpretation that views these kings as rulers who are anti-God figures who have existed and will come in the future. However, he did not attempt to identify them individually. In our view this approach to the kings is destroyed by the introductory reference to the seven hills. The city of Babylon that sits on the seven hills is obviously Rome. This specific allusion is deliberate and must be taken into consideration if the seven kings, along with the eighth, are to be understood in their context.

The majority of readers of John's work have tended to see these rulers as a succession of Roman emperors, although many different reconstructions have come out of this general approach. Difficulties abound in every instance. With which emperor are we to begin the counting, Julius, Augustus, or perhaps Caligula, in whom the monster's tendencies first made their appearance? Julius Caesar was the one under whom the Republic ended and Octavian was the one under which the empire officially began. Are we to count all of the emperor's who spent any time at all in office, or just those who reigned over a more considerable period of time? Early date advocates (pre-AD 70) tend to see Nero as the sixth emperor, counting from Julius Caesar, and then skipping the three pretenders (Galba, Otho, and Vitellius) who reigned in one year, Domitian is counted as the seventh. But the eighth is essentially passed over and given almost no notice at all:

> The seven kings, five of which had fallen, followed the count from Julius Caesar, the first—then, Augustus, Tiberius, Caligula, Claudius, the *five which had fallen*—and Nero, the sixth. He was referred to in the phrase *and one is*—that is, the reigning emperor. It is further stated that *the other*, or the seventh, *is not yet*. The five Caesars had passed before John wrote this apocalypse; and Nero, the sixth Caesar, was reigning at the time Revelation was written. The apocalypse belonged to the Neronic period. Omitting, quite properly the subordinates, or mock rulers, Domitian was the seventh Caesar; and the text specifically stated that he had not come. It is difficult to account for a theory that fixes the chronology of Revelation in the latter part of the Domitian reign when he, *the seventh*, had not come (Wallace, 371-372).

Wallace is, as is his usual status in regard to such things, absolutely certain of his rectitude on this matter, in spite of the fact that the position on the text which he adheres to is a minority viewpoint, entertained by very few of the best conservative non-futurist students of the Apocalypse. His flippant certainty on the date of the writing of the work is also a wonder, since all of the external evidence from the early church writers is allied against his perspective.

On the other hand, those who argue for the late date of the Apocalypse, have a different way of counting the Roman rulers, as this quotation from H. B. Swete illustrates:

> The vision seems to be dated in the reign of the sixth Emperor. Putting aside the name of Julius Caesar, who though he claimed the "praenomen Imperatoris" (Suetonius, *Divus Julius* 76) was a dictator rather than an Imperator in the later sense, the Roman Emperors of the first century are Augustus, Tiberius, Caligula, Claudius, Nero, Galba, Ortho, Vitellius, Vespasian, Titus, Domitian, Nerva, Trajan. It is however more than doubtful whether a writer living under the Flavian Emperors would reckon Galba, Otho, or Vitellius among the August. If we eliminate those names the vision belongs to the reign of Vespasian (AD 69-70), and probably . . . to the last years of that reign, when the accession of Titus was already in sight. . . . The eighth in the series of Emperors indicated in the last note is Domitian. . . "One of the seven" had left a reputation which even in the last years of the century

made his name a terror. Nero was the very impersonation of the Beast, the head (13:9) which seemed to gather into itself all of the worst qualities of the body politic. Nero was gone for the time (*ouk estin*), but he would return as an eighth, the topstone of the heptad, a reincarnation of the Beast, a Nero redivivus though not in the sense that popular rumor attached to the phrase (13:3). Even pagan writers recognized the resemblance between Domitian and Nero; cf. Juvenal 4:37f." (Swete, 220-221).

It is certainly noteworthy that as late as the third century of the Common Era, the name of Nero was commonly associated with that of Domitian at least in Christian circles. In the words of Tertullian (ca. AD 155-240), he was not only a *portio Neronis de crudelitate*—"portion of Nero's cruelty" (*Apology* 5), but a "sub-Nero" (*De pallio* 4; cf. Swete, 221). Swete's analysis is intriguing, but it also has some serious flaws. The idea that John was exiled to Patmos during the reign of Vespasian has nothing at all to commend it. Nothing that happened in the era of that emperor would have led to John's banishment to Patmos or his apprehension of a worldwide persecution (Hailey, 352).

On the other hand, there seems to be little doubt that the author has both Nero and Domitian (and perhaps all of the other persecuting emperors, for that matter) in mind as he pictures this succession of rulers, but he appears little concerned with giving the reader a clear idea of how to understand this group of leaders precisely and with absolute clarity. In our view it is best to say that, "Like the seven hills, the seven kings are a metaphor for the empire" (Blount, 320). As in every other instance where the number seven is employed, it is intended as a figure for completeness rather than as a specific portraiture of the historic leadership of the Roman Empire. What seems to be underscored by the writer in his depiction of this line of rulers is that each one enjoys authority for only a brief season and then disappears from the scene. This is true because they are mere mortals and not gods as so many suppose. Too, he celebrates the fact that five of them "are fallen," using terminology that is associated with violent death rather than by natural causation. Evil rulers have frequently died by assassination. Certainly many of the worst Roman Emperors were struck down by trusted confidants, friends, or even by those who were supposed to protect them from attack. No human leader lingers in high office for long. Whether a ruler is wicked or righteous, he will die the death of all men, and in his own estimation his rule will not be for long.

As G. K. Beale has observed rightly, "Nero serves as a good illustration of the text's idea. Nero lived and died and then reappeared in Domitian in a way similar to that in which the spirit of Elijah reappeared in John the Baptist (Matt. 11:14; Mark 9:13; Luke 1:17; Rev. 11:3-6). That is, Domitian had traits like Nero, as is apparent from Roman writers who compared Domitian to Nero, though Asian provincials probably did not do so. This apparent ceasing and reemergence of evil is a cycle occurring throughout history" (Beale, 870, 871). Certainly, John wants the reader to observe the fact that the "eighth" king is in reality no more than merely one of the seven. He may claim to be more, and may even seem to be more. But he is, in fact, only a human ruler with all of the human limitations of all of the rest. Clearly, number eight is a shadowy figure from the future. Perhaps he represents the final ruler who will fail to acknowledge God and His authority?

The seven have already been identified by John with the different heads of the beast, so he is informing his audience that the beast, the basic source of evil in the sphere of human government, finds a kind of reincarnation in each of the seven. In a way he is each of them, and each of them is the beast. This is true of all of the seven, and it is equally true in the case of the eighth, but John seems to have little interest in the career of the beast in any of his incarnations. Indeed, that is one of the most important reasons for our difficulty in understanding and identifying the exact succession of these seven men (along with the eighth). He does not tell us enough about any of them to make it possible for us easily to make a firm identification.

But that should not be at all surprising to us. John has little interest in what the beast does and he has no great concern for his power. He is only interested in informing his readers that this fellow, like all of the others before him and those who may come afterward, is headed for perdition. He is going to be destroyed after the same fashion that all evil men will be judged and brought to naught. His future is the same as that of every other wicked ruler who has gone before him, from those men who ruled the Assyrian Empire, the Babylonian, the Median and Persian, the Macedonian, and then the Roman. All evil men who fail to recognize the authority of God are destined to the identical end. God will bring them down from their perch on high and cast them into the lake of fire. They will not endure for long, even though it may at times seem so. That is John's message to the seven churches. And that is his lesson for us today. God is the only ruler whose reign will endure forever and whose authority is without limit. Those who fail to give Him the praise and glory He so richly deserves, whether they are kings or paupers, will experience firsthand the power of His might.

C. Judgment upon the Harlot (18:1-24)

After these things I saw another angel coming down out of heaven, having great authority; and the earth was brightened with his glory. And he cried with a mighty voice, saying, "Fallen, fallen is Babylon the great, and is become a home for demons, and a place for every foul spirit, and a place for every unclean and despicable bird. For by the wine of the wrath of her fornication all of the nations are fallen; and the kings of the earth have committed fornication with her, and the merchants of the earth were enriched by the power of her sensuality."

And I heard another voice from heaven, saying, "Come forth, My people, out of her, that you have no fellowship with her sins, and that you receive not of her plagues: for her sins have reached even as far as heaven, and God has remembered her iniquities. Render unto her even as she rendered, and repay her double according to her works: in the cup which she mixed, mingle for her double. How ever much she glorified herself, and lived luxuriously, so much give her of torment and mourning: for she says in her heart, 'I sit a queen, and am no widow, and shall in no wise see sorrow.' Therefore in one day shall her plagues come, death, and mourning, and famine; and she shall be utterly consumed with fire; for strong is the Lord God who judges her.

"And the kings of the earth, who committed fornication and lived luxuriously with her, shall weep and wail over her, when they see the smoke of her burning, standing far away for fear of her torment, saying, 'Woe, woe, the great city, Babylon, the strong city! for in one hour has your judgment come.'

"And the merchants of the earth weep and mourn over her, for no one buys their merchandise any more; merchandise of gold, and silver, and precious stone, and pearls, and fine linen, and purple, and silk, and scarlet; and all kinds of perfumed wood, and every vessel of ivory, and every vessel made of the most rare wood, and of bronze, and iron, and marble; and cinnamon, and spice, and incense, and ointment, and frankincense, and wine, and oil, and fine flour, and wheat, and cattle, and sheep; and merchandise of horses and chariots and slaves; and the souls of men. And the fruits which your soul desired are gone from you, and all things that

were luxurious and splendid are gone from you, and men shall find them no more at all. The merchants of these things, who were made rich by her, shall stand far away for the fear of her torment, weeping and mourning; saying, 'Woe, woe, the great city, she who was arrayed in fine linen and purple and scarlet, and adorned with gold and precious stone and pearl! for in one hour such great wealth has been laid waste.'

"And every shipmaster, and every one who sails anywhere, and mariners, and as many as make their living by sea, stood far away, and cried out as they watched the smoke of her burning, saying, 'What city is like the great city?' And they threw dust on their heads, and cried out, weeping and mourning, saying, 'Woe, woe, the great city, in which all who had their ships in the sea were made rich by reason of her wealth! for in one hour she has been laid waste. Rejoice over her, O heaven, and you saints, and apostles, and prophets; for God has judged your judgment upon her.'

"And a mighty angel took up a stone like a great millstone and threw it into the sea, saying, 'Thus with a mighty fall shall Babylon, the great city, be thrown down, and shall not be found any longer. And the voice of harpers and minstrels and flute-players and trumpeters shall be heard no more at all in you; and no craftsman, of whatsoever craft, shall be found any more at all in you; and the voice of a mill shall be heard no more at all in you; and the light of a lamp shall shine no more at all in you; and the voice of the bridegroom and of the bride shall be heard no more at all in you: for your merchants were the princes of the earth; for with your sorcery were all the nations deceived. And in her was found the blood of prophets and of saints, and of all who have been slain upon the earth'" (Rev. 18:1-24).

This section continues the author's treatment of the great city that he has described as "Babylon." It was represented in great detail in the previous chapter (17:1-18). There he spoke of its coming destruction (cf. 17:16-18). The present chapter contains a series of laments having to do with its fall. The writer opens this portion of the book with the words of a veritable funeral dirge, mourning over the terrible devastation of the mighty city (18:2), and ends it with words of rejoicing over its destruction. There is no sadness over her collapse by the righteous, even though many others are brought to sorrow over it, for as the author notes, with her "sorcery were all the nations led astray. And in her was found the blood of prophets and of saints, and of all who have been slain upon the earth" (v. 24). And, although the jubilant sound of the bridegroom and the bride would be heard no more in her on account of her fall, the demise of the evil municipality paves the way for a wedding which is announced in the chapter that follows (19:1-9).

At the beginning of this chapter an angel comes from heaven announcing, "Fallen, fallen is Babylon the Great." And then an appeal is made to the righteous within the city: "Come forth, My people, out of her, that you have no fellowship with her sins, and that you receive not of her plagues" (v. 4). God's people are called out of the evil city for their protection from the dangerous implications of her horrific fall. Calls such as this are scattered throughout the Bible, in the Old Testament from the time of Abram onward (Gen. 12:1; 19:12ff.; Num. 16:23ff.; Isa. 48:20; 52:11; Jer. 50:8; 51:6, 45; Zech. 2:6-7), and they are present in the New Testament as well (2 Cor. 6:14-15; Eph. 5:11; 1 Tim. 5:22). Compromise with worldliness can be fatal for the people of God, so they must make a clean break with it and shun it altogether. This principle is what is at stake in the divine call for the faithful saints to abandon Babylon. She is doomed, and they must not allow themselves to be drawn into her web of lies and deceit. Rather, they have to hold themselves aloof from her and her sins.

The wicked metropolis is to receive a double dose of her own medicine (cf. v. 6). She mixed it and served it to others, so she will be provided an opportunity to taste what she has forced down the throats of her unfortunate former "guests." The expression "pay back double" *(diplōsate ta dipla)* is an instance of a Greek idiom that occurs frequently in the Greek version of the Old Testament (LXX), in which a verb is followed by a cognate accusative of content (employed characteristically to translate a Hebrew finite verb followed by an absolute infinitive, to intensify the meaning of the verb). The identical idiom is found in pagan Greek, but less frequently than in the LXX. Two other instances of this idiom occur in Revelation (16:9; 17:6). This idiom may not be saying that precisely double what she had mixed would be served up to her, but rather that she would get back "much more" than what she gave to others. That is the probable force of the expression (Aune, 967, n. 6.d.).

It is also interesting to note that the phrase, "Woe, woe, the great city, Babylon, the strong city. . ." is also very familiar language from the LXX (*Ouai, ouai* with the nominative phrase, *hē polis hē megalē* "the great city," which functions as a vocative identifying the one to whom the lament is addressed), is repeated in vv. 16 and 19. Examples of this usage are frequent in the LXX (cf. Isa. 1:24; 5:11, 18, 20, 21, 22; 31:1; Amos 5:18; Hab. 2:6, 12, 19; Zeph. 2:5). Indeed, in the LXX the interjection *ouai* is used with an articular nominative functioning as vocatives in these sentences (cf. Zech. 2:5; Isa. 1:24; 5:8, 11, 18, 20, 21, 22; 31:1). It is clear, therefore, that this author has spent a great deal of time with the Greek version of the Old Testament, absorbing its idiosyncrasies and familiarizing himself with its linguistic intricacies (Aune, 967, n. 10.b-b).

With arrogant pride Rome saw herself as the mistress of the world. Moreover, she saw herself as such without any possibility of personal loss or sorrow. She had visited it upon many others, but she had little experience with it herself. The special rhetoric of her monologue is modeled after Isaiah 47:7-8 where Babylon, the lover of pleasures, says in her heart, "I am, and there is no one besides me; I shall not sit as a widow or know the loss of children." Rome's assertion that she is no widow is not a retort against the suggestion that she is without lovers, but indicates that she has not experienced the debilitating effects of war and loss of life. Her men are victorious in their military adventures. They have not died in great numbers on the fields of battle. They have caused others to experience such losses. There is no mourning in her streets. In fact, her fault is not mere arrogance, but an unquestioning faith in her own inexhaustible resources, unaccompanied by any sense of what depravation meant to others when she visited such things upon them. Over the many centuries of her empire she has brought sorrow and sadness to the wives and children of her enemies, but she has not had to deal with losses and the negative emotions that are associated with them. That is all about to change (cf. Mounce, 326; Caird, 223).

The destruction of the place is then described in elaborate detail. Kings of earth mourn her lost glory. Merchants of earth mourn their lost trade. Mariners of earth mourn their lost shipping. The saints have a different perspective on her, however. They are told to rejoice. All economic considerations aside, God had answered their prayers and provided relief from the oppression she had so heartlessly visited on them. In addition, He had mercifully given them the justice they had for so long been requesting through their earnest prayers. And so, God's judgment on the city is their judgment: "Rejoice over her, O Heaven, and you saints and apostles and prophets, because God has pronounced your judgment against her" (v. 20).

Cycle Five: The Judgment of the Harlot   18:1-24

John's call for rejoicing at the fall of the wicked city, like the earlier call for rejoicing at the fall of Satan (cf. 12:12), may give pause to some modern Christians who live in comfortable surroundings in relative safety. Some have been known to be harshly critical of such language as the prophet employs to describe the devastation of this enemy of God. They have no right to make such judgments, however. They have not known the horrors of religious persecution. They have not seen their Christian brethren hunted down and slaughtered like cattle. They have not known the heartless maltreatment of people whose only crime was to believe in Jesus. If modern students of this book are offended by this exhortation, they should realize that they do not share John's perspective of solidarity with the oppressed. They cannot understand the longing for justice on the part of the exploited and persecuted. Nor can they perceive God's judgment in terms of the punishment and destruction of oppressive and murderous powers. Rome's slaughter of Christians under Nero and Domitian were, for John, only the beginning of what in the end will turn into a more general and worldwide slaughter of God's people (13:7; 18:24). For the prophet of God to rejoice at the undoing of those who have wrought so much pain and suffering on others is, on the human side of the equation, a mark of validation for the righteous actions of God on behalf of those who have prayed so hard for so long seeking vindication. God's judgment on His people's enemies is their temporal vindication.

The chief quarries to which John has gone for his structure of the lament over the city are the prophecies against Babylon in Isaiah 13 and Jeremiah 51, and that against Tyre in Ezekiel 26-27, together with significant segments from the prophecies against Edom in Isaiah 34 and Nineveh in Nahum 3. John's usage of these songs of doom, directed against the tyrannies of former ages, is itself significant in the way he viewed Rome. This city summed up in itself, and even surpassed, the wickedness of the tyrant-powers of the ancient past. Hence, in his song which celebrates her desolation, he concentrates into a single lament the prophecies against all of them (Beasley-Murray, 264).

Above all, however, John is dependent on Jeremiah 51:45-48. There the call for an exodus from Babylon (cf. Rev. 18:4) is followed by the promise that "the heavens and the earth and all that is in them, shall sing for joy over Babylon['s]" doom. John transformed Jeremiah's *promise* of rejoicing into a *call* for rejoicing, and he substituted the "saints and apostles and prophets" for Jeremiah's people on earth. This threefold group comprises those members of the church who have suffered martyrdom at the hands of the Roman state. The last line of v. 20 states that, "God has given judgment for you" against Babylon/Rome. This conclusion requires that the saints, apostles, and prophets especially had to suffer from the cruelty and godlessness of Rome. Thus, verse 20 connects perfectly with 6:9-11; 13:7, 15; and 18:24 (Krodel, 306). This reference to the "apostles" is more than simply an allusion to the death of Peter and Paul in Rome at the hands of Nero, for it is well known that only one of the apostolic band lived a full life and died of old age. And that was the author of the Revelation, John. According to the most dependable ancient tradition, all of the rest of them died as martyrs and the majority of them by crucifixion, but at the time of the writing John himself was imprisoned on the island of Patmos. So, even though he did not die the death of a martyr, he also suffered under the Romans.

At mid-chapter, a rock like a great millstone is cast into the sea by a powerful angel. It turns out that this is merely an illustrative action. It communicates an important truth: "Thus shall the great city be cast down, and shall be found no more at all" (v. 21). A heavy stone that is thrown into the ocean sinks immediately to the bottom. The force of this symbol is abundantly clear. Rome's world-wide empire would be erased with the fall of her capital city. It would be like a stone thrown into the sea. It would be no more. Why this extraordinarily painful visitation? The author responds by saying that it is because "in her was found the blood of prophets and of saints, and of all who have been slain upon the earth" (v. 24). She is a persecutor of Christians, and so God must judge her harshly for these unspeakable crimes against Himself and His people. The passage declares that, as with Jerusalem who went before her, whose inhabitants Jesus reminded that she had effectively inherited the guilt of the people of Israel's earlier history (Matt. 23:29-32; Luke 11:47-51), she would also be held responsible for more than what she in this present generation had done. The Jerusalemites had slain the prophets, and the present generation of persecutor's garnished the tombs of the martyred prophets while simultaneously making new ones. So, unless the bloody city and nation had repented and dissociated themselves from this history of bloodshed and death, they would suffer the cumulative guilt of their own and previous generation's transgressions.

Like Jerusalem before her, Rome also, says John, being the veritable reincarnation of an ancient foe of God's people, Babylon, would likewise suffer the frightening fate of that previous enemy of righteousness. She would reap the hideous harvest of the cumulative guilt of all of the prophets, saints and martyrs of all the ages. What a terrifying prospect!

D. Judgment upon the Beasts (19:1-21)

After these things I heard as it were a great voice of a great multitude in heaven, saying, "Hallelujah; salvation, and glory, and power, belong to our God: for true and righteous are His judgments; for He has judged the Great Harlot, she who corrupted the earth with her immorality, and He has avenged the blood of His servants at her hand." And a second time they say, "Hallelujah." And her smoke ascends upward for ever and ever. And the twenty-four elders and the four living creatures fell down and worshipped God who sits on the throne, saying, "Amen; Hallelujah." And a voice came forth from the throne, saying, "Give praise to our God, all His servants, you who fear Him, the small and the great."

And I heard as it were the sound of a great multitude, and as the sound of many waters, and as the sound of mighty thunders, saying, "Hallelujah: for the Lord our God, the Almighty, reigns. Let us rejoice and be exceeding glad, and let us give Him glory: for the marriage of the Lamb has come, and His wife has made herself ready." And it was given to her that she should array herself in fine linen, bright and pure: for the fine linen is the righteous acts of the saints. And he said to me, "Write, 'Blessed are those who are bidden to the marriage supper of the Lamb.'" And he said to me, "These are true words of God."

And I fell down before his feet to worship him. And he said unto me, "Do not do that: I am a fellow-servant with you and your brethren who hold the testimony of Jesus: worship God; for the testimony of Jesus is the spirit of prophecy." And I saw the heaven opened; and behold, a white horse, and He who sat on it was called Faithful and True; and in righteousness He judges and makes war. And His eyes are a flame of fire, and upon His head are many diadems; and He has a name written which no one knows except He Himself. And He is arrayed in a garment sprinkled with blood: and His name is called the Word of God. And the armies that are in heaven followed Him on white horses, clothed in fine linen, white and pure. And out of His mouth proceeds a sharp sword, that with it He should strike the nations: and He shall rule over them with a rod of iron: and He treads the winepress of the fierceness of the wrath of God, the Almighty. And He has on His garment and on His thigh a name written, "KINGS OF KINGS, AND LORD OF LORDS."

And I saw an angel standing in the sun; and he cried out with a loud voice, saying to all the birds that fly in mid heaven, "Come and be gathered together to the great supper of God; that you may eat the flesh of kings, and the flesh of captains, and the flesh of mighty men, and the flesh of horses and of those who sit on them, and the flesh of all men, both free and bond, and small and great." And I saw the beast, and the kings of the earth, and their armies, gathered together to make war against Him who sat upon the horse, and against His army. And the beast was taken, and with him the false prophet who produced the signs in his presence, with which he deceived those who had received the mark of the beast and those who worshipped his image: they both were cast alive into the lake of fire that burns with brimstone: and the rest were killed with the sword of Him who sat on the horse, even the sword that proceeded out of His mouth: and all the birds were filled with their flesh (Rev. 19:1-21).

1. The Hallelujah Chorus at the Fall of Babylon (vv. 1-6). When the former vision was ended, John informs us that he heard a mighty sound coming out of heaven saying, "Hallelujah; salvation, glory, and power be to our God!" The writer does not identify the source of this thunderous sound; it could represent the concerted voices of a chorus of angels, or else the mighty sound of singing by the glorified church. The word *hallelujah* transliterates a Hebrew idiom that means "Praise Jah" or "praise God." The ending of the word represents the shortened form of the name, Yahweh. Interestingly enough, this term is utilized on four occasions in this chapter of the book (vv. 1, 3, 4, 6) and nowhere else in the New Testament. The Hebrew form of this word is found often in the Psalms, but in most cases the English reader would not be aware of that because it is translated into an expression like, "Praise ye the Lord!" This Hallelujah Chorus is given in four parts, each segment begun with the shout of "Hallelujah!" The third aspect is set off with the words, "Amen! Hallelujah!"

It is worthwhile to note that with the introduction of this section we are rather abruptly reminded that all of the visions in this portion of the document, chapters 17-19, were mediated by an angelic interpreter, who was last heard from directly by the readers in 17:6. Of this heavenly messenger we have by this point almost lost sight: his part in the visions of chapters 18 and 19 was almost more than was to be expected of him at the time, being that he played such an important role there, so much so in fact that if we are not careful we will forget that the whole of John's apocalypse is said to have been conveyed from God "through His angel" (1:1). Thus, even where John does not directly intimate the presence or specific action of an angelic intercessor, it should be assumed by the reader that he is present and very much involved in the process. Evidently the prophet is enabled to hear even the words of God and Christ only through the helpful medium of a ministering spirit.

Of course, for all practical purposes this makes little difference to our understanding of the book. At the same time, however, the inference which John seems to have drawn early in his ecstatic experiences and the colorful visions which crowded into his mind on this occasion were consistent in this one regard. They are universally viewed by him as owing something to the mediation of an angel. This fact should help us to set aside our rather natural first feeling that there is something abrupt and strange in the transition from the scene of heavenly rejoicing in vv. 1-8 to the precepts of the angelic interpreter delivered to John in vv. 9-10 (cf. Kiddle, 380-381).

2. *The marriage supper of the Lamb is announced (vv. 7-9)*. This segment of the work includes the last part of the final hymn of the book of Revelation, and therefore, the last hymn in the New Testament. It is customarily referred to as a "wedding hymn" since it celebrates the nuptials of the Bridegroom and His bride (Christ and the church). A blessing is spoken over those who have been invited to this blessed event: "Blessed are those who have been summoned to the supper of the wedding of the Lamb." The sound seems to issue forth from the throne, for the crescendo is such that John likens it to "the sound of a great multitude, of many waters, and of mighty peals of thunder." Or, like v. 1, it may allude to an overwhelming sound that proceeds from heaven, of either angels or of the heavenly multitudes (cf. 7:9). But, John's response which follows may indicate that it is the angel who thunders it forth, for he seemed so startled by the majestic sound that he attributed divinity to the one from whom it came. It will be recalled that he was similarly inspired with the sound of the Lord's voice when He first appeared to him (cf. 1:15; cf. also 14:2; Ezek. 1:24; 43:2). The explanation for this jubilant singing is given in the following terms:

"Because the Lord God Almighty rules!" The reign of God in its fullest sense is what is ultimately lauded in this Hallelujah Chorus.

The Lamb's marriage supper is heralded here, but it is not described. The notion of a wedding feast is a familiar one to the reader, however, for the idea of the church as the bride of Christ is a common figure in the New Testament. In fact, Israel was previously depicted as the wife of the Lord (Isa. 54:5-6; 62:5; Jer. 31:32; Ezek. 16:8ff.), so this concept was already a well-known one in the parlance of Old Testament theology. The entire prophecy of Hosea was assembled around the theme of Israel as the adulterous wife of God. Even though this was painfully correct, in that Israel had often flirted with other gods and worshipped them adoringly, that Seer looked to the future when the people of God would no longer chase after other lovers: "I will betroth you to Me forever; I will betroth you to Me in righteousness and in justice, in steadfast love, and in mercy. I will betroth you to Me in faithfulness; and you shall know the Lord" (Hos. 2:19f.).

In addition, Jesus employed the motif of the wedding feast to represent His relationship to His disciples in both its present and future aspects. He alluded to Himself as the Bridegroom who had come to His people to make them His own. He asked, "Can the wedding guests fast while the Bridegroom is with them?" (Mark 2:19). John the Baptist also called Jesus the Bridegroom, designating himself as only the friend of the Groom (John 3:29). As well, in His teaching Christ utilized this metaphor. It was to Him the perfect illustration to describe the eschatological coming of the Kingdom (Matt. 22:1-14). In this parable, however, the bride plays no role whatsoever. Rather, attention is focused altogether upon the invited guests, some of whom accepted the invitation while others spurned it.

Obviously, the responsive guests represent those who responded affirmatively to the invitation, while the unresponsive ones represent those people like the scribes and Pharisees who rejected Jesus and His message. Again, Jesus likened the uncertain hour of the arrival of the Bridegroom to the unknown hour of the Second Coming of Christ (Matt. 25:1-13). In this parable, the bride is not identified; attention in this case is altogether centered upon the readiness of the ten maidens. The five wise maidens who found entrance into the wedding feast represent those followers of Jesus who are ready and awake for His coming. The five foolish ones stand for those who will in the final day claim admission, but are unprepared and so will be turned away. The bride plays no role in this story.

Also, as is the case in most every ancient and modern cultural milieu, marriage is depicted as a joyful festival celebration, and this was especially so in Israel as this familiar image was applied to the coming messianic time of salvation (Isa. 61:10; 62:5). On the basis of this well known concept, Jesus pictured the period of His work as uniquely epitomizing a marital time of joy (Mark 2:19-20). The force of this part of His message was that through Him and His ministry God was inviting all who are willing to the wedding feast of His Son, and thus in this demonstration of His grace and generosity He offered His fellowship to those who could be motivated to enjoy it ("as many as you find there, invite to the wedding feast"; cf. Matt. 22:1-14).

In Paul's thought the Old Testament idiom of Israel as the Lord's wife is fully embraced in regard to the body of Christian believers. They are the bride of Christ (Eph. 5:25ff.). In Christ the old bond of the law is broken, and men are free to be joined to Christ, precisely as a wife whose husband has died is free to marry again (Rom. 7:1-4). Because they are bound to Christ, they must abstain from immorality (1 Cor. 6:17). Paul says that he had betrothed the Corinthians to Christ as a pure virgin bride to her husband (2 Cor. 11:2).

In spite of these illustrative metaphors, it is recognized that the consummation of this spiritual relationship is an eschatological event which awaits the return of Christ. There and then the church is to be presented before Him in splendor, without spot or wrinkle or any such thing, that she might be holy and without blemish (Eph. 5:27). It is this eschatological event, the perfect union of Christ with His church, which is announced under the metaphor of the marriage supper of the Lamb. It needs to be noted, though, that John does not describe the marriage itself. He does not do that here and he does not do it elsewhere. This is so because it is not an actual event, but a figure. It is a metaphorical way of alluding to the final redemption of God's people. It will be fully realized when "the dwelling of God is with men. He will dwell with them, and they shall be His people, and God Himself shall be with them" (Rev. 21:3). This is why John is later able to say that the new Jerusalem is like a bride prepared for her husband (Rev. 21:2), and the angel can say that the spiritual city of God is "the bride, the wife of the Lamb" (Rev. 21:9; cf. Ladd, 247-49).

Hence, the post-resurrection church blended together all of these important celebratory ideas as it interpreted the Lord returning in the end time not only as the bringer of the marital festival of joy but also as the noble Bridegroom who united Himself with the church, His bride who anxiously awaited His arrival (2 Cor. 11:2; Eph. 5:23, 33). Here the book of Revelation takes a step further in the development of this symbolic idea. It portrays the perfection of the community of the redeemed in the image of the marriage of the lamb, but at the same time, out of the negative side of the first traditional motif it also achieves an extremely effective contrast. On the one side there is pictured the evil city as a harlot with her importunate ostentation who seduces the whole world with her blasphemous disobedience (17:1-6); and then on the other side there is the community of the saved (the church) beautifully pictured as Jesus' bride with her pure white garment who waits obediently for the anticipated union with her Lord (21:2, 9), the eventual realization of the hopes and dreams of those who love God and long finally to be held in His embrace (cf. Roloff, 212).

3. John worships the angel (v. 10). On account of the Seer's own actions, however, at this juncture the angel takes center stage. The apostle is so caught up in the exhilaration of this moment of divine victory over the forces of evil that the text tells us he fell prostrate before the mighty angel who revealed these things to him. This action met with angelic displeasure, however: "You must not do that! Worship God!" Neither beast nor angel is an appropriate candidate for worship (13:15). Even though his intentions were good, he was nevertheless mistaken to direct his worship toward this magnificent heavenly being. Angels are at best only servants of God, and mere ministers to men: "Are they not all ministering spirits, sent out to render service for the sake of those who will inherit salvation?" (Heb. 1:14). They are creatures of God, just as human beings are. So they are not deserving of worship.

Idolatry can take many forms, including that of angel worship, which John, even though he seemed unaware of it at the time, was attempting in this instance (cf. also 22:8). This tendency to venerate angels was apparently practiced by some of the churches of the region (cf. Col. 2:18; *Ascension of Isaiah* 3.15; Justin, *Apology* 1.6). John's rather transparent point in revealing this human weakness on his own part is purposeful and deliberate. He wants the churches to know that even though in certain circumstances this may be a rather natural human reaction to these beings from that other and higher world, his own mistake shows that this is not an appropriate response to angelic visitation.

As well, this must teach all readers of the book an essential lesson. It is not without purpose that God placed the commandment to avoid idolatry first on His list of warnings to His people (cf. Exod. 20:3, 4). If not even the angel who mediated and interpreted the visions and auditions to John in the Revelation is to be worshipped, how perverse would it be to venerate any other angelic personages, not to mention human emperors or beastly apparitions. Moreover, it is also clear from this experience of the apostle with this particular heavenly being that a genuine angel knows his appropriate place and function in the heavenly administration, refusing both worship and adoration, and properly directing it toward the One who is truly deserving of such veneration. "I am a fellow-servant, with you and your brethren." Thus, unlike the self-deifying Caesars of John's day, angels who recognize their own limitations refuse to be worshipped and so rob God of His much deserved glory (2 Pet. 2:4; Jude 6).

4. *The Rider on the white horse and His armies (vv. 11-16).* Christ is pictured riding on a white horse, arrayed in a garment sprinkled with blood. The armies of heaven follow Him in white. An angel in mid-heaven announces the feast of birds. The feast consists of the flesh of the enemies of Christ. What is all of this about? What does it intimate? Taken as a whole, this is a highly stylized and greatly detailed picture of the eventual defeat of the Lord's foes. They are symbols whose literary context is a book filled with symbols. So, even though they may appear confusing to some readers today, in the biblical background and situation of the book of Revelation they are entirely at home. They are very much a part of the lexicon of John's apocalypse.

The depiction of Christ is powerful in its chosen terminology. He is riding on a white horse, the color white, of course, symbolizing purity and virtue. But the white horse in particular was symbolic of the victorious warrior, the conqueror. In the time of John the Roman generals rode on white stallions when they marched in parades to celebrate their victories. The armies of heaven also are clothed in fine linen, "white and clean," and they also followed Him on white horses. Jesus is called "Faithful and True," terms that have already repeatedly been used to picture His nature (cf. 1:5; 3:7, 14).

Along with this He is called the "Word of God," one of John's favorite expressions for Him through one formulary or another (*ho logos tou theou;* John 1:1, 14; cf. also 1 John 1:1; Rev. 1:2, 9; 6:9; 20:4). He describes His eyes as being "like a flame of fire" (see 1:14; 2:18; cf. Dan. 10:6), and says that on His head were many crowns (*diadema*), picturing His worldwide authority over all nations as the "King of Kings and Lord of Lords" (v. 16; see also 17:14). [It should be remembered that both Satan and the beast are said also to have diadems on their heads in their paltry imitation of the authority of deity (cf. 12:3; 13:1).] These names were written on His robe and on His thigh, John explains. It has been noted that many ancient statues have the name of the person whose likeness is presented in the statuary engraved on the thigh of the statue. The writer may have had this in mind when he offered this description.

He also tells us that Christ "had a name that no man knew, but He Himself." As human beings we may study the theological ideas inherent in the notion of the transcendent Deity, especially in regard to the idea of incarnation, but if the truth is told, these are ideas we may only faintly grasp. Only God Himself knows the true glory and grandeur of the miracle He performed when He blessed this sinful world with the divine/human person and redemptive work of Jesus Christ. That is what John pictures here in this image. Too, he says that this conquering hero is robed with a garment or vesture "dipped in blood" (v. 13). This seems to be an allusion to a well-known messianic text from the Old Testament, namely Isaiah 63:1-3, which universally was applied to the victorious Messiah who had the blood of His enemies spattered on His garments from the winepress of the wrath of God. Some expositors have tended to interpret the blood on His cloak as being His own blood shed for the redemption of the human race, but in general the circumstances of this passage fit more readily the meaning set forth by Isaiah 63:1-3. Clearly the writer wishes to portray Christ in this passage as being a conquering warrior who leads the armies of heaven into battle against the enemies of God. Too, He treads the divine winepress of the wrath of Jehovah God, crushing His enemies beneath His feet. Therefore, the blood depicted as spattered upon His robe must necessarily be that of those enemies and not His own.

Cycle Five: The Judgment of the Harlot   19:1-21

Finally, John explains that "in righteousness He judges and makes war" (v. 11), and "out of His mouth proceeds a sharp sword, that with it He should smite the nations; and He shall rule them with a rod of iron; and He treads the winepress of the fierceness of the wrath of God, the Almighty" (v. 15). The Lord's hot anger (*thumos*) of the wrath (*orgē*) of the Almighty is frightening even to consider. The image of the sharp sword proceeding from the mouth of Christ was seen in an earlier vision (1:16). As Kistemaker rightly observed, "Paul writes that at Christ's return Christ will destroy the lawless one with the breath of His mouth (2 Thess. 2:8), for the battle that the Lord fights is not with a sword, but with His word. This is spiritual warfare in which He battles spiritual forces of darkness in heavenly places (Eph. 6:12). This word coming forth from the mouth of Jesus carries out divine judgment to strike down the wicked (Rev. 19:21; see also 2:12, 16; Isa. 11:4; 49:2). Thus single handedly Jesus strikes down His enemies. The nations that rise up against the Lord will be struck down with His sword, which is a verbal sword, and with the rod of iron He will dash them to pieces as if they were an earthen pot" (Kistemaker, 523).

Likewise, J. Ramsey Michaels queried and then observed:

Is this figure Jesus? Yes, but a better way of putting it is that He is "the testimony of Jesus"—and consequently "the spirit of prophecy" (v. 10)—displayed in visible form. His name, after all, is the Word of God (v. 13), a phrase elsewhere linked closely to "the testimony of Jesus" (1:2, 9; 20:4). Moreover, He is Faithful and True (v. 11), attributes as appropriate to a prophecy or a testimony as to a person (compare v. 9, "These are the true words of God"; 21:5; 22:6). Finally, he recalls a figure described in the Wisdom of Solomon in connection with the death of Egypt's firstborn in the time of the Exodus: "For while gentle silence enveloped all things, and night in its swift course was now half gone, your all-powerful word leaped from heaven, from the royal throne, into the midst of the land that was doomed, a stern warrior carrying the sharp sword of your authentic command, and stood and filled all things with death, and touched heaven while standing on the earth" (Wis. 18:14-16, NRSV) (Michaels, 215-16).

While we do not subscribe to the notion that this writer makes any direct or even indirect allusion to this evocative citation from the Wisdom of Solomon, it is nevertheless true that John does utilize the identical sentiment that pervades the entirety of the Old and New Testaments, and is also reflected in this quote from the book of Wisdom, namely that God's word is "living and active and sharper than any two-edged sword, and piercing even to the dividing of soul and spirit, of both joints and marrow, and quick to discern the thoughts and intents of the heart" (Heb. 4:12, ASV). The "stern warrior" figure from that citation is interesting, but in all likelihood was not unique. Rather, it represented a commonly-held idea about the Word of God, which is reflected both in Hebrews and here in Revelation, e.g. that God fights many of His battles with the sword of the Spirit, and puts Satan and his minions to flight with its effective strokes.

5. *The final battle and the feast of birds (vv. 17-21).* An angel appears next who is "standing in the sun" from a perspective where he could summon all of the birds of the heaven to a feast of dead bodies, the enemies of Jesus Christ. However, one is almost disappointed at this point in the action of the scene. The entirety of the book has led up to this point where the final battle is fought, but then when we reach this juncture we are only told the outcome of it and none of its details. Many expositors have filled in the blanks of the record and have concluded that what is depicted here is the great Battle of Armageddon. They have also set in this void of scriptural information a political figure whom they call Antichrist (even though that terminology is never used by John and is not found at all in the book of Revelation).

In fact, the battle depicted in this scene is a spiritual one that is being fought today and everyday, and will be fought until time is no more and this world is consumed by fire (2 Peter 3:10). It is the unending war between good and evil, God and Satan. For this author's purposes, he centers his attention upon the beast and the false prophet whom he had introduced earlier in the series of visions. He is concerned with the threat they pose to the church of Christ at the time of the writing of this grand missive to the seven churches in Asia Minor. And he is concerned to let his reading audience know what their end will be.

And so, at the conclusion of this vision the enemies of Christ, the first beast (the Roman emperor), and the false prophet (the emperor cult) are cast into the lake of fire. The rest of the army of evil doers are eaten by birds. The author does not identify the birds under consideration, for there are many different birds that feed on carcasses (vultures, buzzards, condors, caracaras, eagles, hawks, crows, ravens, gulls, skuas, and terns). The message

Cycle Five: The Judgment of the Harlot — 19:1-21

of this part of the vision is transparent. Christ will ultimately bring judgment upon all of the forces of evil which set themselves over against the Lord and His chosen people, and even the mighty emperor of Rome and those local enforcers who attempt to enforce his arrogant worship upon the populace will be included, but many others will eventually come and go.

As in other instances where a military judgment is to be brought against a nation, foreign nations are to be used as the rod of God's anger in finally and fatefully bringing them to justice (Isa. 10:5, 6, 15; Amos 9:8-10; Obad. 4; Nah. 2:13; Zeph. 1:2-6; etc.). In other circumstances, God is capable of employing a whole host of different means and methods to bring chastisement and correction upon those who deserve it. He has in the past and He will in the future.

One of the greatest of all moments in the course of this section of the work is found in 17:14, where God claims total and ultimate victory over those who defy Him and attempt to take from Him His much deserved glory both in this world and in the next. He also celebrates the victory of the saints. God will be victorious, but so will His persecuted people. Writes John: "These shall war against the Lamb, and the Lamb shall overcome them, for He is Lord of lords, and King of kings; and they also shall overcome that are with Him, called and chosen and faithful."

At the moment the Lord's people are downtrodden and oppressed, but their time will come! They will experience the exhilaration of triumph. They will see the final end of their enemies. The beast and the false prophet "will be cast alive into the lake of fire which burns with brimstone" (v. 20). The author wants his anxious audience to be certain of the eventual outcome of this magnificent contest. The Lord will be victorious over all of His opponents, whether in time or eternity. He will utterly vanquish them every one. But there is more to remember: He will also graciously allow His faithful ones to share in His eventual supremacy. Their trials and tribulations will be remembered. Not only so, but they will be vindicated and rewarded.

Chapter Eight

Cycle Six: The Final Victory (20:1-15)

A. The Grand Finale

The sweeping vistas of this chapter are quite impressive. They take us from the victory of the martyred saints, the defeat of the Devil and his minions through to the downfall of Gog and Magog, then on to the resurrection and judgment of the wicked, and at last to the everlasting destruction of the enemies of God in the lake of fire. Some of these symbols that are used in this chapter have been like the proverbial prickly pear cactus, hard to handle and downright painful if mishandled. The reader would do well to remember the warning given by the author in 22:18, 19 and not add anything at all to what was said by him, and not subtract anything from his message by ignoring the context or his own self-definition of his material (1:1-3).

So the chapter before us must be read carefully and with reverence and respect for the context as well as for the teaching of Scripture in other more literal passages found elsewhere in the Word of God. The rule of thumb that must always be followed is an approach which allows literal passages of the Bible to interpret the figurative ones. Never the reverse! As amazing as it may sound, some readers of this chapter full of symbols have tended to make it the determinative chapter of the entire Bible in regard to the subject of eschatology or "final things." The one thousand year reign is the most obviously abused symbol found here. The results have proven to be disastrous. Whole systems of theology have grown out of the mishandling of some of these figures. The fact that they are symbols, and are described as such in the introduction to the book, seems never to phase those who are motivated by interpretive speculation in the realm of last things.

Since we have only these few simple figures to go by, the imagination tends to run wild in order to fill in the rather cavernous voids that are left. The result has been a methodical minefield littered with the useless remains of many writers' works who have been tempted into this feckless world of conjecture and supposition. It is best to stay with the text and to read it through the eyes of those who first read it, and not in the light of our own circumstances or situations. Whatever these symbols meant to the Christians of the churches of Asia Minor in the time of the apostle John, they ought to mean the same thing for us today. What they read from it, we should read out of it. Nothing more, and nothing less.

B. Victory for the Martyrs (20:1-6)

> *And I saw an angel coming down from heaven, having the key of the abyss and a great chain in his hand. And he took hold of the dragon, the old serpent, who is the Devil and Satan, and bound him for a thousand years, and threw him into the abyss, and shut it, and sealed it over him, that he should deceive the nations no more, until the thousand years are over: after this he must be loosed for a little while. And I saw thrones, and they sat upon them, and judgment was given to them: and I saw the souls of those who had been beheaded for the testimony of Jesus, and for the Word of God, and who refused to worship the beast or his image, and did not receive his mark on their forehead and on their hand. And they lived, and reigned with Christ for a thousand years. The remainder of the dead lived not until the thousand years were over. This is the first resurrection. Blessed and holy is he who has a part in the first resurrection: over these the second death has no power. But they shall be priests of God and of Christ, and shall reign with Him for a thousand years (Rev. 20:1-6).*

From chapter 12 to this point in the book three enemies have been allied in their opposition to Christ and His people. Of these three the first two were overcome by the victorious Christ in 19:19-20. But, there can be no full, complete victory so long as this third part of the alliance is at large and continuing to oppose God and His people. Therefore, the Devil must be dealt with. In this section of chapter 20 his ultimate fate is indicated. Hence, the overthrow of Satan, and not the reign of 1000 years, is the main theme of the first ten verses of this chapter. Here the Dragon (Satan) is chained and cast into the abyss for 1000 years. During that period, the souls of the martyrs reign with Christ in a spiritual resurrection. In this scene the Devil is overthrown for a time, although not fully and finally at this point, after his two powerful and troublesome agents have been disposed of (19:20). He is bound, or limited in his power (Luke 13:16; Matt. 12:29; Mark 3:27) for 1000 years, a figure which is often used in the Bible as symbolic of a long but unspecified period of time (Deut. 5:10; 7:9; Pss. 50:10; 105:8; 2 Pet. 3:8).

Satan's defeats are heralded throughout the book of Revelation. The fact that the Devil can be and will be conquered is an important message of the writing. He sustained his first great defeat at his "fall from heaven" that followed the incarnation and the earthly work of Christ. His second great defeat is now dramatized by describing him as being "bound" for one thousand years. Cast from heaven at his failure to destroy the Messiah, Satan is now cast from earth into the abyss, his rightful dwelling place. But this is not his final defeat, for he must at last be cast into the lake of fire and brimstone (20:10). Here is pictured the limitation of his power. It is said to restrict his ability to deceive the nations.

What is meant by this "binding" of Satan? Is it literal or figurative? Clearly, it is figurative in nature. The chain with which the angel binds Satan is not a customary string of metal links. That would be a literal and physical chain. Neither is the key to the Abyss a metallic object. Again, that would be a literal and physical key. Neither is the one thousand year period mentioned here an era of normal earthly time composed chronologically of precisely ten centuries. The term "key" appears also in 1:18 where Jesus says that He holds the keys of Death and Hades; in 3:7 He claims that He retains the key of David; and in 9:1 an angel is described as receiving "the key to the bottomless pit." In all of these texts one thing is patently clear, even though obviously highly stylized and symbolic language is employed. The word *key* signifies *authority*. A spirit cannot be literally shackled with a chain, but of course, it may be restricted and limited in its activities by a divine command. Further, a spirit cannot be literally padlocked within a physical room or space with a lock and key, but, once more, the Word of Almighty God has the capacity to limit the movements and activities of the Evil One, and that is what this is all about. The "one thousand years" is no more literal than are these other symbols in the chapter. It describes the time of the martyrs' reign with Christ. Moreover, the epoch of their reign coincides with the period when the Devil is no longer able to "deceive the nations."

Cycle Six: The Final Victory 20:1-6

Certainly this concept is very important to our understanding of this passage, for it is the chief action that is recorded in this part of the chapter. The earthly ministry of Christ and His teaching about the Devil may well provide the key to understanding this colorful figure. It will be recalled that when the seventy returned from their mission to the lost sheep of the house of Israel that they reported that the demons were subject to them in the name of Christ. Jesus replied, "I beheld Satan fall as lightning from heaven" (Luke 10:18). This temporal victory over the demon spirits in this account is thus seen to picture a larger and more important humiliation of Satan himself. At another point in His ministry Jesus was charged by the Pharisees with casting out demons by the power of Beel-zebub, the prince of the demons. In His reply, Jesus declared that if "Satan casts out Satan, he is divided against himself; how then can his kingdom stand?" He continued, "But if I by the Spirit of God cast out demons, then is the kingdom of God come upon you" (Matt. 12:26, 28). The Kingdom of God and the kingdom of Satan are at odds with one another, and where the Kingdom of God is transcendent, then the kingdom of the Devil is frustrated. This he followed up with a parable: "Or how can one enter into the house of a strong man, and spoil his goods, except he first bind the strong man? And then he will spoil his house" (Luke 11:22; Mark 3:27).

The point of this parable is that Jesus is the one who is more powerful than the strong man of the story. The power of the Devil is assuredly recognized by Christ in His characterization of him as a "strong man," but Jesus was more powerful. He bound the strong man and spoiled his house. This was intended to be a representation of what Jesus was doing in His invasion of Satan's realm to "bind" him and then "spoil his goods," that is, cast out his demonic allies and thus impede and obstruct his work. So, the binding of Satan during the earthly ministry of Christ was of the same character as that "binding" of the Enemy which John pictures here in the Revelation. The Devil was to suffer defeat at the hands of the exalted Christ in His efforts to destroy the rule of God in Christ through the beast of imperial Rome.

The Latin word for "one thousand years" is *millennium*. As noted in the Introduction to this book, premillennialists hold that Christ will return prior to the millennium and will personally usher in His reign of 1000 years on the earth. Postmillennialists, on the other hand, are convinced that Christ will return after a millennium has been brought about by the church. Amillennialists, like the present writer, reject the notion that any literal reign of Christ on earth for a literal one thousand year period is intended by this passage. The whole warp and woof of the book of Revelation is opposed to the literal reading of the "1000 year reign" concept as taught by premillennialists and dispensationalists. The Greek word for 1000 is *chilia,* and on this account those who believe in a literal reign of Christ and His saints on the earth for a thousand years are sometimes described as "chiliasts" and their doctrine as "chiliasm." This system of belief was early on attributed to the present passage by Christians from a Jewish background in particular, for this represented then, as it does now, the essence of the Jewish desire for a physical Messianic Kingdom, with its physical wars, its earthly monarch, a literal temple built in Jerusalem, and a this-worldly reign of the Messiah. The sad truth is, however, that all of this is a misunderstanding of the present text of Scripture. For some readers it is an alluring dream of the "last things," even though it has never been viewed by the most astute of interpreters as having much that commends it. At this point a modicum of background information, historically speaking, might well be in order.

Several of the greatest scholars in the early church condemned those who embraced these physical and material ideas with regard to the Kingdom of God. Origen rebuked those who looked for bodily pleasure and luxury in their hope for the Millennium. He remarked that indeed the saints of God will eat during that age, but it will be the bread of life; they will drink, but it will be the cup of wisdom (*De Principiis* 2.11.2, 3). But, it was Augustine who delivered the death-blow to this view. At one point in his career he had personally entertained the literal approach to this passage, and was himself a Millennarian, even though it was always spiritual blessings for which he looked and longed. But, over time he came to see the captivity of Satan as nothing more than the binding of the strong man by the One who is stronger than He (God) which the Lord had promised during His personal ministry. In the thousand years, he saw the whole interval between the first Advent and the last conflict; in the reign of the saints, the entire course of the kingdom of heaven; in the judgment given to them, the binding and losing of sinners; in the first resurrection, the spiritual share in the Resurrection of Christ which belongs to those who have been baptized. Augustine refused to see the Millennium in terms that are crudely literal, and so he spiritualized the entire idea, understanding it as symbolic language describing something altogether different from what these interpreters saw in this text.

Eusebius, the encyclopedic church historian, on the other hand, wrote that some of those who believed in a literal fulfillment of these things were given over to fantastic notions about physical pleasures during this period. For example, Nepos a bishop in Egypt who wrote a book on the subject, entitled *Refutation of Allegorists*. He wrote in order to counter the teaching of Origen of Alexandria and other allegorical interpreters like him who avoided the materialistic conceptions deduced by so many from the Apocalypse, by spiritualizing and allegorizing its language. The Gnostic heretic Cerinthus did this as well. Apparently their imaginations took the text far beyond what any serious attempt at interpretation could provide, seeing this period as "a millennium of desires and pleasures and marriage festivals"; as well as the "delights of the belly and sexual passion, eating and drinking and marrying" (Eusebius, *Ecclesiastical History* 3.28). A tendency toward such surrender to the Judaistic concept of the Messianic Era in addition to materialism and this-worldly thinking has existed during every period when these doctrinal perspectives are prevalent, including in our own day.

Nepos in particular considered himself a literalist in regard to the Revelation of John, as do many who argue for a literal one thousand year Millennium in modern times. Their claim is quite vacuous, however. In fact, their approach is always very creative, adding many elements to the portrait provided by John. For example, John does not mention the second coming of Christ, a physical bodily resurrection, a reign of Christ on the earth, the literal throne of David, the city of Jerusalem in Palestine, or Jesus Christ ever coming back to the earth. Additionally, it does not mention anyone in this resurrection or reign besides the martyrs: "And I saw the souls of those who had been beheaded because of the testimony of Jesus and because of the Word of God . . . and they came to life and reigned with Christ for a thousand years" (v. 4). There is no general resurrection in this passage. That happens later on in the chapter, after the thousand-year period of reign is over (v. 12). So the profession of literalness on their part carries little weight with those who make a careful study of their views about eschatology in connection with this prophecy.

Dionysius (ca. AD 200-265; bishop of Alexandria) met with a strong contingent of Nepos' followers at Arsinoe in Egypt ("where . . . this doctrine has prevailed for a long time, so that schisms and apostasies of entire churches have resulted") and called together a group of them for study and debate in about AD 254 or 255. At this conference the primary promoter of this theory (Nepos himself being deceased by this time), named Coracion, "in the hearing of all of the brethren that were present, acknowledged and testified to us that he would no longer hold this opinion, nor discuss it, nor mention nor teach it, as he was fully convinced by the arguments against it." Furthermore, the ever-brilliant Jerome spoke of those who held to this perspective on Revelation 20 contemptuously, calling them "half-Jews" and saying that "they look for a Jerusalem of gold and precious stones from heaven, and a future kingdom of a thousand years, in which all nations shall serve Israel" (Jerome, *Commentary on Isaiah* 60.1). It is needless to say anything further. It is clear that the best minds of the early church saw this viewpoint as a perversion of the text of Revelation 20 and an abysmal way of understanding what John meant originally to say by what he wrote there (cf. Barclay, 243, 244; Swete, 259ff.).

And so, as we have previously noted, what we actually have here is the reign of "the souls" of the martyrs with whom John is so concerned. The vision has two points of contact and contrast with the Vision of the Two Witnesses (cf. 11:3ff). In each case a definite period of time is fixed: in chapter 11 there are 1260 days, and in chapter 20 there are 1000 years. If the 1260 days in the first instance symbolize the duration of the triumph of paganism under the aegis of the Roman Empire (a relatively short period of time), then the 1000 years in this case just as clearly represent the duration of the triumph of Christianity over government sponsored Roman heathenism.

And so, according to this passage Satan is confined during this period of time "to prevent him from deluding the nations again." Thus, this text plainly implies that throughout the thousand years there was to be a considerable segment of the world population which would otherwise have been susceptible to the attacks of Satan, and therefore a living and breathing element of humanity over and above the conquerors (the souls of the martyrs), who will have proved themselves impervious to these attacks. This impression is immediately confirmed by the twice repeated statement that the conquerors are to reign with Christ, since it would be a singularly empty recognition of their services if they were to reign over a world of which they were the sole inhabitants. If we take these statements seriously, as indeed we must, it inevitably follows that those biblical scholars are misguided who treat the battle of the previous chapter as the end of world history and the wiping out of all members of the human race who have not lost their lives in the great martyrdom.

The battle represents the end of something, but not that sort of end, for it is said that the nations as a whole survive it. These conquerors have been told that they are kings and priests (1:6; 5:10), that they are to reign on the earth (5:10), and that they are to have authority over the nations to smash them with an iron bar (2:27; 12:5). These "nations" are those mentioned in the second psalm (from whence this language is derived) who rise in their wrath against the Lord and His Christ (11:18). They are in fact the peoples among whom the Christians are living, from whom they themselves had been ransomed (5:9; 7:9), and by whom they were to be persecuted (11:2).

They are also the people to whom John was bidden to speak his prophetic message (10:11), to whom the angel of the eternal gospel was sent (14:6), whose conversion the martyrs have confidently celebrated (15:4), and who are now given the assurance of future freedom from Satan's deceptions. The smashing of the nations therefore cannot mean their disappearance from the face of the earth, but rather the breaking of the political power which, with the under girding of idolatrous religion and materialist seduction, has organized them in resistance to the sovereignty of God. Thus John predicts that Christianity will someday smash this power structure and limit the power of Satan to deceive the nations for a very long time.

So, this passage is not about the reign of Christ, but about the reign of the martyrs. It should not be forgotten that Jesus is said to be reigning over His people in literal contexts throughout the New Testament (Eph. 1:20-22; Phil. 2:9-11; Col. 1:15-18; 1 Tim. 1:16, 17; 6:15; Rev. 1:5, 6; 17:14; 19:16). Of course He is also the ruler over all men, but only certain people recognize His authority at this time and yield themselves and their lives to His will for them. Eventually God will allow Him to sit in judgment of the whole earth (2 Cor. 5:10).

But that is not what this passage is talking about. Once more, *it is about the reign of the martyrs*. That must be remembered. At the time John wrote the Revelation these murdered saints were despised by those who had killed them and were about to kill them. Their powerlessness in the face of death was to their enemies an evident token of divine displeasure with them. In reality, the opposite was true. God treasured their sacrifices and would eventually show them to be heroes of the faith. In the mean time they will have to remain patient and wait while the rest of their brethren who are to be martyred are "killed even as they were, should have fulfilled their course" (6:11). This prophecy of John has been beautifully realized, even though it has not been appreciated by many Christians over the years since it was first pronounced. As William Boyd Carpenter, court chaplain to Queen Victoria, explained:

> The millennium-vision is, like so many of the apostolic visions, an ideal picture; it exhibits a state of things which is possible to mankind at any time. The vision has its approximate fulfillment, as the Church, in the faith of the reality of her Lord's victory, carries on her warfare against the prince of this world, and spiritual wickedness in high places. That this approximate fulfillment is not unreal may be seen in the fact that Christendom has replaced heathendom; Christ has taken the throne of the world; the prince of this world has been judged; the ascendancy of Christian thought and Christian principles has marvelously humanized and purified the world. To an Irenaeus, a Polycarp, a Justin Martyr, a Tertullian, the picture of the world during the Christian centuries would have the aspect of a millennium, when contrasted with the age of Pagan dominion and Pagan persecution. In their eyes, accustomed to the darkness of heathenism, the world, as influenced by a widely-diffused Christianity, would seem to be a world in which Christ ruled. They would see, in the acknowledgement, of apostles and martyrs and confessors, the wondrous resurrection-power of God's truth; they would see how they, who fell for Christ, had stepped from their forgotten graves to sit down with Christ. The sovereignty of the world belongs far more to St. Paul and St. John than to Nero or Galba.

Thus, during this period symbolized by 1000 years, the victorious martyrs' cause is raised from defeat to glory, and thus they reign, with the already reigning Christ who made their victory possible (2:26-27; 3:21). The resurrection of the chapter is a spiritual rather than a literal or corporeal one. The physical (or "second resurrection") is said to come after this one. Too, it needs to be recalled that this is a resurrection of "souls" rather than of bodies. Moreover, the concept of resurrection is used more than once in the Bible to picture the revival of a seeming "lost cause" (see also Dan. 12:1, 2; Ezek. 37:1-14; Rom. 11:15). So this is not at all a rare subject in the Bible. That is precisely the meaning here also. Those who speak of multiple resurrections are confused by the usage of this symbolism along with the conspicuous presence of cycles (which they fail to recognize and honor) throughout this document. As we mentioned in the introductory chapters of this book, resurrection and judgment are repeatedly visited and revisited in this work. This does not signify multiples of anything, whether judgments or resurrections. It only signifies the end of another cycle within the literature.

At verse seven Satan is loosed. He again deceives the nations to war against God and His saints. The lesson is that Rome is not God's or the church's final enemy. Others will follow, but at the last the Devil is cast into the lake of fire. The resurrection and judgment of the world is then envisioned by John, and evil men are cast into the lake of fire along with Satan. But, prior to considering these themes, there is the matter of Gog and Magog which must be looked into first.

C. Gog and Magog (20:7-10)

And when the thousand years are finished, Satan shall be loosed out of his prison, and shall come forth to deceive the nations which are in the four corners of the earth, Gog and Magog, to gather them together for the battle: the number of whom is like the sand of the sea. And they went up over the breadth of the earth, and surrounded the camp of the saints, and the beloved city: and fire came down from heaven, and consumed them. And the Devil who deceived them was cast into the lake of fire and brimstone, where are also the beast and the false prophet; and they shall be tormented day and night forever and ever (Rev. 20:7-10).

This vision pictures God's final triumph over Satan. His forces are symbolized by Gog and Magog (Ezek. 38-39), ancient characters standing for the enemies of righteousness. In Ezekiel's case he spoke of powerful enemies of Israel, with Gog from the land of Magog as their fiendish leader. His allies were the prince of Rosh, Meshech, and Tubal. The invasion about which that prophet wrote is often thought to have been the one referred to in the works of the historian Herodotus which occurred in 630 BC (1.104-106).

According to Herodotus, there followed a twenty-eight year period of time wherein the Scythians "became masters of Asia" and "their insolence and oppression spread ruin on every side." Eventually, Cyaxares (reigned ca. 625-585 BC) and the Medes massacred many of them and cast off their rule in order to recover their Median empire.

Josephus (*Antiquities* 1.6) identified ancient Magog with the Scythians, or peoples north of the Black Sea, while the other mysterious names are generally seen as the fearsome tribal groups and their leaders from the south and southeast shores of the Euxine, or Black Sea region. He explained that the Greeks referred to Scythia as *Magogia*. John's reference here has no geographical or ethnic connections, however. For that matter he is not making an allusion to this passage from Ezekiel. Certainly John is not referring to the same parties as Ezekiel had in mind when he wrote. Whatever their original historical, geographical or ethnic associations, Gog and Magog in the parlance of John the apostle was a symbol of the powerful enemies of God and His people. Jewish tradition generally had recognized these rulers of Ezekiel's prophecy as types of world rulers, whose evil power and cunning were directed against Israel. It is this long tradition of Jewish usage that John has in mind as he writes. He employs a set of figures that are familiar ones to any audience that was conversant with apocalyptic imagery at the time. Kaufmann Kohler offers the following general remarks about how the concept was developed for eschatological thought in the Rabbinical and associated materials:

> An important part in the eschatological drama is assigned to Israel's final combat with the combined forces of the heathen nations under the leadership of Gog and Magog, barbarian tribes of the North (Ezek. xxxviii-xxxix.; see Gog and Magog). Assembled for a fierce attack upon Israel in the mountains near Jerusalem, they will suffer a terrible and crushing defeat, and Israel's land will thenceforth forever remain the seat of God's kingdom. Whether originally identical or identified only afterward by biblical interpretation with the battle in the valley of Jehoshaphat (Joel iv. [A.V.iii.] 12; comp. Zech. xiv. 2 and Isa. xxv. 6, where the great warfare against heathen armies is spoken of), the warfare against Gog and Magog formed the indispensable prelude to the Messianic era in every apocalyptic vision (*Sibyllines*, iii. 319 *et seq.*, 512 *et seq.*, 632 *et seq.*; v. 101; Rev. xx. 8; *Enoch*, lvi. 5 *et seq.*, where the place of Gog and Magog is taken by the Parthians and Medes; II Esd. xiii.

5, "a multitude of men without number from the four winds of the earth"; *Syriac Apoc. Baruch*, LXX. 7-10; *Targ. Yer.* to Num. xi. 26, xxiv. 17, Ex. xl. 11, Deut. xxxii. 39, and Isa. xxxiii. 25; comp. Num. xxiv. 7 [Septuagint, Γὼγ for "Agag"]; see Eldad and Medad).

R. Eliezer (*Mek., Beshallaḥ, l.c.*) mentions the Gog and Magog war together with the Messianic woes and the Last Judgment as the three modes of divine chastisement preceding the millennium. R. Akiba assigns both to the Gog and Magog war and to the Last Judgment a duration of twelve months (*'Eduy.* ii. 10); Lev. R. xix. has seven years instead, in accordance with Ezek. xxxix. 9; Psa. ii. 1-9 is referred to the war of Gog and Magog (*'Ab. Zarah* 3b; *Ber.* 7b; *Pesiḥ.* ix. 79a; *Tan.*, Noah, ed. Buber, 24; *Midr. Teh.* Psa. ii.).

The destruction of Gog and Magog's army implies not, as falsely stated by Weber ("Altsynagogale Theologie," 1880, p. 369), followed by Bousset ("Religion des Judenthums," p. 222), the extermination of the Gentile world at the close of the Messianic reign, but the annihilation of the heathen powers who oppose the kingdom of God and the establishing of the Messianic reign (see Enoch, lvi.-lvii., according to which the tribes of Israel are gathered and brought to the Holy Land after the destruction of the heathen hosts; *Sifre*, Deut. 343; and *Targ. Yer.* to Num. xi. 26).

The Gentiles who submit to the Law are expected to survive (*Syriac Apoc. Baruch*, lxxii. 4; *Apoc. Abraham*, xxxi.); and those nations that did not subjugate Israel will be admitted by the Messiah into the kingdom of God (*Pesiḥ. R.* 1, after Isa. lxvi. 23). The Messiah is called "Hadrach" (Zech. ix. 1), as the one who leads the heathen world to repentance (הדריך), though he is tender to Israel and harsh toward the Gentiles (חד ורך: *Cant. R.* vii. 5). The loyalty of the latter will be severely tested (*'Ab. Zarah* 2b *et seq.*), while during the established reign of the Messiah the probation time of the heathen will have passed over (*Yeb.* 24b). "A third part of the heathen world alone will survive" (*Sibyllines*, iii. 544 *et seq.*, v. 103, after Zech. xiii. 8; in *Tan., Shofeṭim*, ed. Buber, 10, this third part is referred to Israel, which alone, as the descendants of the three patriarchs, will escape the fire of Gehenna). According to *Syriac Apoc. Baruch*, xl. 1, 2, it is the leader of the Gog and Magog hosts who will alone survive, to be brought bound before the Messiah on Mount Zion and judged and slain. According to *II Esd.* xiii. 9 *et seq.*, fire will issue forth from the mouth of the Messiah and consume the whole army. This indicates an identification of Gog and Magog with "the wicked one" of Isa. xi. 4, interpreted as the personification of wickedness, *Angro - mainyush* (see Armilus). In *Midrash Wayosha'* (Jellinek, "B. H." i.

56) Gog is the leader of the seventy-two nations of the world, minus one (Israel), and makes war against the Most High; he is smitten down by God. Armilus rises as the last enemy of God and Israel (http://jewishencyclopedia.com/articles/5849-eschatology).

This lengthy quotation demonstrates the impressive array of instances in the literature where this image is used with great effectiveness, some prior to John's writing, and others afterward. In the Enoch literature, it is said that God will destroy them in vindication of his faithfulness toward Israel in the final battle "during the days of the Messiah" (3 Enoch 45:5). As noted above by Kohler, in the Rabbinical writings Gog and Magog had also come to be identified with the future enemies of the Messiah. Likewise, it seems that John also uses these symbols to picture the last fierce enemies of God and Christ, and of Their people, the Church. According to Ezekiel, God uses sword (38:21), fire (39:6), and burning sulfur (38:22) to execute judgment against Gog and Magog. John also employs these same instruments of divine judgment in his vision to describe their downfall (vv. 9-10).

To John these evil culprits will "surround the camp of the saints and the beloved city," but this final assault of Satan and his allies will be short-lived. In his portrait of the battle, the saints do not lift a hand in their own defense. God brings about the end as well as the victory, for: "fire came down out of heaven and devoured them." Interestingly, there is a total lack of detail here. Only a summary depiction of a stunning victory brought about by divine rather than human agency and power. Even though the human imagination is set ablaze with curiosity as to what this might mean, in terms of detail and additional minutia, nothing more is said. But, that is ever the nature of the human mind, and the Lord never in His revelations to men attempts to satisfy that innate inquisitiveness and ever present longing for more information regarding future events.

This is all God wanted His people to know, namely that in the end He will bring about the downfall of their mutual enemies and give the victory to His faithful people. The battle itself is not what is of greatest importance, and certainly not the details of it, but the end result. God and His people will triumph. Evidently that is all they needed to know then and all that we need to know now. The war itself is not a physical one. Burnt out hulks of the machines of war will not mark the place and no earthly map will locate it. In fact, it is no different than the one to which the Apocalypse has made reference repeatedly (16:12-16; 17:14-18; and 19:11-21), that between good and evil, a spiritual engagement. The only distinction to be made is that this particular reference points to one final engagement in that ongoing series of battles. This one is the last one and it ends the war.

So, in John's vision, the Devil and his followers are ultimately judged and punished in Hell: "And the Devil that deceived them was cast into the lake of fire and brimstone, where was also the beast and the false prophet; and they shall be tormented day and night for ever and ever." Meanwhile, the martyrs and saints, earlier pictured groveling upon the ground before the altar in humiliation and seeming defeat (6:9), are perched triumphantly on thrones at the side of their victorious King. Can you see how this message brought hope and comfort to persecuted Christians during the period of their tremendous sufferings?

D. The Great White Throne (20:11-15)

> *And I saw a great white throne, and Him who sat on it, from whose face the earth and the heaven fled away; and there was found no place for them. And I saw the dead, the great and the small, standing before the throne; and books were opened: and another book was opened, which is the book of life: and the dead were judged out of the things which were written in the books, according to their works. And the sea gave up the dead that were in it; and Death and Hades gave up the dead that were in them: and they were judged every man according to their works. And Death and Hades were cast into the lake of fire. This is the second death, even the lake of fire. And if any was not found written in the book of life, he was cast into the lake of fire (Rev. 20:11-15).*

That which John now sees is what he first saw in the beginning of his visions (4:2), a heavenly throne. It is great and it is white in color *(thronon megan leukon)*. Previously a heavenly choir of voices had celebrated the sovereign purpose of God in creation and the redemptive victory of the Lamb. Now the voices have quieted and there is only the throne of God at center stage. This throne is described as "great" in comparison with those thrones that are envisioned at v. 4, the fact of its being white in color is no doubt symbolical of the holiness and purity of the judgment that is to be meted out. Nothing else is left, for the earth and the heaven have "fled away" from the presence of the Almighty (cf. Pss. 18:7-15; 77:16-19; 114:3-5; Hab. 3:6, 10-11).

Scripture says elsewhere that in God's presence the mountains melted away and the ground shook and trembled when God came near (Pss. 102:26; 104; 32; Isa. 36:4; 2:6; Jer. 4:23, 26; Rev. 6:14; 16:20). It will also be recalled how frightening was the scene at Mt. Sinai when God delivered to His people the Law. In this scene all that was thought precious before has now vanished in the blink of an eye. Nothing could more sublimely depict the majesty of the judge or of His throne than the language that John chooses. Everything in the entire creation, the sun, the moon, the stars, the earth with all of its mountains and oceans, not to mention the handiworks of mankind throughout its long habitation of the planet, all of it passes into oblivion. God and His eternal throne is at center stage in John's vision.

This passing away of the earth and the heavens is described also in Isaiah 51:6 as well as in Matthew 24:35 and parallels. That this will take place by a fiery inferno wrought by the divine hand is not related here, but is plainly taught elsewhere (cf. 2 Pet. 3:10, 12; 2 Thess. 1:7-8). God's throne is so preeminent, so central in this portrait of the judgment scene that everything that has ever been created is nothing by comparison. It is as if it never existed at all. In that moment in time nothing else matters. Truly, no one and nothing else will matter. God is the One who will decide the eternal destination of all men at that time. So, in that instant what else or who else could matter more? At the same time, however, it is clear from the verses that follow, that as central to this portrait as the divine throne may be, there is a secondary presence in that scene. All of the family of man will be present also, as John goes on to explain.

This passage, even though it does not say so directly, refers to Jesus Christ as the judge of all of the earth (cf. Matt. 16:27; 25:31; Acts 17:31; Rom. 2:16; Tit. 2:13; Rev. 3:21). The fact that earth and heaven fled away from the divine visage is reminiscent of John's earlier description of the Lord's face: "And His countenance was like the sun when it shines in its strength" (Rev. 1:16). When He walked among men His face was not extraordinary (He had "no form or majesty that we should look at Him, and no beauty that we should desire Him"; Isa. 53:2), for He had truly taken the form of a human servant while He lived as a man (Phil. 2:7, 8). But, in that other realm His divine face is as One who dwells in light that is unapproachable (1 Tim. 6:16), glorious beyond description.

Cycle Six: The Final Victory

20:11-15

And then John sees something more: "I saw the dead, great and small, standing before the throne; and books were opened. Then another book was opened, the book of life; and the dead were judged by their deeds according to what was written in the books" (v. 12). This picture is powerfully reminiscent of Daniel's description of the judgment of God as "ten thousand times ten thousand stood before Him" in the book of Daniel 7:9, 10. What is interesting about Daniel's description of the great judgment is that in that case the Ancient of Days, who sits on the throne, is clearly distinguished from the Son of Man. But, that distinction is not really important, relatively speaking, because the Father and Son are so intimately connected both in Scripture and in reality. Here John envisions the resurrection and judgment of all flesh. In other places in the Holy Scriptures, God is described in His various roles as King, Lawgiver, or Administrator of the creation. Here, though, He is only viewed in one aspect. He is the Judge of men.

This text does not intend to suggest that all of the human race will have died ("I saw the dead . . ."), being that other passages teach that some will be alive when the Lord returns and the judgment is initiated (cf. Acts 10:42; 1 Cor. 15:51; 1 Thess. 4:15; 2 Tim. 4:1; 1 Pet. 4:5). The writer simply states that the dead will be there. They will not be absent because they have died. This is important because the human way of viewing those who have passed on is to see them as "out of sight, out of mind." This is the very reason that Paul had to explain that those who have died will not miss out on the good things that lie ahead for the faithful in his first letter to the Thessalonians (4:15-17). The secular, agnostic, and atheistic mind today sees things thus even now, but with God the dead are still living (Matt. 22:32; Mark 12:27; Luke 20:38); they still exist and will never cease to exist.

It should also be noted that the basis of the judgment is outlined by this author in his revelation of the vision he experienced. He tells us that "books were opened. And another book was opened, the book of life." Daniel 7:10 says, "The judgment was set, and (the) books were opened." The definite article is missing in the Aramaic. What are these books that are alluded to in these two instances? The writer does not say specifically, but it seems that he does not need at this point to say much on that point. All Christians understand the basis of the judgment. After all, this vision in the Apocalypse appears in the final book of the Bible, and the Bible has a long history in regard to this matter. The Bible is a composite book made up of sixty-six smaller books, thirty-nine in the Old Testament and twenty-seven in the New Testament. This, in and of itself, represents a solemn testimonial to the nature of those books that will be utilized as the foundation of that judgment when the Final Assize is brought to bear upon the human family. Our Lord told the Jews, "Do not think that I will accuse you to the Father. There is one who accuses you: Moses, on whom you have set your hope. For if you believed Moses, you would believe Me; for he wrote of Me. But if you do not believe his writings, how will you believe My words?" (John 5:45-47). Jesus also said that His words would judge men in the last day (John 12:48). In this final dispensation of human history, the words of the Son of God are the final words of revelation to man (Heb. 1:1ff.).

Furthermore, nowhere else on earth are the words of Jesus recorded except on the pages of four books in particular: Matthew, Mark, Luke, and John; the four Gospels. They are found nowhere else. Too, the additional words of our Lord, spoken during the apostolic age, were revealed through the medium of the Holy Spirit to His chosen apostles and prophets, and these were set forth on the pages of the other books of the New Testament: Acts, the epistles, and the Revelation (John 16:13, 14). All Scripture is given by divine inspiration and is profitable for doctrine, reproof, correction, instruction in righteousness, so that the man of God may be perfect, furnished completely to all good deeds (2 Tim. 3:16-17). These are the books that will form the basis for the divine judgment. These are the very books that will be opened in the final day. And these are most assuredly the books that were seen in John's vision of the last judgment.

Certainly it is of great comfort to us as human beings to know that the foundation of the judgment exists in written form and is not composed of random thoughts or unwritten words or ideas. How would we know the mind of God if that were the case? If that were what we were left with, how would one prepare for the last judgment? Imagine, if you will, considering the possibility of giving an all-inclusive and final accounting of your life without having any idea of what might be expected of you prior to that examination. Not a very welcome situation to contemplate! And yet that is precisely the situation if there is no revelation of God's will in durable written form. Moreover, that is exactly the nature of the written revelation that is found in Holy Scripture. It claims to be the inspired revelation of the will of God, a virtual guidebook for the lives of those who are minded to obey God during life and spend eternity in His presence when this life is over.

The "book of life" (*hē biblos tēs zōēs*) is also directly and definitively associated with the judgment of all the living. It is thought that this phrase is derived from the custom of the ancients keeping genealogical records (Neh. 7:5, 64; 12:22, 23), and of enrolling citizens for various purposes in society (cf. Jer. 22:30; Ezek. 13:9). Thus, God is said to have a permanent record of all who are under His special care and guardianship. To be "blotted out of the book of life" means, then, to be cut off from the divine favor (Exod. 32:32; Psa. 69:28; cf. also, *Ethiopic Enoch* 108:3). Further, in the New Testament it is the record of those who are to inherit eternal life (cf. Phil. 4:3; Rev. 3:5; 13:8; 17:8; 21:27).

Later Jewish speculation also makes reference to a Book of Death into which are entered the names of the wicked, for which condemnation was reserved (*Jubilees* 30.20-22). Also, in the *Testament of Abraham* it is said that there are two angels at the right and left hand of the judgment seat of Abel, one always writing down good deeds and the other evil. The book, six cubits thick and ten cubits broad, which lies on a table before the Judge, seems to contain the history of every soul, for when it is opened for a certain woman who comes into judgment, it is discovered that her good deeds and evil ones are equal. In yet another text from this same source, Enoch the Scribe of Righteousness seems to make up the account of each soul from two books carried by cherubim (forgiven sins being blotted out of the book that Enoch keeps). In the Coptic *Apocalypse of Zephaniah* there are two angels at heaven's gate who write the good deeds of the righteous and they are carried up to the Lord that He may write their names in the Book of the Living (cf. Simcox, 187). Such speculation regarding things of this sort in these later Jewish sources was considerable. It is not necessary for us to look more fully into them here, being that this is not what the present study is about.

The writer's mention of the resurrection of the dead is also noteworthy. Of course, in the Book of Revelation the idea of resurrection is a recurring one, and one that is dynamic in its range of meaning in those contexts where it is used. Sometimes it is a figurative one, while at other times it represents an allusion to the raising up of all those who have died to new life. This instance appears to picture the true physical resurrection of all the dead, being that it occurs as it does in the biblical timeline. The old fleshly realm has come to an end here, for "Death and Hades gave up their dead . . . (and) were thrown into the lake of fire" (vv. 13-14). It is interesting to note, however, that the term "resurrection" *(hē anastasis)* is not used in this case. He also speaks of the resurrection of the Lord with other words also (cf. 1:18 "I was dead and now I am alive for ever"). The author had spoken of the "first resurrection" earlier in the chapter (v. 5b). That was clearly a symbolic rising from death to spiritual victory. A "second death" is mentioned four times by the writer (2:11; 20:6, 14; 21:8), with no mention at all of a "first death." Clearly he means to suggest that physical death is the first death and that spiritual death in Gehenna is the second one. The second resurrection, even though not described precisely with those words, plainly points to the emptying out of the Hadean world. This is a logical concomitant of what John reveals about this resurrection. Hades is the unseen realm, where departed spirits wait until those spirits are joined with a new and imperishable spiritual body (1 Cor. 15:42-44). If our text says that Hades has yielded up its dead and has been cast into the lake of fire, then the resurrection to which he alludes here must, of necessity, be the final resurrection of all of the deceased. Hades has emptied out. Death itself has ended. Eternity has begun.

Hence, a great lake of fire also comes into John's view. Clearly this is the place called elsewhere in Scripture by the name Hell or Gehenna, the ultimate trash-heap of heaven and earth, where the wicked are finally dispensed with and disposed of. In this case it is called also "the second death" (v. 14), for "into it anyone is flung if his name is not found written in the book of life" (v. 15).

The reader will note that John has had almost nothing to say here about those who are the saved of earth. He has only spoken of the lost and their bitter ending. In the next scene he will turn his attention to this other more favored class of people. He will treat the future of those blessed of God to enjoy the new age, the new heavens and earth, and the city of God, the New Jerusalem.

CHAPTER NINE

Cycle Seven: The Reward of the Faithful (21:1-22:5)

A. The Glorious Future for God's Faithful People (21:1-8)

All throughout John's visions of God's powerful assaults on the old corrupt order of Roman hegemony in the world there have been tantalizing intimations of the coming immortality for the victorious saints. These have come in the form of major themes throughout the Revelation: the promise of the Conquerors, the white-robed multitude, the triumph song of Moses and the Lamb, the wedding feast of the Lamb and His bride, etc. Throughout all of these dark days of persecution the shining clouds of eventual glory have hung low over the camp of the true Israel in their own unique "wilderness wanderings" guiding them relentlessly and unerringly toward their eventual heavenly reward.

Now at last the apostle John stands on his virtual Pisgah and surveys the Promised Land of the blessed Church triumphant. In some ways this is clearly the most important part of the book, as it has also become the most familiar and beloved. At the breaking of the fifth seal from beneath the altar the souls of the martyred dead had cried out pitifully to God in their heartfelt frustration for some sign of divine vindication of themselves and of their cause. They were told to wait yet a little longer. Vindication would come in God's time and on his schedule.

This final cycle of visions provides their rectification. All that they have endured is worth what it has cost. As the hymn writer so beautifully intoned, "Heaven will surely be worth it all!" Of all of the lovely words found in the Word of God, those which are located here in Revelation 21:1-7 must surely be the very most beautiful and precious to those who are facing imminent death or else considering the eventual coming of our Lord in glory and judgment.

> *And I saw a new heaven and a new earth: for the first heaven and the first earth had passed away; and the sea was no more. And I saw the holy city, new Jerusalem, coming down out of heaven from God, prepared as a bride adorned for Her husband. And I heard a great voice out of the throne saying, "Behold, the tabernacle of God is with men, and He shall dwell with them, and they shall be His peoples, and God Himself shall be with them, and be their God: and He shall wipe away every tear from their eyes; and death shall be no more; neither shall there be mourning, nor crying, nor pain, any more: the first things are passed away." And He who sat on the throne said, "Behold, I make all things new." And He said, "Write: for these words are faithful and true." And He said to me, "They are come to pass. I am the Alpha and the Omega, the beginning and the end. I will give to him who is athirst of the fountain of the water of life freely. He who overcomes shall inherit these things; and I will be his God, and he shall be My son. But for the fearful, and unbelieving, and abominable, and murderers, and fornicators, and sorcerers, and idolaters, and all liars, their part shall be in the lake that burns with fire and brimstone; which is the second death" (Rev. 21:1-8).*

In some sense this is the most important part of the book of Revelation, even though it is the easiest to digest and to understand, for even the most casual of readers. Hence, it has become since its first writing, the most familiar to the general world and the most beloved for the people of God. The martyrs and other suffering saints have appealed to heaven for relief, searching all the while for some meaning to it all. As G. B. Caird observed, "Much of John's vision, and much of human history it depicts and interprets, becomes intelligible, credible, tolerable, when we know the answer. Here is the real source of John's prophetic certainty, for only in comparison with the new Jerusalem can the queenly splendors of Babylon be recognized as the seductive gauds of an old and raddled whore" (Caird, 261-62).

John's earlier visions of all of the spiritual unpleasantness: the unholiness, ugliness, and rebellion against God and His Christ, is brought into fuller perspective against the final backdrop of the closing visions of the book. In fact, much of the human history it depicts and interprets as such, becomes, as Professor Caird of Oxford University suggested, intelligible, credible, and somewhat more tolerable, when we know the answer to the ultimate questions of life and when we get some glimpse of the end-point to which history is ultimately headed. Or at least we know that the majority of these questions and our own quavering feelings about them become unimportant in the light of the divine solution to the problems of human suffering. And we do indeed know the most important answers when we see everything in the light of the shining city of God which awaits the faithful. Our perspective assuredly becomes clearer when we catch a glimpse of what John saw from the unique vantage point of the lofty Pisgah of his Apocalypse.

The previous visions have addressed the issue of bringing about the demise of the old world and its woes. In this vision he tells his audience what is to take its place. And so John explains that when it is all over there awaits the Lord's faithful people "a new heaven and a new earth, for the previous heaven and the previous earth are passed away; and the sea is no more." The language which is used by the prophet in speaking of this new existence for God's elect is borne, by necessity, of the speech of the earth, on account of the fact that John has no other language with which to describe it and which his audience would understand as he spoke of it. Human language is filled with similes and metaphors reflecting the life that man lives in this physical world, and so it must be, once more by necessity, the heart and soul of the communicative devices are employed in order to picture those spiritual realities experienced by John in his visions of the future.

So, it could be argued, and has at times been alleged against the Apostle, that he makes the picture of the future life look very much like a luxurious version of this physical planet and the best that it has to offer in the present. That may be true to a certain degree, but in another sense that is a simplistic and unsophisticated understanding of his words. It seems not to appreciate the fact that the one and only medium John had at his disposal for describing the future was that which his audience had already, at least to some extent, experienced in this material world. Naturally, therefore, he borrows from the best and finest features of the world that we mortals have come to know and admire.

The reader should take note of the fact that he begins with heaven, earth and sea. These three realities are very much a part of the present reality, of course, but John gives all three a fresh expression. The heaven and earth of his vision are described as "new." The idea of heaven and earth, taken together as they are in this instance, stand for the whole of the creation of God, and in particular they represent the realm of man's domicile (cf. Psa. 101:25; Acts 4:24; 17:24). So, all of that former aspect of human existence is said to be replaced with a "new" realm of residence for the family of man. And then there is the sea. That sea which figured so prominently in his past visions is said to be "no more." What does he have in mind when he says this? That notion we shall return to momentarily.

So, in a sense it might be said that the future takes on the look of the past. Not in an absolute way, but in a comparative way. Why? Not because that is to be its reality in physical terms, a heaven and earth exactly like the old ones that we have known and experienced, but because that is the only language man has at his disposal to appreciate and understand what this new future reality will be like. Think of it this way: John could not have explained it any other way. Not because this is all of the beauty and ecstasy that heaven will possess, but because this represents the totality of the linguistic framework that we humans have to work with. Just as this present heaven and earth provide for the physical needs and necessities of human existence and maintenance, so the future divine provision will just as adequately and fully provide for our future spiritual life in all of its various aspects. The new heaven and earth will replace the old ones and will satisfy every need of the new spiritual existence just as surely and certainly as the old ones did for the fleshly body of the physical man throughout history.

Moreover, the spiritual counterpart already predicted and even anticipated by the prophet Isaiah were depicted as a final work of the messianic age (65:17; 66:22) and were pictured in precisely these terms also, and, we might add, for precisely the same reason. Some of the other apocalyptic writers apparently thought that the present earth would simply be altered and configured into a more sublime and perfected state (Jubilees 1:29; Enoch 45:1). Still others viewed the future state as requiring the total destruction of the physical earth: "the first heaven will pass away, a new heaven will appear" (Enoch 91:16). This latter view is consistent with the expectation that is set forth throughout the New Testament (cf. Matt. 5:18; 2 Pet. 3:12; Heb. 12:27).

Now it is true that John does not in his Revelation provide us with an account of the demise of the physical earth as is pictured in these other passages, but it is plain that he says nothing here that would contradict these texts. Too, he sees the "new heaven and earth" as effectively replacing the old ones, for he does say, ". . . earth and sky fled away, and no place was found for them" (20:11; cf. Roberts, 179). Such language is absolutely consistent with what we read elsewhere in the New Testament. Additionally, the word for "new" which he chooses in his description (*kainos*) intends for the reader to appreciate this. It means "new in kind" and not just another or a different one. This word at times when it is used implies that which is "unknown" or even "unheard of." Hence, John is not looking for another edition of the same thing. Most certainly he is not seeing in such language the mere physical renovation of the old earth. He is anticipating something altogether new and different in every conceivable aspect. That is what he means by "new."

John also tells his readers that in that future state "the sea" will disappear. This is an especially significant concept, since it has been for him an ever present reality throughout the many chapters of the Apocalypse, just as it had been a daily fact of his life on Patmos since he had been brought there. It surrounded the tiny island on all sides, so no matter which direction you headed, you ended up on the sea shore or overlooking the sea from some lofty height. If it were not for the sea, the Mediterranean, that separated the Apostle from his beloved Christian brethren on the mainland, he would be able to address them directly. Were it not for the sea he could personally comfort them and console them in this period of their tribulation. The sea, as it does oftentimes today, represented a barrier to many human relationships. Indeed, a formidable barrier it was for him at that point in time.

John's picture of what he calls "the sea," however, means far more than merely this, for it takes on a completely different aspect, being that he has used this idea repeatedly in his Apocalypse, and in every instance he has had something very specific in mind as he put it to use. This is a very powerful image which takes its meaning from the perception of the oceans that was common among ancient peoples, some of whom lived near the sea and some of whom sailed the wild oceans to make their living, fishing and trading with foreign nations far away from home. The sea was never still or quiet.

It therefore became the predominant figure for changefulness, surging and roiling uncontrollably and unpredictably as it so often did (cf. Isa. 57:20).

The ocean was also very dangerous. Many ancient mariners who set to sea never returned home. They went out, but never came back. Some became lost and eventually floundered. Some were wind-swept onto islands where they perished. Still others were sunk in stormy weather or else lost forever because their ships broke up on rocky shoals or unexpected reefs. Myths and legends grew up about the dark depths below the ships and what terrible beasts were hidden in that murky and impenetrable darkness. Mighty and powerful ocean creatures were visible at times to sailors, and stories were told of even more horrible monsters that dwelt in the ocean depths. No doubt the sailor's yarns became more fantastic with the passing of time and the telling of more and more extraordinary "tall tales." So, in the end, fear was also very much associated with the sea as a concept and in the popular imagination.

John has made repeated use of the concept of the sea in his visions up to this point, and one thing is perfectly clear by this time to the attentive reader: the sea which he is speaking of is not the physical ocean, even though he clearly intends to inject the notions of changefulness, danger, and fear in his prescription. In his metaphor the sea is in fact the abyss, the spiritual reservoir out of which the beast arises (4:6; 11:17; 13:1; 17:1) and which supports the frightening harlot of chapter 17. John tells us here that there is no future for it—this place of storms and danger, of uncertainty and dark foreboding, of fear and trepidation, of unrest, of suffering and drowning. "To the apostolic age the ocean spoke of separation and isolation, rather than a highway linking shore to shore. For this element of unrest, this fruitful cause of destruction and death, this divider of nations and churches, there could be no place in a world of social intercourse, deathless life, and unbroken peace" (Swete, 276).

In the end, according to John's vision, this seething cauldron of horrors, fraught with unlimited possibilities for evil things, will finally disappear. No one lives on the sea; they may live beside it; but they do not live on it. It is something to be crossed to arrive at one's eventual destination, but there is nothing permanent about it. It is certainly no place to be during a powerful storm. In fact, one does not even want to be in its vicinity during such a mighty disturbance of it, either from above or below. Therefore, "the sea" is one of seven evils John speaks of as having no abiding future, and eventually as being "no more." The others are: death, mourning, weeping, pain (v. 4), curse (22:3), and the dark of night (22:5). Such realities are unpleasant aspects of the present evil world; they have no future beyond a sin-cursed earth (cf. Morris, 237). None of them will be present when the heavenly takes the place of the earthly.

In this passage John introduces to the reader God's magnificent city which He has prepared for His people's future. To John's way of thinking, the New Jerusalem represents the fulfillment of all human dreams for the community and security of life in an ideal metropolis. He calls it "the holy city, the new Jerusalem." In so doing, he equates it with two important biblical concepts. The first is that of holiness or sanctification. This city is holy. This is its principal characteristic. It is set apart from every other city of the past in that it is purely for divine purposes. Sin does not exist there. Thus, the future state of the redeemed will be free from demoralizing sin and evil. It is a place that is "holy" in every possible sense of that word.

And the second obvious trait of this New Jerusalem is that it is truly and in every sense of the expression "the City of God." It will be remembered by all students of the Bible how God promised that He would someday select a city from amongst all the villages, towns and cities of Israel "to cause His name to dwell there" (cf. Deut. 12:11; 14:23; 16:2, 6, 11; 26:2). Eventually that city came to be recognized as the old citadel of the Jebusites (Judg. 1:21; "Jebus," 19:10), ancient Salem, later to be called Jerusalem, king David's capital (2 Sam. 5:6-9). There Solomon built the temple of the Lord and so it became the epicenter of the religious life of the nation. Thus, when the people prayed they said, "Blessed be the Lord out of Zion, who dwells at Jerusalem" (Psa. 135:21), and "Pray for the peace of Jerusalem: They shall prosper who love you" (Psa. 122:6). The beauty of the place was not to be compared with any other. It was called "the perfection of beauty" (Psa. 50:2), "beautiful in elevation, the joy of the whole earth" (Psa. 48:2; Lam. 2:15), "our beauty and our glory" (1 Macc. 2:12) and "the beautiful holy mountain" (Dan. 11:45). So, the heavenly Jerusalem, the future home of God's redeemed ones, is also a place (if it could be called a place) where there is beauty beyond compare. Certainly it borrows its linguistic frame of reference from that first Jerusalem and all of the freighted and highly charged vocabulary with which the ancient Israelites described their nation's capital city.

What is more, according to what we learn from John's vision, everything will be very different there. Practically nothing will be the same. The old things of the physical existence will have passed into distant memory. And it will all be replaced with new and better things. That is the declaration which emanates so forcefully from the throne of God in this scene: "Behold, I make all things new." In so saying, John implies that the unpleasant realities of life in the physical world will have ceased to be. And that is precisely what he says in the verses which follow this important proclamation. After he has declared that "the sea is no more," he suggests that all of the other terrible negatives of life will have passed out of the language of the heavenly sphere. There will be no more tears, death, sorrow, crying or pain (21:4). Those unpleasant experiences will have been forgotten and left behind in that world in which the Lord's people once suffered, wept, and died. Additionally, certain kinds of people will be excluded from that realm. The cowardly, faithless, polluted, murderers, fornicators, idolaters, and liars will be found elsewhere. Their kind will be out of sight and out of mind for they will be in the lake which burns with fire and brimstone (21:8). There will be none of them or of their ilk in that beautiful place.

Furthermore, there will be no temple or tabernacle in the newness of the heavenly realm, for God Himself is everything the tabernacle and temple ever represented, and He will be there in very presence with His beloved people (21:3). Therefore, the city as a whole is its sanctuary, a sacred space, and those who inhabit it will be holy also. Everyday life will be holy, in fact, for God is present every day in every part of the city and, happily, will permeate the life of those who inhabit it. So, there is no need either for a tabernacle or a temple. Those things too are a part of the past.

As well, he tells us that there is no sun, moon, night, or even closed gates in the lovely City of God. The Lord Himself is the glorious light that will shine there on all of its inhabitants, so there will be no need for any of these old realities (21:23, 25; 22:5). In addition, there will be no curse there (22:3). Earth, on account of the presence of sin in that realm, was cursed in the face of man's rebellion against his Creator (Gen. 3:1-6, 17;

Isa. 24:4-6; cf. Rom. 5:12-21; 8:18-25). What John sees in his vision is an altogether new reality, a world which looks beyond the unhappy and often uncomfortable memories of that cursed planet of the past. His portrait of the future pictures a purified and redeemed humanity and a fallen world delivered from the bondage of evil and transplanted into an environment that allows holiness to flourish and righteousness to prosper throughout an endless eternity.

B. God's New Age (21:9–22:5)

And there came one of the seven angels who had the seven bowls, who were laden with the seven final plagues; and he spoke with me, saying, "Come here, I will show you the bride, the wife of the Lamb." And he carried me off in the Spirit to a mountain great and high, and showed me the holy city Jerusalem, coming down out of heaven from God, having the glory of God: her light was like a very precious gemstone, like a jasper stone, as clear as crystal: having a great high wall; having twelve gates, and at the gates there were twelve angels; with names inscribed on them, which are the names of the twelve tribes of the sons of Israel. On the east there were three gates; and on the north three gates; and on the south three gates; and on the west three gates. And the wall of the city had twelve foundations, and on them twelve names of the twelve apostles of the Lamb. And he who spoke with me had a golden measuring rod with which to measure the city, and its gates, and its walls.

And the city lies foursquare, and the length of it is as great as the breadth. And he measured the city with the rod, twelve thousand stadia: the length and the breadth and the height of it being equal. And he measured the wall of it: one hundred forty-four cubits, according to the measure of either man or angel. And the wall was built of jasper: and the city was pure gold, like clear glass. The foundations of the wall of the city were adorned with all sorts of precious jewels. The first foundation was jasper; the second, sapphire; the third, agate; the fourth, emerald; the fifth, onyx; the sixth, carnelian; the seventh, chrysolite; the eighth, beryl; the ninth, topaz; the tenth, chrysoprase; the eleventh, jacinth; the twelfth, amethyst. And the twelve gates were twelve pearls; each of the gates being a single pearl: and the street of the city was pure gold, like transparent glass.

And I saw no temple within: for the Lord God the Almighty, and the Lamb, are its temple. And the city has no need of the sun, or of the moon,

> *to shine upon it: for the glory of God gives it light; and its lamp is the Lamb. And the nations shall walk bathed in its light: and the kings of the earth will bring their glory into it. And its gates will never be closed by day (for there shall be no night there): and they shall bring the glory and the honor of the nations into it: and there shall never enter into it anything unclean, nor anyone who practices what is detestable or false: but only those who are written in the Lamb's book of life (Rev. 21:9-27).*

Every detail set forth by this author is beautiful in its own right, glorious beyond description, but certain features form the main outline of what John saw in his vision of the future glory. What follows is a summary outline of the principal aspects of it:

1. *The New Heaven and the New Earth.* This figure symbolizes perfect acclimation with God. Key to the beauty of this vision is the terminology involved. What man has become accustomed to in this world is what is included in this promissory language. Just as an astronaut traveling into outer space must take with him certain aspects of his normal life on earth (air to breathe, water to drink, food to eat, etc.), so he must see in the heavenly future something of what he has become acclimated to in this life: in this instance, "heavens and earth" along with all of the accoutrements of comfortable survival.

This does not promise a world like the one we have come to enjoy so much, but it does envision an agreeable existence, a continuation of life that will be pleasant and entirely satisfying for the saved. It will not be so foreign and alien that it is not enjoyable. All that is essential for a pleasing and pleasurable future is included in the multi-faceted language of this vision. God's people will never, ever, when they reach that heavenly land, look back and long for the old "heavens and earth" of this present realm. Just as this present sphere, with all of its vicissitudes and problems, has in some sense and to some degree suited us ideally, so that next one will suit us perfectly. That is the force of this lovely figure.

2. *The Tabernacle.* This figure symbolizes perfect communion with God. God had given Moses very specific instructions for the construction and setting up of the Tabernacle in the wilderness (Exod. 25ff). We may conclude from this that he then sought a close relationship with His people. The Old Testament Tent of Meeting was a symbol of the fellowship and mutual communication which took place between God and man in the activities of worship and divine service under that former covenant.

Man communicated his love for the Lord and illustrated it by sacrificial acts of obedience and service. Those activities all centered, in ancient Israel, in various ways about the institution of the Tabernacle. At its holy altar sacrifices were offered which made atonement for the sins of the people and allowed them continuous access to God's mercy and grace. Too, God spoke to His people through prophetic figures like Moses and Aaron as well as by means of the Urim and Thummim (1 Sam. 14:41), and the lot which was cast into the lap (Prov. 16:33). But the centralized shrine was symbolic of unified worship of the Lord and His Word delivered faithfully to them.

Through the Tabernacle, God was communing and communicating with His people. The Temple in its various manifestations took the place of the Tabernacle when a permanent home was found for the Ark of God at Jerusalem in the days of King Solomon. It is not surprising therefore that the visions of John in Revelation include this important Old Testament symbol of the divine presence to picture what was to be in the future. When this present state of things has come to an end, the Lord will allow redeemed men and women to enjoy His presence and fellowship as never before. That is what this reference to the tabernacle of God among men symbolizes in the Revelation.

3. The Sacred City, the New Jerusalem. This figure symbolizes the provision of perfect protection by God. The long description of the New Jerusalem here implies that the ancient city already had been destroyed (AD 70), and that in its place John has in mind to awaken in the hearts of his readers a longing for a new and heavenly city. The old Jerusalem now lies in ruins, having been handed over to the Gentiles. John uses this ancient image (cf. Dan. 7:25; 12:7) in fresh form to portray the abuse of the Church by the heathen power of Rome in Revelation 11:2. But the New Jerusalem in pristine purity and glistening perfection awaits the people of the Lord when they have finished their course, if they have proven faithful.

Every aspect of the description given is of absolute perfection, as is entirely appropriate for the home of the everlasting soul of redeemed man:

a. A Great and High Wall (v. 12). The wall described in this text is enormous. It measures fifteen hundred miles in height! What this wall signifies is security. Perfect protection from all harm is afforded to all those who enter that celestial city. A wall is a metaphor for security (Isa. 26:1; 60:8; Zech. 2:5; 9:8). In the case of a modern city this figure would offer little except symbolic value; methods of warfare have limited the ability of a wall to keep invaders out, but in the ancient world a wall provided considerable protection to the population of a city. People from villages and towns in times of danger flocked to the great walled cities for protection from those who would do them harm or rob them of their possessions. So the meaning of this picture is very evident. God will be the guarantor of safety to His people throughout unnumbered ages.

b. Twelve Gates Guarded by Twelve Angels (v. 12). Gates in the walls signify openings permitting entrance into the city. So the meaning of this symbol is also clear. Abundant entrance is extended to all those who would come to Christ and see His salvation to its end. The saved man has God on his side at every turn in the road. As Paul wrote, "God has not appointed us for wrath, but to obtain salvation through our Lord Jesus Christ" (1 Thess. 5:9); and, again, "There is therefore now no condemnation to those who are in Christ Jesus." There are plenty of gates, and they are opened wide! God wants us for Himself and has made plentiful provision for us to enjoy salvation. Knowledge of the fact that the gates to heaven are wide open for us should animate the Christian in all of his efforts for the Lord. "How much does the hope of victory animate the soldier in battle! When morally certain of success, how his arm is nerved! When everything conspires to favor him, and when he seems to feel that God fights for him, and intends to give him the victory, how his heart exults, and how strong is he in battle! Hence it was a great point among the ancients, when about entering into battle, to secure evidence that the gods favored them, and meant to give them the victory" (Albert Barnes). Here John tells us that God favors us and intends to see us on to victory. The gates of the Eternal City are many and are opened wide, awaiting our arrival! What a comforting thought to the road-weary traveler and the war-weary, bloodied and wounded soldier. The city waits with its gates standing open to welcome him in, whatever direction he comes from, and at whatever time of day or night he makes his final approach. Ancient cities closed their gates at night to guard against an attack in the hours of darkness, but John informs us that there is no night there. The gates are always open (v. 25).

c. Twelve foundations (v. 14) named after the twelve apostles. Unshakable groundwork underlies the city that can never be moved. This is the main concept which lies behind this figure. In this physical world we now inhabit, earthquakes and seismic events of all sorts occur from time to time. The crust of this present world is ever changing, altering, and being reshaped. Any foundation, even though it may be sunk deep into the earth, may crumble in the face of the mighty forces which lie dormant within the stratified layers beneath us and may be awakened in a moment of time. Such seismic events cannot be forecast. They come without warning and lead to tragic results. Buildings collapse in upon themselves and people are crushed beneath the concrete, steel, heavy bricks, mortar, wood, and glass that make up the structures within which we today reside. That is life in this present world, life in the big cities of our present experience. Yet, John informs us that in the world to come the foundations will not be able to be moved. The tremors of earth will not in any wise affect heaven. God has founded the New Jerusalem upon the doctrines, teachings, and promises proclaimed by the Twelve Apostles of the Lamb. These cannot be moved. They are impregnable.

d. The City lies foursquare, measured by the standard of the angels (vv. 15-17). The point of the author is that a vast space lies within the city. It is beyond the capacity of men to measure it. Many modern cities have swelled beyond their capacity to expand. People are so numerous within that leaders frequently have called for birth control and population control. Services such as sewage and garbage collection have been outstripped by the enormous numbers of people who live in these crowded places. People call out for "elbow room." They need to be able to spread out and stretch themselves. This is the curse of big cities all over the world today. Certainly things were much the same in ancient times before the invention of modern machines and methods of sewage treatment, garbage disposal, and water purification and delivery. Modern farming with its usage of crop rotation, heavy machinery, genetic engineering, pesticides, and fertilizers, have increased yields from agricultural land,

and yet some cultures are still faced with staggering overpopulation as challenges to their governments. Disease and even starvation have been the result in certain societies. These are the considerable and daunting challenges of modern cities on this earth, but John tells us that such things are not a problem in that city to which the people of God are going. There is plenty of room for everyone who wants to go there. This suggests that no one will be shut out because there is not enough room for him. The city is spacious beyond our imagining and all who would find their eternal home there will be able to do so. God has made adequate provision for everyone.

e. The Place is Beautiful and Glorious (vv.18-21). Jewels and gold abundantly decorate the city, and its streets are paved with pure gold. Poverty is the curse of many modern cities today, but there is nothing new or different about this. No doubt it has always been so. The burning of Rome in July of AD 64, supposedly at the hand of Nero whom some claim sent out men to act as if drunken and set the area alight, was said to have been on account of the embarrassing old buildings, crooked streets and slums near his palace that he wished to turn into his new Domus Aurea (Suetonius, *Life of Nero* 38:1-3; whether this story is true or not, is uncertain, and in fact it is frequently denied by some modern scholars). One can visit a beautiful modern metropolis and will see the skyline of a picturesque place previous to his visit pictured on post cards and advertisements. Every thing that is seen on such material suited for public consumption, and especially for tourists and out-of-own visitors, will seem beautiful. But, when one visits there he may be forced to drive through neighborhoods that are filthy, run-down, crime-ridden, and suited only for the poorest of residents. Poverty is the bane of the modern city. This is true almost no matter where you go. One side of town may be rich and prosperous. But, there is another, unsightly and embarrassingly poor side to almost every city that we have visited. But, John tells us that this is not the case with the heavenly city, the New Jerusalem. There is no "poor side of town." All who abide there do so in luxury and conspicuous wealth. They want for nothing.

f. No Temple is found within it (v. 22). Man has been a worshipping creature since the dawn of this present world order. The first murder was committed in the context of worship (Gen. 4:1-8). Much of what the Old Testament teaches the sons and daughters of Israel has to do with how and when to conduct various acts of worship and service to God. Worship is a rather natural vehicle for the expression of reverence and thanksgiving, given the rather unique relation between God and man, as Creator and creature. Almost the entirety of the book of Leviticus is dedicated to why and how the sons of Levi were to approach the holy God in a variety of acts of devotion and service. Both tabernacle and temple were centers of worship activities under that spiritual regime. Sacrifices and offerings were the gifts of thankful men and women throughout the history of that covenant. Jesus said that even in the new order that He was to institute worship was still to be viewed as a worthy occupation for the Lord's servants (John 4:24), just so long as it is conducted "in spirit and in truth." Our text explains to us that divine worship is still an appropriate response of redeemed men and women, even in the heavenly sphere. In that delightful place, the Lord God Himself and the Lamb are themselves the temple. Fellowship with God and worship of His divinity are perfectly appropriate and carried out in sinless perfection in the very presence of the object of our worship in that incomparable place. How happy will that be!

g. No sun or moon is needed, for God Himself lights it with His presence (vv. 23-25). At the dawn of creation God spoke the light into the darkness (Gen. 1:1ff.). The world that we human beings have come to know is constituted as a place of light and darkness, balanced between day and night, activity and sleep. Sleep is needed for the body to rest and rejuvenate itself. When the night of sleep is over, then we must go back to work again. Rest prepares us for another day of labor. Darkness is the perfect situation for sleep. In fact, the circadian rhythms of the body may in some cases make it practically impossible to sleep during daylight hours and so to get sufficient rest without the comfortable and familiar circumstance of darkness. Too much darkness, however, also makes it difficult for the body to function normally. Light therapy is sometimes necessary in wintry climates in certain parts of the world where the sun does not shine much during the months of cold. John was well aware of these rhythms of life in this present world and noted in his description of the world to come that life as we now know it will be changed there.

The days of labor for the children of God will then be over. There will be activity, but no need for rest or sleep. Darkness as we have formerly known it will have seen its end. God is light and in Him is no darkness at all (1 John 1:5). And because God is always present with His people there in that future home of the soul, our author tells us that "there is no night there." What a pleasant and wonderful thought!

h. Nothing impure or evil will enter the city of God (vv. 26-27). On this earth every pleasure is mixed somehow or another with pain. We may live in a neighborhood that has a marvelous neighbor on one side but someone who is obnoxious and loud on the other. Joy is blended with sorrow. Beauty is not far from what is ugly or even vile. We enjoy the presence of some truly wonderful people. We could wish always to be around them, and when they are passed on we will ever miss them in our lives. Then there are the others! They make us miserable by their presence and so long as we are around them there is no pleasantness. When they are gone from us we do not miss them. It is a relief not to be in their presence. So it is always in this world to which we have come to be accustomed, but in our heavenly home, the Bible tells us it will be altogether different. Only the good people and pure things of earth will enter to enjoy the presence of God. That place will be perfectly pure and holy. Absolutely nothing and absolutely no one who is wicked will be there. If they were wicked once, like Saul of Tarsus, then they will have changed and become like Paul the apostle of Jesus. No wicked person and no vile habit will see the future state of the Kingdom of God. Evil will have been left behind. That is God's solemn promise. This will be the happy future of the faithful people of God.

William Barclay described it beautifully:

Those who will not lay aside the evil of their ways are barred from the city of God. It is not the sinner who is barred; Christ Jesus came into the world to save sinners. The man who is barred is the man who quite deliberately and with open eyes continues to sin, the man who, knowing Christ's way, and with the offer of Christ's grace open to him, still takes his own way, and still refuses the grace which could cleanse him from his sin. There is a sinner who hates his sin; and there is a sinner who loves his sin. There is a sinner who sins against his will; there is a sinner who deliberately sins. It is not the repentant sinner, but the defiant sinner, who is barred from the city of God (Barclay 2, 281).

4. The River of Life and the Tree of Life are portrayed. Eternal life realized is what these symbols picture. The author's words are such as to inspire and bestir the deepest emotions from within the human spirit. Those first Christians who read these encouraging sentiments may have had some difficulty with a few of the pictures painted by the literary artist's hand elsewhere in the book, but the thoughts which are set to writing here are crystal clear. What they promise and portray is understood perfectly by all who read them:

> *And he showed me a river of water of life, bright as crystal, proceeding out of the throne of God and of the Lamb, in the midst of the street thereof. And on this side of the river and on that was the tree of life, bearing twelve different types of fruits, yielding its fruit every month: and the leaves of the tree were for the healing of the nations. And there shall be no curse any more: and the throne of God and of the Lamb shall be therein: and His servants shall serve Him; and they shall see His face; and His name shall be on their foreheads. And there shall be night no more; and they need no light of lamp, neither light of sun; for the Lord God shall give them light: and they shall reign for ever and ever (Rev. 22:1-5).*

This lovely image pictures the notion of perfect provision by God. Nothing will be lacking; mankind will be given everything he needs and ever will require. At the beginning of chapter 22, the angel shows John a sparkling river which flows crystal clear from the heavenly throne. The background seems to be Ezekiel's earlier vision of the sacred river (47:1-12), which in that case is said to flow from under the threshold of the temple eastward past the altar and ultimately into the Dead Sea where it healed the water of its saltiness so that many fish could again live in it (see also Zech. 14:8 and Joel 3:18).

In John's vision the crystal river is bordered on either side by the tree of life, which bears its fruit continually throughout the year (see Ezek. 47:12). The abundance and variety of the fruit suggest that God's provision is ever new and always more than adequate. Not only does the tree provide fruit to be eaten, but its leaves are therapeutic and bring healing to the nations. The healing leaves indicate the complete absence of physical and spiritual want. Sickness and disease are only a part of distant memory. They are but a vestigial remnant of the human family's historic past. The life to come, existence in the heavenly sphere, will be a life of abundance and perfection.

Thus, the essence of this portraiture is that the paradise of God, the Garden of Eden that was lost to man with the entrance of sin into his world, is in some sense reclaimed in the future abode of the righteous. This scene might be caricatured as "The Tree of Life Regained." All that sin has undone by its ugly and persistent presence throughout the many years of man's presence on the earth will then have been repaired through the sacrificial offering of the Lamb of God who has taken away the sins of the world (John 1:29). How appropriate are the words of God to John as He spoke of what He was planning to accomplish in this resplendent world to come: "Behold, I make all things new!" (Rev. 21:5). Nothing of that sinful aspect of the old world will persist. God's perfect work of redemption will have reached its apex in the coming City of God.

5. The Bride of Christ Adorned for her Husband. This symbol pictures the love of God perfected in those who have loved Him in this world and will love Him more perfectly in that world to come. These chapters also picture the ultimate glorification of the church as Christ's bride (21:2; cf. 19:7, 8), presented to God holy and without blemish (Eph. 5:27). The wedding day has finally arrived because "the bride has made herself ready" and her readiness is symbolized by the purity of her wedding garments. It is not a gown of her own making; like the robes of the martyrs to which they are closely related, rather it is given to her by God (cf. 6:11). It is made of linen which signifies the sanctity of God's people, a sanctity achieved in the great ordeal by those who "washed their robes and made them white in the life-blood of the lamb" (7:14). The bride is, of course, the church, and the members of the church are the guests at her wedding, and their deeds are her wedding-dress (19:7, 8). The perfection of spiritual union between the Lord and his faithful people is thus signified.

6. And they shall see the face of God (vv. 3-4). The meaning of this expression needs no explanation. No blessing of that lovely picture of the future is more precious than the line that reads: "and they shall see His face." It will be recalled that Moses, the great lawgiver of the ancient dispensation, was not permitted to see the face of God because the Lord had declared, "Man shall not see Me and live" (Exod. 33:20, 23). God only gave him a glimpse of Himself as He moved away, a quick view of His back. In this world prophets have only been shown visions of His majesty, but nothing more than this (see Isa. 6:1ff; Ezek. 1:1ff; etc.). No matter how close they were to God in this world, they were always kept at some distance from Him, no matter how intimately they were associated in life. And there is profound meaning to this distance, illustrated in the lives of all of the great apostles and prophets. The sinfulness of man keeps even the best of men from getting too close!

In the ancient world, criminals were sometimes banished from their homeland and from the presence of its king and not ever again allowed to look upon his face (cf. Esth. 7:8; cf. also 2 Sam. 14:24). In some cases this was the sum and substance of their punishment. Being "cast out" is therefore a phrase which is employed in the New Testament to describe those who are likewise banished from the presence of God because they are not worthy to see His face (cf. 2 Thess. 1:9). They will suffer the punishment of eternal destruction, away from the presence of the Lord and from the glory of his might (Matt. 22:13; 25:41).

Jesus taught that only the pure in heart shall see God (Matt. 5:8). John speaks of the great transformation that is to take place in the future when "we shall be like Him, for we shall see Him as He is" (1 John 3:2). Seeing the face of God is an unrealized goal of righteous men in the Bible like the great lawgiver Moses. Here John speaks of the realization of that hope. What has kept man at great distance from the Lord in the former realm (Isa. 59:1, 2), will no longer act as a barrier to perfect communion with Him. In the heavenly city the people of God shall see the face of God. What a splendid thought!

Chapter Ten

The Epilogue (22:6-21)

And he said unto me, "These words are faithful and true: and the Lord, the God of the spirits of the prophets, sent His angels to show unto His servants the things which must shortly come to pass. And behold, I come quickly. Blessed is he who keeps the words of the prophecy of this book." And I John am the one who heard and saw these things. And when I heard and saw, I fell down to worship before the feet of the angel that showed me these things. And he said to me, "Do not do this: I am a fellow-servant with you and with your brethren the prophets, and with those who keep the words of this book: worship God."

And he said to me, "Seal not up the words of the prophecy of this book; for the time is at hand. He that is unrighteous, let him do unrighteousness still: and he that is filthy, let him be filthy still: and he that is righteous, let him do righteousness still: and he that is holy, let him be holy still. Behold, I come quickly; and my reward is with me, to render to each man according as his work is. I am the Alpha and the Omega, the first and the last, the beginning and the end. Blessed are they that wash their robes, that they may have the right to come to the tree of life, and may enter in by the gates into the city. Without are the dogs, and the sorcerers, and the fornicators, and the murderers, and the idolaters, and everyone who loves and tells a lie. I Jesus have sent My angel to testify to you these things for the churches. I am the root and the offspring of David, the bright, the morning star."

And the Spirit and the bride say, "Come." And he that hears let him say, "Come." And he that is athirst, let him come: he that will, let him take the water of life freely. I testify to every man who hears the words of the prophecy of this book, if any man adds to them, God shall add to him the plagues that are written in this book: and if any man shall take away from the words of the book of this prophecy, God shall take away his part from the tree of life, and out of the holy city, which are written in this book. He who testifies these things proclaims, "Indeed: I am coming soon." Amen: come, Lord Jesus. May the grace of the Lord Jesus be with the saints. Amen (Rev. 22:6-21).

The Epilogue
22:6-21

The major visions of the Revelation have now been experienced by John and the great survey of history has been logged into his memory for him to write it down in a book (see 1:11). The Apostle has witnessed the pageantry of history as it was passed before his eyes in the visions that he had seen. The seven seals had been opened on the book of future events. The seven trumpets had sounded to announce impending doom on those who opposed the purposes of God in the world. He had seen from God's perspective the great enemies of the Lord's people, the Great Red Dragon, the Beast, the False Prophet, and Babylon the Great. He had seen the seven bowls of wrath poured out one by one. He had watched as judgments were brought down on these formidable evil characters one by one.

Furthermore, John now knows what the end will be like: that God will secure the victory for His people, just as He did for Israel when she entered the Promised Land. The enemies of God and of His people will be utterly vanquished. Martyred Christians will sit on thrones of glory with their crucified and risen Christ. They will see the Garden of God and eat of the tree of life. They will know the beauty of the New Jerusalem. And beyond all this, they will see the face of God, revel in the company of God Almighty and the Lamb, and bathe in the dazzling sunlight of His holy presence with all of the holy angels and the righteous dead, past and present. What a glorious Revelation it has been!

John has revealed fully what he had been shown. The time has come to close the book on these divine disclosures. The final section is made up of closing assurances and exhortations to the suffering saints of Asia. Especially important are the two texts which, like the latter half of a literary *inclusio* with 1:1 and 1:3, again emphasize the immediacy of the contents of this prophecy for the seven churches of Asia Minor. "The Lord," writes John, "the God of the spirits of the prophets, sent His angel to show His servants the things which must shortly come to pass" (22:6). In verse 10 the angel informs the Apostle that he must not seal up the words of the prophecy of this book, "for the time is at hand." This is a very important communication because it accentuates the immediacy of the message. Many of these readers will remember well what Daniel was told about his visions and revelations, namely that they were not for his time but "for the time of the end" (Dan.

12:4); precisely the opposite of John's explanation. John's directive is not for the future, it is for the seven churches of Asia in the first century AD as well as churches who would experience persecution at the hands of the Imperial power in future years. Secondarily, of course, it applies equally to all who suffer on account of their faith throughout the ages. Nevertheless, it is abundantly clear from this passage that John is not predicting primarily end-time events, but is disclosing explanatory messages for oppressed Christians of his own age.

The following are the main points of John's closing remarks to the churches:

1. A confirmation of the truthfulness and certainty of the message of the Book. "These words are faithful and true," says the prophet. Many promises made to us by other people fall far short of realization. Living in a capitalistic society it sometimes seems that everyone is trying to sell us something. In the course of the "sales pitch" some of the hype is in fact no more than that. Sad to say, but we have become accustomed to being lied to. We have come to expect that much of what is pledged to us in these circumstances will not really pan out. Most politicians are rabid liars. Defense lawyers regularly proclaim defendants innocent who are "guilty as sin." Many preachers "make it up as they go along" rather than producing Bible authority for what they say and do. This is sad, but surely we must know that people in every age of man have had experiences that are somewhat the same. So, John proffers a promise: "The Lord, the spirit of the prophets, sent His angel to show to His servants the things which must shortly come to pass" (v. 6). Eternity itself will proclaim the truthfulness of the promises contained in John's book of prophecy.

2. A blessing on those who keep the prophecy. "And behold, I come quickly. Blessed is he that keeps the words of the prophecy of this book" (v. 7). Within the extensive content of the Book of Revelation there are many commands from the Lord. All of them must be read with an eye toward, not just nonchalantly assimilating them into the mind or uncritically parsing their content without considering their meaning, but also deliberately assessing them in terms of their implications for our lives and with the deliberate intent of keeping them, every one. This spells out the critical difference between ordinary human communications and those things set forth in the Holy Bible, the Word of the Living God.

Moreover, this makes them a constant source of comfort throughout days of darkness, persecution and trial for the Christians of that and every other period of testing—of the sort found here in the Apocalypse of John. Therefore, they also provide a certainty of direction for the child of God.

Holding fast and remaining true to the divine instructions is one of the few dependable means of surviving the storms of change and making our way through the mine fields of troublesome times. Our chart is set for us and our compass is pointed toward heaven, the sacred city of John's visions. Hence, the greatest of all blessings will be enjoyed by those who keep the words of God's book, John's Revelation included.

3. *A certification of the visions of the book.* "I John am he that heard and saw these things" (v. 8). The apostle John certifies at the end of the Book that what he actually saw and experienced is what is recorded in this work. It is a genuine record of God's visions and revelations to him. Apparently he understood that what he had recorded here was so different from what was found in the Gospels, Epistles, and Acts, that there might be a tendency for people, even good and sincere Christian people, to doubt its worthiness as divine revelation. So he provided a written certification that he had written it and that it was not a forgery or a fraud. It was and is the very Word of God.

It could also be said that the ultimate force of this is to reinforce the genuineness of the prophecy for every potential reader: These visions are truly what John saw and heard. And so, these are the things that will come to pass shortly. That which the Lord has promised He will do. It will come on His time schedule, but it will be just as timely as it needs to be in order to accomplish the will and purpose of God in the world. As the prophet Isaiah said,

> For as the rain and the snow come down from heaven and do not return there but water the earth, making it bring forth and sprout, giving seed to the sower and bread to the eater, so shall My word be that goes out from my mouth; it shall not return to Me empty, but it shall accomplish that which I purpose, and shall succeed in the thing for which I sent it (Isa. 55:10, 11).

4. Another warning about angel worship. John was so enthralled by the glorious presence of the holy angel who revealed these great mysteries to him that he fell down to worship this magnificent personage. Having come from heaven where God's glory radiates to all who share that blessed realm, this angelic being shone with the brightness of the divine presence (just as did Moses when he descended from Mt. Sinai). Thus, mistaking the angel for God, he prostrated himself in homage as he would have done for God.

In this matter John was immediately and soundly corrected, as he had been previously: "You must not do this! I am a fellow-servant with you and your brethren the prophets, and with those who keep the words of this book. 'Worship God!'" (v. 9; see also 19:10). Only the Lord is worthy of worship. His angels worship Him. His saints worship Him. Even though they may share something of His nature, they are never worthy of worship. They are part of His creation. God made them just as He made us. God alone must be reverenced as deity! As Jesus said, "You shall worship the Lord your God, and Him only shall you serve" (Matt. 4:10; Deut. 6:13).

5. An instruction about the sealing of the prophecy. "Do not seal up the words of the prophecy of this book, for the time is near" (v. 10). Three times in the book of Daniel the prophet had been told to "seal up" the prophecies of the book for a future time (cf. Dan. 8:26; 12:4, 9). Daniel's words were not to be fulfilled until hundreds of years into the future. Likewise, Isaiah's prophetic projections awaited later realization, and so he used language like that of Daniel (Isa. 8:16; 30:8). The significance of this is evident. Even here in the Revelation, the sealing of a book of prophetic writings has to do with the later actualization of the events and persons in future time (Rev. 5:1; 10:2). The events of the Revelation, however, had to do with the immediate present rather than the future, i.e. the end of the world.

John's writing was specific to the peculiar circumstances of his first audience. He was addressing the needs of the seven churches of Asia, not talking to the final generation on earth, as some confused Bible interpreters have frequently argued. So John was told not to seal up the words of the Revelation. Their fulfillment was soon, not in the far distant future, and certainly they were not intended for the last days of earth. Some of his predictions pertain to the close of the age, but only the final visions.

The thrust of his work intends to comfort these afflicted Asian Christians rather than to describe the end of the world.

6. An assurance that what is true in this world will persist into the world to come. There is no magical transformation of the wicked at death. They are not instantly renovated and reformed by some sort of divine fiat. Neither is this true for the righteous. Those who are righteous in this present world will be righteous in the eternal realm. Likewise, the wicked will be just as evil in eternity as they are in the physical world (vv. 11-13). This is one of the reasons behind their separation to different locations in eternity. They are never very much at home with one another in this world and so they would not be comfortable together in the world to come. So this is a confirmation of the reality that both of them have chosen in this world that quite naturally continues over into the next. Persecutors and oppressors will be swept away into another realm, far distant from their victims in the first world. There is a certain appropriateness to this that needs no supporting argumentation to justify it. Its logical necessity is straightforward.

This is also an unequivocal declaration that the doctrine of universal salvation is patently false. It also flies in the face of the notion that men will receive a second chance in eternity. As well, it contradicts the idea that other men will be able to perform certain powerful rites on our behalf that will change our destination (e.g., baptism for the dead, pay indulgences, etc.). This life is our only chance. We must make the most of the time we have been given. "It is appointed for man once to die and after this comes the judgment" (Heb. 9:27). When the Lord returns, He will come again to punish the evildoers and the filthy. He will also reward those who are holy and good. "Behold, I am coming soon, bringing my recompense with Me, to repay each one for what he has done."

The message of this declaration is that everyone must be ready at all times for the Lord's return. There are no second chances after death!

7. A blessing is pronounced on those who wash their robes. Verse 14 takes the reader back to the picture that is fixed in the mind of those who have come through the great tribulation to stand before the throne of God in celebration of victory. It was said of them (7:14) that they had "washed their robes and made them white in the blood of the Lamb."

No doubt this refers to the same event as is described in John 3:3, 5; 1 Corinthians 6:11; Ephesians 5:26; Titus 3:5; Romans 6:3ff; Colossians 2:12-13; and 1 Peter 3:21. They had been baptized into Christ for the remission of their sins, and so their trespasses had been washed away when the blood of Jesus was applied to their souls at the time of their conversion. The writer warns that entrance into the gates of that precious city, along with the right to the tree of life, is something that must not be passed up.

This is so, writes John, because "outside are the dogs and sorcerers and the sexually immoral and murderers and idolaters, and everyone who loves and practices falsehood" (v. 15). Ancient cities possessed gates that were closed at night. Oftentimes, outside of the city roving bands of predatory dogs roamed looking for food. Occasionally they became bold enough to attack human beings. The wise avoided getting out in the darkness when the gates were shut. They remained in the safety and security of the city. Such a picture of "outer darkness" along with scavenging packs of wild animals was meant to stir the heart with fear and cause the cautious to avoid such dangerous circumstances. The dogs themselves, however, are not meant to be taken literally as canines, for that would be a breach of John's method, employed consistently throughout the book.

Instead, they are a figure which represents something else altogether. As Dr. Lightfoot observed about the expression *hoi kunes*, "dogs": "As a term of reproach, the word on the lips of a Jew, signified chiefly *impurity*; of a Greek, *impudence*. The herds of dogs which prowl about eastern cities, without a home and without an owner, feeding on refuse and filth of the streets, quarreling among themselves, and attacking the passerby explain both applications of the image" (Lightfoot, 141-142). Dogs are regarded as despised creatures throughout the Bible and were used metaphorically at times to stand for unbelievers (cf. Matt. 7:6). This was so, not because the animals were listed among the banned group of creatures for human consumption, but on account of the disgusting habits they exhibited (Prov. 26:11; Luke 16:21). "One must not let dogs enter the holy camp, since they may eat some of the bones of the sanctuary while the flesh is still on them" (Qimron-Strugnell, *Qumran Cave 4*, DJD 10, 52-53, lines 58-59). In the minds of the Qumran covenanters, dogs were banned from Jerusalem because they tended to dig up bones and eat the remaining meat of sacrificial victims. This suggests that some people in Jerusalem at the time did in fact keep dogs as pets in the city, a practice which the sectarians considered as serious transgression.

Moreover, in early Christian literature the term "dog" is applied to those who are unbaptized and therefore spiritually unclean (*Didache* 9:5), as well as to heretics after the fashion of both Paul and Peter (Ignatius, *Ephesians* 7). The proverb, "Do not give that which is holy to the dogs" found in Matthew 7:6 was cited in order to block the unbaptized from the communion table. It was also quoted in the *Gospel of Thomas* (93) and in the *Liber Graduum* (30:11), and in at least two other Gnostic sources referred to in Hippolytus (*Refutation of All Heresies* 5.8.33) and in Epiphanius (*Panarion* 24.5.2; cf. Aune, 1223).

John has three lists of those unbelievers barricaded forever from the Eternal City (21:8, 27; 22:15). The three lists are similar, with 21:27 having only three groups in it, but this is the only one that includes "dogs" on it. The list found at 21:8 includes the "fearful" and the "unbelieving", but otherwise is identical to this one. It is fair to conclude, therefore, that "dogs" is a term utilized in this instance as a replacement for the word "unbelievers." The Old Testament employed the designation as a metaphor to stand for "male homosexuals" (Deut. 23:18), but this usage is not attested at all in the New Testament. Paul applied the canine metaphor to Jewish Christians at Philippi who claimed to be Christians even though their idolatrous actions and beliefs proved otherwise (Phil. 3:2-3, 18-19). Also likened to dogs were professing Christians in the readership of 2 Peter who apostatize from the true faith (2:20-22) by all kinds of corruption, including false teaching (2:1-3, 13-14, 16) and "having a heart trained in greed . . . having followed the way of Balaam, who loved the wages of unrighteousness" (2:14-15). That the canine image describes spiritual counterfeits is seen further by noticing that the first three descriptions of sinners from 21:8 is replaced by "dogs" here at the head of this particular list. Beale says that, "Dogs, as beasts, are concerned only about their physical well-being. The people in 22:15 are "dogs" because they have an insatiable craving to preserve their earthly security, which is a mark of "the beast" (13:15-18)" (Beale, 1141).

At all events, God's holy city will not have any evil at all in it. Wickedness in all of its various forms must remain outside. So, he says, wash your robes and make them white in the blood of the Lamb, and get into that sacred city where there is safety and security. The alternative is not at all appealing!

8. An assurance that the revelation is for the churches. "I, Jesus, have sent My angel to testify to you about these things for the churches" (v. 16). One cannot forget, especially as he reads and reflects upon the message of this mysterious book of visions, that it is written for the seven churches of Asia Minor in the first century AD. Too many gloss over this fact, or else forget it too quickly as they ponder its meaning. Line upon line is written by scholars and preachers who wish to impose their own individual interpretation upon the contents of John's literary artistry. While at the same time they virtually ignore the special situation in which those seven churches found themselves at the time that John addressed his missives and revealed his visions to them. Jesus is not remiss to remind those who read it then and read it now, that it is not a book about the end of the world. It is a Revelation for the churches to which it was originally directed. Its message applied first of all to them and the thrust of its content is written to meet their needs at the time. Secondarily, of course, it is for the benefit of all of the churches for all time, but its first message was for them at the time of its writing. Seven particular congregations who made their home in Asia were the first audience of this book. It addressed their special problems and spoke to their personal hopes and dreams. It is the testimony of Jesus "for the churches."

9. An invitation from the Spirit and the bride. Of course, the Word of the Gospel is the product of the inspiring Spirit of God. He empowered the first apostles and prophets to proclaim the glad tidings of salvation in Jesus Christ, announced to the four corners of the earth, to the Jew first and then to the Gentile also (Mark 16:15, 16; Matt. 28:18ff; Acts 2:38ff; 3:19ff; Rom. 1:16; etc.). The church is the bride of Christ (Eph. 5:25-32). Both are parties to the message of salvation. The church is ever inviting souls to salvation, continuously throughout the ages of her history through the proclamation of the gospel of Christ. In so doing, the church is inviting them into the City of God, the New Jerusalem. She has no greater work than this to do.

Therefore, the New Jerusalem will be filled with people because the church invited them in. Thus, as John wraps up his message to the churches, he reminds them of their important part in this ever present task: to invite lost sinners to the "fountain filled with blood, drawn from Immanuel's veins" (see Zech. 13:1). He also reminds sinners that the invitation is open to them: "The Spirit and the bride say, Come. Let him that hears, say, Come. And let him who is thirsty come; let the one who desires it take the water of life without price" (v. 17). In these words John was doing what he hoped the church would always be doing: inviting lost sinners to drink of the water of life freely!

10. A stern warning about adding or subtracting from the words of the book of this prophecy. Ancient literature was frequently tampered with by those who wished to change the message so that it would conform to their own way of thinking. A few modern writers have given the impression that this practice was harmless and that those who carried on this practice were not ill-intentioned people. Those writers who produced the literary works which appear in the collection of uninspired writings called the Apocrypha and the Pseudepigrapha of both the Old and New Testaments were very often of this stripe. They claimed to be someone who they were not, and they gave the impression that writings which were produced in some instances hundreds of years after the death of the supposed author were actually a previously unknown work from their hand. And so, there are a good number of examples of this sort of thing which existed in the scribal tradition of ancient Israel, and there is some evidence of it even among scribes in the church as well. Altering the words written by an original writer was a crime against the author, then as now. But in the case of Sacred Scripture it is also a crime against its ultimate author, God!

John gives an unsympathetic and severe word of admonition to anyone who might be tempted to alter the wording of his message. "I warn everyone who hears the words of the prophecy of this book: if anyone adds to them, God will add to him the plagues described in this book, and if anyone takes away from the words of the book of this prophecy, God will take away his share in the tree of life and in the holy city, which are described in this book" (vv. 18-19). It will be remembered that "the plagues described in this book" were the punishments visited upon those guilty of the sin of idolatry, including the sentence of death with which the prophetess Jezebel's children were threatened in Thyatira (2:23). On the other hand, the "tree of life" was promised to the conqueror at Ephesus, commended for its opposition to the Nicolaitans (2:6f), and the "holy city" was promised to the Philadelphian victims of Jewish slander (3:12). So John has already clearly defined both the plagues and the blessings involved.

Moses had given similar warnings to Israel about altering the written text of God's revelation when he reiterated the Law to the people in his exhortations which comprise the primary content of the book of the Law called Deuteronomy (4:2; 12:32). Later on, the prophet Jeremiah specifically referred to certain scribes who had turned the truth of God into a lie, by what he described as their "lying" or "false pen" (8:8). Apparently, some then, as now, were tempted to make adjustments to the words they read from the text of God's Word, so as to have its message conform to their own way of thinking. In every case it was condemned with the strongest possible language.

We must not, however, miss the concomitant warning that exists in John's words. Whether one makes an attempt at actually changing the written words, or simply twists the meaning from its original context and purpose is of little consequence at the end of the process. The result is the same. People are confused and deceived by the techniques employed. Souls may be lost, both of the deceiver and of those deceived. So, great caution must be exercised in the handling of the Word of God, not only in the case of the book of Revelation, but throughout. This text testifies to the fact that the Lord will bring such behavior to certain judgment.

11. *A final message: I am coming soon!* As the concluding page of the Revelation is turned, the Lord Jesus has one last thing to say: "I am coming quickly" (v. 20; compare 1:1, 3; 22:7, 10). Of all of the messages this book has to deliver to those of us who read it in the present day, there is not a single one that is more important than this. If we are going to be prepared when the Lord arrives, we always have to be ready for His coming.

Jesus offered several important parables and even a few very direct messages in one of the most extensive teaching sessions of the gospels in order to teach this valuable lesson (Matt. 24:36-51; 25:1-46). Preparation is an issue of eternal vigilance. We can never allow ourselves to relax on this matter. When Jesus comes we must be ready, no matter the day or the hour.

At the same time, John's retort here in his final chapter is nothing short of stunning: "Amen. Come, Lord Jesus!" Jesus used the Greek word *nai* to preface His promise. In response, John used *nai* to preface his words. This is a particle which denotes an affirmation: "yes, indeed." So, Jesus said, "Yes, indeed, I am coming soon." To which John replies: "Yes, indeed, Come, Lord Jesus!"

This should be the heartfelt feeling of every child of God: anticipating eagerly the return of our Lord. But, of course, this can only be so if we are truly ready for Him to come back. Anything short of this will cause uncertainty in the heart along with concern about what the Lord's return may mean for us if we are not prepared for His arrival.

Conclusion

When we have imbibed the important lessons of this final section of the book, we are left once more with the unavoidable impression that the quintessential message of Revelation was written for the benefit of the persecuted saints of the Age of Martyrs. One of the great mistakes made throughout the history of the interpretation of this important religious document has been the tendency to interpret its figures and symbols in the light of the persons and events of the particular age of the interpreter.

This is a grievous error and one which is destined to lead the reader into the quicksand of confusion. This has always ended badly for such interpreters as well as those who are misled by them. God never intended for this book to be read in a thousand different ways by a thousand different readers from a host of different times and circumstances. There is only one way to remedy this state of confusion and this is not ever to start down that road in the first place. This book must be read through the eyes of the people and churches to which it was originally directed. Its meaning must be for them primarily and its lessons for us must correspond with their immediate and long-term needs. Only then will it make perfect sense. Only then will it honor its original setting and circumstance. Only then will its applications for today be appropriate.

Let us be perfectly clear, what it meant for them it must mean for us also, or else it has no meaning at all. Failure to recognize this fact is what has made this the most often abused book of Scripture. And this is no way to treat any book of the Bible. God's message is here for us to discover, understand, and appreciate, so long as we follow the simple rules of logical thinking and plain old common sense. The Lord meant for this to be precisely what He called it, a "Revelation," a spiritual disclosure of how things really are and what will eventually be, not an enigma or a puzzle without a single solution. And this is exactly what it will be for us if we will but allow it to speak to us on its own terms rather than on ours.

For it to be appreciated properly then, it must be read in the context of the Roman oppression that was crushing the Church at the end of the first century AD when it was written. The ultimate victory of the Church over the Roman oppressor and over the world in general is its theme and purpose. Therefore, when we can truly put on "first century glasses" and read it anew with those first anxious saints fearful about the frightening political developments unfolding in the Roman sphere of influence, and of the worrisome prospects about what the coming years might bring for them, then and only then, can we comprehend fully its power and significance for all ages, our own included. John's book of prophecy is a truly amazing document.

Read from this perspective it is filled with effusive encouragement and abiding comfort to suffering saints in every age until its final visions are fully realized when we enter the Lord's shining city to bask in the sunlight of God's holy presence and immeasurable love throughout an unending eternity.

Little wonder that John concluded the book as he did: "Amen, come, Lord Jesus" (22:20).

Afterward

Reading the biblical Book of Revelation is difficult for most people. We have not attempted to dispel this notion, for there is clearly some good reason for this general perception of it. The explanations are varied and sometimes very different. But one thing that oftentimes is clearly missing in the reading of this wonderful part of Sacred Scripture is what one writer called, "a fertile imagination." Some people have it, while others do not. With Revelation, imagination is a must. In fact, that writer went on to say that any person who is either devoid of imagination or else refuses to use it in the study of the book, "will do well to leave this book alone." That is quite good advice. We could wish that many of those who have advertised themselves as "prophecy experts" had given due heed to it! Here is the point he leads the reader to consider:

> This book was written to yield its message by creating an impression, and this impression makes itself realized as one yields himself to the drama that is enacted before him on the stage in Asia Minor AD 90-96. When the play is ended and the curtain falls after the reverent prayer of the writer, "Even so: Come, Lord Jesus," one is left with an overwhelming impression of majesty, reverence, and awe. He feels the assurance of victory in spite of seemingly insurmountable odds; he knows without doubt or reservation that, come what may, Christ is supreme and that no power can take from him the victory which is rightfully his" (Summers, 51).

Throughout our lives we have all listened to speculations about whether the Book of Revelation might mean so-and-so or not, with the so-and-so part changing from time to time and from one circumstance to another. The answers to some of those questions most of us are not able authoritatively to answer. But, quite frankly, we are convinced that any person of average mental ability and intellectual acumen, with just a smidgeon of imagination, will be able to draw a conclusion comparable to the one set forth above in the statement of Ray Summers. In other words, that insightful author got it exactly right on that count. John intends to leave the reader with a very powerful impression of God's thorough mastery not only of His created universe, but also of a situation that might have seemed at the time to be very dark if not totally black regarding the future, maybe even utterly hopeless.

As readers ourselves, we ought to be impressed with the fact that as the book draws to a close God is pictured as sitting firmly on His throne surrounded by myriads of His heavenly hosts, who give Him praise and great glory after His judgment of the Great Harlot. He is unmoved by all that has gone before and even by anything yet to come. There is a roar in heaven like that of "many waters" and "mighty thunders" combined, saying, "Hallelujah: for the Lord our God, the Almighty, reigns" (Rev. 19:6).

In the scene that follows, Jesus appears as a heavenly warrior sitting on a white horse. The armies of heaven follow closely after Him. The peoples of earth are brought under the judgment of God through the power of The Word of God (v. 13). He rules them with a rod of iron and treads the winepress of the fierceness of the wrath of God (v. 15). All of His enemies oppose Him with all their might, but in the end they are brought down to defeat. Their pitiful human power is no match for the divine omnipotence. Christ reigns with His murdered saints at His side for a thousand years, evincing that their cause was never really lost at all. It is just that their time had not yet come. While the saints are ascendant, Satan is limited for a time in an abyss, but after he is loosed temporarily, he is also brought down to consummate defeat himself. His final destination is the lake of fire and brimstone (20:10). Satanic opposition to God and all that is good has met its final end. At last, all men stand before the great white throne of God's final judgment, and the wicked are sent off into the lake of fire (20:11-15).

The next two chapters picture the future for the righteous in the most glowing of terms. God reigns in His new heavens and new earth and in His holy city, the New Jerusalem (chapter 21). The tree of life is brought back into the range of human enjoyment, almost as if in some sense the original and altogether pleasant Garden of God (Eden) were restored to human experience. Once this picture portrait of the blessed future of the redeemed is given, John turns to a series of practical statements and assurances for his readers in the latter half of the final chapter.

One thing is certain: by this point in the reading of the Book, the reader who is paying careful attention is brought to a state of mind that is precisely as described by Summers: an "overwhelming impression of majesty, reverence and awe." God has brought human history to its close with the ease with which He had called it all into being with the simple words, "Let there be. . . ." He had defeated every enemy and dealt out judgment to all of the evil ones who opposed Him, even the mighty Satan. He had rewarded the faithful with a new order of things beyond the imaginings of those who trusted him for deliverance. Even the dead have been brought back to life and are permitted to participate fully in the blessings of the new order of things. So, the reader is left only to wonder at God's phenomenal power and marvelous might.

It is further to be noted that the author of the work attempted at this juncture in the process to impress upon the minds of his readers the need for energetic action in the light of all that has been seen and heard in this Revelation. This was not a drama without a message, or a book without a point. And so he said,

Blessed are they that wash their robes that they may have the right to enter in by the gates into the city (the New Jerusalem) (22:14; see also 7:14).

Those who would like to share in the good things so described must by all means take quick action to prepare for the Lord's eventual return and the closing out of this world of sin and death. They are to "wash their robes" in preparation for glory, a clear reference to New Testament baptism in water for the remission of sins (Mark 16:16; Acts 2:38; 22:16; 1 Pet. 3:21), and induction into the body of Christ, His church (Gal. 3:27). Furthermore, there is an engaging appeal to all others who might consider this invitation to the heavenly joy that awaits obedient believers:

And the Spirit and the bride say, Come. And he that hears, let him say, Come. And he that is athirst, let him come: he that will, let him take the water of life freely (22:17).

Says John, God's Holy Spirit and the church of Christ call out to everyone who is thirsty for that water of life proffered in Christ with a simple yet appealing summons: "Let him come." Come and get it! The door is open for now. But perhaps it will not be so for long. So do not delay to do what is needed in order to enjoy these good things of God, but also to prepare adequately for those frightening, but inevitable results that will come to all of the wicked who have ignored this wonderful invitation.

Now, you may not be able to understand everything about the Book of Revelation; many of its fantastic images may still elude you completely even after having read this book, but I would venture to guess that you have no problem at all with this part. No doubt, you "get it" without any reservation. That part is easy. Clearly the Book wishes to imbue you with an overwhelming sense of God's might and power and then, with darkly foreboding warnings for some and bright pictures of the future for others, to move us all to trusting faith and obedient service in the Kingdom of His Son. It is our solemn prayer that it will indeed do both things for every reader, just as it has for most sincere students throughout the years since its inception at the hand of the venerable apostle John.

Works Consulted

Aune, David E. *Revelation 1-5*. Vol. 52a, *Word Biblical Commentary*. Waco, TX: Word, 1997.

———. *Revelation 6-16*. Vol. 52b, *Word Biblical Commentary*. Nashville: Thomas Nelson, 1998.

———. *Revelation 17-22*. Vol. 52c, *Word Biblical Commentary*. Nashville: Thomas Nelson, 1998.

Badham, F. P. "The Martyrdom of John the Apostle." *American Journal of Theology*, 3.4 (October, 1899): 729-740; and, 8.3 (July, 1904): 539-554.

Bagnall, Roger S., Roberta Casagrande-Kim, Akan Ersoy, Camhur Tanriver, and Burak Yolaçan. *Graffiti from the Basilica in the Agora of Smyrna*. Institute for the Study of the Ancient World. New York: New York University Press, 2016.

Bailey, James L. and Lyle D. Vander Broek. *Literary Forms in the NT: A Handbook*. Louisville, KY: Westminster/John Knox Press, 1992.

Baines, W. G. "The Number of the Beast in Rev. 13:18." *Heythrop Journal* 16.2 (April, 1975):195-196.

Banks, E. J. "Thyatira." Vol. 5, *International Standard Bible Encyclopedia*. (2977-2978). Grand Rapids: Eerdmans, 1939.

Barclay, William. *Letters to the Seven Churches*. Nashville: Abingdon, 1957.

———. *The Revelation of John*. 2 vols. *The Daily Bible Study Series*. Philadelphia: Westminster, 1960.

Barnard, L. W. "Clement of Rome and the Persecution of Domitian." *New Testament Studies* 10.2 (January, 1964): 251-260.

Barnes, Albert. *Notes on the New Testament Explanatory and Practical: Revelation*. Grand Rapids, MI: Baker Book House, 1951.

Works Consulted

Beale, G. K. *The Book of Revelation.* Edited by I. Howard Marshall and Donald A. Hagner. *New International Greek Testament Commentary.* Grand Rapids, MI: William B. Eerdmans Publishing Company, 1999.

Beasley-Murray, G. R. *Revelation. New Century Bible Commentary.* Grand Rapids: Eerdmans, 1987.

Bettenson, Henry, and Chris Maunder, eds. *Documents of the Christian Church.* Fourth edition. Oxford: University Press, 2011.

Bialik, H. N., and Y. H. Ravnitzky. *The Book of Legends: Sefer Ha-Aggadah: Legends from the Talmud and Midrash.* Trans. W. G. Braude. New York: Schocken Books, Inc., 1992.

Blount, B. K. *Revelation: A Commentary. The New Testament Library.* Louisville: John Knox Press, 2009.

Boring, M. Eugene. *Revelation. Interpretation.* Louisville, KY: John Knox Press, 1989.

Bultmann, Rudolf. *History and Eschatology: The Presence of Eternity.* Gifford Lectures. New York: Harper, 1962.

Caird, G. B. *The Revelation of St. John the Divine. Harper's New Testament Commentaries.* New York: Harper & Row, 1966.

Carpenter, William Boyd. *The Revelation of St. John the Divine; with Commentary.* Ellicott's Bible Commentary. Cassell & Company, 1903.

Chaniotis, Angelos. "Negotiating Religion in the Cities of the Eastern Roman Empire." *Kernos* 16 (2003): 177-190.

Charles, R. H. *A Critical and Exegetical Commentary on the Revelation of St. John.* 2 vols. *International Critical Commentary.* Edinburgh: T&T Clark, 1920.

Clemen, Carl. "The Sojourn of the Apostle John at Ephesus." *American Journal of Theology* 9.4 (October, 1905): 643-676.

Collins, John J. *Crisis and Catharsis: The Power of the Apocalypse.* Philadelphia: Westminster Press, 1984.

———. "Introduction: Towards the Morphology of a Genre." *Semeia* 14 (1979): 1-20.

———. "Introduction: Early Christian Apocalypticism." *Semeia* 36 (1986): 1-12.

Edwards, James R. "Archaeology Gives New Reality to Paul's Ephesus Riot." *Biblical Archaeology Review* 42.4 (July/August, 2016): 24-32, 62.

Erdman, Charles R. *The Revelation of John*. Philadelphia: Westminster, 1936.

Fairchild, Mark R. "Laodicea's 'Lukewarm' Legacy: Conflicts of Prosperity in an Ancient Christian City." *Biblical Archaeology Review* 43.2 (March/April, 2017): 31-39.

Field, Henry M. *The Greek Islands and Turkey after the War*. New York: Charles Scribner's Sons, 1885.

Fiorenza, E. S. *The Book of Revelation: Justice and Judgment*. Second edition. Mineapolis, MN: Augsburg Fortress, 1998.

Gill, David W. J. "Erastus the Aedile." *Tyndale Bulletin* 40.2 (1989): 293-301.

Graf, F. "An Oracle Against Pestilence from a Western Anatolian Town." *Zeitschrift für Papyrologie und Epigraphik* 92 (1992): 267-279.

Gsell, Stéphane. *Essai sur le règne de l'empereur Dominien*. Bibliothèque des Ecoles françaises d'Athènes et de Rome, 65. Paris: Thorin et Fils, 1894.

Hailey, Homer. *Revelation: An Introduction and Commentary*. Grand Rapids, MI: Baker, 1979.

Harrison, Everett F. *Introduction to the New Testament*. Grand Rapids, MI: Eerdmans, 1964.

Hemer, Colin J. *The Letters to the Seven Churches of Asia in Their Local Setting*. Grand Rapids, MI: Eerdmans, 1989.

Hendriksen, William. *More Than Conquerors*. Grand Rapids, MI: Baker Book House, 1967.

———. *Three Lectures on the Book of Revelation*. Grand Rapids, MI: Zondervan, 1949.

Humble, Bill, and Fair, Ian. *The Seven Churches of Asia*. Nashville: Gospel Advocate Company, 1995.

Works Consulted

Hunter, Archibald M. *Introducing the New Testament.* London: SCM Press, 1967

Hvalvik, Reidar. "Barnabas 9.7-9 and the Author's Supposed Use of Gematria." *New Testament Studies* 33 (1987): 276-282.

Jenkins, Ferrell. *Studies in the Book of Revelation.* Temple Terrace, FL: Florida College Bookstore, 1993.

Jones, Brian W. *The Emperor Domitian.* London: Routledge, 1992.

Johnson, Luke T. *The Writings of the New Testament.* Philadelphia: Fortress Press, 1986.

Kiddle, Martin. *The Revelation of St. John. Moffatt New Testament Commentary.* New York: Harper, 1940.

Kistemaker, Simon J. *Exposition of the Book of Revelation. New Testament Commentary.* Grand Rapid, MIs: Baker Academic, 2001.

King, Daniel H. "Overview of the Book of Revelation." *Overcoming with the Lamb: Lessons from the Book of Revelation.* Ed. Ferrell Jenkins. Temple Terrace, FL: Florida College Bookstore, 1994.

———. *The Book of Revelation. Bible Text Books.* Athens, AL: Guardian of Truth Foundation, 2010.

Klein, W. M, C. L. Blomberg, and R. L. Hubbard, Jr. *Introduction to Biblical Interpretation.* Dallas: Word Publishing, 1993.

Kohler, Kaufmann. "Eschatology." *Jewish Encyclopedia.* 5.209-218. http://jewishencyclopedia.com/articles/5849-eschatology.

Krodel, Gerhard A. *Revelation. Augsburg Commentary on the New Testament.* Minneapolis, MN: Augsburg Publishing House, 1989.

Kümmel, Werner Georg. *Introduction to the New Testament.* Trans. A. J. Mattill, Jr. Nashville: Abingdon Press, 1965.

Ladd, G. E. *A Commentary on the Revelation of John.* Grand Rapids, MI: Eerdmans, 1972.

Liddell, H. G., R. Scott, and H. S. Jones. *A Greek-English Lexicon.* Oxford: Clarendon Press, 1968.

Lightfoot, J. B. *St. Paul's Epistle to the Philippians.* London: Macmillan and Co., 1869.

Longman, Tremper, III. "The Divine Warrior: The New Testament Use of an Old Testament Motif." *Westminster Theological Journal* 44 (1982): 290-307.

McDowell, Edward A. *The Meaning and Message of the Book of Revelation.* Nashville: Broadman Press, 1951.

McGinn, Bernard. "Revelation." *Literary Guide to the Bible.* Ed. R. Alter and F. Dermode. Cambridge: Harvard University Press, 1990, 523-543.

Michaels, J. Ramsey. *Revelation.* Vol. 20. *IVP New Testament Commentary Series.* Downers Grove, IL: Inter-Varsity Press, 1997.

Milligan, William. *The Book of Revelation. The Expositor's Bible.* New York: Hodder & Stoughton, 1889.

Mitten, D. G. *The Ancient Synagogue of Sardis.* New York: Committee to Preserve the Ancient Synagogue of Sardis, 1965.

Morris, Leon. *The Revelation of St. John. Tyndale New Testament Commentaries.* Grand Rapids: Eerdmans, 1969.

Mounce, R. H. *The Book of Revelation.* Vol. 19, *NICNT.* Grand Rapids: Eerdmans, 1977.

Patterson, Paige. *Revelation.* Vol. 39, *The New American Commentary.* Nashville: B. & H. Publishing Group, 2012.

Pfeiffer, Charles F., ed. *The Biblical World: A Dictionary of Biblical Archaeology.* Grand Rapids: Baker Book House, 1966.

Pfeiffer, Charles F. and H. F. Vos, *The Wycliff Historical Geography of Bible Lands.* Chicago: Moody Press, 1967.

Phillips, J. B. *The Book of Revelation: A New Translation of the Apocalypse.* New York: Macmillan & Co. Ltd., 1957.

Plummer, Alfred. *Revelation. The Pulpit Commentary.* Grand Rapids: Eerdmans, 1950.

Works Consulted

Prichard, Bob. *Revelation through First Century Glasses.* Nashville: Gospel Advocate, 1997.

Ramsay, W. M. *The Church in the Roman Empire before AD 170.* 5th ed., 1897. Grand Rapids: Baker, 1954 reprint.

———. *The Letters to the Seven Churches.* New York: A. C. Armstrong & Son, 1904.

Reddish, M. G. *Revelation.* Macon, GA: Smyth & Helwys, 2001.

Richardson, Donald W. *The Revelation of Jesus Christ.* Richmond: John Knox Press, 1939.

Rist, Martin. *The Revelation of St. John the Divine.* Vol. 12, *The Interpreter's Bible.* Ed. G. A. Buttrick. New York: Abingdon, 1957.

Roberts, J.W. *The Revelation to John: The Apocalypse. Living Word Commentary.* Ed. by Everett Ferguson. Austin, TX: Sweet Publishing Company, 1974.

Roloff, Jürgen. *Revelation: A Continental Commentary.* Trans. J. E. Alsup and J. S. Currie. Minneapolis: Fortress Press, 1993.

Seager, A. R. "The Building History of the Sardis Synagogue." *American Journal of Archaeology* 76 (Oct. 1972): 425-435.

Seiss, J. A. *The Apocalypse: Lectures on the Book of Revelation.* Grand Rapids, MI: Zondervan, 1900.

Simcox, W. H. *The Revelation of St. John the Divine. Cambridge Greek Testament.* Cambridge: University Press, 1909.

Smallwood, E. M. "Domitian's Attitude toward the Jews and Judaism." *Classical Philology* 51 (1956): 1-13.

Southern, Pat. *Domitian: Tragic Tyrant.* Abingdon, Oxon: Routledge, 1997.

Strack, Hermann L., and Paul Billerbeck. *Kommentar zum Neuen Testament aus Talmud und Midrasch.* Band III. Munich: C. H. Beck, 1926.

Summers, Ray. *Worthy Is the Lamb.* Nashville: Broadman, 1951.

Swete, Henry Barclay. *The Apocalypse of St. John.* Grand Rapids: Eerdmans, 1968.

Sweet, J. P. M. *Revelation. Westminster Pelican Commentaries*. Philadelphia: Westminster Press, 1979.

Unjhem, Arne. *The Book of Revelation*. Philadelphia: Lutheran Church Press, 1967.

Wall, Robert W. *Revelation*. Vol. 18, *New International Biblical Commentary*. Peabody, MA: Hendrickson Publishers, 1991.

Wallace, Foy E., Jr. *The Book of Revelation*. Nashville: Foy E. Wallace, Jr. Publications, 1966.

Wasson, Donald L. "Domitian." *Ancient History Encyclopedia*. https://www.ancient.eu/domitian/.

Weizsäcker, Carl von. *The Apostolic Age of the Christian Church*. Trans. James Millar. 2 vols. New York: G. P. Putnam's Sons, 1894.

Wishart, Charles F. *The Book of Day: A Study in the Revelation of St. John*. Oxford: Oxford University Press, 1935.

Zahn, Theodor. "Der Ausbruch des Vesuvs vom J. 79 n. Chr. nach seinem Eindruck auf Heiden, Juden und Christen." In *Festschrift zu Adolf Schlatters 70. Geburtstag*. Stuttgart: Calwer, 1922, 151-169.

www.ingramcontent.com/pod-product-compliance
Lightning Source LLC
Chambersburg PA
CBHW072322170426
43195CB00048B/2220